ABOUT ISLAND PRESS

Island Press is the only nonprofit organization in the United States whose principal purpose is the publication of books on environmental issues and natural resource management. We provide solutions-oriented information to professionals, public officials, business and community leaders, and concerned citizens who are shaping responses to environmental problems.

In 2003, Island Press celebrates its nineteenth anniversary as the leading provider of timely and practical books that take a multidisciplinary approach to critical environmental concerns. Our growing list of titles reflects our commitment to bringing the best of an expanding body of literature to the environmental community throughout North America and the world.

Support for Island Press is provided by The Nathan Cummings Foundation, Geraldine R. Dodge Foundation, Doris Duke Charitable Foundation, Educational Foundation of America, The Charles Engelhard Foundation, The Ford Foundation, The George Gund Foundation, The Vira I. Heinz Endowment, The William and Flora Hewlett Foundation, Henry Luce Foundation, The John D. and Catherine T. MacArthur Foundation, The Andrew W. Mellon Foundation, The Moriah Fund, The Curtis and Edith Munson Foundation, National Fish and Wildlife Foundation, The New-Land Foundation, Oak Foundation, The Overbrook Foundation, The David and Lucile Packard Foundation, The Pew Charitable Trusts, The Rockefeller Foundation, The Winslow Foundation, and other generous donors.

The opinions expressed in this book are those of the author(s) and do not necessarily reflect the views of these foundations.

ABOUT THE CHESAPEAKE BAY FOUNDATION

With programs that focus on environmental education and resource protection, and with active support from more than 110,000 members, the Chesapeake Bay Foundation (CBF) has made "Save the Bay" the region's rallying cry since 1967. CBF works throughout the Chesapeake's 64,000-square-mile watershed to protect and restore the bay. The foundation employs a staff of 120, with headquarters and a state office in Annapolis, Maryland; additional state offices in Richmond, Virginia, and Harrisburg, Pennsylvania; and field stations all over the region. Funding for CBF is provided by its members, grants from corporations and foundations, individual major gifts, state contracts, and earned income. Approximately 95 percent of CBF's $20 million annual budget is privately raised. CBF is a 501(c)(3) not-for-profit organization. For more information, visit its Web site at www.cbf.org.

The original *Turning the Tide* and this revision were funded by The Abell Foundation, Baltimore, Maryland.

TURNING
the TIDE

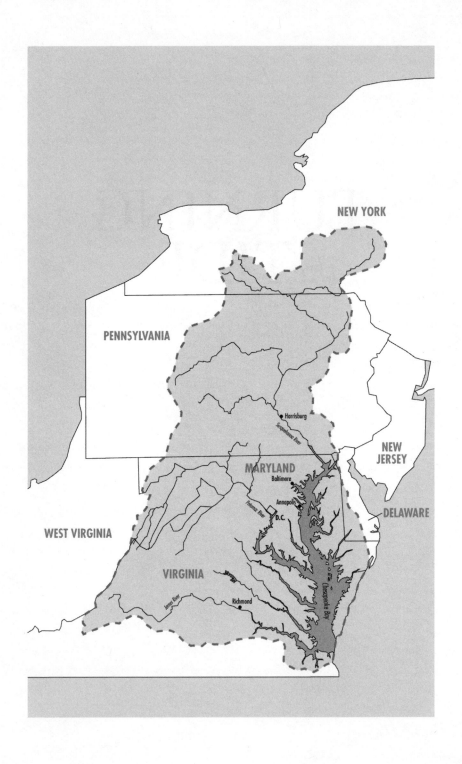

NEW YORK

PENNSYLVANIA

Harrisburg

Susquehanna River

MARYLAND

Baltimore

Annapolis

Potomac River

D.C.

NEW JERSEY

DELAWARE

WEST VIRGINIA

VIRGINIA

James River

Richmond

Chesapeake Bay

TURNING
the TIDE

Saving the Chesapeake Bay

REVISED AND EXPANDED EDITION

TOM HORTON

Chesapeake Bay Foundation

ISLAND PRESS
Washington . Covelo . London

ISLAND PRESS is a trademark of The Center for Resource Economics.

Library of Congress Cataloging-in-Publication data.

Horton, Tom, 1945–
   Turning the tide : saving the Chesapeake Bay / Tom Horton.—2nd ed.
rev. and expanded
      p. cm.
Includes bibliographical references and index.
   ISBN 1-55963-548-7 (cloth : alk. paper)—ISBN 1-55963-549-5 (pbk. : alk. paper)
   1. Water quality management—Government policy—Chesapeake Bay
Watershed (Md. and Va.) 2. Land use—Government policy—Chesapeake Bay
Watershed (Md. and Va.) 3. Land use—Environmental aspects—Chesapeake Bay
Watershed (Md. and Va.) 4. Estuarine area conservation—Chesapeake Bay
Watershed (Md. and Va.) I. Title.
   HC107.A123H67 2003
   363.739'4'0916347—dc21

2003001911

British Cataloguing-in-Publication data available.

Printed on recycled, acid-free paper

Design by Sans Serif Design

Manufactured in the United States of America
10 9 8 7 6 5 4 3 2

CONTENTS

LIST OF FIGURES

FOREWORD

In 1967, a handful of people identified the early signs of a deteriorating Chesapeake Bay that, if left unchecked, would lead to its destruction. This group founded the Chesapeake Bay Foundation (CBF) with a single mission—to save the bay. There was a great deal worth saving. Despite its handicaps, the Chesapeake Bay was then producing one-quarter of the nation's oysters, one-half of all its blue crabs, and a staggering 95 percent of its soft-shell crabs. In addition, nine out of every ten striped bass (called rockfish on the bay) caught from North Carolina to Maine were born in the Chesapeake Bay.

Ironically, the bay's tenacious productivity in the face of increasing pollution left the majority of residents complacent. The small group of CBF members kept pushing, however. Today, CBF claims more than 110,000 members. They still are determined to save the bay—an even more pressing agenda than when CBF was founded. The bay is now a far different place from what it was in 1967. Overfished and stripped of much of its valuable habitat, its once legendary bounty is now just that, legendary. The population of oysters has declined so much that when CBF first published this book in 1991, it was compelled to call for a total moratorium on oyster harvests. The CBF believed this would allow the population to rebuild itself, much in the way a moratorium on the harvest of rockfish had been successful over the six previous years.

The 1991 recommendation was met with almost universal opposition, however, from politicians, fisheries officials, and even the media. It was soundly defeated. Today, the rockfish population in the Chesapeake is considered nearly fully restored, while oysters are worse than ever. As of press time, the 2002 season was the worst oyster harvest in the bay's recorded history.

So what has happened to the Chesapeake Bay since 1991? What is its current condition? Is it getting better, or worse? What are the primary sources of pollution? Why don't government agencies stop the pollution?

To answer these questions, and many more, CBF decided a comprehensive reassessment of the bay's condition, including recommendations to improve it, was needed. This was no easy task, for CBF defines the bay as the entire watershed—from the headwaters of the Susquehanna River in New York State, through Pennsylvania, most of Maryland, and a large part of Virginia, to the Atlantic Ocean—more than 64,000 square miles. The watershed's total area comprises nearly one-sixth of the Atlantic seaboard. Understanding how this system functions is the first order of business. Tom Horton, principal author of both editions of *Turning the Tide*, brings to life complex scientific principles in a comprehensible and engaging style. He describes how the Chesapeake, once called the "crown jewel of the world's estuaries," lost its ability to function the way nature intended. "Degraded," "abused," and "polluted" all describe the current condition of the bay. But the bay is not "dead," at least not yet. For amid the toxic waste, filled wetlands, and oxygen-starved waters, there lies a body of water fighting for survival.

And live it will, if we give it half a chance. Two decades of intense private and public effort to save the bay have averted immediate disaster. In 1991, I wrote in this foreword that "there are signs that we may have seen the worst." Sadly, the last decade has seen no improvement and many scientists believe that the bay may actually get worse over the next few decades unless we have the guts to make fundamental changes. Simply "treating" our wastes before discharging them to the air and water, for example, will not be enough. We must alter the processes—both individually and collectively—in order to reduce the amount of pollution we create in the first place. *Turning the Tide* presents detailed recommendations on how to achieve such reductions, to stop the loss of valuable habitat, to improve fisheries management—in short, how to save the bay.

These strategies to help save the Chesapeake Bay can serve other coastal bodies of water as well. They can be employed everywhere, from San Francisco Bay to Tampa Bay. *Turning the Tide* will be valuable to anyone who wants a better understanding of how nature works and how modern society works against her.

In fact, the Chesapeake Bay is a superb model of the planet as a whole. Not only does the bay encompass a large and diverse geographic region that includes every possible environmental abuse, it is also a largely enclosed system in which most pollutants accumulate.

The Chesapeake Bay is a microcosm of the planet, and our efforts to save it constitute a living experiment for the management and protection of the earth as a whole. Valuable scientific and political experience can be gained as we grapple with some of the more subtle forms of pollution—those that flow not from an easily identifiable source, such as an industrial discharge pipe, but rather from all the little things that each of us does on a day-to-day basis: the pollutants in car exhaust, the sediment released from a construction site, the manure that runs off a farm, the freshwater wetlands filled to build a new house, the trees cut down for road construction. Multiply these routine impacts by the 16 million people who live here (to say nothing of projected growth), and the tremendous stress on the system becomes apparent.

Turning the Tide reminds us that progress on the environmental front must not be measured by the number of new programs in place or the amount of funding appropriated. We must look to the very resources we are trying to protect, such as wetlands, oysters, crabs, and water quality, and measure improvement or decline in them over time.

Again from my 1991 foreword, I wrote, "As we go to press our optimism is tempered by an all-too-predictable reaction to a faltering economy. Even though there has been general agreement that a healthy environment and a robust economy are simply two sides of the same coin—one cannot exist without the other—lines are now being drawn in the sand as adversarial feelings reemerge to replace cooperation and coalition-building. The rhetoric is heating up as environmental programs are being fought, clean water regulations are targeted by industry lawsuits, and funds dedicated for conservation projects are diverted to balance the government's books."

Twelve years later, and as Yogi Berra once said, "It feels like déjà vu all over again."

In spite of the fact that as little as one cent of every tax dollar is spent on the environment, environmental programs are still being cut to "reduce the burden" on the taxpayer. What lunacy!

Perhaps nowhere is the irony greater than in our approach to energy and transportation policies. This nation's insatiable appetite for foreign oil (and lots of it!) only exacerbates the problems of terrorism and global instability. In spite of September 11th, an impending war with Iraq, and the clear linkage of fossil fuel combustion with air and water pollution, America has failed to take even the most basic steps toward energy conservation.

Consider that in the twelve years since 1991, average gas mileage standards for automobiles and SUVs have gotten worse, not better, and individuals are each driving more miles every year. To add insult to injury, automakers are still allowed to produce SUVs that emit far more pollution than cars of similar horsepower under a loophole in the federal law that considers the SUV a "truck," not a "car." Legislation considered by the U.S. Senate in 2001 would have closed this loophole and raised minimum mileage standards. It was overwhelmingly defeated, including negative votes by every bay area senator except Maryland's Paul Sarbanes. Environmentalists, however, will not give up now any more than we have in the past when ideologues masqueraded as fiscal conservatives while trying to gut environmental protection and restoration policies.

At the Chesapeake Bay Foundation, our membership is not only growing, but each member is giving more annually, demonstrating a resolve to save the bay that has never been greater. Our volunteer board of trustees and our full-time staff are dedicated to doing everything within their power to reduce pollution, restore habitat, and better manage the bay's fisheries. History may yet record that a well-meaning but ultimately timid society lost the Chesapeake Bay in the early years of the twenty-first century, but we don't think so. Rather, we believe that wiser leaders will prevail, leaders who realize that saving the bay, a national treasure, is one of the best ways to demonstrate that humans can, in fact, learn to marry environmental and economic prosperity for the good of all. To paraphrase the great Everglades conservationist Marjorie Stoneman Douglass, "Saving the Chesapeake Bay is a test. If we pass, we get to keep the planet."

William C. Baker
President, Chesapeake Bay Foundation
February 2003

PREFACE

Saving the Bay, Failing the Bay: The Last Decade and the Next

A parable for our times: Imagine you have vowed to climb a mountain. To make it, you need to reach a way station, not that far from the top, by a certain hour. The hour comes, and you are well short of your objective. Disappointing, but no disaster, you figure. You have covered a lot of ground, will make the way station soon enough, and will eventually reach the peak.

Or so it seems. But now, with each step upward, the incline becomes steeper. And there has been a dismaying error—the way station is not nearly as close to the top as your map said. And the breeze is becoming a headwind. If you ever do make that peak, the wind will be blasting like a freight train up there. At least you won't have to stay on top for long. But then you ask for the first time, How long *will* I have to hang on there? The answer comes: FOREVER. And, suddenly, the hour seems late.

Unfortunately, this parable is not about mountain climbing, nor is it one bit fanciful. It is about how all of us in the bay region, despite moving in the right direction, are failing our pledge to restore the health of the Chesapeake Bay.

Consider the following assessment:

In sum, then, the picture is one of encouraging improvement on portions of a few rivers; evidence that a species or two are capable of rebounding from depressed levels; continued declines in resilience; and the lukewarm satisfaction that conditions would have been much worse had we done nothing to offset

the polluting effects of rapid growth in both human and farm animal popula-
tions.

Nearly eight years after the historic agreement to restore the bay's health
made by Maryland, Virginia, Pennsylvania, the EPA, and the District of Co-
lumbia in December 1983, there still is no discernible trend toward a system-
wide comeback. (Turning the Tide, *1991, p. 36)*

It has now been twenty years since the historic restoration agreement
and more than a decade since those words were written. Just as our
mountain climber had covered a good deal of ground, we, too, have made
some major achievements:

- Striped bass, bald eagles, and brown pelicans have made impressive
  comebacks, to levels of health as good as or better than anything seen
  in several decades. American shad, still quite depressed, are showing
  encouraging upturns. More than 800 miles of historic shad and herring spawning rivers blocked by dams have been reopened.
- For the first time in history, we are restoring and creating some types
  of wetlands faster than others are being destroyed. By fall 2002, we
  had planted almost 2,280 miles of streamside forests, important as
  wildlife habitat and as filters for pollutants washing from farmlands
  and developed areas.
- Smart Growth, a new and encouraging approach to channeling development away from open spaces and into existing developed areas,
  has taken hold in Maryland and is becoming a national movement.
- Even as population has grown and sewage flows have increased, improved technology has continued to reduce the two key bay pollutants, nitrogen and phosphorus, in sewage discharges.

Other bay-shaping events in the decade since *Turning the Tide* was first
published include the following:

- There were outbreaks in 1997 on three Eastern Shore waterways of
  Pfiesteria piscicida, a toxic alga suspected of killing fish and causing
  memory loss and other health problems among watermen and state
  employees testing water quality there.
- Air pollution's contribution to the polluting nitrogen that has devas-
  tated oxygen levels and underwater grass abundance in the bay was

barely suspected a decade ago. Now it is documented as a major impact. And the bay's newly defined "airshed" extends well beyond the boundaries of its 64,000-square-mile watershed, to as far away as the smokestacks in the Ohio River Valley.

- The blue crab, the bay's last great commercial fishery, has plunged to historic low levels of abundance.

Meanwhile, the literal bottom line on the last decade is that vast volumes of the bay's deep waters remain deficient in the oxygen vital to aquatic life. The underwater grass meadows, rich habitats that once lushly carpeted perhaps half a million acres of shallow bay bottom, remain at around 15 percent of their former abundance. And the levels of nitrogen and phosphorus in the bay, the root causes of its systemwide impairment, dropped little in the last decade.

The excesses of phytoplankton, or floating algae, fertilized by the nitrogen and phosphorus, remain as high as ever, clouding the water, blocking light that the grasses need to grow, consuming oxygen as the algae die and decompose. Also clouding the water, and getting serious attention only in the last few years, are the 5.7 million tons of sediment, or dirt, running into the bay from farms, developments, and eroding streambanks and shorelines. This is about three times the estimated annual sediment entering the bay before European settlement. Targets for reducing it, perhaps by 2–3 million tons annually, are only now being worked out, and no one knows whether such reductions are achievable.

The Chesapeake Bay Foundation's comprehensive annual State of the Bay Report index, compiled since 1998, has remained at 27–28 on a scale of zero to 100—well short of the goal of "40 by 2010" (see Appendix A). So there is much news to report, and a lot of facts and figures to update, in this first major revision of *Turning the Tide*. But the conclusions from more than a decade ago, which I highlighted earlier, can serve this edition with all too little change. Regarding the bay's bottom line, the big news is that there's not much news. We still face the question raised on the first Earth Day, in 1970, in an extraordinary issue of *Fortune* magazine wholly dedicated to the environment: ". . . whether a high technology society can achieve a safe, durable and improving relationship with its environment?"

We still don't know the answer. But there are new questions, central to the future of the state-federal Chesapeake Bay Program, acclaimed internationally as a cutting-edge attempt to restore a huge, natural system: What will make this decade better than the last decade? What lessons do we draw from the paltry results of an "acclaimed" restoration attempt that has been operating in earnest for nearly two decades? This new edition of *Turning the Tide* is dedicated to answering those questions.

Of course, there is no legal deadline that says we cannot revise this book in another ten or even twenty years, chronicling the same scenario of "battles won—war going not so well." But just as our mountain climber finds the hour getting late, the slope becoming steeper, and the wind picking up, we have real reasons to fear for the bay restoration effort should this decade resemble the last two.

First, remember what we have set about is restoration, not holding the line (which is more like what we have been doing). We can get a glimpse of what true restoration means—also a lesson in why we're lagging—by focusing on nitrogen, the element that is the bay's biggest and most ubiquitous single pollutant. Nitrogen is a good indicator for the myriad ways in which modern lifestyles affect the bay. It comes from nearly everything that underpins the way we live—burning fossil fuels to heat homes and run cars; fertilizing lawns and farms and golf courses; flushing toilets. In the mid-1980s, nitrogen entering the bay from all sources—polluted air, sewage, land runoff—totaled roughly 360 million pounds. In contrast, nitrogen entering the bay when Captain John Smith explored it in 1607 is estimated to have been about 50 million pounds. We had increased it by an astounding sevenfold—mostly in just the last half century, scientists think. In 1987, the bay restoration program set a goal of reducing nitrogen by 40 percent. That was the bare minimum scientists thought would clear up the water enough to bring back underwater grasses and oxygen. But shortly after the goal was set, it was redefined to mean 40 percent of "controllable" sources of nitrogen. "Uncontrollable" was arbitrarily defined to include close to half of all nitrogen sources—the air, and all the runoff from New York, West Virginia, and Delaware, states on the outskirts of the watershed that were not then part of the program. (They have recently joined, but they are only just beginning their own restoration efforts.) With these deductions the 2000 goal became a 21 percent reduction, a far cry from the 40 percent originally envisioned, and in 2002 not yet achieved. At this writing, it appears we may achieve the goal a few years behind schedule. But recent studies suggest that the methods of measuring the reductions overstate our true progress.

For more than a decade, reducing the nitrogen entering the bay was our mountain climber's way station, which now turns out to be farther away from the peak than our climber thought. For real overall improvement in the bay, the best science says we need to decrease nitrogen by 150 million pounds annually. New goals to reach this level by 2010 are being refined now. That reduction is about twice as much in this decade as we have accomplished in the last two. Some people have argued that to set so realistic a goal may be too daunting, that it will just discourage people. But, in retrospect, the opposite was true during the last decade—having set a goal, even one quietly acknowledged as semi-bogus, there was scant incentive to push beyond it. The kinds of new and visionary thinking necessary to bring about true progress won't come from setting under-achieving goals that look doable by merely tweaking the status quo.

A second concern about letting another decade pass like the last arose at an extraordinary gathering in 2001 that brought together former political leaders from Virginia, Maryland, and Pennsylvania—pioneers who put the bay's restoration on the public agenda some two decades ago. All were old enough to have known the Chesapeake at its twentieth-century best. All feared that each new generation since has experienced a bay more degraded than the one before it. That point of view inevitably leads to lower expectations and less pressure on politicians to do right by the bay, they said. Retired Maryland state senator Bernie Fowler, who virtually began the bay restoration after becoming alarmed at declines in his native Patuxent River during the 1960s, had this to say:

> There's going to be no memory banks in those computers at EPA that can re-cite the ten bushels of crabs one person used to catch out there, and all the hardheads . . . and the shuckers in the oyster houses up and down the river, all singing harmony while they worked. If we can't make some headway soon, today's children will never, never have the hope and the dream of bringing the water back, because they just won't have any idea how enriching it used to be.

Similarly, at age fifty-seven, the author often writes and speaks about what an important connection with the bay the American shad made for him on their annual spring spawning runs through the little farm town where he was a kid in the 1950s. The fact that his beloved shad fishing has been closed for lack of shad since 1979 isn't what worries him most—it is that he has raised two kids, now twenty-one and twenty-four, who have never caught a shad—and who aren't overly worried about bringing back what they have never had. What to their father is rich memory and anguish is to them history. And the same thing can happen with generations who do not remember wading for soft-shell crabs in the clear water of the grass beds, or anticipating winter's fat, raw oysters and the sight of skipjacks setting sail to catch them.

It is unlikely, even if the bay continues for much longer in an unrestored state, that political leaders and decision makers will admit failure. What is likely is that they, and we who live around the bay, will redefine success and change the concept of "restored" to some more achievable state of health.

Another major concern is this: Just as our climber faces a constantly increasing slope and wind on the way to the peak, the bay restoration gets tougher every decade—and not just politically, as public memories of a truly healthy estuary recede. It gets tougher because more than a million new people move into the watershed every ten years to join the 16 million or so here already. Today's population is double what it was in 1950. Simultaneously, our modern lifestyles continue a decades-long trend— environmental stresses rising even faster than population, the result of the increasing per capita consumption of land, energy, and water, and the increasing pollution that is a by-product of those appetites. Think of what this trend means for measuring real progress in bay restoration. Defining what constitutes real progress is a major aim of this book. Real progress in restoring the bay must not only dramatically reduce the current pollution but also completely offset all the environmental impacts of the human populations yet to come. From a restored bay's standpoint, it must seem as if the next million residents (and the next million) never exist.

It is not widely appreciated that the goals of the bay restoration program for reducing nitrogen and phosphorus have long acknowledged the need to offset constantly increasing population levels within the watershed. Accordingly, whatever pollution limits we eventually achieve are to become absolute caps. Pollution should never be allowed to rise again, no matter how many people move in. To actually achieve these caps is to confront the frightful, freight-train wind, gaining velocity every year, against which our climber, to stay on the peak, must fight forever.

Today's environmental problems stem both from *how many* people live in a place as well as from *how* they live there. But the entire focus of bay restoration, and of virtually all the energies of environmental management nationwide, is on reducing people's impacts on nature, as if it did not matter how many people there are.

Thus, even the latest federal-state agreement for the bay's restoration, *Chesapeake 2000*, takes this perplexing approach: "There is a clear correlation between population growth and . . . environmental degradation in the Chesapeake Bay system." And it adds that the 3 million new people expected in the watershed by 2020 "could potentially eclipse" all past gains in water quality and habitat protection. But the agreement proposes nothing about population growth except the need to accommodate it. We have already seen the folly of bay restoration goals that treated several large sources of pollution as uncontrollable. Continuing to regard population growth as uncontrollable will mean repeating this mistake on a grander scale.

Chapter 5, "The Ultimate Issue: People," presents the question of whether population should be stabilized as well as arguments for doing so. Whatever the outcome of that necessary national debate, it must not detract one iota from current efforts to reduce human impacts on the bay. This is where most of our gains are going to come from in the next decade or two, given the long time frames involved in stabilizing population. And there is enormous scope for gain in reducing per capita consumption of natural resources. Polls taken throughout the last half century show that for most Americans, material well-being long ago passed the point where additional getting and spending make us happier. Nowadays, acquiring "more stuff" correlates better with having more stress.

And while Americans today may be no happier than previous generations, we are substantially "bigger" in terms of our impacts on nature.
Consider our reliance on burning fossil fuels such as coal and oil, which
are major sources of the nitrogen polluting the Chesapeake. Counting all
the energy needs, from food to heat to transportation, the average American now requires about the same amount of daily calories as the average
sperm whale. In both energy use and nitrogen pollution, we are about
seventy-five times bigger than our hunter-gatherer ancestors, leaving ecological footprints as we tread the earth that are several times larger than
individuals of even a few generations ago. Thus, even if we could wave a
magic wand and stop all growth of population throughout the bay's watershed, we would still be left with a huge task of restoration because of
past and current abuse of the region's natural assets. But it is equally clear
that the effort it takes just to offset rapid population growth is a significant reason for the slow progress with bay restoration.

Some people would place faith in technology to avoid wrestling with
limiting the population, and indeed, some of our greatest hopes for
restoring the bay will lie with continuing technological advances. Available right now, or within a few years, are automobiles that cut nitrogen
pollution by 90 percent compared to the so-called cleanest models now
on the road; sewage treatment plants that reduce nitrogen by at least half
from current discharges; and promising, cost-effective techniques for development of land that dramatically reduce impacts on water quality
downstream.

But experience shows it is grossly misleading to assume that what is
possible will become panacea—or even a significant part of the solution.
Cars that average or exceed fuel standards of 30 miles per gallon have
been available for many years. But average auto mileage has been getting
lower and lower, slipping below what it was twenty years ago, as Americans now flock to gas-guzzling SUVs and trucks, and the federal government waffles on mandating higher mileage standards. ("Fifty-two percent
of vehicles on the road are pickup trucks—God Bless America," trumpets
a Goodyear tire ad.) As for the new, "low-impact design" standards for
land development, which hold such promise for minimizing impacts on
water quality, only a few new developments actually use them—even in

Maryland's Prince George's County, which pioneered and proved these techniques. Change is hard. What is technologically and economically possible and what is probable are seldom the same.

Also, ask yourself, what if we could invent a car with zero pollution, that used no fuel, and was completely recyclable—would you want to see three times the traffic and roads and parking lots even with such "perfect" technology?

If we can no longer ignore population growth, then what do we do about it? Chapter 5 reviews the prospects. Ultimately, the major part of the solution must happen nationally. The United States could either lower the current, record-high numbers of foreign immigrants, or persuade people to have fewer children, or seek a solution that combines both means. There are compelling reasons—environmental, economic, and social—for the whole country to consider stabilizing population. But even if population is stabilized nationally, people from the rest of the country may continue moving into the Chesapeake watershed, as well as into other environmentally sensitive areas. And limiting Americans' freedom to move about would likely be harder, and certainly less desirable, than reducing immigration or fertility rates. Nor will any actions we take make a big difference for another generation or so, because of the "population momentum" from existing citizens who will be entering their reproductive years. Until then, no matter what we do about how many of us live here, we will rely mostly on reducing the impacts of how we live and use our land.

But a national debate on population has to start somewhere. Perhaps there is no better place than the watershed of the Chesapeake, where the nation's Congress and its president live, and where it becomes clearer every year that we are unlikely to attain and sustain the restoration goals we have set by considering such a huge part of the problem off-limits and uncontrollable.

It seems likely that before trying to reach consensus on stabilizing population, a few other questions must be resolved. Chapter 5 begins by examining how population growth is, or isn't, linked to economic prosperity and quality of life. That they may be linked would certainly be news to Europe and Scandinavia, which have both low population growth and high standards of living. But in the United States, many decision makers still operate on the "grow or die" model. It is time to look critically at such assumptions, to begin asking ourselves and our legislators: If 2 million people moved here in the next decade instead of the 3 million projected, would we be worse off? Also, to whom are we most responsible—the 16 million here, or the millions not yet arrived?

Lessons Learned

Population growth is only one of many reasons the bay has remained unhealthy during more than a decade of restoration. What other lessons and observations can we draw from our experience to make the next decade better than the last? There are several areas, listed here in no particular order of priority, where marked improvement is essential.

LEADERSHIP

Political leadership is crucial to the bay, because the agreement that joins the principal states of its watershed and the federal agencies in restoring it is largely voluntary. "Its strength is that it was the only way we could come together," said Joseph Gartlan Jr., longtime bay champion and former Virginia state senator, at the April 2001 gathering of leaders who began the restoration. The group doubted that political leadership exists today to restore the bay to health. They felt that the situation exists partly because citizens have not been mobilized to push politicians to make the bay environment more of an issue in election campaigns.

The scope of the leadership problem is broadly illustrated by almost uniformly weak environmental records of the past decade across Virginia, Maryland, and Pennsylvania and in the U.S. Congress. This deficiency helped make the 1990s a period of half-measures, of diverting environmental groups' energy toward preventing backsliding, thwarting an aggressive push for true restoration.

Consider the environmental voting records of legislators during the last decade, based on scores compiled by the bipartisan League of Conservation Voters in Maryland and Pennsylvania, and by the Sierra Club and Clean Water Action environmental groups in Virginia:

- Out of a possible 100 for the decade, Maryland's House of Delegates averaged 55 percent and its state senate 60 percent.
- Pennsylvania's house averaged 50 percent and its senate 35 percent. (Excluding one session where only one vote was scored and the senate got a zero, its score for the decade was around 45 percent.)
- Virginia's house averaged 50 percent and its senate 48 percent.
- The U.S. Congress, as scored by the League of Conservation Voters, averaged 48 percent in the House of Representatives and 46 percent in the Senate. During one four-year stretch, from 1997 to 2000, the Senate's leadership voted 0 (zero) on the league's selected environmental issues, and the House leadership averaged 8.

At the gubernatorial level, the league rated only Maryland's Parris N. Glendening. He received an overall grade of B for his first four years and a B-plus for his second term. He was the exception. It is fair to say no Virginia or Pennsylvania governor during the 1990s would have received nearly so high a grade. Virginia's spending on natural resources protection amounted to just 1 percent of its budget, ranking forty-ninth among the states. The current administration of President George W. Bush shows little promise of environmental leadership, threatening to turn back progress in areas of air and water quality that are critical to restoring the bay.

In addition, an often bitter partisanship has ruled the politics of environment during the last decade and a half. The bay restoration owes much of its early support to Republicans in state and federal offices from all three watershed states. But more recently, the Republican party has consistently been on the wrong side of too many environmental issues. Democrats, while better, have not shown remarkable leadership. This partisanship in recent years kept the governors of the three bay states from showing an effective, united front in lobbying for federal cleanup funds.

It is too easy just to criticize politicians. Many legislators and governors of the past decade who were notably weak on the environment remained broadly popular with their constituents. The environmental community needs to rethink how to build a consensus for the bay that reaches well beyond its own members.

ACCOUNTABILITY

As noted, decisions over time have watered down earlier goals of reducing bay pollutants from 40 percent to nearly half that. We must set clear standards that can be checked and enforced, and that will translate to real progress. The latest state-federal agreement, *Chesapeake 2000,* which will guide bay restoration for the next decade, marks a real improvement. It calls for reducing the major pollutants in every river system enough to resolve the baywide declines in oxygen and underwater grasses. It sets a goal of increasing oysters tenfold by 2010 and another goal of protecting 1.5 million more acres of open space from development by decade's end.

Chesapeake 2000 is by far the best restoration agreement yet. But is it good enough? It is all too full of "will strive" in areas that cry out for "will do." "Individual responsibility" in the draft agreement was reworded to "individual stewardship." A pledge to "reduce the rate of harmful sprawl development" of forest and farmland in the watershed fails to set a high enough standard for protecting forests, which constitute the least-polluting land use in a watershed where runoff from the land is among the most intractable sources of pollution.

The wording of this goal became contentious. The drafters settled on the final wording, "harmful sprawl," but whether this means something different from and worse than plain sprawl, or whether "harmful" is simply an adjective reminding us of sprawl's destructive power, is left to interpretation. The CBF, knowing how harmful sprawl can be and certain of the drafters' good intent, interprets it as an adjective.

Chesapeake 2000 says virtually nothing about goals for reducing air pollutants that form an equally large source of bay pollution. We are at the beginning of 2003 and already falling well behind schedule (see Chapter 2) in setting specific cleanup goals called for in the agreement.

There is also the matter of tracking cleanup progress to make sure it's really happening. We did not do this during the last decade in areas like agriculture, with its strongly defended tradition of voluntary cooperation. For example, when a toxic algae outbreak occurred on three Eastern Shore waterways in 1997, with possible links to the runoff of poultry manure, subsequent investigations revealed a shocking lack of progress by both the poultry industry and the chicken farmers in handling manure.

The voluntary nature of farm pollution cleanup also thwarts efficient targeting of resources, which tend to get spent where farmers are receptive, not necessarily where they do the most good.

There is also growing evidence that we have spent the last decade giving too much credit for pollution control to a host of so-called BMPs, or best management practices. Examples include ponds that check the damaging gush of stormwater into streams from streets and parking lots, and manure storage pits built on dairy farms so the manure can be spread when crops will use its nitrogen and phosphorus, reducing amounts that wash off in rainfall. Record keeping of how these management practices function in the long run and of whether they are maintained after installation is minimal. And it is apparent that many BMPs are essentially Band-Aids, whose application masks the need for more fundamental changes in the way we develop land and farm it. Some BMPs are better than others, but it seems unlikely they can ever substitute for inherently less-polluting ways of using the land.

MONEY

You get what you pay for, and in January 2003 the Chesapeake Bay Commission, working with the environmental leaders and managers throughout the bay region, estimated that it will take approximately $19 billion during this decade to reach the land-protection and water quality goals in the latest bay restoration agreement. It may seem like an insurmountable sum, but if apportioned among all those who live in the watershed, it works out to about 35 cents a day, per person, if spread over a decade, and 43 cents per day if spread over the remaining eight years of this decade. If costs are spread across the nation (e.g., for air pollution), the cost per capita is further reduced, and there is already $6 billion earmarked for protection and restoration programs, leaving $13 billion to be identified.

The commission's report, *The Costs of a Clean Bay: Assessing Funding Needs Throughout the Watershed,* breaks down the costs of protecting the bay's resources as follows: $1.4 billion for living resources such as oysters, crabs, and migratory birds; $1 billion for underwater grasses, wetlands, forests, and stream buffers; $11.5 billion for water quality—primarily for removing nitrogen, phosphorus, and toxic chemicals from sewage, urban storm water, air pollution, and boat discharges; $4 billion for land conservation redevelopment and revitalization of urban areas, transportation systems, and public access to the bay; and $0.7 billion for environmental education and community engagement.

If well spent, the money will result in spectacular re-greening of the watershed as buffers are planted, forests are protected, and wetlands are restored and in water clear and clean enough for a resurgence of underwater grasses and a more balanced web of life in the bay.

The $19 billion is probably a minimum. We have spent the last decade allocating hundreds of millions of dollars on such things, never asking what were the real needs for a successful restoration. The bay's economic value was estimated in 1989 to be almost three-quarters of a trillion dollars. Governor Mark R. Warner of Virginia, in remarks made as he was named chairman of the Executive Council of the Bay Program in October 2002, called the Chesapeake the region's economic engine. He noted that its restoration would greatly enhance its value. So, consider: If you bought a car for $20,000, would you begrudge spending $70 a year to maintain it? That's the same proportion we would spend to restore the bay.

We can never express the bay's worth solely in dollars and cents. But we can say with some confidence that if we don't soon put our money where our goals are, we're asserting that a healthy Chesapeake isn't worth a few dimes a day from each of us.

THE MYTH OF "VOLUNTARY"

If assessing our progress during the last fifteen years does nothing else, "it should explode the myth that the bay restoration works because it's a voluntary program," says scientist Michael Hirshfield, a past CBF vice president. Because the overarching restoration agreement among the states and the federal agencies is voluntary, it is easy to forget that the actual work is frequently driven by rules and regulations. Some of our greatest progress has come from the following:

- An outright ban on phosphate laundry detergents, which dramatically reduced loads of polluting phosphorus from sewage treatment plants.

- A ban on catching striped bass, which is credited with bringing the species back in record numbers.
- Similarly, bans on hunting geese and on commercial crabbing during certain days and months have been the only medicine strong enough to stop declines. Protective wetlands laws, court-ordered deadlines for sewage treatment plants to upgrade and for toxic dumping to cease, and protective zoning on open spaces also underlie a good deal of the progress to date.

The ecologist Barry Commoner, in his 1975 book *Making Peace with the Planet,* noted that our few real environmental successes—cleaning up lead, PCBs, DDT, nuclear fallout—resulted from outright bans, rather than trying to negotiate "how much the environment could tolerate." This is not to say that all the rules and regulations, bans and moratoriums conceivable could restore the bay without the cooperation of millions of citizens. But cooperation often works best when backed by good laws. (Consider how effective voluntary speed limits would be on our nation's highways.) Despite the need for them as backstops for voluntary efforts, the nation's clean water and clean air laws are under threat of weakening and reduced enforcement as we begin the twenty-first century.

GOOD SCIENCE

In many of the bay's biggest controversies—Did we need to control nitrogen pollution? Were striped bass really in trouble? Were crabs actually being overfished?—it was bay scientists who laid the foundations that mobilized citizens and enabled decision makers to choose wisely. Maintaining and funding robust research programs and monitoring programs, which year after year collect the data on water quality, fish abundance, and a host of other items, are fundamental in all three bay states. Trying to make decisions without good monitoring is like having a doctor make a diagnosis without taking your temperature or feeling your pulse.

DEFINING REAL PROGRESS

Progress is too often the kind that has been characterized as rowing ahead at 3 knots, when the current is moving against us at 4. Consider the

Baltimore newspaper editorial that proclaimed "Victory at Fort Meade" after a compromise had been reached on the fate of 9,000 acres of fields and forests owned by the U.S. Army—surplus military land proposed for development, but championed by local governments and the state for a wildlife refuge. The army, the editorial noted, had agreed to the refuge and would develop only 1,400 acres.

Was that a victory? Or was it a decline of nearly 3 square miles of open space in an already congested part of the bay's watershed and a sure increase in pollution from development? Huge portions of the bay's wetlands, forests, oysters, and submerged grasses have been destroyed since European settlement. Every time we compromise these aspects of the bay's nature, we are dealing with systems that have already been hugely compromised. So when we lose an acre of wetlands on the Chesapeake, we are losing not only an acre, but an acre of the remaining 42 percent of all wetlands that the bay watershed used to have. We are dealing not with protecting forest, but with protecting the last half of our forest. Similarly, we are protecting the last 15 percent of the underwater grasses and the last few percent of the oysters.

"Compromise, when it comes to the bay, is the halfway house to surrender," said Rogers C. B. Morton, the late Republican congressman from the Eastern Shore of Maryland, speaking at a 1968 conference on the health of the bay. Compromises are inevitable, but maybe less so if we learn not to regard them casually as victories for nature.

Real progress must mean improving the Chesapeake's vast system, not just holding the line or slowly eroding in the face of any increases in impacts on the environment from a human population that continues to grow across the Chesapeake region.

As with our mountain climber, the hour is late. Another decade without real progress may jeopardize both local and national support for restoration of the Chesapeake. At the time of this book's completion, in the winter of 2003, there is a consensus within the community of environmentalists and bay managers that much more needs to happen, NOW. But political leadership, watershed-wide, remains questionable, and public support to push that leadership toward real bay restoration is not what it needs to be.

There is no doubt that this decade can be one of dramatically greater progress than the last. We have barely scratched the surface of what is possible. The need to check population growth is still a debate waiting to happen, but we are now setting more realistic cleanup goals. The technology is available to make great strides forward, and concerted attempts are under way to raise billions of new dollars to mobilize it. Science will never have all the answers, but it now tells us enough about what is necessary to restore the bay. We have no real excuses for waiting.

ABOUT THIS BOOK

This book is organized into six chapters. Chapter 1, "The Bay Connects Us, the Bay Reflects Us," lays the groundwork for a fundamental reconsideration of the Chesapeake as a living, connected entity, an *ecosystem*, where rivers and the sea, people and trees, oysters and agriculture all interact across six states and 64,000 square miles to shape the quality of life on land and in the water. It explores what makes the bay not only more productive of life than almost any other place on Earth, but also terribly vulnerable to modern environmental stresses. It introduces the concept of *resilience*, the enormous ability of the bay's plant and animal communities to filter and buffer pollution. When we lose oyster reefs and underwater grasses, forests and wetlands, we lose more than habitats for aquatic and terrestrial life. We cripple nature's ability to maintain itself.

Chapters 2 ("Pollution"), 3 ("Harvests"), and 4 ("Resilience") are the heart of the book. They detail what we know about the state of the Chesapeake. They build on the ecosystem concept, extending our analysis from the forested mountain slopes and creeks, downriver and downslope through the Piedmont and Coastal Plain farms and cities, to the marshes at water's edge. They follow the land as it slips away into rich, shallow-water habitats of tidal mudflats and submerged underwater grass beds and, further from shore, into oyster beds and finally the deep channels. Chapter 2 looks at the obvious and not-so-obvious ways in which we put pollutants into the bay. Chapter 3 shows how sometimes the real problems involve how much life we take out of the water when we catch fish, crabs, and oysters faster than they can reproduce. Chapter 4 gauges how we are doing in preserving the natural habitats—on land and underwater—that help the system cope with the stresses of pollution and overfishing.

Chapter 5, "The Ultimate Issue: People," is about how many people can live here and how much impact each person can make on the environment—two sides of the same coin. It examines the need for changes in our individual habits—from the homes we demand to the cars we drive and the energy we use. It examines both the rampant sprawl development that is frittering away our natural landscape and prime farmlands, and some promising solutions to sprawl.

Chapter 6, "Recommendations," presents a series of goals and recommendations for bay restoration, using a tough litmus test for each strategy: Can it work well enough so that even as millions more people move into the region, the bay's environmental health still improves?

While this book is principally a report card on the state of the Chesapeake Bay, we in the bay region are not alone in our concern for our fragile environment. Nearly two-thirds of the nation's population now live in the narrow margins of the continent near the coastlines (Atlantic, Pacific, Gulf of Mexico, and Great Lakes), a trend that promises only to increase. Worldwide, half the people live on about 5 percent of the planet's surface, and much of that 5 percent is near the coasts.

The environmental struggles of the Chesapeake region are being joined from Puget Sound in Washington State to Galveston Bay in Texas, from Pamlico Sound in North Carolina to Penobscot Bay in Maine. Moreover, environmental declines similar to the Chesapeake's are now documented in Europe, Mexico, Australia, South America, China, and Japan. The Chesapeake is now one of more than fifty so-called dead zones—coastal waters around the globe with large volumes of *anoxic* (without oxygen) water. There is no record to date of any dead zone being restored to health.

While the Chesapeake does not exhibit every problem of every coastal region, it nonetheless has much to recommend it as a model. A world-class coastal resource in major decline, it has been the focus of years of unprecedented efforts toward restoration, even as more people arrive every year to use its natural resources. Few other places afford a better laboratory. The successes and failures recorded here represent nothing less than a national and an international test of the possibilities for reconciling growing human demands with the integrity of the natural environment.

PART I

The CHESAPEAKE ECOSYSTEM

1

The Bay Connects Us, the Bay Reflects Us

The Small, Skinny Bay

The Chesapeake Bay is on our maps and in our minds as a large and dominant body of water, fringed on either side by tidewater Maryland and Virginia, ending at Norfolk to the south and at Havre de Grace to the north. Although the bay is commonly described as 195 miles long and from 4 miles to 30 miles wide, it is a system about twenty times that size. Nearly fifty significant rivers and thousands of streams, creeks, and ditches penetrate deep into the surrounding land. They extend the bay northward to Cooperstown, New York, site of the Baseball Hall of Fame; as far west as Pendleton County, West Virginia; southward in Virginia to Lynchburg and Virginia Beach; and eastward to Seaford, Delaware, and Scranton, Pennsylvania.

All of the land thus encompassed, sprawling 64,000 square miles between upstate New York and southeastern Virginia, slopes toward the

Chesapeake Bay. Every drop of rain that runs off these lands flows toward the bay. So does the discharge from every sewage pipe, every industrial outfall and uncontained oil spill, every Styrofoam coffee cup casually tossed into a ditch. When soil erodes from farmland, or from a forest bull-dozed for development, the sediment can head only in one direction—bayward. This is the drainage basin, or *watershed,* of the Chesapeake Bay; and on such a map the bay appears neither dominant nor long and broad—just a smallish pool of water on the receiving end of all our activities, wise and foolish, across the vast lands of the watershed.

Even placing the bay in the context of its watershed may understate the degree to which the land can influence its waters. This is because the bay's considerable length and breadth conceal how skinny it is. There is little water in it—the Chesapeake is very, very shallow. About 1,000,000 feet long from head to mouth, and up to 100,000 feet wide, it averages only 21 feet in depth. Acre for acre across the lands of its watershed, the bay has less than one-tenth the volume of water of most of the world's other coastal bays to absorb and dilute whatever pollutants wash from farms and cities around it. (See Figure 1.1.)

The Great, Green Filter

To understand how watersheds and their waters interact, start by visiting and comparing two kinds of small streams anywhere in the Chesapeake basin—one in a mostly forested area, the other in an urban-suburban set-ting. Notice how when it rains in the wooded stream valley, the leaves and branches of the forest intercept and deflect the raindrops, softening the impact of those that reach the ground. The rain that falls is literally sponged up by the dense vegetation and the deep leaf duff of the forest floor. Only in very intense storms will the stream's channel receive enough runoff to go rampaging destructively down its course, cutting at its banks and scouring its bed.

By contrast, the paved areas, house roofs, and compacted soils of the urban-suburban stream's more developed watershed will channel as much as 100 times the amount of water from the same rainfall into the stream course; and the runoff will occur several times more quickly,

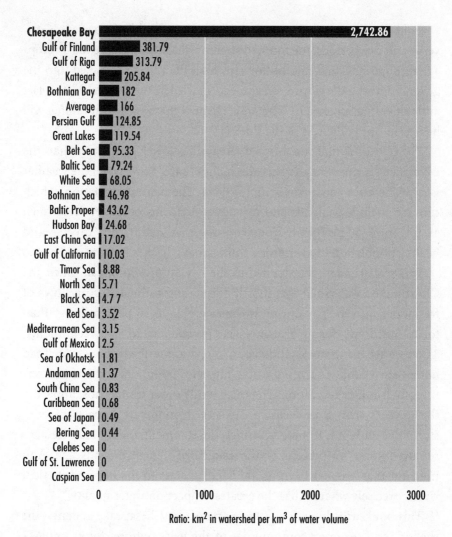

Body of Water	Ratio
Chesapeake Bay	2,742.86
Gulf of Finland	381.79
Gulf of Riga	313.79
Kattegat	205.84
Bothnian Bay	182
Average	166
Persian Gulf	124.85
Great Lakes	119.54
Belt Sea	95.33
Baltic Sea	79.24
White Sea	68.05
Bothnian Sea	46.98
Baltic Proper	43.62
Hudson Bay	24.68
East China Sea	17.02
Gulf of California	10.03
Timor Sea	8.88
North Sea	5.71
Black Sea	4.7 7
Red Sea	3.52
Mediterranean Sea	3.15
Gulf of Mexico	2.5
Sea of Okhotsk	1.81
Andaman Sea	1.37
South China Sea	0.83
Caribbean Sea	0.68
Sea of Japan	0.49
Bering Sea	0.44
Celebes Sea	0
Gulf of St. Lawrence	0
Caspian Sea	0

Ratio: km^2 in watershed per km^3 of water volume

FIGURE 1.1. The Shallow, Vulnerable Bay. Chesapeake Bay, compared to other coastal and inland bodies of water, has a huge drainage basin for the amount of water it contains, a ratio of 2,742.86 square kilometers of land for every cubic kilometer of water. The principal reason is the Chesapeake's extreme shallowness; its average depth is less than 22 feet. [R. Costanza, Gund Institute for Ecological Economics, University of Vermont]

without the rough, spongy surfaces of the forest to slow its passage. Conversely, in dry periods, the forested stream will continue to be fed by seepage through its banks and bottom from all the rain that soaked into the ground. On the developed stream, too much left the watershed too fast and not enough soaked in. The same channel that raged with rainfall will lie nearly empty the rest of the time.

The upshot is that the forested stream has lower peak flows than the developed stream when it rains and higher "base" flows when the weather is dry. The forested stream is more stable. The natural vegetation, which can also include wetlands and meadows, performs other services—such as filtration of pollution from runoff—that maintain a diverse and healthy population of everything from aquatic insects to trout and bass.

This scenario can be extended to the bay. In pre-European times, the Chesapeake's watershed was mostly forest, and estimated peak flows of freshwater into the bay during storms were 25 to 30 percent lower than today. Base flows during droughts were probably 10 to 15 percent higher. Thus, we see that natural landscapes, in relation to the bay, are more than homes for wildlife, sources of wood, filters for pollution, and pleasant settings for outdoor recreation. They also wring order from chaos, impart to the whole system a *resilience,* a capacity to moderate impacts of both storm and drought. In modern times, development and agriculture have removed some 40 percent of the watershed's original landscape. And much of that loss has been on the lands closest to the bay and its tidal rivers, precisely where it has the greatest impact on water quality.

This book will show how other parts of the Chesapeake system—the shellfish and sea grass communities of the bay's bottom, for example— also buffer the bay against both natural and human disruption. And it will explain how, as we continue to change the original nature of the system's resilience, we risk destabilizing it beyond recovery.

The Amputated Bay

The tributaries, or rivers and streams, of the watershed are much more to the bay than a collector system sending pollution downstream. They are highways and habitat for spawning fish, a vital link in the bay's fabled seafood production. For thousands of years, great schools of herring and shad glutted the bay each spring, extending like living fingers of the ocean to the farthest upstream limits of the drainage basin. Starting far out at sea, these fish ran up Virginia's James River, past Jamestown and Hopewell. Racing through Richmond, pushing ever upward, they turned into the Rivanna, pressing on to Charlottesville and beyond. The shad sought the rivers, while the smaller herring continued up streams no wider than a person's stride. Even larger numbers of both species thronged Pennsylvania's Susquehanna, the bay's biggest river, embarking on the longest migration of any fish in eastern North America. They mounted the watershed as far as Binghamton, Elmira, and Cooperstown in New York State.

Fish that run up rivers from the sea to spawn are called *anadromous*. The bay has several such species, of which the shad and herring are perhaps the most ambitious voyagers. (See Figure 1.2.) Like the salmon of the West Coast, they appear to be drawn back to the waters where they were born by homing in on a sort of "organic bouquet," or scent that is unique for each river and stream in the vast drainage basin. In navigating from their ocean home, the fish may also be guided by the angle of the sun, the earth's magnetic field, currents, temperature, the amount of salt in the water, or a combination of all these. Exactly how they find their way home remains a mystery.

Come autumn, usually on nights when the moon is dark and a storm has just passed, an even more curious traffic stirs throughout the circulatory system that weaves together the bay and its basin. In the streams of lands as distant as the West Virginia mountains, the rolling farmland of Virginia's Shenandoah Valley, and the swampy river bottoms of Maryland's Eastern Shore, eels are stirring, undergoing physical changes to prepare them for the reverse of the shad's spawning trip. The eels will move downstream through the bay, homing in, along with eels from all over North America and Europe, on the Sargasso Sea, their universal spawning grounds.

Species that run down rivers to the sea to spawn are called *catadromous,* and eels are the bay's only full-fledged example of this behavior. Migrating eels may reach nearly 4 feet in length and weigh more than 6

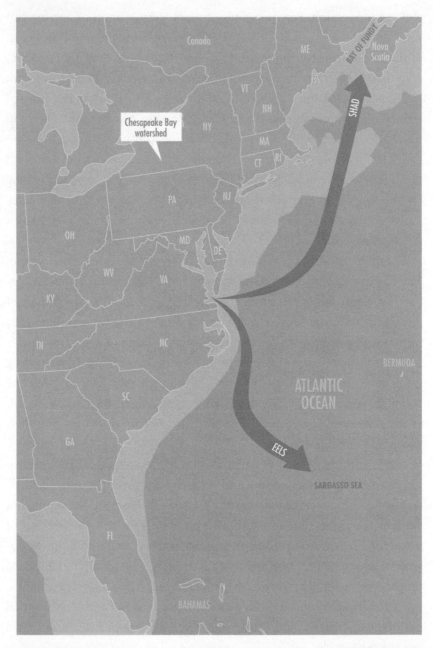

FIGURE 1.2. Living Connections with the Oceans. Many species associated with the Chesapeake roam far and wide. Two prominent voyagers are eels, which spawn in the Sargasso Sea, and shad, which range as far north as the Bay of Fundy, returning to the Chesapeake to spawn.

pounds. The parent eels all die upon spawning, sinking into the depths of the Bermuda Triangle. Great, slow currents seize the helpless young, which at that stage of life resemble transparent willow leaves, and transport them across the ocean. Months, even years, later, as tiny eel-like forms, or elvers, they arrive near the mouths of Chesapeake Bay and other inlets of the Atlantic coast. There is not even the possibility of a "bouquet" imprinted at birth to explain how they wriggle their way from there to every capillary of a watershed they have never experienced. We only know that what draws them back is a powerful force that has been working for millions of years.

During the last century and a half these living connections, anadromous and catadromous, between the oceans and the bay watershed have weakened considerably. Early settlers in Pennsylvania rejoiced as the shad runs in early spring saved them from winter's near-starvation. Now, no living Pennsylvanian would remember those glad migrations. Overfishing during the spawning runs up the bay was intense. In the mid-nineteenth century, shad were taken by the ton in huge haul seine nets that would sometimes block an entire river.

But the death knell for the great spring runs sounded with erection of insurmountable dams on the James and the Susquehanna, beginning in the 1800s. In effect, these and thousands of smaller dams and stream blockages have cut off thousands of miles of historic spawning waters. The runs of shad, herring, and other species continue, in weakened measure, to this day on some rivers and streams. But it is well to remember, as we try to restore the former vitality of the bay, that its health is linked to the whole scope of the watershed. And with respect to fish migration, we are currently dealing with a partial amputee.

An Unruly Beast—The Estuary

Just as the bay branches upstream throughout a sixth of the Atlantic seaboard, downstream at its mouth it is open to the full scope of the ocean. The resulting collisions of sweet and salt—fresh river water flowing seaward and ocean water pushing inland—make what we call an *estuary*. The Latin verb *aestuare*—to heave, boil, surge, be in commotion—

gives fair warning that this place is no mere river, running in only one direction for all time. Nor is it a lake, its waters turning over sedately once or twice a year as the surface layers cool and warm. Neither does it feature the predictable currents and constant, salty chemistry of the oceans. Estuaries are among the liveliest natural systems of the planet. They are the aquatic world's three-ring circuses of motion, productivity, and changeableness. There are about 850 such places in North America, from Long Island Sound to San Francisco Bay, but none among them so large and potentially bountiful as Chesapeake Bay.

I say "potentially" because the modern-day Chesapeake is a system in deep trouble, struggling for survival. In these pollution-conscious times, we are always asking, What is the quality of our waters? How are they doing? Do they and the life they hold seem to be coming back or going sour? If we were to observe and monitor the bay for a few days, or even a few years, to try to give it a grade, we might end up exasperated, wanting to flunk it solely for unruliness. That is the essential nature of estuaries—neither ocean nor river, but a transition zone, an edge where both systems overlap and struggle to assert themselves. That nature makes for a complicated and quirky system, one that is taxing both to creatures who would live in it and to those who would understand it, a system that needs all the stabilizing mechanisms (like its forested lands) it can get. But it is also a system capable of sustaining more life, more productivity for its size than virtually any other place on Earth. To see the method in the bay's apparent madness—to develop a frame of reference for asking, "How's the bay doing?"—it helps to begin when the only history was written by wind, river, and rock.

A Rare Flower—The Geologic Bay

The present Chesapeake Bay is just the latest in a long line of bays here. Indeed, there may well have been at least ten bays here during the last 5 million years. For most of the last half-million years, there has not even been an estuary at this point on the coast, just the narrow river valley carved by the mighty Susquehanna across the coastal plain and the continental shelf. A second channel was cut by the James, the two joining around Norfolk. The ancient riverbeds today form the bay's main shipping channels.

Intermittently throughout geologic time, the earth's climate has cooled so that large portions of today's oceans became bound up in the polar ice and glaciers. Sea level then was as much as 100 meters (325 feet) below where it is today, the surf breaking more than a hundred miles east of the current beaches. Only in the relatively short (measured in tens of thousands of years) interglacials, the warmest periods between ice ages, do the ice melt and the heave and surge of the rising seas gorge the coastal river valleys and inlets. During those brief, geologic summers, estuaries such as the Chesapeake swell and blossom like rare flowers within the nooks and crannies of the continental fringes, only to wither away with the onset of the next ice age and the reabsorption of the seas into the polar ice.

Today's Chesapeake began to fill about 10,000 years ago as the rising sea level reached the bay's present mouth and backed up the river flows from the Susquehanna and the James. The slope of the lower river channels was so slight that the flooding proceeded rapidly up their valleys. Around 9,000 years ago, the head of the newborn bay had almost reached Baltimore, though it was much narrower and shallower than today. Some 6,000 years ago, as Sumerians in Asia were inventing writing, the bay had widened and deepened, assuming something like its present form. By 3,000 years ago, as Rameses II ruled Egypt and Troy was sacked, the Chesapeake as we know it today had formed.

Perhaps there were a few seconds of geologic time then when the estuary could be said to have been in equilibrium, neither coming nor going; but ever since, its channels have been filling in with the sediments that continually wash from its shores and from the lands of the watershed. As it fills, its waters eventually will be squeezed upward and outward, to spread in a wide, shallow film across much of today's Eastern Shore. They will also inundate the western shore's low-lying peninsulas from Aberdeen, north of Baltimore, on down to the marshes of Guinea in Gloucester County, Virginia, at the mouth of the York River. This process will take a few thousand years unless human influences—dredging, for example, or the accelerating rise in sea level fueled by global warming—override expected climatic and geologic events. Ten thousand years from now, perhaps only a marsh will commemorate where the Chesapeake dwelled.

The great estuary will be gone. Or will it? Water will still flow from the watershed, will still seek its level in the sea, slowly carving new channels into the sediments left behind, setting the stage for the next coming. And even a quarter-million years hence, as the glaciers lie heaviest on the land and the seas have shrunk back off the continental shelves, who can say that November's eels and April's shad will not continue to come and go in a few, remnant tributaries of the coastline, safekeeping in their genes and instincts the annual rituals of once and future bays?

Slosh and Burp—The Wind's Will

The bay's geologic variability is mirrored on time scales as short as the everyday circulation of water. Tides send a charge of water rippling up and back down the 195-mile basin twice in every twenty-four-hour day. These tides, two highs and two lows every day, stretch as far up the bay's rivers as Washington on the Potomac and Richmond on the James. Many creatures of the estuary synchronize their lives to these periodic movements of water. The abundant periwinkles that scale the stalks of marsh grass to stay above the rising tide will continue their up-and-down migrations far from their native bay. (People who once took Chesapeake periwinkles to Alabama found them on the living room floor the next morning. As the tide rose back on the Chesapeake, the periwinkles had scaled the walls of their aquarium in Birmingham.) Likewise, crabs taken from Tangier Island, Virginia, and put into a tank in Pittsburgh, Pennsylvania, will shed their shells in accordance with the tidal clockwork back on Tangier.

Nothing would seem more regular and predictable than the tides, and that is true as far as when each high and each low occur. But how high and low they go is quite another matter. Because of the Chesapeake's long and shallow shape, movement of water in it is ruled to an unusual extent by the caprice of wind. A northwest blow may literally shove much of the bay's water out the mouth of the estuary and hold it there for days. High tides still come on schedule, but there is not much to them. On the other hand, the succeeding lows are memorable, exposing thousands of acres of normally submerged bottom—just one of the many stresses that life in the estuary must deal with. Conversely, a steady northeast wind may pile water up in sections of the bay several feet above normal, flooding low-lying shorelines with salty water, severely limiting the kinds of plants and animals that can survive there.

Certain winds may also have potentially harmful effects by triggering *seiching,* or sloshing motions, within the bay's deeper waters, tilting them from the eastern shore to the western shore, much like the motion you can set up by wiggling your hips in the bathtub. This in turn can cause the bay to "burp," or heave up, oxygen-poor waters from its deep channels into shallower areas—another in the long line of unpredictable and stressful phenomena encountered by life in estuaries. On the Chesapeake, local winds tinker as much as 90 percent of the time with the regular cosmic clockwork (like the moon's gravitational pull) that drives the tides. An extreme wind, such as a hurricane, may temporarily increase the volume of water in the bay by more than 30 percent. Winds routinely play the bay like a concertina, pumping and squeezing its normal water volume upward and downward by 10 to 20 percent.

Such variability is far more than a statistical curiosity. The fortunes of seafood lovers from Harrisburg to Norfolk depend on the wind's caprice. It affects the yearly availability of the succulent blue crab. Historically, about half of the nation's entire harvest has come from the Chesapeake. As many as a quarter of a billion individual crabs may be taken in a good year; but like most everything else in the estuary, the numbers of crabs can fluctuate wildly. In Maryland waters, the catch once went from 36 million pounds to 10 million, then back to 27 million, all in a four-year period.

All the bay's crabs are hatched near its mouth, in sight of the Chesapeake Bay Bridge-Tunnel between Cape Charles and Virginia Beach. Here, tides and currents conspire to flush most of the helpless larvae, or *zoea,* into the open ocean. There, dozens of miles out on the continental shelf, is the other boundary of the system that begins in the forested hills of West Virginia and New York. And the baby crabs drifting toward the point of no return from the Atlantic are highly dependent on winds, prevailing from just the right direction at just the right time, to get back into the Chesapeake. Thus, part of the answer to the annual ups and downs of the crab harvest may literally be "blowin' in the wind."

The Only Constant Is Change

As if it were not enough that the bay is shoved around at the wind's will, consider that it also flows two ways at once (Figure 1.3). Since the freshwater from its rivers is lighter than the salt water pushing up from the ocean, the fresh spilling off the watershed runs atop the salt. So the bay on its surface is usually heading toward Norfolk, while on its bottom it is Baltimore-bound. The tides, of course, still move up and down the bay, reversing at times the effect of the two-layered flow; but for a particle of water near the surface, the net movement, tides notwithstanding, is downstream, whereas a particle near the bottom will likewise work its way up-bay.

FIGURE 1.3. Mixing and Flows of Water in the Estuary. Freshwater flows out of the bay, riding over an incoming wedge of salt water from the ocean. Stirred by winds and currents, the layers mix. The tides flow in and out, with two highs and two lows every day, but the net movement of water is usually downstream on top and upstream on the bottom. [Adapted from White, *Chesapeake Bay: A Field Guide*]

A lot of life in the bay has evolved to hitch free rides on this two-way circulatory train. The feeble-swimming *larvae,* or early life stages of many fish and crabs, are able to sink or rise in the water to ride the flows of salt and fresh up or down the bay, moving from where they are born to areas with better food or growing conditions.

But what is fine for these wayfarers presents a major problem for other bay creatures that survive best by staying put near where they were born. These include larval oysters and many other species of *plankton,* the tiny, floating plant and animal communities that abound in the nutrient-rich waters of the estuary. They cope by intermittently rising toward the surface and then sinking toward the bottom, performing a roughly circular movement that lets them maintain stability in a system that constantly tries to wash them either to Baltimore or out to sea.

It all seems quite neatly worked out: fresh on top, salty on the bottom, one layer flowing south, the other north—this is the "classic" bay circulation. But the bay hardly ever seems to play by the rules for long. The willful wind is one reason; another major one is the great bursts of water issuing from the mighty Susquehanna River at the bay's head. Carver of the bay's channel in geologic time and source of nearly half of all of the bay's freshwater, the Susquehanna dominates circulation and water quality for nearly half the estuary's length. When Mother Susquehanna clears her throat, delivering billions of tons of new rainfall throughout the estuary, it can set the lesser river mouths of her children to chattering, flip-flopping their normal flow patterns up and down both shores of the Chesapeake.

So it was that one of the first long-term measurements of the bay's circulation found that the estuary was flowing in classical pattern—out (seaward) on top and in on the bottom—less than half the time. The rest of the year the flows went any of the following ways, always returning to the classic pattern within days:

In on top, out on the bottom.
In on top, out in the middle, and in on the bottom.
Out on top, in in the middle, and out on the bottom.
Out on the top, middle, and bottom.
In on the top, middle, and bottom.

The classic two-layered flow does occur more often than any other pattern; but for plankton, larval fish and crabs, or environmental managers attempting to track the movements of pollutants through the estuarine system, there are never firm guarantees of where things will end up in Chesapeake Bay.

Invisible Fences

As much as any single factor, the bay's layered flows define the patterns of life within the estuary. They call the tune to which everything there must dance; they zone the bay and its rivers into biological regions as distinct as mountain and plain on the land—all because of a very simple thing that happens among the layers. They mix. Not totally, or we would no longer have layered flows, but they mix some. And, voilà! We suddenly have a system that is not only fresh as a lake (in its upper reaches) and salty as an ocean (at its mouth), but also everything in between—an almost infinite range of habitats for aquatic life, depending on each species' level of tolerance for salt. The amount of salt in water is expressed in parts of salt per thousand parts of water (by weight). Freshwater has a salinity of 0 (zero) parts per thousand, while the ocean is around 35 parts. The salt gradations also extend in the water from top to bottom. An exquisite ability to differentiate among these salinity variations is how the oyster larvae maintain position in the bay, rising and sinking periodically to stay in about the same place. Salt also contracts and expands the boundaries of spawning and nursery areas for crabs and fish, and dictates the kinds of vegetation that grow in marshlands and underwater grass beds. It limits and unleashes diseases and parasites and pests such as jellyfish, enhances the reproduction of oysters (saltier is better), and influences where blue crabs migrate, mate, and shed their shells.

If we go out and measure salinity up and down the bay on any given day, we will get a picture of neat compartmentalization, lines of salinity, or *isohalines*, grading from saltier to fresher as we move up-bay. But like almost every other "snapshot" of the ever-shifting estuary, this one also tends to be misleading. In fact, the isohalines are routinely sent scuttling down and up the bay like fallen leaves before the gusts of autumn. The reason is that some times of the year—and some years—are wetter or dryer than others.

In some years, nearly three times more river water flows into the bay as in other years (see Figure 1.4). This current pushes the ocean's influence south, just as dry years let it advance up the bay. Even whole decades can vary tremendously: Nearly every year of the 1970s was wet, well above the average annual inflow, while almost all of the 1960s were bone dry. It is probably no coincidence that the wet 1970s, when a lot of pollution was washing off the lands of the watershed, ushered in an era of marked environmental decline in the bay.

The estuary, after extended wet periods, can resemble a freshwater lake as far south as the Potomac; and a year later, if the rains are scant across

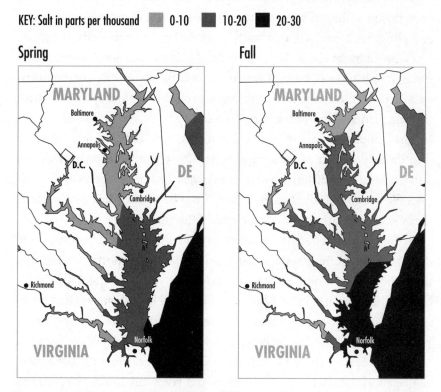

FIGURE 1.4. Salinity: Spring and Fall. Higher river flows in the spring push back the ocean's salty influence; in autumn, drier weather diminishes river flow and the ocean marches up the estuary. [Adapted from Cronin, *The Biology of the Estuary,* and White, *Chesapeake Bay: A Field Guide*]

the watershed, salinities as far north as the Maryland Bay Bridge can reach as high as 22 parts per thousand (25 is average at the bay's mouth).

Most species of aquatic life have a narrow range of tolerance for salinity—either they can't stand it or they need the full strength of the ocean salt. Many of the bay's dominant species are among the minority that can tolerate wide swings in salt. Even so, the bay's dramatic gyrations in this basic parameter of life in water add considerably to the stress of living in an estuary.

If You Harvest the Bay, Pray for Drought

The up-and-down swings in the water moving off the watershed can also have major pollution consequences. Consider the quantities of nitrogen and phosphorus and soil that wash from the land and are delivered to the Chesapeake by its rivers. Up to a point, this input is a good thing. Nitrogen and phosphorus, both of which occur naturally in soil, are the nutrients that fertilize much of the bay's growth of *phytoplankton* (tiny, floating plants). They also nourish the bay's submerged grass beds, which in turn support a host of higher life-forms. Similarly, sediment flowing into the estuary is a necessary ingredient for phytoplankton growth and also acts as a sort of fertilizer to its marshes. Sediment accumulation allows the marsh to build higher, to keep from being drowned by a sea level that has been rising ever since the end of the last ice age.

In the last several decades, however, principally through large increases in discharges of human sewage, farm fertilizers, and animal wastes, and through deforestation and land development, we have dramatically increased the watershed's contributions of essential ingredients such as nitrogen, phosphorus, and sediment to the point they have become major pollutants of the Chesapeake, an issue discussed in more detail in Chapter 2.

The difference between a wet year and a dry year across the bay's basin can be enormous in terms of pollution. Wet years can double the amounts of nitrogen and phosphorus that are washed off the land—a difference of more than a hundred million pounds a year (Figure 1.5)—and the difference in sediment runoff can be billions of pounds. Wet years, or more specifically, wet springs, can also cause so much freshwater to flow down

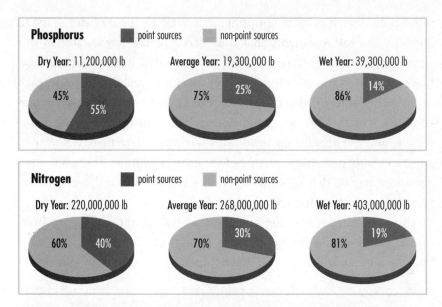

FIGURE 1.5. **Wet and Dry Years Affect Bay Pollution.** Rainy years produce more runoff from city streets and country highways, suburban lawns, construction sites, and farm fields. The runoff, called nonpoint source, carries with it pollutants of all kinds, including the bay's two most troublesome, nitrogen and phosphorus. The relatively constant flow of pollutants from the pipes of sewage plants and factories, called point sources, carry more of the burden of pollution in dry years than in wet. [EPA Chesapeake Bay Program]

the bay that it does not mix normally with the salty, heavier, bottom layers. This condition, known as *stratification,* amounts to something like clamping a lid over the bottom waters. With the normal mixing processes thwarted, sometimes for months, bacteria consume most of the oxygen in the bottom layers, and no more can get churned down from the surface. This natural phenomenon seems to have been worsened by pollution (discussed in detail in Chapter 2). The bottom line is that massive regions of the bay now often become as devoid of oxygen as outer space. Large areas that still look clean and vital to the eye of a boater sailing across them may, beneath the surface, be as hostile to fish and crabs as the driest desert.

While those who farm the land often pray for rain across the watershed to increase their harvests, the watermen who harvest the modern, troubled bay would, on the whole, prefer it dry—the less runoff, the less water pollution. It is often tempting, following a couple of dry years, to attribute the improvements that may occur in the bay's water to our many and expensive efforts to restore the estuary's health. The real test, however, is to wait until after a few wet years, or even a wet decade, such as the 1970s, and see what things look like. It may be no coincidence that conditions in the bay worsened dramatically during the 1970s. Conversely, one might seize on conditions during an extremely wet year to paint an overly pessimistic picture of the estuary's future. Though human pollution may be the bay's bad actor, it is still Nature, with wet and dry years, who sets the stage. (See Figure 1.6.)

This variability is why the unglamorous task of monitoring environmental conditions in the bay for long periods of time is so critical, as is tracking accurately the ups and downs among its creatures. Monitoring—

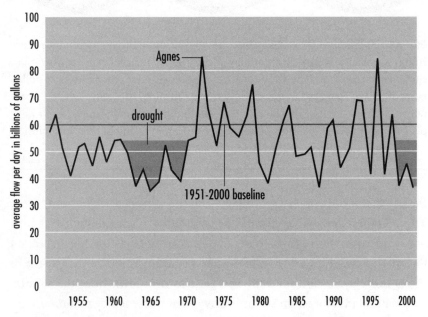

FIGURE 1.6. **Historic Variations in the Bay's Freshwater Streamflow.** Differences in rainfall and subsequent runoff of polluted stormwater (Figure 1.5) not only influence the bay annually but can color whole decades. The 1960s were drier than average, with relatively little runoff, whereas the 1970s were much wetter than average, with high runoff. Tropical Storm Agnes made 1972 one of the wettest years ever recorded. The late 1980s and 1990s were both dry periods. [USGS, Chesapeake Bay Program]

think of it as taking the bay's temperature, feeling its pulse—is expensive and its payoff long term. Like planting trees in city parks, it can be tempting to cut back on monitoring in tight budget years. No one will notice for a while. But, as much of the foregoing text has shown, the natural variability of the estuary is huge. The total biomass of fish in the bay, from minnows to big ones, for example, is estimated to vary as much as tenfold from year to year. It can take years, even decades, of careful observation to see patterns and trends that will let us sort out the signals of human-induced impacts from all the normal "background noise," or static. Without comprehensive monitoring, effective management of a dynamic system like the Chesapeake Bay is impossible. Without it, day to day, year to year, the only thing we can be sure of is that the bay won't be the same as it was the day, or year, before.

Avalanche! A Bit of River Goes a Long Way

We talk a lot about how much the water flowing from the bay's watershed influences it. So it may come as a surprise to learn that the entire river flow is only a tiny fraction of the 18 trillion or so gallons that is the volume of the bay and its tidal tributaries. If the bay were to be drained, and dammed to keep the ocean out, the rivers would have to run for half a year to refill its basin, assuming average rainfall.

But think of that freshwater input as a catalyst—those two or three drops of chemical you add to a big glop of epoxy glue to make it a powerful cement. Or think of leverage—how using a long pry-stick multiplies your muscle power to move a big rock. So it is that freshwater, as it proceeds down the bay, stimulates more and more of the heavier ocean water to slide up the bay underneath it. You can observe this effect by partitioning an aquarium, filling one half with freshwater, dyed blue, and the other with salt water, dyed red. Pull out the partition and watch the salt run under the fresh.

The effect in the bay is a bit like an avalanche, gathering power as it moves downslope. As the freshwater layer moves ever seaward, it mixes with and pulls increasing volumes of the salty, lower layers upward and back toward the sea with it. By the time this process reaches the Virginia capes, the volume of river flow has been amplified from three to nine times. And to compensate for what is flowing out of the bay, the ocean is pumping a correspondingly large volume of water in along the estuary's bottom.

So it is that a relatively small flow of freshwater into the bay can energize the circulation of the whole system by a factor of several times. Many other estuaries do this, but few so forcefully as the Chesapeake. This robust circulation, in turn, underlies the bay's world-standard capacity for productivity, as shown in the next section.

And so the bay goes—and comes—and goes; here and gone with the ice ages, up and down with the tides, in and out with the layers of salt and fresh (also out and in, in-out-in, and more); the wind blows, the bay burps, a zillion crabs are lost at sea; it rains in Pennsylvania, and in Virginia salinity retreats, fish nursery areas shift, the bay bottom gasps for oxygen. How are we to make sense of such a place, where land and water mingle so, and the seas and the rivers make such an infernal commotion?

Monitoring is a start. Some scientists think powerful computer graphics might be the only way to visualize what is going on, and they can already run simple programs that digest several years of data on things like changes in the bay's oxygen content and animate them. We are already, on a limited basis, tracking and counting the migrations of fish with photoelectric cells in the banks of spawning rivers; and satellites give us increasingly accurate and lovely color pictures of plankton densities, sediment concentrations, and more. Perhaps the day is not far off when we can portray all this coming and going à la Disney—and then what a shifting, shimmering, quixotic creature old Chesapeake will appear.

Such a notion may be fanciful, but the extremely variable character of the estuary is not, and it raises a very real question: Why, with all the uncertainties and stresses associated with its behavior, is an estuary like the Chesapeake so incredibly rich with life?

Productivity—The Bay's True Value

By any measure but its own historical bounty, the modern bay remains richly productive. To value its natural systems against the economics of dredging, sewage treatment, or other human projects that cause environmental harm, we often invoke the bay's production in commercial terms: more than 100 million pounds of seafood landed annually with a dockside value of tens of millions of dollars. (We land close to 400 million pounds of seafood annually if we include the coastwide catches of menhaden rendered into oil and fertilizer at Reedville, Virginia.) From the bay also comes a major portion of the nation's blue crab catch and, before overharvest, pollution, and disease decimated the stock, 15 percent of its oysters. It is spawning grounds for an estimated 70 percent of the East Coast's striped bass. All this from a mere pinprick on the North American coastline that contains a few billionths of the planet's water.

Estimates of the Chesapeake's total worth, including all bay-related economic activity, range into the hundreds of billions of dollars. But all the dollar and seafood-landings measures only hint at the true biological worth of the estuary. Scientists who compare the richness of life among Earth's different regions of land and water prefer to look at their *primary production*. This is the overall production of plant life—the basis everywhere for the food webs that ultimately sustain the large fauna, such as rockfish, waterfowl, and humans. Primary production can range from cactus in a desert region, to agriculture's corn and soybeans, to lichens in the Arctic and plankton and seaweeds in the water.

The land–water edges, where estuaries lie, excel at "crop" production, towering over all the earth's other land- and waterscapes, natural and managed. The only systems invented by humans that come close to estuaries are intensive rice culture in flooded river plains and year-round cropping of sugarcane in the tropics, but these efforts require large inputs of human time and expensive fertilizers and pesticides. An estuary does the work for free. All we have to do is not impair (or these days, *repair*) its natural functioning.

It is not surprising that estuaries, with their rich broth of nutrients from coastal rivers and wetlands, have a primary production about five times the average for the oceans as a whole. But actual estuarine production of fish is more impressive still—about ten times higher than the oceanic average. And among the world's estuaries, the Chesapeake Bay is a star, with a fish production (per unit of primary production) one hundred times or more that of the oceans as a whole.

So how does the bay get more oomph out of every ounce and pound of primary production than almost anyplace on Earth? To begin understanding the secrets of this enormous capacity for life, one needs no Ph.D.—only a pole several feet in length and a canoe, although you can make do in many places with old sneakers and the willingness to wade out from one of the marshes or beaches along the estuary's shoreline. Probing the bay's waters this way (or *progging,* as the watermen say), you will quickly discover a profound truth: You can touch bottom easily almost everywhere. If you know people who boat on the bay, ask if they have ever run aground. If they say not, they most likely never leave the dock.

The Chesapeake Bay is quite shallow. At nearly 200 miles long, and up to 30 miles wide, it looks like a lot of water out there; but that water is spread thin. The average depth of the bay is around 21 feet, or 27 feet if we don't include its tidal rivers—less than halfway from pitcher's mound to home plate. It has been estimated that 10 percent of the bay is less than 3 feet in depth and that 20 percent is less than 7 feet. In this simple fact— that its bottom lies very near its top—rests much of the bay's uniqueness as well as its vulnerability to modern pollution.

Its shallowness means that sunlight, the first essential for plant growth, can penetrate a large part of the Chesapeake's waters. This light and warmth, combined with the continuous flow of nutrients, minerals, and dissolved gases from the estuary's dozens of rivers, supports large stocks of phytoplankton. Similarly, excellent potential growing conditions for rooted underwater grasses extend to at least half a million acres of shallow bottom. Here is the bay's second engine of primary production, huge underwater meadows of grasses. More than a dozen varieties of these plants occur throughout the bay, ranging from wild celery near the head of the estuary that can barely tolerate salt to eelgrass near its mouth that thrives in oceanic salinities. Collectively, the grasses are referred to as *submerged aquatic vegetation* (SAV). They are not only food for waterfowl; they are also high-quality, "keystone" habitats—nurseries, hiding places, and breeding grounds—for shrimp, crabs, fish, seahorses, and a host of less familiar life-forms in the food web. In addition, the sunlit shallows also foster rich growths of *benthic* (bottom-dwelling) algae.

Where its broad shallows merge with the land's edge, the Chesapeake forms a quarter-million acres of tidal marshes, or wetlands. The grasses and other marsh plants that grow here extend food and habitat as lush as anything the underwater grass beds offer for up to thousands of feet inland. In effect, with its phytoplankton, underwater grasses, benthic algae, and tidal marsh plants, the bay's primary production engine is running on four cylinders, while other natural regions of the planet run mostly on one (plankton in the open oceans, forests on the uplands, for example).

Doing More with Less

Despite the rich table the Chesapeake sets for its aquatic life, it is an unpredictable hostess. The watershed's rivers don't deliver nutrients in anything like a constant manner (remember wet and dry years, and the dynamic and variable nature of estuaries). In general, there is a glut each spring, when river runoff is high, and a famine during the winters and some summers when the rivers run low. Plants and animals in the estuary have to live year-round and need a fairly steady supply of food. But how are they to get three squares a day from such a quirky system?

The bay, it turns out, is a system elegantly adapted to do more with less, to recycle—something we humans are just beginning to realize makes a lot of sense in our own lives. Recycling works like this: The phytoplankton absorb nitrogen and phosphorus from the water and grow. As they die, or get eaten and passed through a larger creature's digestive tract, their remains fall to the bay bottom—a never-ending shower of nutrients. Then, the many kinds of bacteria that are abundant in shallow estuaries rapidly decompose the remains, freeing the remaining nitrogen and phosphorus for reinjection back into the water to fuel new plankton growth.

Recycling is further aided by the bay's two-layered flow and the mixing between its top and bottom layers. These unique circulatory patterns mean that nitrogen and phosphorus don't just shoot down the rivers and out into the oceans—not by a long shot. On average, a particle of water (with the dissolved materials it carries) takes around half a year to pass from the Susquehanna to the ocean. This long *residence time* gives the recycling processes plenty of time to work. Think of it like swishing a gulp of a tasty drink around in your mouth for a long time, getting all the goodness out of it before spitting it out.

All bodies of water—oceans, rivers, and lakes—recycle nutrients to an extent. The bay happens to pull it off better and faster and more times than just about any of them. For example, less than a third of all the nitrogen, an essential nutrient that enters the bay by the hundreds of millions of pounds each year, ever escapes to the ocean. Recycling is enhanced further in the bay by its extraordinary shallowness. Nutrients that fall to the bottom are never far from the top. Tidal currents and wind churn the bottom sediments back into the water, where sunlight and phytoplankton begin the cycle of growth all over again.

Another way nutrients get quickly back into action in the bay is through uptake by *benthos,* the worms, clams, and other bottom dwellers that eat the nutrients and are in turn eaten, passing their calories up through the food web. Again, it all works so well here because the bottom is so very close to the top. The ocean's average depth, by contrast, is 12,000 feet, nearly 500 times that of the bay. Nutrients there fall to such depths that they never get back into the action on any meaningful time scale; and the oceans, except for their shallows, are relative deserts of primary production.

These days, there is a downside to the Chesapeake's tremendously efficient recycling. It was fine to make the most of nitrogen and phosphorus when the watershed was mostly forested, as relatively few nutrients flowed in from such lands. But now we are overloading the estuary with both of these nutrients from human sewage, from fertilizers washed off lawns and farms, and from polluted air. The effect, given the bay's ability to maximize use of nitrogen and phosphorus, is a bit like pouring kerosene on a fire. The system is producing too much phytoplankton, which in turn is causing depletion of vital dissolved oxygen and clouding the water, cutting off indispensable light that the underwater grasses need to grow.

We might sum things up by saying that the estuary has a higher metabolism than most other regions of the earth. Such terms, usually applied to higher life-forms, make it sound as if the bay were a coherent, living organism; and indeed, the more we discover about the sophisticated interaction of its parts—from ocean to oyster to watershed—the more intricately connected all the parts seem to be.

Ordering the Bay's House

For example, look at how scientists think the estuary handles the big variations in delivery of food via its rivers, which gush and shrivel according to the rainfall across its watershed. The underwater grass meadows, which in their prime may have carpeted half a million acres or more of bay bottom, play a role here that goes far beyond their better known values as habitat for crabs and fish and food for waterfowl and wading birds.

The grasses' maximum growth occurs in the spring, around the time that the bay in most years gets its maximum freshwater runoff, a time when most of the nitrogen and phosphorus it will see for the whole year is circulating through in a matter of weeks. The grasses as they grow can absorb large quantities of this phosphorus and nitrogen. The grassy bottom may, in effect, be functioning as a bank or warehouse, enabling the bay to smooth and damp its peaks of food energy. As an added benefit, the grass beds clear the water by trapping and filtering tremendous loads of sediment that enter the bay as runoff. And they dampen wave energy, reducing the shoreline erosion that is another source of excessive sediment in the modern bay.

From late summer through early winter, when river and nutrient flows are low, the grasses die back and decompose, a process that scientists think provides a nifty timed release of nutrients, allowing the recycling machinery to sustain the estuary's improbably large production. Grasses also store nutrition in their roots, a prime food source for wintering swans and geese that excavate them from the shallow bottoms. It is ironic that just when we most need the grasses to regulate the current nitrogen-phosphorus pollution of the bay, the excess nutrients have helped kill off nearly 90 percent of the grass beds.

There is a term scientists apply to individual creatures—and increasingly to whole natural systems—to describe mechanisms that work like the bay's grasses to maintain order and stability and to limit swings away from the conditions best for survival. It is called *homeostasis* ("staying the same"). A familiar example is the way we sweat when we're hot, to let evaporative cooling bring body temperature back toward a normal 98.6°F. A lovely example in a big, natural system is the life cycle of certain Pacific salmon, which return, fat and sleek, after years of roaming the oceans, to spawn and die in the streams and rivers where they were born. These waters, which must nourish the newly hatched salmon, are naturally nutrient poor because of the barren soils of their watersheds. But by dying and decomposing there, the adult salmon effectively fertilize the nursery with nutrients harvested thousand of miles out to sea.

Estuaries, as discussed earlier, are among the most dynamic, variable, potentially chaotic, and even stressful aquatic systems. Their functioning, from daily plankton production to their geologic filling and draining, is characterized by rapid and severe swings of behavior. Such places would seem especially in need of mechanisms like the underwater grasses and the marshes to smooth out the peaks and valleys—all the more so since we continue to destroy the forest, another major stabilizing influence, throughout much of the watershed.

This is not to say that even the pristine Chesapeake ever resembled a steady-state system such as the tropical coral reefs, where life has proceeded for millions of years within exceedingly narrow, stable ranges of temperatures, water clarity, and salinity. Indeed, scientists are just beginning to investigate how the Chesapeake's extraordinary seafood production may be related to its pulsing nature—from the flux of its rivers amid wet and dry and the caprices of wind churning its shallow waters to the exodus and homecoming of its many species of migratory fish. They think this essential pulsing, combined with the bay's complex, underwater circulatory patterns, may concentrate pockets of unusually rich food resources within the estuary at various times and places.

Over time, the Chesapeake ecosystem has evolved ways to flourish within the dynamic context of the estuary. When all these coping mechanisms are functioning well, we may say the system is resilient—that it can fluctuate with respect to river flows, salinity, sediment, nutrients, or whatever, but always return to equilibrium. Maintaining the bay's resilience depends not only on restoring a healthy aquatic system, but on maintaining and restoring woods and wetlands throughout the lands of its watershed. Without both, restoration of the bay's health is not possible.

Oysters Are Much More than Hors d'Oeuvres

It is on the shallow bay bottom, along with the grass beds, that we find yet another element of resilience, on the order of the forests, marshes, and underwater grasses. You may know this elegant mechanism of homeostasis as the old, gray oyster (variously rendered as "aryster," "oistuh," "erster," and "arschture"). The eastern oyster, *Crassostrea virginica*, is a good example of how we sometimes underestimate the importance of bay creatures by considering them mainly as they relate to our bellies and our commerce. For more than a century, dating from the 1860s, our huge harvests of the tasty bivalve were synonymous with Chesapeake Bay's incredible bounty.

In retrospect, it is clear that the towering peaks of oyster production during the late nineteenth century were not sustainable. Rather, they simply represented a short-term mining of the wealth accumulated on the bay's bottom. The edible oyster meat harvested in Maryland waters alone during the peak of that exploitation was equivalent to the yield from 160,000 head of prime steers. It is a testament to the resilience of the estuary and the oyster that harvests could remain at what was still considered world-class levels (1–3 million bushels a year) almost until the last decade of the twentieth century. Overfishing combined with disease, mismanagement, and pollution have now reduced the oysters in the bay to just a couple percent of their numbers before heavy harvesting began after the Civil War.

Just 2 percent left—think about that. And think of what it would be like to live in your house if you had lost 98 percent of the plumbing, or 98 percent of the heating and air-conditioning system, or 98 percent of the roof. In losing the bay's oysters, we have lost much more than a plentiful supply of appetizers, or even a vital portion of our seafood economy. We have destroyed a vital filter, an important recycler, a major habitat for other creatures, and, like the underwater grasses, a banker of food energy.

After their free-floating larvae attach to other oyster shells and become *spat* in the first weeks of life, oysters never move. They have traditionally been superabundant in the bay because its vigorous circulation brings them plenty of food and because their food is phytoplankton, which grows so well in the sunlit shallows (the bulk of oysters grow in water 30 feet deep or less). They are superb filterers, feeding by gaping their shells slightly and pumping bay water through their gills at rates up to 2 gallons per hour.

In addition to growing fat oysters, this process has at least two other important consequences for the estuary's health. By sucking in sediment that clouds the bay's waters and depositing it on the bay bottom as compacted fecal matter, the oyster acts to clear the water, thereby helping sunlight penetrate and grow more underwater grasses and beneficial kinds of plankton. It has been estimated that the pre-1870 stocks of oysters in the bay filtered a volume equal to that of the entire Chesapeake every few days, compared to a "filtration time" of nearly a year for today's diminished stocks. (Although they did not live everywhere in the bay, there is no doubt they made a major impact on water clarity. In modern times, expansion of filter feeders such as mussels and clams has caused dramatic clearing of the water in the Great Lakes and San Francisco Bay.)

Moreover, the oyster, like the grasses, seems to have been a banker and recycler of the huge pulses of nutrients that surged off the watershed in the wet springtime. Oysters filter the lush, nutrient-fertilized spring plankton bloom through their gills, using some of it for growth, but also depositing nutrient-rich feces on the bay's bottom—which, you will recall, is never far from the top. From there, these nutrient packages can be speedily recycled into production again. Feeding on plankton also acts to clarify the bay's waters.

Nowadays, the situation with the cloudy, oxygen-deprived bay and its depleted oysters is similar to an aquarium that has lost most of its filter. In addition, a healthy oyster bed was also the bay's equivalent of the tropical "live bottom" coral reef, its hard surfaces and millions of crevices providing habitat for a whole host of marine life. This community in turn attracted larger fish to feed, as well as sea ducks and loons. Young crabs also seem to prefer oyster bottoms as wintertime habitat over almost any other part of the Chesapeake. Only in recent years have scientists and bay managers come to appreciate how important were the physical structures of these reefs. Decades of intensive dredging, beginning more than a century ago, has broken apart and flattened the reefs that once posed hazards to navigation and that probably begot the term that watermen still use for an oyster bed: oyster "rock."

In a sense, today's bay is a natural system that has literally flipped—from clear to clouded, and from being rooted in great, bottom-dwelling communities of oysters, underwater grasses, and benthic plankton to an estuary adrift, dominated by the excesses of free-floating plankton, or algae.

The Chesapeake Ecosystem

We may never know precisely the extent to which the Chesapeake's shallow bottom—its grasses and its oysters—regulated its own environment, but the concept is not far-fetched. The Amazonian rain forest, for example, is well documented as maintaining a microclimate of the very moist conditions ideal for its own perpetuation. Cutting it down destroys those conditions, making regrowth of the original jungle impossible. Similarly, the Swiss Alps once were forested, but after clear-cutting by the Romans, they never recovered. The climate without the trees was too dry, and the mountain soils without a protective cover of forest lost their fertility to erosion. The climate protected the trees, which protected the climate, and so on, and so on.

It is all a circle, an interconnection, or *ecosystem* of plants and animals and people, of air, water, and soil. And these parts cannot be understood or valued apart from the patterns by which they connect and influence one another. This is how we must learn to understand the Chesapeake Bay—not just as water, or watershed, or seafood and sport, but also as an interrelated system of buffers and banks, of filters and traps and sinks, all working together to keep the bay's house in order, to maintain resilience.

Clear the forests, and you disrupt the rhythms and quality of the rivers' flows. Kill the underwater grasses, and you lose more than duck food and ducks (and duck hunting, with its rich tradition and history); overharvest oysters, and you remove more than can be measured in pounds or bushels or dollars, or even by the thrill of watching graceful and historic oyster skipjacks dredging the "rocks" under sail. Fill the marshes, and the losses of their rippling green and golden beauty and abundant birdlife are only the most obvious changes for the worse; you have also lost a vital pollution buffer between watershed and water, and diminished a primary source of energy for estuarine productivity. Damage parts, and you damage patterns. The ecosystem we call the estuary will in each case decline in its ability to rebound and regroup from the natural and humanmade forces that constantly buffet it. Resilience will be lost.

What the Animals Are Saying

The damage humans have done to the bay and its watershed is nothing short of staggering. And with more millions of people moving into the region, the odds may seem long against a major turnaround. Indeed, this book details many alarming trends. But reading all the reports in the world cannot provide a full sensibility of this marvelous, 64,000-square-mile creature called Chesapeake. The best way to start saving the bay is through direct contact with parts of its system, whether it be casting for rockfish with a rod, watching a great blue heron with binoculars, sitting in a duck hunting blind, or feeling the ooze of the bay bottom squishing up through your bare toes. Sometimes it is best to quit analyzing the bay and just listen to what its creatures have to tell us.

It may seem surprising, given the reputation of estuaries for producing and attracting huge quantities of species, that not many kinds of creatures live in the Chesapeake. To be sure, many kinds visit at various times of the year, either descending from their upstream, freshwater habitats or moving in from the oceans to feed or spawn. But in terms of full-time residents, both freshwater systems and the oceans, though less productive than estuaries, support many times more varieties of life.

This seeming paradox simply reflects the estuary's basic nature—lots of food production on the one hand, but also tremendous variability in environmental conditions: salinity that can swing from oceanic to lake-like and back; temperatures in the shallows that may freeze to the bottom mud in winter and soar above 90°F in summer; water quality in the rivers that can change with an overnight rainfall. As a bay scientist once summed it up, "The chow's great if you can stand the hassle."

That is just the point, and it may be the bay's best hope for coming back in the new century—much of what has survived here is able to stand a lot of hassle, is adaptable, tough, resilient to its core. So it is that blue crabs, while they find salinities highly suitable around the middle of the bay, near Tangier and Smith Islands, also flourish in the freshwater reaches of the bay's tributaries and the near-ocean of its mouth; and they do better than one might expect in grossly polluted sections such as Baltimore Harbor and Norfolk's Elizabeth River.

Oysters, though they can't move away from pollution, are able to survive days, even weeks, of depressed oxygen in the water by clamping their shells shut and switching their entire metabolic process. If overharvesting of big oysters, which are mostly females, creates problems for reproduction, male oysters are able to change their sex as needed to compensate. Even in their current, depleted state, oysters are still capable in some years of excellent reproduction.

Rockfish, harvested down to only a few percent of their previous numbers in the Chesapeake, have proven capable of an astounding comeback after a moratorium on fishing gave them just a few years of breathing room. Great blue herons, one of the few birds found year-round on the bay and in every county of its five-state watershed, prefer to dine on soft crabs, small fish, toads, and snakes, but when food is scarce they have been observed eating baby kittens and even a full-grown muskrat. Canvasback ducks, after pollution killed most of their normal food (the underwater grasses), changed their diet almost completely to small clams. Wild Canada geese turned to feeding in grain-fields, with great success. Submerged aquatic grasses, which remain hugely depressed, will often sprout vigorously in areas that have been barren of them for many years, if a dry year temporarily clears the water there.

In sum, although the bay we are trying to restore is a crippled version of the original, healthy system (see Figure 1.7), its primary inhabitants are anything but fragile and nothing if not adaptable to change. They are the

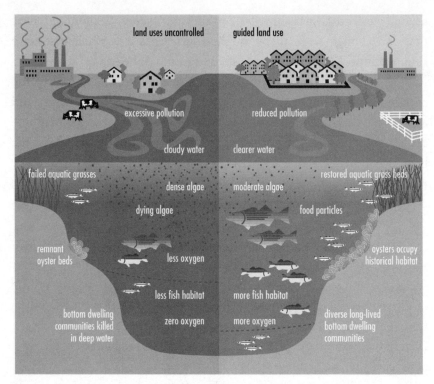

FIGURE 1.7. **The Bay We Have (*left*) and the Bay We Want (*right*).** The bay we have is polluted by far too much nitrogen, its plants and animals stressed by cloudy water that is often low in oxygen. Many species have been diminished by loss of habitat and overfishing. The bay we want has good water quality that nurtures a diverse, healthy community of plants and animals. [After K. Mountford, Chesapeake Bay Program, and others]

opportunists, the plants and animals that are best able to rush in and colonize new habitats during the intervals—brief in evolutionary time—when fertile estuaries such as the Chesapeake occur during the short warming spells between the long ice ages. If you have ever hooked a rockfish or a shad on a line, felt it tug for its freedom; tried to pry apart a living oyster's shells; or attempted to pick up a big-clawed, feisty jimmy (male) crab, then you know—the bay vigorously, vitally, desperately wants to live. Given half a chance to thrive, its inhabitants will not be shy grabbing it.

Vicious Cycles in Reverse

History is replete with environmentally damaging projects, from damming rivers to spraying pesticides, where the negative impacts turn out to surpass anything anticipated. It is another legitimate hope for the bay's recovery that restorative actions will also have unanticipated positive benefits, one building on another, a kind of vicious cycle in reverse. In areas such as Richmond, Virginia, on the James River, where long-standing dams have been breached to allow the passage upstream of spawning shad and herring, the river above and below the dams has unexpectedly blossomed with a variety of other new aquatic life. If current efforts to reduce nitrogen, the bay's most ubiquitous pollutant, start to improve oxygen in the depths, scientists expect a cascading effect. In the presence of more oxygen, the bottom sediments should begin to turn more of the nitrogen buried there into harmless gas. This conversion would further reduce pollution and improve oxygen, which would reduce more nitrogen—the vicious cycle in reverse. And if we can boost oysters significantly—a tenfold increase by 2010 is our goal—they will filter and clarify more water, which at some point will stimulate more underwater grasses to grow, which will help clarify the water further.

Perhaps such a cycle can happen with people, too. On clear, calm days the Chesapeake is a literal mirror, beautifully reflecting the moods of the light and the passage of the day. It also mirrors, in its health, the ability of some 16 million twenty-first-century residents of the watershed to coexist with the natural system. Currently, the bay reflects more effort than progress, and there is a tendency always to think in terms of more people moving in, having more impact. Inevitably, the watershed collects our pollutive sins. Perhaps it can work the other way, connecting us all to care for what's downstream. We know the awful power of millions of people having too much environmental impact. What would be the power of millions were we to take serious restorative actions, a mammoth, vicious cycle in reverse?

PART II

STATE *of the* BAY

The health of the Chesapeake Bay depends largely on three factors:

- The pollution factor: what we put into the bay that harms the water, plants, and animals there.
- The harvest factor: what we take out of the bay, that is, how many fish, crabs, and oysters we catch.
- The resilience factor: how well we maintain the natural features of the bay ecosystem, from forest to marsh to oyster reef, that help it cope with stresses from the first two factors.

Many parts of the bay ecosystem, of course, are all the more important because they overlap these three categories. For example, oysters, whose enormous capacity to filter and cleanse pollution from the water is a part of the bay's resilience, also provide a seafood harvest. The chapters in this section examine our progress in eliminating pollution, managing harvests, and maintaining resilience.

First, however, let's define progress, the "new and better measures" of it mentioned in the preface. If we measure it, as we often do, by the money and manpower expended on bay restoration and by the increasing sophistication of our environmental regulations and scientific knowledge, then we have been making progress fairly steadily since the first Earth

Day in 1970. But if we measure it by the responses we see to date in the bay's water quality, its fisheries, and its resilience, its ability to rebound from environmental insult, then progress is more muddled. If we compare progress to the official, watershed-wide goal of "restoration"—regaining a Chesapeake environment roughly equal to that of forty to fifty years ago— then we see the last decade, like the one before, as one of mainly preventing further degradation, of running hard to stay in place. Within that overall context, there have been a few solid successes, genuinely hopeful trends, and advances in scientific understanding of the bay. Still another way to look at progress is whether it is enough to offset not only our current pollution, but that which is to come from millions more people who will be living and working around the bay in just a few more decades.

The examples that follow show the broad trends of the last decade. They are discussed in more detail in Chapters 2 through 4.

POLLUTION

Less of the bay's total pollution load enters from the pipes of sewage treatment plants and industries, though these still have significant impacts on water quality. Far greater amounts enter in the runoff from farms and developed areas and in the fallout from polluted air. And these diffuse sources are proving the most difficult to control.

- Real progress has been made, and should continue to be made, in controlling one of the bay's major sources of pollution, sewage treatment plants, even as the population they serve grows. The septic tanks that serve suburban and rural households not connected to sewer lines remain an unregulated and fast-growing source of pollution. Portions of two major bay rivers, the Potomac and the Patuxent, where sewage treatment plants are dominant sources of pollution, have become healthier.
- Air pollutants that affect the bay's water, poorly understood ten years ago, are now acknowledged to be one of the greatest causes of the bay's ills. Automobiles, power plants, and airborne ammonia from animal manures are all major air pollutants. None is adequately regulated to restore water quality, though real progress has been made

with power plant emissions. Better controls on power plants have also led to an improvement in acid rain for the first time in decades.

- Controlling polluting runoff of fertilizers and manure from agriculture, which occupies about a quarter of the entire watershed, has proven more frustrating than imagined a decade ago. So far, farmers' widespread adoption of voluntary plans to control their runoff has not had much effect on water quality. Promising techniques to improve the situation exist, and are getting some use, but there is no assurance they will make a large impact in the next decade.

- The polluted stormwater runoff from developed lands has become the fastest-growing source of bay water quality problems. The current use of artificial ponds and silt fences to catch runoff from development is proving inadequate compensation for the loss of natural filtering when asphalt and concrete replace forests, fields, and wetlands. The sediment, or dirt, that runs into the bay was not even targeted for reduction until the latest (2000) bay restoration agreement. Now it is thought that reductions of 40 percent or more from the 5 million tons entering the bay annually are necessary to restore water quality. There is little prospect of doing this in the next several years.

- An unprecedented outbreak in 1997 of the toxic dinoflagellate *Pfiesteria piscicida* was associated with losses of brain function in watermen. Suspicions that the outbreak was linked to pollution from agriculture resulted in Maryland's enacting the bay region's first mandatory water quality controls on farming.

- In the bulk of the bay and its main river, the Susquehanna, there were no strong trends of improvement or further deterioration of water quality during the last decade. However, there are encouraging signs that one major pollutant, phosphorus, is declining and preliminary evidence of a decline in nitrogen.

- An encouraging new way of setting standards for water quality is emerging. After decades of regulating pollution mainly from industries and sewers and largely ignoring runoff from agriculture and urban lands and from airborne pollution, the bay states are approaching water quality from a "fish-eye" view, setting cleanup standards based on how much pollution, regardless of the source, that the bay and its rivers can stand and still remain healthy.

HARVESTS

Although we may never fully sort out the relative influences of pollution, disease, and overharvest on the declines of the bay's widespread fisheries, it is amply clear that overfishing has been a major culprit, and the one we can most immediately control.

- Populations of striped bass, or rockfish, have rebounded sharply after more than a decade of generally poor reproduction in most of their bay spawning areas. A few other species, such as weakfish, bluefish, and croakers, are doing better as a result of management actions and, in some cases, favorable climate conditions.
- Shad, the subject of an intensive restocking effort using fish raised in hatcheries, are showing highly encouraging signs of a comeback, but it will be years, and probably decades, before they fully recover on all bay rivers.
- Crabs are at historic low levels because of overfishing, habitat loss, and natural cycles. An encouraging new bi-state management plan between Maryland and Virginia is a first step toward managing this last great bay seafood harvest on a sustainable basis.
- Despite ambitious goals and serious efforts to restore them, oysters continue at low ebb in the Chesapeake, as diseases devastate them.
- Menhaden, one of the bay's most important species, are scarce. Management plans are, for the first time, beginning to recognize the importance of menhaden beyond conventional economic valuations as food for larger fish—that it is a major consumer of the algae that pollute the bay.

RESILIENCE

The concept of resilience is not as commonly understood as pollution and fisheries harvests, but it is just as vital to the bay's health as good sewage treatment and proper conservation of seafood resources. Resilience lies in the forests and wetlands of the bay's watershed, which filter and cleanse stormwater running off the land and stabilize the environment of the bay's rivers and streams by absorbing water during storms and releasing it during droughts.

Resilience also includes the bay's submerged grasses and its oyster beds, which perform similar cleansing and filtering and stabilizing functions in the water. And it springs from the rich and extensive habitats that offer extraordinary spawning and nursery and feeding areas to support the bay's fish and fowl.

When we say of any natural system, "leave it alone and it'll come back," we are talking about resilience.

- We continue to lose forests, already down to around half their historical coverage of the bay watershed. The loss is actually worse than it seems from such watershed-wide figures, as the greatest losses have come from the lands closest to the bay and its tidal rivers, precisely where the forests are most needed from a bay water quality standpoint. The distribution of forests is as important as the total acreage.
- Wetland losses from human activities are reversing for the first time in history, the result of programs to restore and create new wetlands faster than we drain and fill them. However, natural losses from a rapidly rising sea level are likely to degrade and destroy many more wetlands in the next several decades than we can conceivably create.
- The decline in submerged grass beds, whose health is one of the best indicators of bay water quality, seems to have bottomed out in 1984 and reversed modestly in the last few years. Acreage remains far below levels of two decades ago, and there is no signal of a widespread comeback.
- Our ability to contain the suburban sprawl that is converting huge quantities of open space to developed land across the bay's watershed remains grossly inadequate.

To restore and maintain the Chesapeake Bay in the long term, we are going to need, at a minimum, to keep its remaining natural systems intact and to enhance them. There are obvious limits to regaining the watershed's historical forests, and there is evidence that natural, uncontrollable losses of wetlands to rising sea level are increasing. Therefore, we must be all the more zealous in controlling pollution, in "helping out" an ecosystem that cannot help itself as well as it once could.

We must not only reduce the current level of human impacts enough to restore the bay; we must also reduce those impacts enough to offset more than a million people a decade who will be moving into the watershed. One open question, discussed in Chapter 5, is whether we can restore the bay without stabilizing population in its watershed.

Are we on track to make that kind of progress? What does it mean for the bay? Let's examine where we stand and where we are headed in the categories of pollution, harvest, and resilience.

Pollution

Agriculture

Agriculture intimately involves us directly with the soil, water and other living creatures of God's creation . . . the nature of that relationship—whether it is in harmony with the Creator's plan or in opposition to it—determines whether we are either responsible stewards . . . or irresponsible destroyers.

—Gregory D. Cusak, Iowa Department of Agriculture

Think of the bay as a great tree that is rooted by its river systems in every nook and cranny of lands covering fifteen times the area of the waters to which they drain. And since the bay is so very shallow—average depth about 21 feet—there is very little water beneath its broad surface to absorb and dilute pollutants from the land. So whatever people do on the watershed greatly influences the quality of the water.

Agriculture involves more than a quarter of the bay's 41-million-acre watershed. It covers an area nearly twice as large as Maryland, and it is one of the most important sources of pollution from the land to the water.

Development and reversion to forest shrank farm acreage by more than a third during the last half century. But the tonnage of "nutrients" spread on each acre of cropland—the nitrogen and phosphorus in commercial fertilizers and animal manure—doubled and even tripled to produce today's bounteous harvests. In addition, modern agriculture has packed cows, hogs, and poultry into farms in densities 5 to 100 times greater than in the 1950s (Figure 2.1). Their manure, an estimated 88 billion pounds a year, generates nearly 600 million pounds of nitrogen a year, the largest single pollutant degrading the bay. This is more than triple the nitrogen produced in wastes from all 16 million people in the watershed.

If it were applied evenly across the watershed's agricultural lands, all the manure that farm animals produce could be spread without excess on crop- and pasturelands at current fertilization rates. But hauling manure more than a few miles is too expensive for farmers. With animals more concentrated than ever (Figure 2.2), and with the acreage of available farmland on which to spread their wastes still shrinking—by more than 10 percent since 1985—many areas of the watershed end up with more manure than crop- and pastureland can use. One five-county region of Virginia, for example, has an estimated 800 million pounds a year more manure, mostly from poultry, than its farms need for fertilizer. Total manure produced in the bay watershed has not changed much in the last fifteen to twenty years, but more of it now comes from chickens, whose wastes have relatively high amounts of nitrogen. Thus, manure nitrogen has actually risen an estimated 17 percent since the early 1980s.

Meanwhile, sales of commercial chemical fertilizers—nonmanure nitrogen and phosphorus—have remained about the same throughout the watershed, even in areas with excesses of manure. This statistic indicates that many farmers may still be spreading too much nitrogen and phosphorus on the land. Offsetting this somewhat is the fact that crop yields have risen about 10 percent on average in the last decade—so crops are actually absorbing more fertilizer per acre than they used to.

The bottom line, however, is that large acreages of soils in the bay's watershed, and the groundwater underlying them, have become polluted in the sense that they are saturated with more nutrients than the soil can hold. The excess nitrogen and phosphorus move into waterways and thus into the bay. Some of the excess—mainly nitrogen—trickles through the

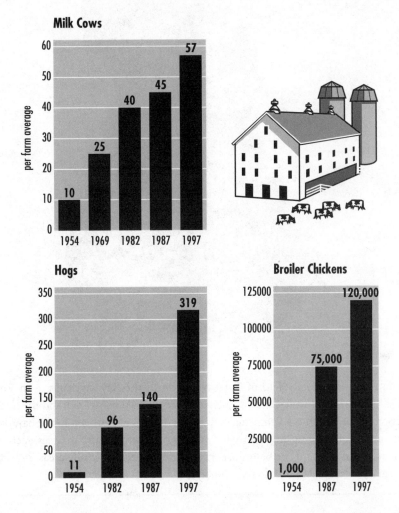

FIGURE 2.1. **The Concentrations of Animals on Pennsylvania Farms.** The growth of animal husbandry in central Pennsylvania has been intense over the past twenty years, especially for hogs and broiler chickens, while the population of milk cows has also grown steadily. The concentration of animals on small acreages of land raises huge risks of manure runoff into tributaries of the Susquehanna and, ultimately, the Chesapeake. [EPA Chesapeake Bay Program]

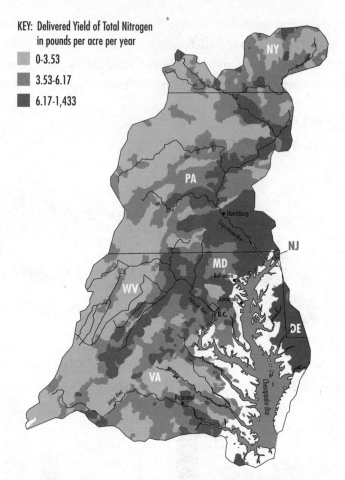

KEY: Delivered Yield of Total Nitrogen
in pounds per acre per year
- 0-3.53
- 3.53-6.17
- 6.17-1,433

FIGURE 2.2. Delivered Yield of Total Nitrogen to the Bay. Agriculture in Virginia's Shenandoah Valley, the Susquehanna valley in Pennsylvania, and the midsection of the Delmarva Peninsula delivers high loads of nitrogen to the bay, but note also high loading from heavily settled urban and suburban areas such as northern Virginia and the Baltimore-Washington Corridor. White areas indicate no data available. [U.S. Geological Survey]

soils in groundwater or moves in airborne forms. Or it flows in surface runoff, which is how most phosphorus moves bayward.

As a direct result, one of the bay's biggest problems is that its waters have become overfertilized, or *eutrophic*. Too much nitrogen and phosphorus are entering the bay. They fuel explosive growth of suspended,

TABLE 2.1. Sources of Bay Pollution*

Source	Nitrogen to Bay (million lbs/yr.)	% Percent	Phosphorus to Bay (million lbs/yr.)	% Percent
Agriculture	117	38	9	44
Developed land	48	20	5.3	26
Forest	42	14	0.4	2
Subtotal for all land	207	68	14.7	71
Other (includes sewage, septic, and air**)	97	32	5.9	29
Total	304		20.6	

*Estimates for 2002, EPA Bay Program. Land runoff is for an average rainfall year. In wet years, it will be a larger percentage of total pollution; in dry years, a smaller portion.
**Measures only air pollution that falls directly on water. Most air pollution falls on land and is counted in runoff from forests, developed land, and agriculture).

drifting plant life, or *algae,* that is so extensive that these tiny, single-celled plants cloud the water and block out light needed by the bay's underwater grasses for growth. Then, when the algae die, they sink to the bottom, where the bacteria decomposing them consume large quantities of oxygen. Indeed, many parts of the bay can become so low in oxygen that they are as hostile to fish and crabs and other aquatic life as a desert. Polluted land equals polluted water.

Of all the nitrogen and phosphorus polluting the bay, more than two-thirds is carried in *runoff*—rainwater, flowing above and below ground—from the 41-million-acre watershed. And agriculture is by far the dominant source of this runoff from the landscape.

BOX 2.1. Nitrogen

The primary pollutant of the Chesapeake Bay is nothing toxic or scary sounding. Nitrogen is one of Earth's most common elements, 78 percent of our atmosphere, and a vital building block of all plant and animal tissue. It is also concentrated in all human sewage and animal manure, is in agricultural fertilizers, and is released into the air and water every time we burn oil, coal, and gas. In just the past half century, human activities have doubled the amount of nitrogen in circulation worldwide. Humans "have altered nitrogen more than any other element," says Stanford University ecologist Peter Vitousek. By contrast, human changes to atmospheric carbon dioxide, blamed for global warming, represent an addition of only about 10 percent.

Nitrogen's well-documented damage to the Chesapeake Bay, a theme that runs throughout this book, is turning out to be the problem of coastal waters everywhere. More than half the 127 coastal bays in the United States are tainted by excess nitrogen, and similar problems— losses of aquatic oxygen and seagrass habitats—are turning up in Scandinavian fjords, Chinese harbors, and Australia's isolated Great Barrier Reef. "People are noticing it in their own areas, but they don't realize it's happening in every other bay and pond and shoreline of the world," says Boston University ecologist Ivan Valiela. A National Academy of Sciences report calls "nutrient pollution [primarily nitrogen] . . . the greatest pollution threat faced by the coastal marine environment."

The dramatic doubling of global nitrogen is overwhelming natural systems adapted by a long evolution to much lesser amounts. If the history of the planet were compressed into a single year, this enormous change occurred just twenty-five seconds before midnight on the last day of December.

The sudden change is rooted in agriculture's desperate, 10,000-year search for ways to boost crop yields, a dream finally realized in the early twentieth century, when a new industrial process enabled humans for the first time to extract limitless amounts of potent nitrogen fertilizer from the air.

On the eve of the twentieth century, the demand for more nitrogen was such that a prestigious chemist, Sir William Crookes, challenged the British Association for the Advancement of Science: World population, he said, would soon outstrip agriculture's ability to feed people. Only more nitrogen fertilizer could push up grain yields that had risen only sluggishly since the time of the Greeks and Romans. In the atmosphere of the planet, Crookes said, lay a limitless reservoir, some 4 quadrillion tons of nitrogen—if only it could be tapped.

But the nitrogen there is N_2 gas, a molecular form that was not useable for growing crops. Throughout evolution, nature had devised only two ways to turn a tiny bit of this nitrogen, 90–140 million tons a year worldwide, into fertilizer form. Lightning rips N_2 molecules apart, allowing them to recombine with oxygen and hydrogen to enrich soils as they fall to Earth in rain. And bacteria in the roots of alfalfa, soybeans, and other nitrogen-"fixing" plants, or legumes, can convert atmospheric nitrogen for plant growth.

Within a decade of Crookes's speech, two German chemists, Fritz Haber and Carl Bosch, had worked out a way to wring nitrogen from the air cheaply and in large quantities. Both would win Nobel Prizes for their process, which even today remains the basis of operation for giant fertilizer-making factories around the world that convert nearly 100 million tons a year of inert, gaseous atmospheric nitrogen into anyhydrous ammonia, a potent plant growth elixer of nitrogen and hydrogen. Some leading food policy experts like ecologist Vaclav Smil of the University of Manitoba consider this "the most significant invention of the twentieth century." Vitousek estimates without all the extra nutrition we now get from thin air, we could not support about 2 billion of the world's 6 billion people.

While fertilizer production is the leading source of the planet's excess nitrogen problem, the burning of fossil fuels also liberates large quantities. Like nitrogen in the atmosphere, this too has been mostly locked up underground in coal and petroleum deposits until recent decades. Worldwide, smokestacks and tailpipes are sources of about one-fourth of excess nitrogen. Indeed, the Chesapeake Bay gets nearly a third of its nitrogen pollution from the air nowadays.

Demand for energy and fertilizer continues to rise worldwide, though countries like the United States have seen a leveling off of fertilizer use. Worldwide, not one of more than fifty water bodies badly polluted by nitrogen, including the Chesapeake, has returned to health, according to Robert Diaz, a researcher at the Virginia Institute of Marine Science. But one vast, unplanned experiment has proven that recovery can start if the nutrient overload decreases enough. It is happening in the Black Sea, for decades the world's worst and most persistent "dead zone," as oxygen-deprived areas are known. The collapse of the Soviet Union, and of the economies dependent on it throughout the watershed of the Black Sea, caused nitrogen entering the sea to fall by approximately 50 percent. By the late 1990s oceanographers found the sea's huge dead zone had nearly disappeared, according to scientist Laurence D. Mee of Britain's Plymouth University. The fisheries there remain devastated, and economic rebound could easily wipe away most of the pollution gains. Nonetheless, the Black Sea's experience does show that sharp reductions in nitrogen can begin the restoration process that is the goal here in our bay.

THE CLEANUP EFFORT IS STRUGGLING

A primary goal of the early Chesapeake Bay cleanup effort was to reduce the agricultural nutrients that get into the water (as well as nutrients from other sources, such as sewage) by 40 percent of 1985 pollution levels. The reductions were supposed to be permanent. In effect, they were meant to "cap" any further increase in nutrients polluting the bay, even if nutrient sources such as human and farm animal wastes continued to grow.

In 1987, when the bay cleanup began in earnest, there were fond hopes that helping the bay would be largely a win-win solution for farmers, a matter of education and modest financial help from government. By purchasing less chemical fertilizer and using manure more efficiently to grow crops, by adopting a host of so-called best management practices (BMPs), farmers could realize cleaner water while cutting expenses and reducing soil losses from erosion.

BMPs are as varied as the landscape across the bay's 64,000-square-mile watershed. They range from storing manure in concrete pits so that it can be spread when crops need it, to planting seeds directly into unplowed soil—a practice known as conservation tillage, which minimizes the runoff of soil and nutrients. Other BMPs involve changing field slopes to retard runoff, planting trees or grasses along field edges to filter runoff, fencing cattle from streams so they don't pollute the water and cause bank erosion, and planting winter cover crops to take up excess fertilizer from the soil after the main crop is harvested.

Across the watershed, tens of thousands of BMPs have been implemented, including the widespread adoption by farmers of "nutrient management plans," which spell out how much fertilizer is needed per acre.

And the results? The EPA's Chesapeake Bay Program estimated in 2002 that all these BMPs and others, applied for more than a decade, had reduced agriculture's nitrogen pollution by about 23 million pounds, or 15 percent, and reduced phosphorus by about 2 million pounds, or 18 percent. Those numbers are far short of the sought-after 40 percent reduction and even more disappointing in light of new science that indicates nitrogen and phosphorus must be cut by tens of millions of pounds more than previously assumed to restore bay health.

But the reality is that even the EPA estimate of nutrient reductions since the 1980s may be overly optimistic. Recent studies by the U.S. Geological Survey (USGS) that looked at the actual—not estimated—levels of nitrogen and phosphorus in seven major bay waterways have found that most showed no significant change, or only modest reductions. The only river in which nutrient levels fell significantly was Maryland's Patuxent, where water quality is dominated by sewage treatment plants that have adopted new cleanup technology. On the other rivers, land runoff, the bulk of it from agriculture, dominated water quality.

Some of the disappointing lack of a downward trend in pollution, the USGS studies stated, might be explained by the fact that later years of the study, which looked at 1985 to 1998, were wetter, washing more nutrients from the landscape. Another possibility was that nitrogen travels mostly through groundwater and can take years in some areas to seep out into waterways. Thus farmers might actually have made reductions in pollution that won't show up for some time in the bay and its rivers. Where farmers have adopted "no-till," or farming with minimal plowing, more nitrogen might also end up being stored, long term, in the topsoil.

But overall, the researchers felt that agriculture's modest reduction of pollution is still an overestimate. That finding was bolstered by two others: The USGS saw no evidence that farmers are buying significantly less fertilizer or generating much less manure, the two major sources of nutrients in agricultural runoff; nor did it see nutrient loads in the rivers drop during the drier years of 1999 and 2000, when fewer nutrients might be expected to wash from the landscape.

A more intensive, small-scale study of German Branch, a little stream feeding Maryland's Choptank River, showed similarly perplexing results. More than two-thirds of the lands drained by German Branch on its winding, 10-mile course are in farming. Starting in 1989, a host of state, local, and federal agricultural and environmental agencies, plus scientists from the Smithsonian, have spent countless hours and perhaps $1 million devising various techniques to reduce nutrients running into German Branch. Equally critical, farmers throughout the stream valley have cooperated with plans to conserve soil, reduce fertilizer use, and adopt a range of other BMPs.

But again, nutrient levels in German Branch, more than a decade later, have not changed much. "It is difficult to identify any positive water quality results," summed up a state report.

A CASE STUDY: CENTRE COUNTY REVISITED

In 1990, the author visited several dairy farms in Centre County, Pennsylvania, to assess what was then a new attempt throughout the bay's watershed to reduce pollution from agriculture. Smack in the middle of the Susquehanna River basin, source of half the freshwater running into the Chesapeake, Centre County's nearly 1,000 farms were judged by bay cleanup officials to be fairly typical of the progress being made.

At that time, Centre County apparently did not lack for examples of progress, and a few farmers were demonstrating real ingenuity in keeping polluted runoff out of the bay. Not surprisingly, though, the county as a whole was nowhere near the 40 percent reduction of nitrogen and phosphorus that was the goal for all sources of bay pollution.

Farmers and scientists at nearby Penn State University and water quality managers identified several key obstacles to progress:

- Far too much of the Chesapeake Bay cleanup money available to farmers was going into capital-intensive manure pits, concrete storage structures popular with farmers but only marginally effective as pollution controls. The added manure storage did give farmers more control over when they put manure on their fields, and correctly timing this spreading to springtime, when crops are growing, can significantly reduce polluted runoff. But the volumes of manure were far too great for such pits to store from one spring to the next; and the pits, experts concluded, took money away from more effective alternatives.

- The voluntary nature of agricultural cleanup made it hard to target solutions and money to farms and techniques where it would be most effective, as opposed to where farmers were willing to do it.
- Money was woefully inadequate to help farmers, strapped by years of low grain prices, make rapid progress.
- Several effective pollution controls were getting little push: fencing cattle away from streams, planting winter cover crops to capture pollution before it worked its way through groundwater into waterways, and planting streamside forests and wetlands, all to filter and absorb polluted runoff before it got to waterways.

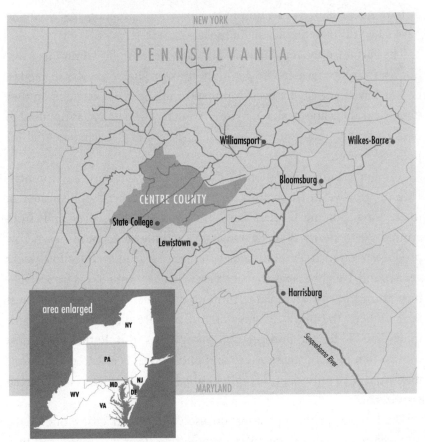

FIGURE 2.3. **Centre County, Pennsylvania.** Centre County, so named for its location, has State College located on its southern edge. It is primarily agricultural land, draining to the headwaters of several important Susquehanna tributaries.

Ten years later, the author revisited Centre County, talking with farmers and other experts to assess progress. A small dairy farm of fifty cows that had been lauded in 1991 for making some initial cleanup progress has changed very little. Manure is still spread almost daily, year-round, and the farmer doesn't use one of the newer-generation manure spreaders that allows more precise calibration of how much is actually applied to each acre to match what crops need. When it rains, or the ground is frozen, and runoff from spreading would be especially bad, "you try to work around that," the farmer says, "but . . . " On the plus side, he has fenced all his cattle off from the trout stream that runs through his land, as have his neighbors. Streamside fencing is one program that seems to have taken off in Pennsylvania in the last decade.

The farmer now supplements his dairy income by trimming cows' hooves for other farmers. To get more milk production, cows in the last decade have increasingly been confined to the barn, he explains, so they don't wear their hooves down naturally. Such confinement, as opposed to pasture grazing, concentrates manure and creates a larger potential for polluted runoff.

Another farming operation that was perhaps the most environmentally progressive in the county ten years ago remains sophisticated in many ways, but the farmers have increased the cows they milk from around 80 to nearly 800. That massive volume of manure—each cow produces around 100 pounds a day—must be spread every couple weeks year-round. Neighbors say that at times when the ground was frozen, manure from this operation came running onto their properties. For most farmers here, the untimely spreading of manure means they can't take much "credit" for the nitrogen and phosphorus in it. Rather, they must assume that most of the nitrogen and phosphorus is lost to the environment, and they must continue purchasing large quantities of commercial fertilizer.

The farmers in this operation do use winter cover crops, one of the best techniques for soaking up excess pollution from agriculture; but they say that very few places in the county do this. They estimate that "about 20 percent" of the county's farms use the most up-to-date pollution control techniques. They add, however, that these are mostly big farms, so their statement covers considerably more than 20 percent of Centre County's farm acreage. They belong to a crop management association, whose members pay $5–$6 an acre for expert advice on applying no more nitrogen, phosphorus, and pesticides than they need. But membership is small—thirty-five farmers, about what it was a decade ago. "Many others could benefit from it, but with fifteen to twenty years of low grain prices, they see it as an extra cost," one of the farmers said.

The farmers say they know they must upgrade their manure handling—more to comply with impending federal regulations than from any pressure from Pennsylvania's own, outdated nutrient management law. They are investing nearly half a million dollars to install a state-of-the-art waste-handling system. The operation is too big to qualify for Chesapeake Bay pollution control grants, but the farmers wish such grants—about $60,000 a year in Centre County—could be targeted more effectively: "I've seen some places build expensive manure pits, and a few years later they're out of business," he said.

Another farmer revisited after a decade says nutrient management— matching the application of nitrogen and phosphorus as closely as possible to what crops need—has been on a definite upswing in the last decade. A major problem with utilizing the nitrogen and phosphorus in manure remains, however. A large number of farmers, including this one, use no-till, or conservation tillage—inserting seeds in narrow slits cut into the field with a special planter—which minimizes conventional plowing. This practice, strongly encouraged by agricultural experts and environmentalists alike, saves labor and energy and significantly cuts soil erosion. However, farmers say it makes it impossible to work manure into the soil effectively. And that problem, in turn, means that most of the nitrogen and phosphorus in the manure are lost to the environment, including into runoff to waterways.

Beth Hirt and Scott Heckman, government nutrient management specialists who work with Pennsylvania farmers, say that overall there has been progress. Indeed, one of the farmers they are advising is employing a range of pollution control techniques that simply could not have been found on a farm in the bay watershed ten years ago. But he is "way above average," Heckman says. Hirt pushes alternatives to manure storage pits, but the pits remain popular. Only about 90 of the county's 900 or so farms have nutrient management plans, though they tend to cover the larger acreages, she says.

Les Lanyon, an agricultural researcher at Penn State University, says some farms definitely have cut back on nitrogen. For the first time in his career, he has seen corn crops in Lancaster County suffering from too little fertilizer. The big picture, though, Lanyon argues, "is that we've gotten the easy guys, the farmers who could obviously save money by cutting back on crop nutrients." What are left are large numbers of farmers for whom cutting back on nitrogen and phosphorus enough to meet Chesapeake Bay restoration goals will mean spending money that many of them don't have. Ironically, the trend to big dairy farms, which makes manure handling more challenging, may be good in that big operations can afford the investment in state-of-the-art waste handling, Lanyon says. But if agriculture is to meet bay goals, he says, "it's going to take more of a societal commitment [i.e., public spending] to value water quality as much as we expect farmers to."

The overwhelming impression from revisiting Centre County is that some progress has occurred, but certainly nothing like the 40–50 percent reduction in nitrogen and phosphorus pollution that scientists say is needed to restore the bay's water quality. Furthermore, while some upcoming changes in federal and state nutrient management rules could well make a positive difference, it seems more likely that a visit to the county in 2010 could find far less progress than needed. The leadership, the mandate, and the money to make big gains in clean water are not there.

THE OUTLOOK: SOLUTIONS ARE AT HAND

The more we understand the reasons for failing to reduce bay pollution from agriculture, the clearer it becomes that there are huge opportunities to make this decade different from the last. The good news for the next decade is that, in hindsight, we have barely scratched the surface of the possibilities for more bay-friendly farms.

Many of the BMPs in which farmers put faith are clearly not the way to make reductions in nutrient runoff everywhere. No-till, for example, with its limited plowing of farm fields, makes it difficult to mix manure rapidly into the soil on farms that spread it. Changing this can substantially cut polluted runoff.

Here's another example: The widespread construction of concrete pits and sheds to store manure has theoretically given farmers more control over when they spread it on fields. But in practice, very few farmers are able or willing to spread manure only during the growing season. Application of manure at times when crops can't use it remains all too common, increasing the runoff of nutrients into the bay. Manure storage is also expensive, taking up a share of pollution control dollars out of proportion to its clean water benefits.

Ironically, one BMP proven to be especially cost-effective in removing farm pollution has been little used to date. Known as cover cropping, it involves planting certain winter crops, such as rye and oats, not long after the farmer's main, cash crop has been harvested. Cover crops can remove as much as 25 pounds of nitrogen per acre from groundwater before it has a chance to move off into waterways. In the spring, they may be plowed under or killed with herbicides that cause negligible toxic runoff before planting another crop, such as corn, or they may be harvested as grain. Cover crops improve soil quality by adding organic matter to the land and over a few years can reduce the amount of nitrogen fertilizer farmers need to add each year.

Cover crops require extra management to perform well. Planting must be precisely timed, and farmers must have a good idea of how much nitrogen they gain from plowing the crops under, to know how much to take "credit" for before fertilizing again. Cover crops have been better evaluated under coastal plain conditions than in steeper, cooler parts of the watershed.

But their potential for bay cleanup is great. If planted each winter on even half of the watershed's 6.4 million acres of croplands, cover crops would go a long way toward helping agriculture meet bay cleanup goals—keeping tens of millions of pounds of nitrogen out of the water. Cover cropping targets the most difficult to control of farm nutrients— nitrogen—which quickly dissolves in rainwater and "escapes" underground, out of reach of other controls. In contrast, phosphorus generally sticks to soil particles, and any number of good farming practices that stop soil erosion also help control phosphorus runoff.

Currently, however, less than 5 percent of the watershed's croplands are enrolled in cover crop programs, mostly in Maryland. Virginia has no cover crop program, and Pennsylvania's is limited to a small percentage of its farms. A large part of the reason is that farmers are wary of the additional labor and expense involved, which increases in hilly, cold portions of the watershed. However, where Maryland has made financial assistance for cover crops available at $25 an acre (limited so far to a few million dollars a year), farmers have been quick to plant them.

This cost, with millions of acres of cropland in the watershed, might seem high. But compared with what it costs to remove nitrogen from sewage discharges and from urban stormwater runoff, cover crops are an affordable cleanup technique, at a couple of dollars per pound of nitrogen removed. And there is good reason to believe that if planting them becomes widespread, and if farmers incorporate such planting as standard practice, the costs would fall considerably. It might also be cost-effective to expand cover cropping in selected years, following serious droughts. In dry years, crops grow poorly, leaving much more fertilizer in the soil to pollute the bay. The bottom line: Cover crops are no silver bullet and may work better in some places than in others, but their potential is vastly underrealized.

There is also great promise in shifting land that now grows grain for livestock to grazing pastures. Like cover cropping, this practice could significantly cut polluted runoff to the bay. For example, Bobby Prigel, a Baltimore County dairy farmer, has recently stopped confining his dairy cows to the barn, let their milk production fall by 30 percent (and their manure production), and planted permanent, grassy pasture where he used to grow corn. He grosses less money, but he also spends far less on feed and medicine, uses fewer pesticides and fertilizers, and has less soil erosion. His profits are greater, and he has more time for himself. "Life is a blast," he told the *Baltimore Sun* (January 29, 2002). Innovative grazing techniques that involve frequent rotation of beef and dairy cows from pasture to pasture hold broad promise for increasing farm profitability while reducing bay pollution. This modern return to old-fashioned grass farming also has proven health benefits, producing meat with more "good" fatty acids and fewer fatty acids of the type harmful to human health.

Another promising approach to reducing the amount of nitrogen and phosphorus farmers apply to the soil in the first place is gaining attention across the bay watershed. It assumes that even with the current, widespread adoption of nutrient management plans that prescribe how much fertilizer is needed for each acre, farmers are still applying more than they need (see Box 2.2). Farmers might do this for several reasons: as insurance that they will get optimum growing conditions, because nitrogen fertilizer is cheap, or because they have more manure than they know what to do with.

BOX 2.2. Farms, Fertilizer, and the Chesapeake Bay

Why would any farmer use more fertilizer than he or she needs? This sensible-sounding question is many a farmer's heartfelt response to evidence that excess nitrogen and phosphorus fertilizer washing from farms is polluting the bay.

But it's not that simple.

First, farmers can't predict the weather when they fertilize each spring, so they apply enough to make the best of their crop, assuming they get a good growing season. Often they may add a bit extra, just for insurance. Some years, especially when there's a drought, growing conditions aren't the best. Crops don't reach their maximum growth potential and so don't take up the maximum amount of fertilizer, leaving an excess to run off in rainfall to the bay.

Even more important, the modern grain cropping in wide practice around the Chesapeake is what agricultural scientists call an inherently "leaky" system. They mean that the most widely grown annual grain— corn—even in the best growing year, stops growing and using fertilizer by mid-August. But natural microbial action in the soil keeps on making more nitrogen available until cold weather stops this activity. This release of nitrogen comes from organic nitrogen bound up in topsoil by the thousands of pounds per acre. The bottom line is that growing corn generally ends up leaving anywhere from 15 to 30 pounds per acre of nitrogen available to move through the soil and groundwater into waterways.

Similarly, even soybeans, which "fix" nitrogen from the air and don't need any from the farmer, release nearly as much excess fertilizer as corn into groundwater when their nitrogen-rich root system decays after the growing season and harvest. Finally, a lot of farmers substitute animal manure for more expensive commercial fertilizer. Many manures have only a bit more nitrogen in them than phosphorus—but plants need several times as much nitrogen as phosphorus.

So to put on enough nitrogen, the farmer has to spread lots more phosphorus than plants can use, again leaving an excess in the soil with the potential to run off and cause water pollution. The same problem can occur when a farmer agrees to spread sludge from sewage treatment plants on fields. Virtually every county in Maryland now shows farm soils with excessive phosphorus—often on half or more of all farms tested.

In sum, it is not so much that farmers use more fertilizer than they need, but that they are operating within a farming system that is imprecise and leaky.

Research indicates that many farms might cut fertilizer by as much as 25 percent with little or no loss in yields of crops they harvest in most years. Farmers, however, are not likely to experiment, especially with grain prices at or near historic lows. They feel they need to squeeze every bushel they can from their land. So a coalition of agricultural and environmental interests is seeking up to $20 million a year from the $17-billion-a-year federal 2002 Farm Bill to pursue a "yield reserve" insurance program, along with other innovative practices. The yield reserve program would provide incentive payments for participation and insure farmers who reduce fertilizers against any resulting loss of yields.

A vital research question that needs to accompany any such program, some scientists caution, is the extent to which farmers are really overapplying nutrients. In some regions, it seems obvious that they are, but in other places, no one really knows. To the extent that they are overapplying nutrients, a yield reserve program could be a great stride toward cleaner water. Where farmers already are carefully managing their fertilizers, it might have less effect.

Further reductions in pollution from farms could come from stepping up ongoing programs to plant forested buffers between fields and waterways (see Chapter 4, "Resilience") and to create and restore wetlands that intercept runoff from fields. Both of these techniques, gaining favor in all three major bay states, have great promise in filtering out nutrients. In regions with extensive livestock in pastures, programs that encourage farmers to fence animals off from streams hold great benefit for curbing both sediment and nutrients. Of the two bay states where this is most important, Pennsylvania has made a good effort on streamside fencing, but Virginia has just begun.

The most significant development in the effort to re-vegetate stream banks to filter polluted runoff has been the Conservation Reserve Enhancement Program (CREP). An infusion of federal and state money has made this voluntary program profitable enough for agricultural landowners that farmers in a few areas have expressed concerns about taking too much land out of production, especially with the prospect of extra incentives for 300-foot buffers. This is a complex issue now being hotly debated in Maryland, but the program is valuable enough that ways to deal with the concerns are gradually being worked out. Lands revegetated under CREP are frequently marginal soils. Enrollment in the program has jumped by an order of magnitude in recent years. Continuing to restore ditch and stream banks to natural vegetation will be critical to achieving water quality goals for the bay.

VOLUNTARY OR REGULATORY?

Looking back at the past decade, one of the biggest differences between trying to control farm pollution and controlling other pollution sources has been the largely voluntary nature of the former. Throughout the years, lawmakers have agreed with agricultural interests to exempt farming from most environmental regulations (see Box 2.3). Thirty years after the federal Clean Water Act began to regulate many other sources of pollution, agriculture is responsible for about 60 percent of the nation's water quality problems. How to hold farmers more accountable without impairing the flexibility and profit they need to stay in business is an on-going baywide and national issue.

**Box 2.3. Examples of Agricultural Exemptions
from Environmental Laws**

- Virginia's Chesapeake Bay Preservation Act stipulates a mandatory 100-foot buffer next to waterways, but only 25 feet for farmers with an approved water quality conservation plan.
- Federal and state nontidal wetland regulations allow farmers to develop any nontidal wetland that has been farmed since 1985. All on-going agricultural activities are essentially exempt from normal wetland protections.
- Maryland's Critical Area Act declares agriculture to be a "protective" use of the shoreline, the same as forests. It requires only a 25-foot buffer (versus 100 feet for other uses) and allows other variances for farming from its restrictive zoning on shorefront development.
- Pennsylvania's Clean Streams Law exempts farmers from keeping live-stock out of streams.
- Virginia, Maryland, and Pennsylvania state sediment control laws exempt all agricultural activities, such as plowing, from getting grading permits.

To date, the voluntary nature of farm cleanup has slowed progress several ways. There has been little accountability. Are farmers installing and maintaining the BMPs and following the nutrient management plans they have agreed to (and in many cases been paid for)? What are they doing with excess manure? No one knows. Money for BMPs currently is spent where there are farmers willing to carry out such practices. But research by the USGS is making it clear that the practices are not all equally cost-effective.

Variations in soil types, in drainage above and below ground, in near-ness to waterways, and in other factors dramatically affect how much pollution actually gets from fields into the bay. Farms near big rivers, for example, may have more impact than those bordering smaller streams, because natural processes in small streams, where they remain healthy, can remove a lot of nutrients. A purely voluntary approach may skip putting resources into the worst-polluting farms, as it is often the best farmers who tend to sign up for BMPs.

Voluntary programs also have until recently required substantial investments by the farmers themselves. For farmers just trying to survive another year, investing heavily in conservation for the sake of the bay, which may be many miles away, is a low priority. Programs such as CREP, and to an extent cover cropping in Maryland, have demonstrated that where money is available, farmers will respond. Voluntary agricultural cleanup has also been hindered in many areas by understaffing and lack of commitment by the local agencies charged with giving technical advice to farmers. Many USDA and agricultural extension service employees still focus primarily on their traditional mission of soil conservation and increasing agricultural productivity. Nutrient reduction is a new objective that often adds to their already full plate of things to do.

However, when a motivated, effective local technical agent is focused on nutrients, the results can be astounding. Bobby Whitescarver, a government agricultural advisor in the Shenandoah Valley and the Chesapeake Bay Foundation's 2002 Conservationist of the Year, almost single-handedly has been responsible for a quarter of the CREP projects in Virginia. Chris Strohmeyer, an agricultural technician in Chester County, Pennsylvania, restored 22 miles of streamside forest buffers and 84 acres of wetlands in one year—while working on such restoration only a third of his time. But such energetic, dedicated people are the exception, not the rule. All too often, agricultural advisers and their staffs are content with the status quo and at times may even resist the conservation programs they are hired to implement.

During the last decade, all three bay states have passed their first laws to regulate agricultural pollution. Pennsylvania's was the first, passed early in the 1990s, but not implemented until 1997, and only after it had been severely watered down. It applies to only a small fraction of the state's agriculture, around 1,000 farms statewide, although they are large ones. It has major loopholes. The most glaring is one that lets a farmer sell his manure to a broker, who then does not have to account for whether it is spread responsibly, in accordance with crop needs. Pennsylvania legislators have acknowledged the need to plug this loophole, but it remains. The state also faces substantial imports of manure from other states.

Pennsylvania's law still lets manure be spread on the basis of how much nitrogen crops need—a major weak point, since crops need far more nitrogen than phosphorus, yet manure is rich in both. The upshot, in a 2001 paper by EPA and USDA scientists, is that soils across the bay watershed are becoming saturated with excess phosphorus—an estimated 40 million pounds from manure alone and more than 100 million pounds from manure and fertilizer combined. This is a potential time bomb, as phosphorus at very high levels can begin to run off in spite of BMPs that normally stop it. In Maryland, virtually every county now has more phosphorus than plants need in soils on anywhere from 25 to 90 percent of all farms sampled.

Thus, in Pennsylvania, what was heralded a decade ago—somewhat wishfully—as a "pioneering" law is now clearly behind the times. Both Maryland and Virginia have passed more recent agricultural pollution control laws that just reached the implementation stage in 2002. Both require a move to spreading manure on the basis of phosphorus—critical if manure is to be managed on the land in an environmentally sound way— and both make farmers more accountable for what they do with their fertilizers. Virginia's law is targeted narrowly at poultry, while Maryland's is broader.

Maryland is the only state so far that has attempted to make poultry processors responsible for what happens to the manure from their chickens. Processors own or control virtually every phase of raising chickens, selling or loaning chicken growers everything from feed to medicine, to money to build chicken houses. But up to now, processors have argued successfully that the manure from those chickens is solely the responsibility of the farmers who raise them.

Meanwhile, the federal government has finally issued long-awaited rules to reduce pollution from large, concentrated animal operations nationwide. Some bay-region agricultural experts say that the new federal rules are dismayingly weak and could undercut state efforts to take a tougher stand.

RETHINKING AGRICULTURE—V-8S AND 4-CYLINDERS

It is essential not to point fingers at farmers as culprits in bay pollution. They are part of a food system that includes everyone who eats. We need to understand modern agriculture in context—as the engine of a high-tech food system that has evolved in the last half century to produce huge surpluses of meat, dairy, and grains as cheaply as possible. National pursuit of a cheap food policy has for decades meant keeping the costs to the environment "off the books," an oversight we are only recently beginning to try to account for. Paying to produce food in a nonpolluting fashion is a societal responsibility to which people must now pay serious attention.

The measures outlined in the preceding section, if pursued widely and diligently, can go a long way toward ensuring that farms and the bay co-exist in good health—but probably not all the way. We can compare today's agriculture to a powerful, V-8 automobile engine. If we need better gas mileage (or bay water quality), we can tweak a lot of things—add on-board computers, drive more responsibly, lighten the vehicle. But in the end, we still have a V-8. And if we need really big improvements to mileage, we may have to consider a 4-cylinder.

So it is with current systems of farming. When all is said and done, although we can get considerably more environmental "mileage" out of it, we are still left with a V-8. For example, a number of agricultural soil scientists now think it is virtually impossible to grow annual grains, such as corn, without leaving excessive nitrogen in groundwater. Such crops grow only long enough to use nitrogen through mid-August. Meanwhile, natural cycles keep liberating more nitrogen well into autumn, as bacteria convert it from organic form in the soil to a form that runs off in groundwater. More effective weed-killing chemicals now largely suppress emergent weeds that might once have taken over, growing and using nitrogen as the corn quit. The average acre of topsoil holds thousands of pounds of bound up, organic nitrogen. So there is always plenty to be released by bacterial action, no matter how carefully a farmer manages his fertilizer applications. Cover crops, assuming they are used, can take up some but not all of this excess.

Consider another example: Studies by Norwegian nutritionist Marina Bleken show that the grain-fed meat so predominant in American diets takes around three times as much nitrogen fertilizer to produce a pound of protein as producing it through growing grains alone. Bleken estimates that the overall American diet requires nearly twice as much nitrogen fertilizer as the so-called Mediterranean diet, often recommended by nutritionists in the United States. The latter diet is based on vegetables, grains, and cereals, similar to what Italians ate during the 1960s. It is considered varied, tasty, and healthy—and far from meatless, still incorporating about half our country's world-leading 270 pounds a year per person meat consumption.

The mountains of manure produced by our meat-intensive diets pose a larger pollution control challenge than thought a decade ago. Researchers for the USDA now think that in addition to amounts reaching the bay via surface runoff and groundwater, large amounts of manure nitrogen—an estimated 145 million pounds a year—become airborne as ammonia. Some, but by no means all, of this runs into the bay.

In sum, today's agriculture is a system that fundamentally "leaks" large amounts of pollutants, much as a V-8 engine is fundamentally a gas hog. Just as we will probably always need V-8 engines for certain jobs, we will likely always need high-production agriculture to feed a growing and urbanized population. However, just as we have a variety of cars on the road—and need more of the fuel-efficient varieties—we also need to diversify agricultural products and services with ones that serve our needs but are less polluting. It seems likely that we will need to go beyond current available conservation practices to make our agricultural system fully compatible with a healthy bay.

Such changes cannot occur at the expense of farmers, already strapped by years of low prices for many of their crops. Estimates of bay restoration needs by the CBF and state governments thus include $2 billion in the next decade to bring about a dramatic re-greening of agricultural lands. About 700,000 acres of forest, an area about twice the size of Baltimore County, need to be planted along 50,000 miles of streams to filter and buffer polluted land runoff. Another 1 million acres of cropland would be taken out of production and put in natural vegetation under this restoration scenario.

Longer range, agricultural experts recommend diversifying farming in the watershed to include alternative crops to corn and soybeans, including perennials more in sync with natural nitrogen cycles. For such things to happen on a wide basis, there needs to be a shift in federal farm subsidies, which total billions of dollars annually, moving away from the current system that is weighted heavily toward rewarding increased crop production to a system that compensates farmers with "green payments" for environmentally sound practices. Modifying the way growers raise meat—letting cattle graze in pastures instead of confining them to barns and feeding them grain—would both cut polluted runoff and provide health benefits (remember farmer Bobby Prigel's story).

Ecologically, the "closed circle" concept of recycling animal wastes back into the soil to grow the crops that feed the animals is an appealing one both to environmentalists and to farmers, who can save money on commercial, chemical fertilizer. But it does not work well with the huge numbers of farm animals in the bay watershed. Pennsylvania is the nation's second leading dairy state, fourth in eggs and eighth in swine and turkeys. Virginia is fourth in turkeys and eighth in meat chickens. Maryland is seventh in the nation in chickens, and neighboring Delaware is ninth.

The upshot is that the bay region imports huge quantities of feed—and the nitrogen and phosphorus in that feed—from outside the watershed. Shipping the manure back to where the feed came from—all over the nation and the world—would be the only way to ensure ecological balance, but it would be too expensive. Applying manure to soils is also difficult, because many soils need lots of nitrogen and little or no phosphorus, and farmers can't apply them separately in manure, as they can with purchased, chemical fertilizers. Farmers need to be able to sell manure as an economically valuable resource rather than be faced with a disposal problem.

Some promising alternatives exist. Perdue Farms, one of the watershed's and the nation's largest poultry processors, has invested millions in a plant to turn poultry manure into pellets that it is selling to farmers in the Midwest to enhance soil productivity there. It uses 80,000 tons of chicken manure a year—7–10 percent of what is produced in Maryland and Delaware. A proposed electrical power plant, endorsed by the CBF, would use some 400,000 tons more of the area's chicken manure—about half of all produced in the area. Critics have complained that such a plant would need a state subsidy to be competitive with oil- and coal-fired power plants. But that need occurs partly because of the billions of dollars in federal subsidies that oil and coal companies already get.

Conclusions

- Runoff of agricultural nitrogen and phosphorus from both chemical fertilizers and manure is the dominant pollution source on all but one of the bay's seven major tributaries. It has declined only very modestly, despite a great deal of activity across the watershed to control it.
- In retrospect, efforts have not been and still are not focused, effective, or funded well enough to make real progress in improving agricultural pollution in the next decade.
- There are huge opportunities to change this prospect. Planting winter cover crops on millions of acres to sop up nutrients before they run off is one place to start. Currently, cover crops are grown on less than 5 percent of croplands.
- Manure, in most places, must be spread strictly on the basis of how much phosphorus crops need, because soils across the watershed are becoming dangerously saturated. Pennsylvania lags behind Maryland and Virginia in dealing with this issue.
- The federal Farm Bill must be restructured to pay all farmers for green practices on crop- and pasturelands. Now it mainly pays a limited number of large farmers based on how much grain they grow—grain that largely goes to feed animals in large confinement operations, a huge source of polluted runoff.
- The planting of forested buffers and the creation or restoration of wetlands between farm fields and waterways must continue to be accelerated. Fencing farm animals out of streams also needs wider application.
- The traditional voluntary approach to reducing farm pollution must be further modified to make farmers accountable for what they do with their manure and fertilizer. All three bay states have begun to do this. Pennsylvania's relevant regulations, however, are badly outdated. Proposed federal regulations need to be strengthened and put into effect now.

- Farmers are not the culprits. They are part of a national food system geared to produce abundant, cheap food that has ignored the costs to the environment for decades. Rectifying this situation in the bay watershed will take several billion dollars over the next decade. Such costs must be borne by all who eat, the watershed's 16 million citizens.
- Modern agriculture is a fundamentally leaky system, sending excessive pollution to waterways even with the most careful attention to clean water by farmers. Ultimately, farmers' incomes must be diversified with less-polluting products, such as growing native grasses for energy production and growing trees as a way of sopping up the excess carbon dioxide causing global warming, plus rental payments for restoring forested buffers on stream banks. In addition, consumers need to consider a less-polluting diet. The Mediterranean diet, which would use about half the meat of the current U.S. diet, would require only a little more than half the fertilizer that farmers use now and result in far less manure.
- Fledgling attempts to burn excess manure for power and to ship it back in pellet form for use on midwestern farms should be strongly supported and expanded.

Sewage—Real Progress, but Big Tests to Come

The pollution of sewage of our ever increasing population and the waste from our rapidly growing industries is affecting the entire fish and oyster industry in and around Hampton Roads.

—Virginia Commissioners of Fisheries, 1919

In contrast to the struggles to control nutrient pollution from agricultural runoff, the cuts in nitrogen and phosphorus from human wastes have been a bright spot of progress in the last few decades, with potential for even bigger reductions ahead in these two key bay pollutants. And this improvement has happened even as population has increased by more than a million people.

Across the watershed, about 12 million of the bay region's 16 million citizens flush their toilets into centralized sewage systems that dump directly into the bay and its rivers (the rest are connected to individual home septic tanks, discussed later). Currently, there are 298 major treatment plants that account for almost all the sewage flowing to the bay, with 8 more plants scheduled to come on-line in the immediate future. Fifty industries also each pipe as much nitrogen and phosphorus to the bay as do some major sewage plants.

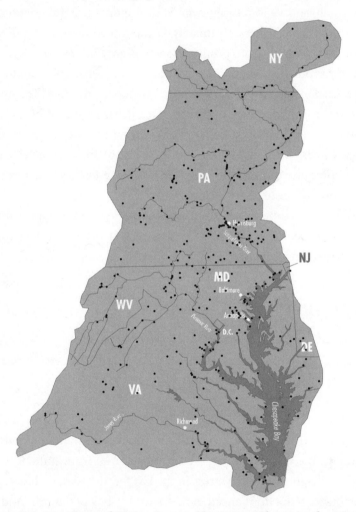

FIGURE 2.4. Locations of Major Sewage Treatment Plants in the Watershed. The pattern of major sewage treatment plants (those that discharge more than 0.5 million gallon of wastewater per day) mirrors the patterns of human population in the Chesapeake watershed.

Nitrogen from these municipal and industrial pollution sources fell from 88 million pounds a year to 64 million pounds between 1985 and 2000. Phosphorus during the same period fell from about 12 million to 6 million pounds a year. Sewage has thus been the sole source of major, documented cleanup gains in nutrients entering the bay.

And if all of the above treatment plants and industries were to employ currently achievable, state-of-the-art cleanup techniques, they could remove at least another 45 million pounds of nitrogen each year, with substantial reductions in phosphorus to boot. Such progress, however, is by no means guaranteed to happen.

Looking back, it should not be surprising that the largest pollution gains came from these so-called point sources (i.e., from specific pipes, as opposed to the nonpoint source runoff from farms and suburbia). Laws, programs, and technologies to control wastes from sewage plants and industries have been maturing for decades. Billions of dollars have been invested in them, dwarfing the sums spent on controlling nonpoint runoff. A lot of the expense was shared by millions of sewer users or among major industries, as opposed to a relative handful of farmers in the case of agricultural pollution.

In addition to this "maturing process," two major breakthroughs helped. During the mid- to late 1980s, all bay region states and the District of Columbia banned the use of phosphate laundry detergents. This painless change in a single consumer product, multiplied by millions of homes whose wash water flowed to sewage treatment plants, reduced phosphorus discharges by 30 to 50 percent. The ban was bitterly opposed by the detergent industry, which launched a scare campaign that said it would cause widespread human-health problems and that consumers, disgruntled by dirty, gray laundry, would revolt. In fact, no one noticed.

The second leap forward came from introduction of a new technology during the 1990s (see "Eco-thriller" below) that allowed larger, cheaper reductions in nitrogen at sewage treatment plants than anyone had foreseen. The achievements on some bay rivers have been striking:

- The District of Columbia's giant Blue Plains treatment plant on the Potomac River has cut nitrogen by 8 million pounds a year and reduced phosphorus from more than a million pounds to 100,000.

Blue Plains, the largest advanced wastewater treatment plant in the world, serves 2 million people in Washington, Maryland, and Virginia. Thus about 12 percent of residents in the six-state watershed of the Chesapeake flush to this one plant. The reductions of phosphorus—the key polluting nutrient in the upper, freshwater portions of the bay and its rivers—have allowed a remarkable comeback in the environment of the Potomac around Washington, especially underwater grasses, fish, and waterbirds. A similar comeback, however, has not yet occurred further downriver, where nitrogen levels control algae growth. Part of the reason is that Blue Plains has only recently been able to address nitrogen, while it has been doing exemplary phosphorus control for over two decades.

- On Maryland's Patuxent River, whose heavily developed drainage basin made sewage the dominant pollution source by the 1970s, nitrogen from treatment plants has fallen more than 50 percent and phosphorus more than 80 percent, even during a period when population in the river basin has leapt by more than a third. The runoff from developed lands and airborne fallout now pollutes the river more than sewage.

- On Virginia's James River, the bay's third largest tributary after the Susquehanna and Potomac, nitrogen has dropped by a whopping 11 million pounds a year. This improvement has come jointly from improvements in the Hopewell, Virginia, treatment plant and from Honeywell's private industrial facility on the river there. Honeywell has become a mentor in the EPA's Businesses for the Bay program, helping other industries reduce their pollution.

- In Pennsylvania, which is working with industries on nutrient reductions, the Osram Sylvania plant on the Susquehanna in Towanda has changed a manufacturing process and reduced its annual nitrogen discharge by a million pounds.

ECO-THRILLER

Almost certainly, you have never heard of Clifford W. Randall, a mild-mannered professor of environmental engineering at Virginia Polytechnic Institute in rural Blacksburg. But Randall could star in an eco-thriller, a tale of international intrigue and raw sewage, of power politics, vast monies, and the reduction of nitrogen and phosphorus—as the fate of a great estuary hangs in the balance.

A plot outline follows. It all really happened.

Begin in 1956, in the sewage plant in Lexington, Kentucky, where young Cliff Randall is working his way through the University of Kentucky, forming a lifelong interest in treating wastewater. Up on Chesapeake Bay, the living is good—plenty of oysters to slurp and ducks to shoot, a cornucopia of crabs and rockfish, hardheads and trout. A decade passes. Some people are becoming worried about declines in the Chesapeake, especially where sewage flows are increasing; but the declines are still easily dismissed as part of natural ups and downs.

Randall, now an assistant professor at the University of Texas, with his Ph.D. in sanitary engineering, is fascinated by a mystery down in San Antonio, where he's been hired to evaluate several sewage treatment plants. One of them seems to be working far better than it was designed to do, taking out large quantities of nitrogen and phosphorus. Removing nutrients from sewage takes wastewater treatment to a whole new level—like taking aircraft from propellers to jets. At this time, sewage engineers know how to do it, but only in ways that use lots of chemicals, are horrendously expensive and energy intensive, and create lots more sludge to dispose of.

The oddball Texas plant seems to do it naturally, biologically—a great breakthrough if anyone can figure out how it is happening and copy it. About the same time, a similar miracle is occurring at Back River, the main sewage plant for Baltimore. It is written up in a scientific paper around 1971, but no one much notices.

People are, however, beginning to notice declines in the Chesapeake during the early 1970s that are less and less explainable as natural cycles. Too much nitrogen and phosphorus, the verdict will be. By then Randall has moved to Virginia Tech in Blacksburg, where he and others are rolling along toward understanding new, nonchemical ways of nutrient removal from sewage.

They are rolling along toward a brick wall, as it turns out. An eminent professor at Berkeley explains the miraculous San Antonio plant—

chemicals were doing the nutrient removal all along—they were present in the region's groundwater. His thesis is widely accepted—also utterly wrong; but that won't be apparent for years. Meanwhile, as a result, any funding for Randall's biological nutrient removal dries up for a decade.

Now, flash to the Chesapeake's Patuxent River in the mid-1970s, where University of Maryland scientists are locked in a struggle over nutrients in sewage. On the outcome rests the fate of the river and ultimately the bay—also, quite likely, the scientists' reputations and jobs. They have staked everything on their cutting-edge research that says, in essence, their own state government and the federal EPA are going to kill the bay by allowing too many nutrients in sewage. The scientists stated as much in a lawsuit brought by southern Maryland counties against the state of Maryland and the EPA.

Though the EPA's and Maryland's resistance is couched in arguments over chemistry, the real issue is money. If they agreed to do with sewage what the scientists say is necessary, the costs, using conventional chemical treatment methods, could run into the billions.

Meanwhile, Randall has never lost faith in finding a biological way to cleanse sewage cheaply and efficiently. In 1982, he attends an international pollution conference in Capetown, South Africa, and finds, sequestered from the world by its apartheid policies, that that small nation has already pioneered biological nutrient removal (BNR). The man who launched South Africa's effort, James Barnard, had made his breakthrough after studying an obscure paper—the one published on Baltimore's Back River plant years before.

By 1984, Randall and his colleagues at Virginia Tech are making real headway, proving that a Virginia plant can be modified for BNR for just 2.5 percent more funding than far inferior standard treatment would require. By contrast, another Virginia plant, using standard nutrient removal, had cost 400 percent of conventional treatment. In 1985, Randall chaired the Chesapeake Bay Restoration Program's scientific and technical committee. He met the University of Maryland scientists from the Patuxent River and threw his support behind their argument for increased nutrient removal. With the prospects now bright for doing it relatively cheaply with BNR, Maryland agreed, and eventually EPA acquiesced. "Cliff provided the economic and technological key that allowed the scientific truth to be accepted," says Chris D'Elia, one of the University of Maryland scientists who risked their careers in demanding nutrient removal more than a decade ago.

D'Elia, now head of the University of Maryland's Sea Grant Program, nominated Randall for a prestigious bay science medal: "This guy made a major contribution to science, saved the taxpayer a bundle, and cleaned up Chesapeake Bay," D'Elia says. "It was like cold fusion, except BNR works." Today, BNR and associated sewage treatment techniques have accounted for the bulk of the progress in cleansing the bay of its nitrogen. Costs have plummeted, from an estimated $35 per pound of nitrogen removed to an amazing $2–$4 a pound.

OBSTACLES AHEAD

If it were only a matter of technology, then sewage and industry could provide huge, additional cleanup in the next decade—enough to get the bay states at least a third of the way to the water quality needed to restore the Chesapeake's health. But a number of roadblocks must be removed before that has any chance of happening.

Pennsylvania, for example, has moved only slowly to install modern nitrogen controls on its 143 sewage treatment plants throughout its Susquehanna River basin, the source of nearly half the bay's freshwater. Against a backdrop of marked reductions in sewage nitrogen in the last decade or so, nitrogen from Pennsylvania's plants has actually gone up by more than a million pounds a year. By 2010, if current trends continue, Pennsylvania will become the single largest source of nitrogen from sewage among all bay rivers, despite far larger numbers of people living in Maryland and Virginia.

It all comes down to money. Maryland has spent about $240 million on sewage upgrades in the last decade or so and Virginia about $150 million. Pennsylvania has spent less than $10 million in the part of the state (about a third of Pennsylvania) that drains to the Chesapeake. An estimated $3 billion to $4 billion over and above current spending will be needed throughout the entire watershed to realize the full benefits of technology by 2010. Maryland currently plans to upgrade all its major sewage treatment plants

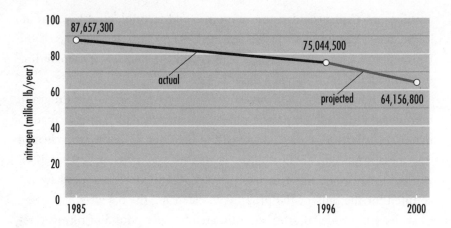

Total Phosphorus: Delivered Loads

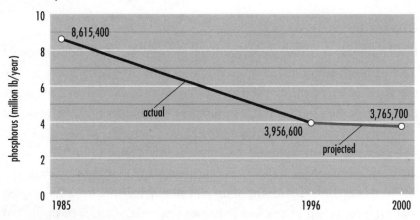

FIGURE 2.5. **Progress in Reducing Point Source Pollution of the Bay.** Progress in reducing both nitrogen and phosphorus is real but currently much too slow to achieve the goals of *Chesapeake 2000* by 2010. [EPA Chesapeake Bay Program]

close to the limits of technology during this decade. Virginia plans up-grades to about 13 out of 72, and Pennsylvania plans upgrades to 12 of 123 plants. Neither Virginia nor Pennsylvania plans upgrades as stringent as Maryland's. Overall, half of all sewage flowing to the bay is now treated with the latest technology; the planned upgrades will increase that figure to about one-third of the plants but 80 percent of the flows.

Here is another way to compare how the states have cleaned up their sewage: Virginia has the largest flows of sewage in the watershed—562 million gallons per day (mgd) from its major plants. Next is Maryland (469 mgd), then Pennsylvania (291 mgd), followed by the District of Columbia (159 mgd). If, however, we use 2000 data to rank them by which state has the least pollution per gallon, the order shifts.

The District's sewage, all from the advanced Blue Plains treatment plant on the Potomac, carries the lowest amount of pollution, that is, the cleanest concentrations of both nitrogen (75 pounds per million gallons) and phosphorus (0.9 pound per million gallons). Maryland ranks second, with 85 pounds of nitrogen per million gallons and 5.1 pounds of phosphorus. Pennsylvania and Virginia plants both carry relatively high loads of pollution, around 120 pounds of nitrogen per million gallons; Virginia carries 7.6 pounds of phosphorus, and Pennsylvania, 12.7 pounds.

As for industry, despite the big, voluntary cuts in nitrogen made by Honeywell on the James and Osram Sylvania on the Susquehanna, there are no federal or state requirements limiting nitrogen from industrial pipes. The federal government is currently developing guidance on this issue that the states could adopt.

Comparing industries' contributions of nitrogen and phosphorus in the bay states, again based on year 2000 performance, Virginia has the largest overall discharges (293 mgd), followed by Maryland (116 mgd) and Pennsylvania (76 mgd). However, Virginia industry is cleanest in terms of nitrogen released (37 pounds per million gallons of discharge), but highest in phosphorus (7 pounds). Maryland industry is highest in nitrogen (70.5 pounds) but lowest in phosphorus (3.55 pounds). Pennsylvania industry is in the middle, with 61 pounds of nitrogen and 5.55 pounds of phosphorus.

A caution: As with any technology, sewage treatment plants and the infrastructure that serves them don't always run right. Major problems include inadequate maintenance, deteriorating underground pipes and pumping stations, and waste flows that exceed their capacity. In addition, some areas have sewers that also collect stormwater, causing overflows of raw sewage at the treatment plant during heavy rainstorms. Historically, federal and state governments have hesitated to levy large fines against sewage treatment plants that pollute as a result of the above factors, although that situation is improving.

Maryland is one of the few states in the nation to conduct a thorough study of what it would take to repair all its faulty sewer infrastructure and treatment plants. The price tag is more than $4 billion, which would require new spending of $80–$140 million a year for several years. Baltimore City alone faces more than a billion dollars in needed repairs but stands under a court-ordered consent decree to make them. Washington, D.C., has told Congress it needs more than a billion dollars over twenty years for giant, underground basins to collect and hold overflows of stormwater and sewage after heavy rainfalls until it can be pumped through the Blue Plains plant for treatment.

LIMITS TO SEWAGE TREATMENT

Despite the periodic pollution episodes caused by aging sewer lines and plants, sewage plants around the bay are generally doing a better job. In the next decade, and maybe beyond, if we spend the money and employ proven technologies, we can count on large, cost-effective water quality improvements from sewage. But what happens as population and wastewater flows continue to rise, as we reach the point of taking out all but the last part of nitrogen or one-tenth of a part of phosphorus per million parts of wastewater? The mammoth Blue Plains plant already removes phosphorus to an average concentration of 0.18 part phosphorus per million parts of wastewater, and it removes nitrogen to an average concentration of about 6.5 parts per million. It can't do much better without extensive redesign, so with the anticipated increase in the Washington area's population, the total discharge of both nutrients is likely to begin edging back up over the next decade if the D.C. Water and Sewer Authority is not careful to limit new hookups.

In addition, there is no reason to expect another outside boost to the efficiency of sewage treatment such as occurred during the late 1980s from phosphate detergent bans throughout the watershed. Current technology can reach 3 parts nitrogen per million in this decade—on average, twice as clean as the best plants are now—and 1 part per million seems possible. To exceed those levels, however, may be pushing hard against the limits of both technology and cost.

This likelihood is why the bay restoration agreement contains a commitment to "cap" the nitrogen and phosphorus from sewage and other sources of pollution. In other words, even if population doubles and triples in the future, that growth will not be allowed to erode environmental progress. Somehow—no one is quite sure how—as sewage treatment reaches cleanup standards healthy for the bay, it will hold there even as population rises. Such caps are even more critical as states, such as Maryland, begin to pursue Smart Growth policies, which aim to keep people from developing the countryside and create incentives to make them settle more densely around areas served by central sewage systems.

But as long as we pursue present policies of using the bay and its rivers to dilute our wastes, it is difficult to see how we will hold such caps in the long run unless population in the watershed stabilizes (see Chapter 5).

Already, in 2001, an early test of the so-called cap strategy occurred. Fast-growing Howard County, Maryland, sought to expand one of its sewage treatment plants on the Little Patuxent River, resulting in loads that would have increased as more people moved in. After lengthy negotiations and pressure from the CBF, the county agreed to a goal of holding nitrogen discharge levels even as growth occurs. In addition, it will look for projects to cut nitrogen in other ways, such as creating natural forest buffers along rivers and streams to filter pollution from stormwater runoff. In return, the state and environmentalists agreed to a goal for capping nitrogen instead of a legal requirement.

This is only a shadow of the debates to come over capping pollution from sewage. Ultimately, perhaps, as the recent Bay Program report "Holding the Line on Nutrient Pollution" stated: "This will force us to rethink how we grow or expand . . . to question growth as a measure of prosperity. It raises the long-term issue of limits to growth in all sectors . . . of measuring the quality of life by something other than the level of resource consumption."

SLUDGE—AVOIDING A SHELL GAME

It is important to ask, What is the ultimate fate of the pollutants removed from sewage before it enters the bay? The short answer is, A lot of them go into sewage sludge, the semi-solid residue produced in mountainous quantities by advanced treatment plants. Around 700,000 tons of sewage sludge (by dry weight, after water is removed) are generated each year in the bay watershed. Blue Plains, in the District of Columbia, by far the largest plant in the bay region, piles up more than 100,000 tons of sludge each year.

One of the lessons of all environmental cleanup, still not well learned, is that we have to be careful of taking a pollutant out of one place—air or land or water—only to put it in another where it continues to cause problems. It is occasionally possible to destroy pollutants partially—for example, turning dissolved nitrogen in bay water to nitrogen gas—but more often pollutants are just shuffled from one medium to another, a variation of the old shell game.

Rich in phosphorus and nitrogen, and declining in toxicity as industries increasingly "pre-treat" the waste they send to sewage plants to remove its more noxious elements, sludge has gained wide acceptance for spreading on farmland as a fertilizer in many parts of the watershed. Virginia and Pennsylvania even import sewage sludge, up to 100,000 tons a year, from as far away as New Jersey and New York.

All three bay states attempt to spread sludge on the land in an environmentally safe manner, matching it as closely as possible with the fertilizer needs of crops. However, just as farmers do with manure, they are still applying it on the basis of how much nitrogen crops need. This may result in buildups of too much phosphorus in the soil, creating the potential for the nutrients removed from sewage to follow another path (farm runoff) back into the bay. This return of sludge is not always a problem. For example, depending on the sewage plant, the phosphorus in the sludge can be bound up with iron, preventing it from becoming a threat to water quality even if it enters the bay.

Overall, sludge in the watershed has a small environmental impact compared to manure. Amounts do not appear to have increased much in the last decade, as newer, biological sewage treatment processes generated less sludge than did older, chemical treatments. Some states are beginning to market their sludge to home gardeners as a soil builder. Maryland disposes of about 43,000 tons a year this way. The ultimate fate of this sludge, as with sludge used in agriculture, depends on home users being responsible for applying it properly and keeping it out of waterways.

SEPTIC TANKS—OUTHOUSE TECHNOLOGY
IN THE TWENTY-FIRST CENTURY

While sewage treatment plants continue reducing pollution at great expense, nearly a quarter of the watershed's population gets by on the cheap with a fifty-year-old, polluting waste treatment technology that is little more than an out-of-sight version of the old outhouse: the septic tank.

Living in housing that ranges from mobile homes to mansions, these people are users of the watershed's estimated 1.3 million septic systems. Pennsylvania has nearly 400,000, followed by Virginia with 373,000 and Maryland with 317,000. Septic systems function out of sight, out of mind. Many people aren't sure they even have one. If you don't pay a regular water and sewer bill, chances are, you do.

Septic systems are tanks, usually concrete, buried in the backyard, collecting wastewater from the home's plumbing. The solids settle to the bottom of the tank and are gradually liquefied by bacteria. Liquid waste flows out the top part of the tank into an underground drain field, where the soil filters and detoxifies bacteria and viruses. From the human health standpoint, septic tanks are an improvement on the outhouse. But they are perhaps even more harmful to the health of the bay. That is because they directly inject all the nitrogen in human wastes into the groundwater, where it has the potential to reach the bay via streams and rivers (how much actually reaches bay tributaries varies from place to place). Septic tanks usually do not increase phosphorus, the other worrisome nutrient in human wastes, because it binds to soil particles rather than moving through the groundwater like nitrogen.

An urban resident hooked to a modern sewage treatment plant produces about 2 pounds of nitrogen a year for the bay to deal with. A septic system user produces 9 pounds, nearly five times as much nitrogen, and although some of the septic system's nitrogen is removed by soils or by the root zones of forests before it reaches waterways, it still has the potential to be more polluting than the treatment plant.

Furthermore, the trends with septic systems are mostly heading all the wrong way. Sewage treatment plants are improving, and by decade's end may be able to lower per-capita nitrogen to a pound a year. Meanwhile, the septic tanks used to serve all new development outside sewer areas are improving scarcely at all, despite the availability of better technologies for septic systems. Watershed-wide, nitrogen from sewage is about 20 percent of the bay's total burden, while nitrogen from septic is around 5 percent. But 50 percent of recent development in some suburban counties relies on septic systems. Nitrogen from septic tanks in the Patuxent River basin has risen an estimated 38 percent in the last fifteen years. In another decade or two, septic systems could be a comparable source of nitrogen, baywide, to sewage treatment plants, even though the septic systems serve only a quarter of the watershed's households.

While sewage treatment plants have some problems with breakdowns, an estimated 30 percent of septic systems are failing (they need to be pumped out regularly in order to function properly, and many older ones are made of metal and are rusting out; also, drain fields eventually clog up and stop working). Septic failure presents real problems with bacterial pollution. Ironically, such a clogged-up septic tank is no worse a discharger of nitrogen than a brand new one and may even be better if it bubbles wastes to the surface where some nitrogen might escape as a harmless gas.

Maryland is the only state in the watershed that has made a serious legislative attempt to give a tax credit to homeowners who replace conventional septic systems with newer technology. A coalition of developers, real estate agents, and farmers defeated it, largely on the basis of cost. New, proven designs that make septic systems 60–90 percent less polluting than older designs can add a few thousand dollars to the cost of conventional systems, but in Texas and Louisiana, where hundreds of thousands of these less-polluting septic tanks have been installed, costs quickly fell to about $1,000 extra. This price tag would be comparable to about two years of sewage bills. Homeowners need to recognize that there is a cost to treating sewage, whether through sewage bills or upgrading a septic system.

There is also a real question of equity: Why should people who choose to live outside designated growth areas served by sewers get off cheaply and add more pollution to boot? With states such as Maryland now pushing Smart Growth programs to channel development into designated growth areas, requiring less than the best septic technology, even as sewage treatment plants undergo expensive upgrades, amounts to a subsidy to development of rural open space.

Environmentalists have traditionally viewed septic systems as a check on explosive development, a rough substitute for good land use planning. Building lots must have adequate size, well-drained soils, and at least a minimum required slope for the septic tanks to work well enough to get approval from health authorities. However, the downside of this check probably has been worse than the upside. Health rules concerning septic tanks have tended to steer development into low-density sprawl patterns that consume more open space and are economically costly, often directing growth to prime farm soils where septic tanks work well.

Improved, less-polluting septic tanks, along with "waterless" composting toilets that don't send any nitrogen to waterways, worry some environmentalists because of their potential for allowing development on soils and slopes that are now protected because they won't drain well enough to permit conventional septic systems. But the answer to that concern is better land use, not continuation of polluting, outdated waste treatment systems. Currently, there seems little prospect for a significant change to less-polluting septic systems either on new development or in replacing older, failed systems.

Conclusions

- Sewage treatment has been the only major, proven success in reducing the bay's crippling load of nitrogen and phosphorus. It is also the pollution source currently best targeted with money, a mature legal and regulatory framework, and good technology.
- Progress has been uneven. Pennsylvania has lagged badly and could become the bay's largest source of nitrogen from sewage by the end of the decade, despite having far fewer people than other regions of the bay watershed.
- More money will be critical to the further progress needed from sewage treatment to realize improved baywide water quality by 2010. Some $3 billion to $4 billion beyond present state spending is necessary to take best advantage of new cleanup technology. Billions more will be needed to repair aging sewer lines and older treatment plants,

and to eliminate overflows of raw sewage caused when stormwater floods treatment plants.

- Using the best technology available on all major sewage treatment plants could eliminate more than 40 million pounds of nitrogen a year out of an estimated 100- to 150-million-pound reduction needed from all sources of pollution to restore the bay.
- Long-term, current policies to cap total pollution from sewage treatment plants must hold firm as population soars. On some rivers, the population is already nearing the point where it is bumping against the limits of sewage cleanup technology. This limit may come with phosphorus sooner than with nitrogen.
- About 25 percent of the 16 million people in the bay watershed, including a substantial portion of new growth, continue to use outdated, highly polluting septic system technology to treat wastes. Unless the states require new, less-polluting septic systems for all new development and replacement of all failing systems, septic tanks have the potential to offset much of the progress at sewage treatment plants.

Air

This most excellent canopy, the air.

> —William Shakespeare

Across every square inch of their collective 2.6-million-acre surface, the bay and its tributaries are in constant contact with the atmosphere. And these days, the atmosphere is no longer so excellent as Shakespeare would have it. Air pollution is heating it up like a greenhouse, ripping holes in the ozone layer, injuring both human and aquatic health, and turning the heavens sour with acid rain.

Just as the health of its waters is linked to the health of its watershed, the Chesapeake Bay is also a creature of its *airshed*. Indeed, dramatically cleaner air is a requirement for restoring and sustaining the bay's health and will have huge benefits for human health, too. The airshed—the region that encompasses most airborne sources of bay pollution—covers about 418,000 square miles, more than six times the size of the watershed. Its borders are imprecise, changing with the direction of the wind. But for most of the year, the net flow of air to the bay is from west to east. The bay thus receives the fallout of pollutants emitted to the air from the urban centers of Baltimore, Washington, Richmond, and Norfolk, from

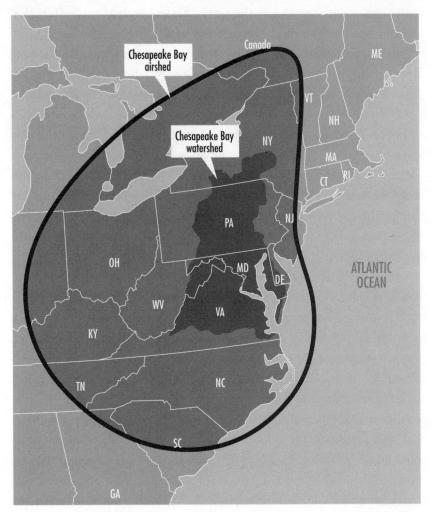

FIGURE 2.6. The Chesapeake's Airshed. The land area draining to the Chesapeake is easy to define and much smaller than the area from which air pollution comes to the bay. On any given day, weather conditions (especially winds aloft) determine which sources send pollutants to the Chesapeake. However, the airshed commonly encompasses this region shown. [EPA Chesapeake Bay Program]

as far afield as the great industrial complexes of the Ohio River Valley, from the hog farms in North Carolina, and from pollution sources in Kentucky, Indiana, and Canada.

About 60 percent of these pollutants come down when rainstorms wash them from the air, and the rest come as "dryfall," the steady, slow sifting down from above during the rest of the year, much as dust accumulates on a window ledge or a car roof. Air pollutants enter the bay both directly, settling onto its waters, and indirectly, falling onto the lands of the watershed, from where portions of them enter runoff to waterways.

The bay states and the nation have been working for decades to control air pollution, with some success; but most of those efforts have been governed by concern for what affects human health. We are just beginning to recognize the need for even more stringent measures to protect aquatic health. Indeed, air pollution was not even considered a "controllable" impact by the federal-state bay restoration program during the 1980s and 1990s. Now it is acknowledged to be one of the largest challenges in the cleanup program.

The air pollutes the bay in several ways. The largest impact is from nitrogen, which is in turn the bay's single greatest problem, at the root of its widespread declines in oxygen and the underwater grass habitats so vital to crabs and fish. As of 2002, scientists estimated that 98 million pounds—almost a third of the nitrogen entering the bay each year—came from air pollution. That is more than half again the amount that comes from sewage treatment plants.

Airborne nitrogen comes from a variety of sources. The burning of coal and petroleum products creates oxides of nitrogen, which easily travel hundreds of miles, raining down on the land and waters as they go. Power plants, cars, and trucks are the biggest culprits. Nitrogen also comes from airborne ammonia gas, a less-understood pollutant but one that probably trails only nitrogen from fuel combustion as a bay problem. The major source of this ammonia is animal manure from the heavy concentrations of cattle, hogs, and poultry in the bay watershed and airshed. Agriculture-intensive Lancaster County in Pennsylvania alone is estimated to generate 37 million pounds a year of ammonia nitrogen (only a fraction of which actually gets into the bay, after working its way through

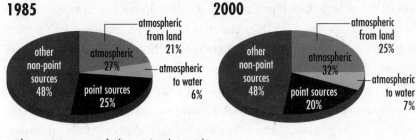

1985

other non-point sources 48%

atmospheric 27%

point sources 25%

atmospheric from land 21%

atmospheric to water 6%

2000

other non-point sources 48%

atmospheric 32%

point sources 20%

atmospheric from land 25%

atmospheric to water 7%

other non-point sources: fertilizer, septic tanks, natural sources
atmospheric from land: vehicles, electric utilities, industry
point sources: wastewater treatment plants, industry

FIGURE 2.7. **Increasing Share of Air Pollution.** Over the period 1985–2000, air pollution reaching the bay rose from about the same as point sources to more than half again as much. It is now a major contributor to the Chesapeake's problems. [EPA Chesapeake Bay Program]

the soils and vegetation). A major question about agricultural airborne nitrogen is how far it travels. Evidence so far suggests the measure is miles, but not hundreds or thousands of miles as with nitrogen from power plants.

Just adding up the pounds or tons of nitrogen from any of the above sources does not always give a true picture of its impact on the bay. For example, sources closest to the bay will deliver more pollution than similar-sized sources farther away. With major highways such as Interstate 95 running like a great river of exhaust fumes close by the Chesapeake for its entire length, automobile nitrogen likely has more impact than that from Ohio River Valley power plants, which falls in the far northern and western parts of the watershed.

Similarly, farm animals concentrated closest to the bay on the Delmarva Peninsula and in Lancaster County, Pennsylvania, may have more immediate impact proportionate to the size of their nitrogen emissions. Although about half the airborne nitrogen in the bay's huge airshed comes from outside the states of the watershed, there is no excuse for the bay states to delay cleaning up their own air pollutants while efforts are made to gain cooperation from more far-flung pollution sources.

Equally important are preserving and expanding the kinds of landscapes within the bay watershed that most effectively trap and filter air pollutants before they reach the water and minimizing landscapes that do just the opposite. Consider the striking differences between forested and developed regions of the watershed. Airborne nitrogen falls on all watershed lands at the rate of 6–9 pounds per acre each year. But where it falls on forests, about 1–2 pounds of nitrogen actually make it into waterways, as the natural vegetation incorporates the rest in growth (see Chapter 4, "Resilience," for a fuller discussion). Where it falls on impervious surfaces—roofs, streets, parking lots, sidewalks—the full load of nitrogen readily washes off. Even when it is subsequently trapped by stormwater control ponds, the pollution ultimately reaching the bay far exceeds that from forests, wetlands, and other naturally vegetated lands.

PROGRESS—WILL THE AIR DO ITS SHARE?

There has been little or no real progress in reducing airborne nitrogen in the last decade or so, despite significant reductions from power plants and cleaner tailpipe emissions from vehicles. There are two principal reasons for this failure. (1) More people are driving more cars, and driving them a lot more often, offsetting the benefits of better pollution controls. In the bay's watershed, vehicle miles traveled (VMT) has been rising four times as fast as population since the 1970s. (2) Nitrogen from animal manure has not been regulated at all, and this source increased an estimated 17 percent between 1982 and 1997, according to USDA research. Airborne nitrogen from North Carolina hog farms, which are in the bay's airshed, increased sixfold in the last two decades. The bottom line is that air pollution has gone from causing an estimated one-quarter of the bay's nitrogen burden to nearly one-third.

Is there likely to be real progress made in the next decade? Keep in mind that scientists estimate nitrogen entering the bay needs to be reduced by around 40 percent to see restoration of its oxygen levels and underwater grass habitats. Air pollution's "share" of that total would be a reduction of nearly 40 million pounds a year. Bay managers have estimated we might get a 14-million-pound reduction from a "business as usual" approach, mainly from requirements of the current federal Clean Air Act that will result in cleaner emissions from power plants by 2010.

It is possible to eliminate close to the whole 40 million pounds—if federal and bay-state governments pushed power plants and automobiles to use the cleanest technologies available; if sprawl development were checked, thereby reducing the use of personal vehicles and favoring mass transit; and if agriculture were required to begin capturing the ammonia that now escapes from manure. (Europe and Scandinavia already are beginning to require ammonia controls to some extent.)

But the reality, at the beginning of the twenty-first century, is that even the progress expected from the existing Clean Air Act is uncertain. The administration of President George W. Bush, drawing heavily on advice from the coal, oil, and gas industries, has made increased production the centerpiece of its proposed energy policy, opposing any serious push for energy conservation. The administration argues that its proposed alternatives to the current Clean Air Act will ultimately result in even better air quality, but analyses by environmental groups show expected cuts in airborne nitrogen may be less than under current rules.

As for automobiles, VMT continues to rise, and fuel economy has been sliding slowly backward since 1988 as millions of Americans line up to buy pickup trucks and SUVs. These relatively heavy vehicles not only guzzle gas but also take advantage of loopholes in the Clean Air Act that allow them to emit more pollution per gallon of gas than automobiles (see Chapter 5). The U.S. Senate in 2002 overwhelmingly rejected attempts to require higher-mileage vehicles. Of the six senators from the bay states of Maryland, Virginia, and Pennsylvania, only one, Paul Sarbanes, voted against higher-mileage, less-polluting vehicles.

The impacts on the bay of vehicle choice are substantial. Based on U.S. EPA tests of tailpipe emissions, a large SUV produces twice as much nitrogen as a midsize station wagon each year, in addition to many more smog-forming hydrocarbons and other pollutants that harm human health and add toxic chemicals to the bay. If the bay states were to require the same level of emission controls now in common use on standard automobiles in California, the measure would reduce nitrogen by more than 90 percent from the current emissions of SUVs and pickup trucks in the Chesapeake's airshed.

As for agricultural ammonia, there is no move to regulate it. The progress to date is that it is now recognized as a "significant and growing" piece of the bay's nitrogen problem. Monitoring across the Delmarva Peninsula shows a sharp rise in this source of nitrogen during recent decades, closely tracking the rise of poultry-growing in the region. It is particularly significant that ammonia nitrogen appears to be the form most readily utilized by the bay's algae, whose excessive growth is at the root of oxygen losses and underwater grass declines.

Air pollution control is also generally more cost effective at its sources than at its points of entry into the bay, which are mainly the runoffs of rainwater from paved surfaces across the watershed, washing nitrogen and toxic chemicals that have fallen from the atmosphere. Capturing and treating such urban runoff, especially from existing developed areas, is several times more expensive than reducing it at the tailpipe and the smokestack level.

We have the scientific knowledge and the technologies to dramatically cut air's contribution to the bay's excess of nitrogen, but we are not on track to make more than a fraction of the reduction needed for the air to do its share in restoring water quality. Also, even should we make short-term reductions in airborne nitrogen, there is no comprehensive policy to cap those levels, as there is with nitrogen from sewage treatment plants. So the levels could rise again as population and energy demands grow.

Box 2.4. How Clean Is Clean Air?

What was the air quality like when the bay was completely healthy, say, 400 years ago? We can get an inkling by comparing U.S. monitoring re-sults for two major sources of nitrogen from remote American Samoa with the equivalent numbers for the Chesapeake. Airborne ammonia there is deposited on the land and water at about 10 percent of the lev-els commonly found here. And oxides of nitrogen are deposited at lev-els around 2 to 5 percent of the bay's airborne load.

AIRBORNE MERCURY

Polluted air also deposits toxic chemicals and metals across the bay's lands and waters, including a particularly troublesome one, mercury (see also "Toxics and Bacteria," this chapter). Mercury is a naturally occurring metal that has always entered the air and water from volcanoes and vents in the seabed. But humans have increased mercury by an estimated two to five times these natural levels. Sources range from leakage by batteries thrown into landfills to the emissions of waste incinerators, but by far the largest source of new mercury in the environment is burning coal in power plants. Forest fires also release a lot, but that is mostly from mercury originally deposited from polluted air.

Mercury in the water takes on a form called methylmercury, which accumulates in the muscle tissue of fish and crabs. It is one of the leading causes of health advisories (see "Toxics and Bacteria," this chapter) that urge residents to limit eating fish from the Chesapeake watershed. Pollution control technologies exist to reduce airborne mercury from power plants by at least 80 percent, though the EPA's recently announced mercury reduction effort calls for less. Opposition from the coal industry and an administration that has made burning coal a major piece of its energy policy leave progress here uncertain. As with nitrogen, forests and other natural vegetation can soak up large amounts of airborne mercury, while lands that we pave pass much of it on to waterways.

At any rate, significantly reducing mercury in the bay is a long-term process, since our industrial society has been loading the air, soils, and vegetation with it for more than a century. Even if new inputs from the air drop sharply, mercury will continue to leak from the land and be released from vegetation when it is burned for decades. To an extent, the salt in the waters of the middle and lower bay moderates the impacts of mercury, which tends to accumulate to higher levels in fish in freshwater.

ACID RAIN

Acid rain is another airborne threat to the bay that has a toxic impact on its fisheries. Between the 1960s and the mid-1980s, rain falling across much of the Northeast was first documented as becoming substantially more acidic. One long-term monitoring station below Annapolis showed a tenfold increase in acidity between 1974 and 1985. During the 1990s, a national policy to reduce acid rain through Clean Air Act regulations on power plants achieved an unprecedented 40 percent reduction in the sulfur oxides that rain down as sulfuric acid. Nitrogen oxides, the other major source of acid rain, have risen slightly. But for the first time in decades, there is evidence that the acidity of rainfall in the bay region, while still far from normal, is decreasing.

The most vulnerable bodies of water are small streams and the upper, freshwater reaches of tidal rivers, which are often critical spawning areas for fish. Severe storm events can cause pulses of highly acidic water, stressing or killing fish eggs, juveniles, and small aquatic animals that are important as food for young fish. Acid rain also can release aluminum, one of the most abundant elements in the earth's crust, from streamside soils, and aluminum in the water can be lethal for aquatic life in quantities as low as a few parts per billion parts of water. Shad, herring, and yellow perch—and to a lesser extent, white perch and rockfish—spawn in upstream reaches of bay tributaries that are potentially vulnerable to acid problems.

Research to link acid rain with fish declines in the bay indicates that it is not usually the major factor. It does, however, seem clearly linked to the virtual wipeout of yellow perch in certain streams on Maryland's western shore. Where these streams have been dosed routinely with lime to counteract the acid, yellow perch spawning has improved. Vulnerability of streams varies widely, depending on the capacity of each one's soils to buffer the impact of acid rainfall. In general, coastal plain streams of the bay's western shore and the lower Eastern Shore seem most vulnerable. Since the effects of an acidic pulse can be short-lived, it is unlikely that all acid rain's impacts can be picked up with the random, sporadic monitoring that has been done to date.

The acidity of streams across the watershed has neither improved nor worsened in the last decade. Sulfur oxides should continue to decline if the existing Clean Air Act is maintained, but nitrogen oxides could rise or remain fairly stable. While power plant emissions of both these acid rain components are falling, nitrogen oxides from motor vehicles continue to increase.

Conclusions

- Air pollution, not even considered a "controllable" impact ten years ago, is now recognized as the source of nearly a third of the bay's nitrogen problem.
- The bay's airshed is more than six times the size of its watershed. Despite the fact that much of the air pollution affecting the bay comes from far outside the region, pollution sources closest to the bay and its rivers are most important to control.
- Each acre of natural landscape—forests and wetlands—soaks up large amounts of the air pollutants that wash into the bay in rainstorms. By contrast, impervious surfaces—roads, roofs, and parking lots—pass most of the pollutants to waterways.
- It is far cheaper to reduce the nitrogen and toxic chemicals in air pollution at their sources—tailpipes and smokestacks—than to capture and remove them from urban runoff after they are deposited on paved surfaces throughout the watershed.
- Little or no progress has been made in reducing airborne nitrogen. Cleaner emissions from power plants have been offset by increased nitrogen from vehicles and from farm animal manure. It is possible to reduce the bay's current nitrogen load from air pollution by as much as 40 percent, but current plans seek no more than a 15 percent reduction, and even that is not guaranteed.
- Mercury in air pollution, primarily from coal-burning power plants, is a leading cause of health advisories on eating fish from the bay watershed. The EPA has proposed to reduce it during the next decade.
- Acid rain, another airborne threat to bay fisheries, has gotten somewhat better during the last decade, as the Clean Air Act has forced power plants to cut sulfur oxide emissions.

Susquehanna—The River That *Is* the Bay

I drain a thousand streams, yet still I seek
To lose myself within the Chesapeake . . .

—from "We Heard the River Singing," a Susquehanna sonnet

If you want to look at whether efforts to control pollution from the land are winning or losing, there's no better place to start than the Susquehanna River. It drains more than 40 percent of the Chesapeake's 41-million-acre watershed. It has more than half the bay's agricultural lands and among the world's highest concentrations of farm animals and manure. It is along the Susquehanna, more than any other bay river, that agriculture has the greatest influence on water quality.

And the Susquehanna, in turn, determines the water quality of the upper Chesapeake—in fact, the upper Chesapeake is the tidal portion of the Susquehanna. From the river's entry into the bay proper around Havre de Grace, Maryland, to the Patuxent River nearly 90 miles south, about 90 percent of the bay's freshwater comes from the Susquehanna. For the nearly 200-mile length of the bay, it constitutes about 45 percent of all the freshwater (see Figure 2.8).

The influence of Susquehanna water, flowing out of New York and Pennsylvania, can extend far down the bay's main stem, playing a role in low oxygen levels in all the western shore rivers down to Virginia's Rappahannock. A study of severe water pollution in Rock Creek, in Anne Arundel County, Maryland, found that most of the problem was poor water quality entering the creek from the upper bay, not the water running from the relatively tiny watershed of the creek.

Compared to many other bay tributaries, the Susquehanna is a pipeline for pollution, less equipped to filter out and absorb nutrients, such as nitrogen, that enter it from sewage and from farm runoff. It lacks the tidal action and tidal wetlands that now appear to be trapping half of the nitrogen coming down rivers like Maryland's Patuxent before it ever reaches the bay. Scientists suspect the Patuxent is more typical of most bay rivers, which means controlling nitrogen before it enters the Susquehanna is even more critical.

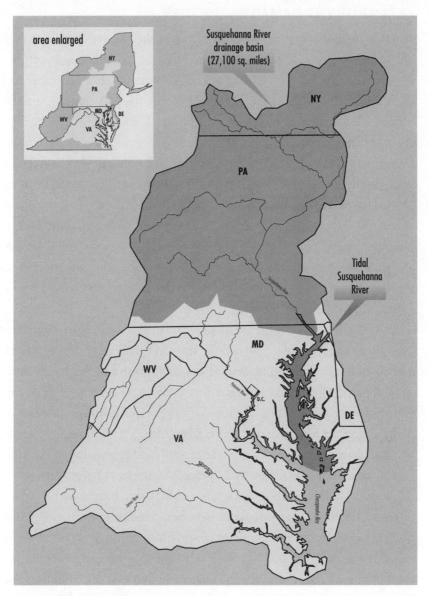

FIGURE 2.8. The Susquehanna River Is the Bay. The Chesapeake Bay is actually the lower valley of the Susquehanna, "drowned" by tidal waters as sea level has risen over the past 15,000 years. The Susquehanna provides about half the freshwater that enters the bay, including more than 90 percent of what comes in above the mouth of the Potomac.

EXTENT OF THE DAMAGE

The Susquehanna is one of the few places in the bay system where there are some long-term records of actual levels of polluting nitrogen and phosphorus flowing to the Chesapeake. Nitrogen levels in the river as it flows into the bay rose at least threefold during the past century, with the bulk of the increase coming between the late 1960s and the 1980s. Since the mid-1980s, measurements by the U.S. Geological Survey have found no significant trends, up or down, in nitrogen coming down the river, despite estimates by EPA's Chesapeake Bay Program that better farming practices were reducing it substantially.

Several factors might account for some of this apparent lack of progress: wet years in the 1990s washing more pollutants from the land and time delays of several years for nitrogen to move through groundwater from farms to waterways—improvements in the water would lag behind improvements on the land.

Also, Pennsylvania, while it has plans to upgrade nitrogen removal at its sewage treatment plants, has done little in this respect during the last decade on the Susquehanna. Sewage is a small source of the river's nitrogen (10 percent) compared to agriculture (about 50 percent), but its contribution has been rising as population grows. Another increase in pollution on the Susquehanna comes from nitrogen in rainwater washing off lands paved for development. Developed land is growing in the basin even as farmland has shrunk by 12 percent in the last fifteen years.

The bottom line on the Susquehanna is that agriculture's reductions in nitrogen, the bay's main pollutant, have been modest at best, while nitrogen from sewage and development is actually growing. By 2010, Pennsylvania could easily be the bay state with the largest nitrogen pollution from both land runoff and sewage treatment. Some of this pollution does flow from New York's portion of the Susquehanna drainage basin, but it is less than a sixth of Pennsylvania's contribution.

The river has shown an encouraging downward trend in phosphorus, the bay's other major polluting nutrient. This is partly due to better agricultural practices and also to large cuts—about 40 percent—from Pennsylvania sewage plants that contribute more than a quarter of the river's phosphorus. Phosphorus in the runoff from developed lands is a small but growing source of pollution to the Susquehanna.

TIME BOMB AT CONOWINGO

While phosphorus trends in the river are improving, there is a virtual time bomb ticking away behind the 110-foot-high dam at Conowingo, near the Susquehanna's mouth. The dam currently "traps" 50–70 percent of the sediment washing downstream from Pennsylvania and New York. The result is that the bay receives only a little more polluting sediment now than it did in pristine times when Pennsylvania and New York were all forested (see also "Sediment," this chapter). Since phosphorus tends to bind to soil particles, the dam also keeps some 40 percent of the river's phosphorus load from washing to the Chesapeake. In the next two to three decades that protection will end, as the reservoir behind Conowingo fills to the "equilibrium" point, where it begins passing most of the sediment and phosphorus on downstream. Smaller dams above Conowingo have already stopped trapping.

No solution is at hand, though a multistate task force has begun looking at options. A loss of trapping at Conowingo would cause major problems for water quality in the upper bay and also for dredging the economically vital ship channels serving the Port of Baltimore. The port is already struggling to dispose of all the sediment it must dredge each year to keep the channels open (see "Dredging," this chapter). The sediment and phosphorus trapped behind Conowingo could be dredged out and disposed of on land, possibly in abandoned strip mines in western Pennsylvania.

But it would take an estimated 100 railroad cars a day, forever, each loaded with dredged sediment, just to keep even with the excess that will begin flowing downstream when the dam fills to capacity in a few decades. The costs, assuming a disposal place can be found, are estimated at $30 million a year, according to the Susquehanna River Basin Commission in Harrisburg. A small bright side to dredging behind the Susquehanna dams is that the trapped materials include an estimated 20 million tons of potentially valuable coal that have washed down from Pennsylvania mines over the decades.

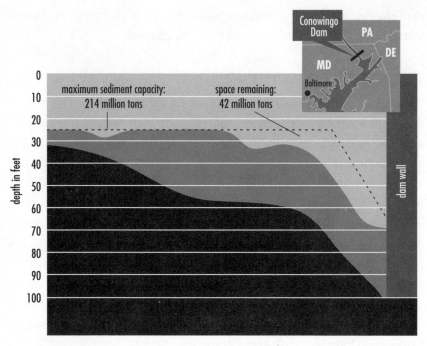

FIGURE 2.9. Conowingo: Storing the Silt. Since Conowingo Dam was closed on the Susquehanna in 1928, the pool above it has filled rapidly with silt, much of it carried down from Pennsylvania. The diminished capacity of Conowingo Reservoir to hold additional silt poses a serious threat to the upper Chesapeake. [U.S. Geological Survey]

DRYING UP THE RIVER

The Susquehanna's water quantity, as well as its quality, is important to the bay, and that quantity is under considerable stress. The loss of the river's freshwater to a variety of users—industry; farm, lawn, and golf course irrigation, and power plants—is growing rapidly. Golf courses alone have increased their water use nearly fifteenfold in recent years.

Most of the time, all this loss is hardly noticeable in a river whose daily flow averages in the tens of billions of gallons. But in drought times, users may take as much as a quarter of all the water going to the bay. And by 2025, they will be taking closer to half of the river in dry times.

Such times are precisely when it is critical for Conowingo Dam to be releasing downstream some of the water it would normally be storing.

Such releases supply oxygen and cool water to keep the river below the dam healthy for fish. Federal regulations specify these releases, but the fish face powerful competition for Susquehanna water. The city of Baltimore is drawing more and more from the Conowingo pool for drinking water for a growing metro population. The giant Peach Bottom nuclear plant must cool its reactors with water from the pool—or shut down and darken much of Philadelphia if water levels fall too close to its water intake pipes.

POLITICS OF THE BAY

While the Susquehanna dominates bay water quality, the two states that affect the river's water—Pennsylvania and, to a lesser extent, New York—own not a square foot of the Chesapeake. They will receive relatively little of the economic and cultural benefits of a restored Chesapeake. And other looming, expensive water quality problems, such as acid mine drainage and failing sewage infrastructure, will compete for cleanup resources.

It was justly hailed as a major achievement in 1983 when Pennsylvania chose to join Maryland and Virginia in a formal bay restoration agreement, something it was not obligated to do. But realistically, keeping the Chesapeake cleanup high on Pennsylvania's political agenda requires a better effort than all three states and the federal government have demonstrated during the past decade.

It is obviously in Pennsylvania's interest to do better for the bay—but only to a limited extent. Closer to home, the low flow conditions and excesses of nutrients and sediment that affect the Chesapeake downstream have major water quality impacts upstream, too. In Pennsylvania's latest (1998) statewide water quality assessment, nutrient pollution had worsened since 1981 in all of eleven large, public-use lakes. The assessment also found more than 4,000 miles of streams were degraded, out of a total of about 13,000 the state looked at (70,000 additional miles of stream were not assessed). Agriculture, the bay's main problem in Pennsylvania, was also one of the two major sources of stream degradation.

Actions needed to help the bay are often the same as those needed to help Pennsylvania's lakes, ponds, and streams. However, the key pollutants within Pennsylvania are phosphorus and sediment. Nitrogen, which causes major problems when it enters the bay downstream, is not nearly so large a problem in the fresh and flowing waters upstream (though when concentrated in groundwater, it can pollute drinking water wells, a serious problem in parts of Pennsylvania). The other major source of stream pollution in Pennsylvania, acid mine drainage from past coal-mining practices, does not directly affect the bay. Cleaning it up could, however, expand the spawning areas available as efforts to restore fish migrations from the bay throughout the Susquehanna drainage push further upriver.

Conclusions

- Restoring the bay is heavily dependent on reducing sediment and nutrients flowing down the Susquehanna River, source of nearly half the freshwater in the Chesapeake.
- It is a political challenge of the bay's restoration that Pennsylvania, the state most responsible for Susquehanna water quality, will benefit relatively little from a restored Chesapeake. Actions needed to solve Pennsylvania's own pollution problems will also help the bay— but not to the extent necessary to restore the bay.
- In the last decade, Pennsylvania has significantly reduced phosphorus pollution from sewage plants and, to a lesser degree, from agriculture. It has allowed nitrogen pollution from sewage and development to grow, and it has made only modest reductions at best in runoff of nitrogen from farms. Agriculture remains the dominant source of bay pollution.
- Decisions must be made on dredging out the sediment and phosphorus now being trapped behind Conowingo Dam. By 2030, the dam will be so full it will stop trapping, thereby causing problems for water quality and for dredging ship channels in the bay. Well before 2030, the dam will begin passing more sediment and phosphorus.
- Nitrogen contamination of wells is a threat to human and farm animal health in parts of the watershed.
- Losses of Susquehanna water are growing as industry, power plants, irrigation, and thirsty cities draw on the river. Water quality is linked to sufficient water quantity.

Sediment—Dirt's Long, Slow Dance

If we soared as high as eagles and lived as long as redwoods, comprehending the bay as a whole through the centuries, only then might we fully appreciate how its rivers and channels shift and change in lifelike ways as we change the lands they drain. Only from on high, through time, could we watch how the rivers responded to the lumberman's historic mass shearing of their forested slopes and to the farm plow's breaking the watershed's virgin soils. Fattened with new sediment eroded from the land, waterways filled their old, deep gorges, built lush wetlands in their meanders, extended fertile floodplains to either side, and pushed out broad deltas and shallow tidal flats from their mouths.

From the human perspective, all this has seemed about as exciting as watching dirt move. But moving dirt is as much a talent of rivers as moving water—and we are just realizing that centuries' worth of sediments, stored up in the river systems of the bay, may be haunting us for centuries to come. Our ignoring dirt's complex dance through the bay's vast network of tributaries is ending, as the bay states finally begin grappling with the difficulties of controlling the bay's "forgotten" pollutant, sediment.

An estimated 5 million tons of sediment, about 400 pounds each second, enter the bay every year. Bay restoration agreements prior to 2000 contained no goals for limiting sediment specifically (they did set goals for controlling phosphorus, which moves into the bay bound to sediment). But sediment is very much a pollutant on its own. It clouds the water, cutting off light to vital underwater grass habitats. It is just as big a problem to these habitats as the algae caused by excessive levels of nitrogen and phosphorus, on which most control efforts have focused to date. Sediment also physically smothers oyster beds and the eggs and young of fish. And because phosphorus fertilizers applied to farms and suburban yards bind tightly to soil particles, sediment is a major pathway to the bay for that polluting nutrient. In addition, excess sediment necessitates more dredging to keep ship channels open. This is both expensive and environmentally damaging when the dredged materials have to be placed somewhere (see also "Dredging," this chapter).

The sediment now entering the bay annually is estimated to be about three times what left the pre-European, mostly forested watershed. Even "good" soil conservation practices, by today's agricultural standards, can permit up to forty times as much sediment runoff as that from a forest. And bulldozing for construction sites can cause sediment runoff that is ten times worse than farmland runoff. Current estimates recommend reducing sediment by 40–60 percent (2–3 million tons a year) to restore the bay's water clarity enough to bring back underwater grasses that once covered half a million acres or more of the bay bottom.

The science of how to reduce this flow of dirt is probably twenty years behind that of reducing nitrogen and phosphorus. That lag in knowledge has developed because the way all this dirt moves from the land into the bay is anything but straightforward. Where it comes from and which of its sources are most critical to control—and at what cost—are also not well understood.

Consider a 1980s study of the Monocacy River, a tributary to the Potomac, which drains extensive farmland in Carroll and Frederick Counties in Maryland. An astounding 90 percent of all the soil washed into the Monocacy during the past two centuries remains there, captured in its channels, banks, floodplains, and deltas. Some, or perhaps all, of this material will eventually end up polluting the bay as it is scoured downriver by rainstorms and floods. There is no way to know how much will be retained permanently upstream and how much will move—or when it will move. We only know that whatever happens will be in the river's own, sweet time. Meanwhile, reducing soil erosion from lands in the Monocacy's basin is still a good idea, both for the immediate health of smaller, upland waterways and for the long-term health of the bay. But the lag between reducing soil erosion upstream and seeing water quality improvements in the bay may be a long one.

Consider another study, that of Coon Creek in Wisconsin, a well-researched, agriculture-dominated tributary of the Mississippi River. Through 150 years the lands drained by Coon Creek saw huge changes, from deforestation and plowing to an era of increasingly better soil conservation. Sediment washing off the lands along the creek was cut in half between 1853 and 1975, and cut in half again by 1993. Yet, because of the creek's complex responses in storing and releasing sediment, the tons of dirt actually delivered to the Mississippi remained virtually unchanged during the entire 140-year period.

Bay managers face even greater complications. For example, it may be that the type of dirt is more important than the total amount of dirt. A recent study on the Susquehanna River, the bay's biggest tributary, indicated tens of thousands of tons of sediment coming from the erosion of streambanks each year in just a tiny portion (68 square miles) of the bay's 64,000-square-mile watershed. By weight, this is more than the sediment washing each year from far larger acreages of farm fields. But the runoff from fields tends to be finer, lighter soil particles, whereas streambanks tend to be coarser, heavier particles. And it is the "fines" that may travel fastest to the bay and remain suspended in the water for days at a time, becoming resuspended from the shallow bottoms of the bay every time there is a good wind, clouding the waters all out of proportion to their share of the tonnage of sediment entering the estuary.

The sources of sediments also shift, depending on what part of the bay one looks at. Overall, the vast majority, by weight—maybe as much as 80 percent—is delivered by river flow. But in the mid-bay, down to about the Potomac River, and especially on the flatlands drained by rivers of the Eastern Shore of Maryland and Virginia, the great bulk of the sediment comes from shoreline erosion. Another potentially important source of sediment, unquantified to date, may be from the thousands of acres of bay wetlands that are slowly dissolving (see also "Edges of the Bay" in Chapter 4, "Resilience") because they cannot keep up with rising sea level. So controls on sediment will vary, depending on location and on the type of sediment that is doing the most damage.

Sediment flowing to the bay will also jump markedly in another few decades unless action is taken to dredge the millions of tons accumulating behind dams on the Susquehanna River. Since construction of the high dam at Conowingo in 1928, the bay has been getting a "free ride." The 110-foot dam traps 50–70 percent of the sediment coming down the bay's largest tributary each year, limiting sediment to almost the levels that once came from a totally forested watershed. But the dam will reach its trapping capacity around 2030 and begin passing most of that sediment on (see also "Susquehanna," this chapter).

The fact that shoreline erosion along the bay and its lower rivers is a large source of sediment sometimes raises arguments in favor of more shoreline development. The more homeowners settle there, it is claimed, the more they will protect the shoreline against erosion with stone riprap, bulkheads, and dikes. Some politicians say we need to encourage as much waterfront development as possible to generate the tax base to pay the high expense of such extensive "armoring" of the shoreline.

Such a policy, however, would not only destroy shallow-water habitat, some of the bay's most productive area, but also ruin beaches used for nesting by diamondback terrapins, horseshoe crabs, and waterbirds. It would run counter to attempts in both Maryland and Virginia to keep as many of the bay's edges as possible in natural vegetation to filter and buffer its waters from polluted runoff from the uplands. It is already too easy for shoreline owners to "harden" their waterfront with bulkheads and stone riprap; they are granted low-interest government financing and issued permits virtually as a guaranteed right of any owner. This policy has led to erosion controls even in areas that are not eroding that much. (See also "Nontidal Wetlands" in Chapter 4, "Resilience.")

Here's a better way to look at the problem: Shoreline erosion has always occurred in the bay, yet it is only in recent decades that water clarity has worsened to the point of losing huge acreages of underwater grasses. The thick growth of submerged grasses that once lined much of the bay's shallow edge provided a highly efficient means of clarifying sediment from the bay's waters. This may seem like a "chicken-or-egg" situation—the grasses stopped the sediment, but the sediment killed the grasses. However, the grasses died because of the combined effects of sediment and increasing amounts of nitrogen and phosphorus from sewage and land runoff. Reducing those two pollutants might well let the grasses reestablish themselves, and that rebound, in turn, would control sediment, leading to more grasses.

In addition, a resurgence of the grasses would decrease shoreline erosion dramatically in many areas. Growing so long and thick that they literally lay matted on the surface, the underwater grass beds were highly effective buffers against waves rolling into the shoreline, eroding it.

Controlling sediment pollution in the bay region is likely to be one of the most difficult areas in which to show real progress during the next decade. Setting at least some broad goals in the next few years is a start on what promises to be a long journey.

Conclusions

- Sediment is only now being recognized as a critical pollutant of the bay. Goals to be set soon will call for reductions of 40–60 percent to restore water quality.
- No one knows how to achieve that level of reduction. Techniques will vary from one part of the watershed to another, depending on the source of sediments and the types of soils that do the most damage.
- Forests produce far less sediment than any other land use in the watershed.
- Developing the bay's edge is not an effective or desirable long-term approach to reducing shoreline erosion.

Dredging

Our 25-year plan [for disposing of dredged material] is always a 25-year plan—we just push it back a year every year, and as long as there is a port, we'll be looking.

—Port of Baltimore official

How much dredging must we really accept? The answer is not known, because until now, the question hasn't been seriously asked.

—Maryland citizens' task force on dredging

To grasp the challenge of keeping Baltimore's port, with its tens of thousands of shipping-related jobs, economically viable, you must comprehend a million cubic yards of "spoil," or sediments, dredged to keep shipping channels open. Think of a mammoth cube with every surface the size of two side-by-side football fields, a solid mass roughly 100 yards high and wide and deep. That is a million cubic yards. And every year, on average, Maryland's Port Administration must dredge four to five such

cubes and—more to the point—must find someplace to put all of this
without degrading the environment. On the bay's lower end, Virginia
currently dredges another 2.5–3.0 million cubic yards a year.

And all the above is for just the routine maintenance dredging. Maryland projects at least an additional 20 million cubic yards of new work in
deepening, widening, and straightening channels to accommodate bigger
ships and to lessen the chances of collisions. Virginia plans to increase
dredging to a total of 5 million cubic yards a year as it moves forward
with plans to deepen channels going into its ports of Norfolk and Hampton Roads near the bay's mouth.

In a historic shift, Maryland has recently agreed with the Chesapeake
Bay Foundation to phase out, by 2010, the age-old practice of simply
dumping dredge spoil back into the bay, a practice with harmful impacts
on fish and water quality. Though it is too early to say for sure, the decision has the potential to change the way dredging and spoil disposal are
planned and carried out. The agreement made a priority of finding new,
beneficial uses for dredge spoil and opened up the port's planning process
to citizens and environmentalists. The CBF has seen an unprecedented
shift of energy toward more responsible dredging and disposal on the
part of state and federal agencies involved in it.

That is not to say that finding environmentally acceptable solutions
will be easy, or cheap. The agreement to phase out open water disposal
took away immediately a 4-mile-long deep spot near the Bay Bridge that
the port had been hoping to use to contain several years' worth of dredge
spoil. This plan had been hotly opposed by citizens of nearby Kent Island
and by others around the state. The debate finalized a shift in focus that
was already going on—to find "beneficial" and "innovative" uses for
dredge spoil.

One technique has been to create, or re-create, islands in the bay built
of dredged spoil, restrained by dikes from slumping back into the bay.
The first of these containment islands, which occupies the site of eroded
Hart and Miller Islands off Baltimore County, has become a popular site
for boaters and birdwatchers. A second one, under construction, will oc-
cupy more than 2 square miles on the old site of Poplar Island, an island
off Talbot County that has nearly vanished to erosion from wind and

waves. When finished, the new Poplar Island will feature more than 500 acres of forest rising to some 100 feet above the bay, extensive wetlands, bird nesting habitat, and several hundred acres of restored underwater grass meadows. It will hold more than 38 million cubic yards of spoil.

But even that capacity pales before the 100 million cubic yards of new capacity the Port Administration needs every twenty-five years—just for maintenance dredging. Poplar Island has been largely a win-win proposition, meeting both dredging and environmental needs. The bottom there, hard clay where the old island had eroded away, was relatively unproductive of bay life according to the U.S. Fish and Wildlife Service. But that emptiness is not always the case. Other places where dredging interests have in the past eyed sites for more spoil islands would cover bottoms that support shellfish, crabs, underwater grasses, or striped bass spawning areas. A large part of the bay's incredible fecundity is due to all the life that uses its bottom.

On the positive side, the agreement on ending open water disposal has led to new emphasis on using spoil to restore other eroded natural bay islands. This is generally better than past moves to look for open water sites where artificial spoil islands could be built. But even if other eroded islands are restored, the impacts on the environment from spoil disposal will have to be examined on a case-by-case basis.

And the need for disposal remains pressing—just pursuing maintenance dredging could mean, in the next century, building the equivalent of five more islands, each 2 square miles in size and 40 feet high. And the costs rise sharply the further spoil has to be barged to potential island restoration sites from the upper bay, where most of the dredging is done. Poplar is costing nearly half a billion dollars, or about $400,000 an acre. To date, attempts in Maryland to put dredge spoil inland, on farmland around the edges of the bay, have ended in controversy.

Virginia, with its major ports of Norfolk and Hampton Roads closer to deep water than Baltimore's, has enough capacity at an existing dredge spoil location, Craney Island, to last at least through 2050, according to the Army Corps of Engineers, but of course the state's dredging needs won't end then.

RETHINKING DREDGING NEEDS

In Maryland, a citizens' committee appointed to analyze the Port Administration's proposals to widen and deepen the northern approaches to the bay through the Chesapeake and Delaware Canal is beginning to think the unthinkable. The committee discovered major flaws in an economic analysis by the U.S. Army Corps of Engineers purporting that the project would have benefits greater than its costs. The citizens noted that roughly two-thirds of all dredge spoil generated in the bay each year comes from keeping open the northern route, which carries a small and declining fraction of the Port of Baltimore's large ships. The southern approaches, with ships entering the bay's mouth in Virginia and moving north to Baltimore, have larger, deeper channels already. Maryland officials to date consider any scaling back on dredging the northern approaches unthinkable and likely to give a competitive advantage to other ports.

So the search for more beneficial ways to deal with dredge spoil continues. On their success depends how much we will ultimately have ports designed for the bay or a bay designed for ports.

THE SMALL PICTURE

When most of us think of dredging, we think of mountains of muck being removed from deep channels that lead to major ports such as Norfolk or Baltimore. However, a fair amount of dredging takes place every year for access to small marinas, community harbors, and myriad federally maintained channels used by watermen and recreational boaters. Though the volume of sediments generated by these smaller projects is much less than those generated by dredging major ports, it can be significant locally, because it brings with it the same issues: where and how to dispose of material and how to stem the environmental impacts from it.

Conclusions

- Environmental progress in phasing out the overboard disposal of dredge spoil has heightened the need to find other, environmentally acceptable places to put it. Using dredge spoil to restore eroded bay

islands has promise, but too much island building could have serious impacts on the bay's rich bottom habitats.
- The time has come for Maryland to give serious consideration to doing less dredging of its northern bay approaches, as use by large ships declines.

Stormwater Pollution

In the 1980s, the acreage of lawns in Maryland surpassed the acreage in corn, the largest agricultural crop.

—Maryland Turfgrass Survey

Although the largest amount of polluted runoff from the lands of the bay watershed still comes from agriculture, the fastest-growing part of the runoff problem comes from clearing and paving agricultural lands and other open space for development. While farm acreage seems destined to shrink, development currently knows no bounds.

By 1985, after nearly 400 years of settlement, some 3 million acres of the watershed had been developed. In the 25 years between 1985 and the end of 2010, close to another million acres of forest and farmland will shift to roads, cities, towns, and suburbs. And that development won't be spread equally—the great bulk will occur close to the bay and its tidal rivers, where its impacts on water quality will be greatest.

Watershed-wide, it is estimated that runoff from development, also known as urban stormwater, contributes 15–20 percent of the bay's nitrogen and phosphorus, and 9 percent of its sediment. Stormwater runoff is also linked to elevated levels of toxic chemicals in parts of the bay's faster-developing rivers (see "Toxics and Bacteria," this chapter).

Runoff's long-term potential to offset water quality improvements from reducing other pollution sources is evident from looking at Maryland's Patuxent River, which drains the fast-growing Baltimore-Washington metropolitan corridor. The Patuxent's drainage basin is as developed now as the whole bay watershed is going to be in a few more decades.

Between 1985 and 1998, nitrogen and phosphorus levels in the Patuxent declined more than in any other bay river. The decline resulted mostly from new sewage treatment technology, which cut the river's phosphorus input from 58 percent to 27 percent and nitrogen input from 47 to 29 percent.

Meanwhile, development drove up phosphorus from urban runoff from 15 percent to 40 percent of the river's total burden, according to EPA estimates derived from a computer model of the bay watershed. The model estimated that nitrogen in urban runoff rose from 29 percent to 47 percent. Based on these estimates, it will not take many more years before urban stormwater significantly erodes the gains made in sewage treatment—gains that cost several hundred million dollars.

Urban stormwater runoff is perhaps the leading cause of degradation of the bay watershed's nontidal, small tributary streams. A Maryland survey during the mid-1990s concluded that about 90 percent of the state's 9,000 stream miles were in fair to poor health (almost half were poor). Causes ranged from acid mine drainage to agricultural impacts.

But wherever development had "hardened" more than 10–15 percent of a stream's natural watershed with impervious surfaces—roads, driveways, houses, and the like—that stream was almost never healthy. Even the cumulative effects of residential development on large lots with trees are enough to raise a stream's watershed to that 10–15 percent hardened threshold that presages damage.

CHANGES IN THE LANDSCAPE

In Maryland, the acreage in turfgrass for home lawns, golf courses, cemeteries, median strips, and grounds of public and commercial buildings now covers around a million acres. Corn, the largest crop in the state, covers only about half that. Turfgrass also covers more than a million acres each in Virginia and Pennsylvania. One survey showed that two-thirds of Virginians and 40 percent of Marylanders regularly used pesticides on their lawns. Nationally, the EPA estimates that the runoff of such chemicals from home lawns can be higher, per acre, than from farmland. An unknown but growing amount of fertilizer is also spread on lawns, with some golf courses using more than farmers, per acre, to grow their plushy, manicured greens and fairways.

The impacts of runoff from this very substantial and rapidly growing acreage are difficult to quantify. In university tests, turfgrass tends to be very good at absorbing runoff before it gets into waterways, but real-world studies are showing that development compacts soils so much that runoff from suburban turfgrass is often much higher than thought. Healthy topsoil, for example, can store 6 inches of rainfall. But a typical, newly sodded lawn in a housing development might be able to store only half an inch.

Even more is known about pollutants that come from impervious surfaces. The quality of rainwater washing off urban pavement can be shockingly polluted, especially the "first flush," in which dry-weather accumulations of pollutants that have fallen from the air, from car exhausts, and from accumulations of oxygen-demanding organic matter such as grass clippings all wash into storm drains and creeks. Pets are estimated to deposit more than 7 million pounds of feces annually on streets in Washington, D.C., alone.

Rains in the Harrisburg area (both shores of the Susquehanna) annually flush to the river around 2 million pounds of nitrogen, a third of a million pounds of phosphorus, and 8.5 million pounds of organic matter from leaves, grass clippings, and garbage that create a demand on the water's oxygen when it decays. Similarly, in Baltimore, the amount of copper (a metal toxic to aquatic life) that washes off in rainfall is equal to the amount that comes into the harbor from industrial discharges.

National surveys of urban stormwater have detected more than half of the EPA's list of more than a hundred "priority pollutants" in runoff. These pollutants either are acutely toxic or are known or suspected carcinogens. Stormwater that is channeled through sewage treatment plants in some urban areas may so overwhelm a plant's capacity in big rains that it is forced to release poorly treated sewage as well as the polluted runoff (see "Sewage," this chapter). Where stormwater does not go to sewage treatment plants, it dumps directly into waterways. The next time you are tempted to dump anything into a storm drain, remember that as far as the bay is concerned, you are dumping it directly into a natural stream or river.

HARD LIFE FOR STREAMS

While urban runoff's biggest impacts on the bay are nutrients and, in some areas, toxic chemicals, it is the sheer physical, hydraulic impact of such runoff that is the major destroyer of streams throughout the watershed. Most people think of impervious surfaces as just roads and parking lots, but they also include roofs, driveways, sidewalks, patios, and even cars. It does not take extreme urbanization to harden as much as half of a developed piece of land. Once that has happened, rain that used to soak into the soil is collected and focused by gutters, drains, curbs, and storm drains, then shot toward streams at high velocity. The stream is subjected to fierce flooding and erosion for a few hours. Then, when the surge has passed, the stream dries out, no longer fed by the slow seepage through its bed and banks. The water that used to seep underground, replenishing the stream in dry weather, has all run off in the new, impervious environment (Figure 2.10).

This feast-or-famine flow wreaks havoc on the stream's habitat. It is easy to see if you compare an urban creek to a rural one. In the urban setting, the channel will be widened and the banks eroded. After a rain, the creek will surge wildly with water, then run almost dry within hours or a

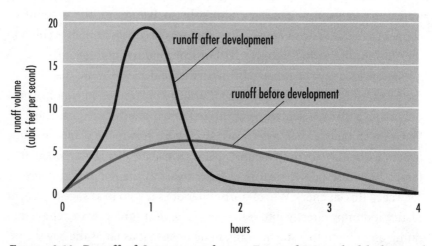

FIGURE 2.10. Runoff of Stormwater from a Forested Watershed before and after Development. As we have changed the bay watershed "from filter to funnel," replacing forests with roadways, parking lots, and roofs, we have diminished its capacity to absorb rainfall, filter it, and release it gradually. Instead, the "first flush" of urban and suburban stormwater runs off fast and heavy, sweeping pollutants along with it, so flows between rain events often drop to drought levels. [EPA Chesapeake Bay Program]

day. The country creek will be more stable, rising less in rainstorms, falling less in droughts. It will be, in short, a better place for a fish to live.

Hundreds of studies both regionally and nationally have found that as the amount of paving in a stream's watershed goes up, aquatic life in the stream declines, even if there are no specific pollution sources present. Such degradation can start by the time 10–15 percent of a stream's watershed is hardened, which is equivalent to putting it all into suburban homes on 1- to 2-acre lots, or a typical small park or cemetery. By the time imperviousness reaches 25 percent—a typical townhouse development easily exceeds that level—most streams support very little life. Brook trout, a native fish that needs very high water quality, often succumb when imperviousness of a stream watershed exceeds 2 percent. Increased runoff from paved-over watersheds also causes flooding downstream, with substantial potential for loss of property and, sometimes, human life. Ironically, farmers on the edge of some fast-growing communities in Virginia's Shenandoah Valley are beginning to worry about flooding in their low-lying pastures from upstream development.

MUDDIED WATERS

Whenever it rains, an acre of land where the natural vegetation has been cleared for construction can flush dozens of times as much soil into waterways as can well-managed farmland and hundreds of times as much as a forest, according to Richard Klein, a Maryland-based expert on sediment pollution. A certain amount of sediment is healthy for the bay. It is a source of nutrients and silica needed for the growth of plankton, which support the higher food chain, and some of it is captured by marshes as a source of building material to keep ahead of rising sea level. Thus, a sediment-free bay would be quite clear but less productive.

But in modern times such needs have been far exceeded. The abrupt inflows of thousands of tons of soil from construction, rapidly running into a stream, can be as deadly as a spill of oil or raw sewage—perhaps more so, because sediment never degrades, but keeps getting resuspended by tide and storms and wind to cloud the water. Sediment pollutes by smothering fish eggs, by tearing at the fragile gills of just-born fish, and by covering gravel bottoms that are prime habitats for fish spawning and for aquatic insects. Further downriver it may cover oyster reefs, leaving no clean shell exposed where the free-floating young of oysters can attach to form their own shells. Sediment also clouds the water, cutting off sunlight that must penetrate to the bottom to grow the submerged grass that is critical habitat in rivers and the bay.

Sediment in recent years has joined nutrients on the list of major bay pollutants (see "Sediment," this chapter). Without huge reductions in sediment, restoration of critical habitat such as underwater grasses won't happen. Baywide, 90 percent or more of sediment comes from sources other than urban stormwater runoff. But to focus only on the bay and its tidal rivers ignores a great deal. The bay's watershed contains more than 100,000 miles of streams and rivers above the influence of tide, and half of this mileage either supports or has the potential to support trout, whose various species are quite vulnerable to sediment. A *Trout* magazine article in 1989 listed seven of America's top ten trout streams as lying in the Chesapeake watershed. This part of the bay's drainage network also supports fishing for smallmouth bass, and it was a world-class spawning and nursery ground for shad and herring before dams blocked their traditional annual migrations. With a major goal of bay restoration to remove those blockages from thousands of miles of waterways (see Chapter 3, "Harvests"), the impacts of sediment even far upstream from the main Chesapeake are critical to success.

No matter how much we relate to the bay, it is on the smaller streams that most of us live. Virtually no one in the watershed lives more than half a mile, about a 15-minute walk, from a stream. The bay is our larger heritage, but the little waterways are our daily, neighborhood connections to it.

REAL SOLUTIONS AND BAND-AIDS

During the last two decades, all of the bay states pursued two major strategies to control and reduce sediment and nutrients from urban stormwater runoff. For sediment, they required construction sites to erect "filter fences"—the straw bales and black cloth staked into the ground around road-building and other development sites. They also required the building of settling ponds to catch and filter the muddy water draining from soils exposed by development. In the last decade both requirements have become standard practice, and they are a lot better than nothing. But neither is particularly effective.

For starters, success in controlling sediment in runoff is judged on having an approved control plan in place—not on how much sediment actually leaves the site, and not on the impact on water quality. Simply put, there are no meaningful standards. At best, silt fences and settling basins might control 85 percent of sediment by weight, and often as little as 50 percent. But the very fine, light sediment particles, those that don't weigh much but can float for days before settling out and spread out to cover acres of water, are the ones most likely to escape and cloud the water in the bay and its rivers. A development site might have to catch as much as 93–98 percent of the total sediment to remedy this problem, according to the national Center for Watershed Protection, based in Ellicott City, Maryland.

The wide use of silt fencing and settling ponds is nonetheless an important start. Effectiveness varies hugely from county to county and township to township around the watershed. Frequent government inspections are critical to ensuring such systems are maintained. While all three bay states have oversight authority for local sediment control, only Maryland has used it much to make some counties beef up their sediment control staffs and budgets, according to the Watershed Protection Center. But even at best, such approaches are essentially Band-Aids, added after the damage is already done.

The real keys to reducing sediment in urban stormwater runoff lie in limiting to the greatest extent possible the acreage that must be cleared of its natural vegetation in the first place and in carefully phasing construction so that as little soil as possible is exposed to rainfall at any given time. Similarly, leaving permanent buffers of natural vegetation between waterways and construction is critical. Currently, none of these techniques is routinely employed around the watershed to limit sediment from development, though some counties are requiring more carefully phased construction.

Again, with postconstruction, developed lands, catchment ponds have been the major weapons in the arsenal of stormwater controls for more than a decade. Tens of thousands of stormwater ponds have been constructed throughout the watershed—3,000 in Fairfax County, Virginia, alone. You see them everywhere, from schoolyards and highway interchanges to the back of housing developments and on the edges of shopping centers. The technique, Band-Aid though it is, has helped. Ponds control about 30 percent of the nitrogen in urban runoff and about half the copper, for example. And they take the edge off the destructive rush of stormwater that scours and erodes stream channels.

But urban stormwater remains a bay pollution source that continues to grow, even as goals for bay restoration call for huge reductions in pollution. Stormwater ponds release water that is often so warm it is deadly to fish life in small streams. The ponds are also sources of mosquitoes. Such ponds now form a large and costly infrastructure; for example, Prince George's County, in suburban Maryland, spends more than $6 million a year to inspect and maintain ponds as they fill in. Many jurisdictions are delaying dealing with the true cost of maintaining thousands of ponds.

The real solution to urban stormwater lies in designing every newly developing landscape to mimic the nature being displaced, to filter the rainfall more like the forests, using stormwater ponds only as a last resort. Consider Somerset, a suburban housing development of 200 single-family homes on 85 acres in Prince George's County. Homes in Somerset lack gutters and downspouts, and the streets have no sidewalks or curbs—nothing to collect and focus rainfall and send it cannonballing into streams.

Careful grading done during Somerset's development directs rainfall in slow-moving sheets to grassy swales that further slow its movement, so it can soak in or evaporate. Much of it ends up draining into "rain gardens," clumps of tastefully landscaped shrubs. In reality, these are scientifically designed, with several feet of layered soil, gravel, and mulch, to capture and filter large quantities of stormwater, removing pollutants and recharging the belowground water table.

Somerset, one of a few "low-impact design" communities pioneered in Prince George's, is "just a first cut," says the county's stormwater chief, Larry Coffman. Coffman feels such techniques can eventually allow even developments with considerably more than 15 percent impervious surface to occur with minimal impact on waterways.

A new generation of stormwater regulations has shifted guidelines for development from Band-Aid approaches toward mimicking natural flows—cooler, cleaner, and slower. But nowhere in the watershed are such techniques rapidly becoming common practice by developers. Maryland leads the pack, followed by Pennsylvania and Virginia, but even Maryland's law only requires developers to let the first quarter inch of rainfall soak in before running off. Studies indicate that allowing the first inch and a half of rain to soak in would dramatically remove more nitrogen and toxic metals, though it would cost developers more.

The large potential for helping the bay is evident in some estimates made by the Chesapeake Bay Commission, representing the legislatures of Maryland, Pennsylvania, and Virginia. Using rain-garden-type approaches to let stormwater infiltrate the ground, watershed-wide, could cut nitrogen from urban runoff as much as 40 percent—by some 16 million pounds. By combining them with approaches such as reducing impervious surfaces and filtering runoff through wetlands, developers could cut nitrogen by an estimated 24 million pounds.

But the bottom line is that real progress with urban stormwater is still largely conceptual. It is occurring slowly enough that the problems could get worse in the coming decade before they get better.

AN OUNCE OF PREVENTION

The other part of the stormwater puzzle lies in making older developed areas less polluting. Such urban retrofit is being tried on an experimental basis in several parts of the watershed, most notably, the Anacostia River in Washington, D.C., and Gwynns Falls, a tributary to Baltimore Harbor. Baltimore County, Maryland, has used retrofit to stem the pollution of a reservoir, Loch Raven.

Retrofitting may involve a range of techniques: frequent street sweeping; laws aimed to discourage people from letting their animals relieve themselves on the sidewalk; placing rainbarrels to catch the water from gutter downspouts, letting it slowly seep from holes in the barrels so it can soak into the ground. Rain gardens appear to have great promise in urban retrofit. A modest one planted in Bladensburg, Maryland, is able to catch and cleanse the runoff from an entire strip mall.

As part of *Chesapeake 2000*, the most recent restoration agreement, state and federal governments have pledged to set examples for reducing runoff pollution and stormwater damage to streams in both old and new development on the 13 percent of the watershed's lands under their ownership. A project completed at the heavily urbanized Washington Navy Yard on the Anacostia River cut toxic chemicals significantly and is regarded as a model for retrofitting older, developed areas.

Longer term, reducing air pollution from cars and power plants, which would have many benefits for human health, would also greatly reduce the pollution in urban runoff. Much of the toxic metal and nitrogen in urban runoff actually comes from what falls onto pavement from the air. (See "Air," this chapter.)

Washington, D.C., has proposed spending up to $1 billion to construct huge underground vaults to divert and hold stormwater that now is discharged into sewer pipes, overwhelming municipal treatment plants and sending raw sewage into rivers. After the rain, the stormwater could be sent to the sewage plant for treatment.

To date, most urban retrofits have proven relatively expensive, per pound of pollutant removed. Rain gardens may improve on that statistic, but in general, it will be far cheaper to prevent polluted runoff up front, by designing developments to mimic nature.

Conclusions

- While the largest amount of polluted runoff from the lands of the bay watershed still comes from agriculture, the fastest-growing part of the runoff problem comes from urban stormwater runoff—the sediment, chemicals, and nutrients from developed lands.
- Urban stormwater runoff is arguably the leading cause of degradation of the bay watershed's nontidal tributary streams. The sheer physical force of stormwater cannonballing from paved surfaces is more destructive to stream habitat than any pollutant.
- Hardening as little as 10–15 percent of a stream's watershed with streets, roofs, driveways, and other impervious surfaces significantly

degrades water quality. That figure is equivalent to residential development on 1- to 2-acre lots.

- State and local attempts to reduce pollution from urban stormwater runoff have improved during the last decade, but not nearly enough to keep its impact from growing. Traditional, add-on approaches, such as silt fences, ponds, and catch basins to intercept sediment and other pollutants, don't work well enough.

- Techniques that do work are based on designing the developed landscape to mimic nature, letting stormwater filter slowly into streams through the soil and groundwater, cooling and cleaning it in the process. Reducing impervious surfaces; carefully phasing construction to expose the least possible amount of soil to rainfall; and leaving buffers of forests, fields, and wetlands along waterways are other proven techniques. These could cut nitrogen by nearly 24 million pounds a year in stormwater runoff, if applied watershed-wide.

- The states have begun to embrace these concepts, but they are still not widespread in development practice. The impacts of urban stormwater runoff on the bay seem likely to get worse before they get better.

- Retrofitting older, developed areas to reduce stormwater impacts is expensive. Reducing air pollution, which falls on paved areas and washes into the bay, could go a long way to reduce these impacts.

Toxics and Bacteria

What do you mean, I can't eat the fish I catch out of my home river?

—Angler in Baltimore Harbor

The least understood pollution impacts on Chesapeake Bay are those from the large array of toxic chemicals discharged into the air and water of the region. Some can do damage in amounts as low as a few parts of pollution per trillion of water. Others can build up, bit by bit, over years to dangerous levels in creatures and humans, or react with one another to have impacts that are more than the sum of their parts. Toxics can also have hard-to-detect, sublethal effects, not visibly harming a species but lessening its ability to reproduce, weakening its immune system, or damaging individuals of the next generation.

Toxics come from industrial wastes, auto exhaust, coal- and oil-burning power plants, farms and golf courses, the bottom paint on boats, manufacturing wastes, leaky landfills, the ballast water discharged from visiting ships, and the cleaning products, cosmetics, and pharmaceuticals flushed down sinks and toilets in every home. They include industrial metals such as arsenic, copper, cadmium, and mercury, and chemical compounds such as DDT, PCBs (polychlorinated biphenyls), and a range of pesticides used in farming and lawn care. All these have been found throughout the bay's waters and its bottom sediments. Groundwater, the source of drinking water for millions of people in the watershed, also routinely shows low levels of chemical contamination. In specific sites and for specific chemicals, groundwater contamination has been a serious health threat.

Fish, shellfish, and crabs have shown a range of toxics in several studies in Maryland and Virginia's bay and rivers. While none of these toxics are good for us or for the Chesapeake, science has not yet directly linked toxics in the bay to significant effects in humans or to widespread aquatic health problems. That lack of direct linkage may say as much about the state of our understanding as about the state of the bay.

There are well-documented concentrations of toxic chemicals in hot spots on three industrial rivers: Baltimore's Patapsco, Norfolk's Elizabeth, and Washington's Anacostia. Several other regions that had been thought free of any significant contamination have recently proven more toxic than expected. Mercury, a toxic metal produced by coal-burning power plants, has been documented throughout the watershed.

The first part of this section looks at what is known about the role of toxics in the health of not only bay species but also humans who eat seafood from the bay. Also of concern, given the millions of oysters and clams slurped raw from Chesapeake waters each year, is the level of bacteria from sewage and polluted stormwater runoff in bay waters. A bay that was thriving with marine life would still be half a loaf if there were hazards to human health in sampling its delicacies.

The latter part of this section discusses a different problem—one that can arise from more than a dozen species of tiny, floating plankton, or algae, that grow naturally in the bay. These can go for months or years, doing no harm, until poorly understood combinations of natural events and human pollution trigger outbreaks. Such "blooms" of toxic algae in bay waters have killed fish and shellfish and produced severe, short-term memory loss in humans exposed to them.

IS BAY SEAFOOD SAFE TO EAT?

If you fish for your dinner in the bay region, chances are good that your catch will fall under a state health advisory, urging you to limit how much of your catch you consume. Health advisories, which are voluntary, range from striped bass in the Potomac to walleyes in the Susquehanna, from blue crabs in Baltimore's Patapsco to smallmouth bass in Virginia's Shenandoah and white perch in Maryland's Elk River. In all, sections of virtually every Chesapeake tributary are affected, as well as lakes, reservoirs, and nontidal streams. Areas not under advisories are not necessarily clean, as chemical sampling of fish hasn't been done yet in many areas, including much of the bay proper.

Depending on the place and the species, the health advisories urge limiting consumption to as little as one meal a month—less if you are pregnant or a child. In a few areas, mostly industrial, they urge no consumption at all. The advisories don't apply to fish and crabs in restaurants or in stores and markets, since these are presumed to come from a wide mix of places besides the Chesapeake. Contaminant levels in commercially caught seafood are also regulated by the U.S. Food and Drug Administration (FDA) under a different set of criteria that are, in many cases, less stringent than the health advisory criteria used by the EPA and the bay states. Mercury, for example, is allowable up to 1 part per million (ppm) of fish by the FDA, whereas state and EPA health advisories apply to levels above 0.3 ppm of mercury (mercury in levels of 0.2–0.3 ppm appears common in striped bass in parts of the bay that have been sampled). Health advisories are based not on the idea that anyone could get a harmful dose of toxic chemicals from a single meal, but on the risks entailed in consuming bay seafood regularly for half a lifetime.

Thus, the year 2001 saw a dramatic expansion of bay fish consumption health advisories, and the main reason was not an increase in contamination but wider sampling of toxics in seafood, combined with more realistic estimates of how much seafood people are eating (twice as much as previously assumed). The bulk of the contamination that has caused the health advisories involves a handful of chemicals and metals that persist for long periods in the environment:

- PCBs used for decades as electrical insulators in cables and transformers. They can cause cancer and prevent reproduction in mammals and birds. The manufacture of PCBs was banned in the 1970s, but those already in the environment do not readily break down and thus pose a hazard for many, many years. They "bioaccumulate," or "biomagnify," in animals, becoming more and more concentrated as they move up the food chain from lower to higher organisms. PCBs are still illegally dumped and wash into the aquatic environment from soils onto which they have leaked. They are also recycled into the food chain from contaminated bay bottom sediments.

- Mercury, a metal acutely toxic to a wide range of animals and plants. It also is a powerful cause of birth defects in humans. The largest source of mercury comes from coal-burning power plants, some as far away as the Ohio River Valley (see also "Air," this chapter). Mercury also comes from improper disposal of batteries and fluorescent lightbulbs, from agricultural chemical use, and from some consumer products. Like PCBs, mercury persists in the environment and bioaccumulates through the food chain. Unlike PCBs and other chemicals, it accumulates in the muscles of fish, not in their fatty tissues, so measures such as trimming the fat and not eating fatty organs and the roe (eggs of fish) won't work to reduce mercury in a seafood meal.

- Pesticides, including DDT, dieldrin, and chlordane, all banned for years because of their toxic effects and tendency to bioaccumulate. They are still washing into the bay and its rivers from soils on the land where they were used years ago.

For the most part, there are few clear trends of either increasing or decreasing levels of toxics in seafood samples from the bay between the 1970s and the present. This deficiency is due to a lack of long-term monitoring. Oysters do not accumulate toxics as much as fish and crabs do, and to date have a clean bill of health, baywide, as far as chemical contamination goes.

Three indicators of toxic problems, all of them birds who live at the top of the food chain and feed heavily on bay fish year after year, are looking up. Bald eagles, ospreys, and brown pelicans, whose numbers sank to historic lows in the region as the pesticide DDT accumulated in their systems, have rebounded strongly in the last decade.

Of the three major contaminants behind the bay's health advisories, mercury is perhaps the most worrisome. It is the only one still being produced, and with the current national push to burn more coal, mercury entering the environment could actually increase. The U.S. EPA recently relaxed the regulations for power plants. It is possible to reduce mercury by 80–85 percent with activated carbon technology, but that process is more expensive than current pollution controls. The coal industry often blames forest fires for emitting as much mercury as power plants. It is indeed released by burning trees, but where did the mercury in the vegetation come from in the first place? Probably from polluted air. We need to control all sources, not argue over who contributes more. Airborne mercury can travel hundreds of miles, but coal-burning power plants closer to the bay probably are the most potent sources of it.

While there is no reason to suspect that toxic chemicals in the bay are having major or widespread impacts on human health, it is nonetheless sobering to realize that in virtually every place scientists have sampled to date, they have recommended limiting human intake of bay seafood because of chemical contamination.

BACTERIA AND HUMAN HEALTH

Is it safe to swim in the bay? Will eating raw seafood make you sick? These questions are most often related to the threat of bacterial contamination, which around the bay may come from malfunctioning septic tanks or sewage plants and broken sewage pipes, as well as from animal waste runoff, runoff from urban streets, or the overboard discharge of boat toilets around marinas. Historically, it was concern in the oyster industry about contamination by Baltimore's raw sewage that forced the city in 1909 to open the first modern sewage treatment plant in the nation (an alternative plan considered by city fathers was to spray the sewage on the land in an area now known as Glen Burnie).

The number of beach closings and advisories has steadily increased nationwide from 1988 through 2001. In 2001, a survey by the Natural Resources Defense Council (*Testing the Waters*) showed Maryland with 262 closures and warnings, up from 111 in 2000. The closures were partly due to better monitoring. Stormwater runoff was the leading cause of the high bacteria levels, with sewage spills at 29 percent and agricultural runoff at 16 percent. Virginia did not report a single beach closing or advisory in 2001, which raises questions about the quality of its monitoring.

Closure of shellfish areas is another indicator of toxics and bacteria in bay waters. Both Virginia and Maryland monitor these levels closely because oysters and clams, unlike most other seafood in this country, are traditionally eaten uncooked. Extremely serious problems, such as hepatitis and parasitic infestations, can result from eating shellfish taken from polluted waters. Shellfish waters are graded along a spectrum ranging from "approved" for harvesting to "prohibited," with several levels of restriction in between.

In a 1995 survey, Maryland and Virginia ranked considerably better than the nation as a whole in percentage of shellfish acreage restricted for harvests due to bacterial contamination. According to the National Oceanic and Atmospheric Administration (NOAA), 9 percent of waters in Maryland were restricted and 6 percent in Virginia, compared to a national average of 31 percent. And less than 6 percent of all Chesapeake waters were prohibited for all shellfish harvest, compared to 25 percent nationwide. Virginia's restricted acreage has fallen slightly in the past decade, from around 95,000 acres to around 90,000. Maryland's restricted acreage has remained stable at around 110,000 acres during the last decade.

Major reasons reported for contamination of shellfish waters in 1995 were urban runoff (40 percent of restricted areas), unidentified sources (39 percent), and wildlife (38 percent). In many cases, more than one source is the cause. Wildlife such as resident geese, nonmigratory fowl that don't fly north for the summer, is an increasing source of bacterial contamination around the Chesapeake. Septic tanks were reported as responsible in 32 percent of shellfish restrictions, nationwide. Some restricted acreage is listed as waters maintained as buffers around sewage treatment plants in case there is an unexpected discharge of raw sewage.

As of 1997, NOAA data showed Chesapeake Bay with 1 percent of its shellfish beds prohibited for harvest, another 6 percent restricted, and 2 percent conditional. Delaware Bay, by comparison, had 17 percent of its beds prohibited, and the Atlantic coastal bays of Maryland and Virginia had 3 percent prohibited.

TOXICS AND THE BAY'S HEALTH

While human health problems from toxics and bacteria in the bay appear relatively minor, there are larger concerns about the impacts on the species that live there. The bay continues to be plagued by downturns in reproduction of a number of its fish species. Low levels of the same toxics that pervade the bay are frequently found in their tissues and in their eggs; and exposing eggs and larvae to the waters of their spawning rivers can cause significant mortality.

Because of air pollution, the rainfall across the bay watershed in recent decades is far more acidic than what once was considered normal. Bay species such as striped bass, herring, shad, and white and yellow perch have been documented as potentially vulnerable to acid rain. But there is nothing conclusive linking their health in the Chesapeake to acidity, and overfishing has usually proven the dominant source of declines in bay fish. Such vagueness has hampered efforts to link parts per million, billion, trillion, and quadrillion of toxic chemicals to impacts on the bay's health during the last decade.

Some impacts, however, are more certain:

- A current U.S. Fish and Wildlife Service study of bullhead catfish in the urban Anacostia River in Washington, D.C., found that more than half of the fish sampled had active tumors caused by highly toxic chemicals known as PAHs, or polycyclic aromatic hydrocarbons. These compounds are increasing in the bay. They come from burning fossil fuels in power plants and cars, with cars now becoming the dominant source because the number of miles people in the bay watershed drive each year has risen four times faster than population since 1970. Individual automobiles since then have become much less polluting, but the higher mileage they are driven offsets that gain, and PAHs have not been a target of new auto cleanup technologies.

- Studies have shown that oysters in laboratory experiments become more susceptible to diseases when exposed to PAHs and to tributyl tin (TBT), a toxic in boat bottom paint.
- Marine organisms are damaged when exposed to creosote used on bulkheads and docks. Similar impacts come from exposure to so-called salt-treated timbers used in marine construction, which are actually treated with copper, chromium, and arsenic.
- In the Patuxent River, researchers have shown that plankton can concentrate traces of toxic metals from the water, passing it on up the food chain to higher organisms.

Two areas of the bay heavily polluted with toxic chemicals are Baltimore Harbor and the Elizabeth River in Norfolk, where urban-industrial centers have engulfed the shorelines for more than two centuries. Concentrations of metals such as cadmium, lead, and arsenic, as well as organic chemicals, including pesticides and PCBs, occur there at levels several times those in more natural environments. Fish samples from the Elizabeth show a high incidence of tumors, fin rot, and eye cataracts. Fish exposed in a laboratory to water containing polluted sediments from Baltimore Harbor showed a higher death rate than those exposed to water containing uncontaminated sediments—even when concentrations of harbor sediment were 100 times lower than concentrations of clean sediment.

The pollution of these two areas existed long before the bay's more widespread, modern-day decline. Indeed, the evidence is that the great bulk of the toxics entering the two locations has stayed there—the result of circulatory patterns by which chemicals dumped over many years are trapped and settle out, rather than flushing vigorously into the main bay.

The toxics reported to have been discharged to the air and water by industries around the Chesapeake have declined by 67 percent since 1988. Despite that positive trend, which seems likely to continue, enough poison has accumulated around Baltimore and Norfolk that their waters probably will never be high-quality environments. Because of that problem, and because the bulk of the threat appears trapped forever within these already polluted localities, there is often a tendency to write their rivers off in terms of their fish and wildlife. Another area in the same urban-polluted category is the Anacostia River in Washington, D.C.

The other side of the equation, however, is that these are the areas where huge numbers of the bay region's people live and work and have most of their opportunities to make frequent contact with the water. Recreational crabbing, for example, draws people to Baltimore's Harbor by the hundreds on summer days, and crabbing is actually carried out on a commercial basis within the Elizabeth River. Similarly, city dwellers in both places catch and consume substantial numbers of fish locally. A recent Maryland program to promote fishing interest in Baltimore Harbor was completely overwhelmed when more than a thousand youths showed up—three times the number expected—clamoring for their promised rods, reels, and plastic tubs of earthworms.

Meanwhile, several sections of bay rivers previously thought to be clean have turned out to be moderately toxic. To an extent this finding reflects progress—Chesapeake restoration programs have made major efforts in the last decade to examine the bay for toxics. Very little was known before, outside of the old, industrial hot spots. Now contamination is documented in broad areas of the James, Potomac, Patuxent, Chester, Severn, Magothy, Middle, and Back Rivers. Several others have been found relatively clean, and several remain to be tested.

The sources of contamination in these newfound areas are not always clear, but airborne contaminants, particularly from automobiles and power plants, constitute one source. Another is the urban stormwater runoff from developing lands in their watersheds. Finally, the affected rivers may have circulation patterns that trap contaminants that come in with the tide from the bay proper. Even as the old industrial regions reduce toxic chemicals from discharge pipes and smokestacks, other regions seem to be growing more toxic from an array of diffuse sources such as auto exhausts and the runoff from pavements.

One further source of chemical contamination in the bay is the periodic dredging of old, contaminated sediments in industrial areas. Dredging for navigation or disturbances by storms can resuspend these toxic sediments in the water, putting them in new contact with aquatic life.

KILLER ALGAE

Sometimes human pollution sets the stage for the Chesapeake's natural organisms to run riot. Of the hundreds of species of tiny, floating plants, or algae, in the bay, fifteen are known to be capable of producing toxins under certain conditions. What sets them off is not well understood. It can be a combination of weather and other natural conditions, over which we obviously have no control; it can also be the excessive amounts of human-caused pollutants—a factor that we could control. The elevated levels of nitrogen and phosphorus in the bay are not directly linked to such algae becoming toxic, but they do stimulate algal growth. Unpredictable explosions of algae, or "blooms," can quickly spread throughout dozens of square miles of the bay and its rivers, with devastating results.

In the summer of 1997, Maryland's lower Pocomoke River and other creeks in the region experienced the bay's first recorded outbreak of *Pfiesteria piscicida,* an alga that produces a toxin and is found in nontoxic form throughout the Chesapeake. *Pfiesteria* was implicated in the subsequent death of thousands of fish and in ailments recorded in two dozen bay watermen and state water quality workers that ranged from rashes to severe, short-term memory loss. Scientists are still researching just what combination of events triggered the outbreak, as well as whether causes other than *Pfiesteria* were responsible for the fish kills. Researchers from North Carolina, which had experienced larger attacks of *Pfiesteria* earlier, think it was a combination of nutrients, weather, water circulation patterns, and the presence of large numbers of fish, whose excretions somehow cause *Pfiesteria* to attack them, releasing a potent neurotoxin in the process.

The Pocomoke was temporarily closed to all fishing and water recreation, at a cost of millions to bay seafood harvesters and marketers. There remains a lively scientific debate as to whether a common fungus was also at work, possibly in conjunction with *Pfiesteria,* in causing the fish kills; but the human health evidence, well documented by medical teams from the University of Maryland and Johns Hopkins, points strongly to *Pfiesteria*'s devastating handiwork. The outbreak caused such a furor that Maryland, and later Virginia, subsequently passed strong legislation to keep manure and other sources of nutrient-laden farm runoff out of bay rivers. Everyone realized that a spread of *Pfiesteria,* or something similar, in the future could easily ruin the bay's huge recreational and seafood harvesting economy.

The Chesapeake region has had other, less-damaging brushes with algae. For example, a bloom in 1992 of *Cochlodinium heterolabatum* covered close to a hundred square miles. This alga had been occurring routinely within Virginia's York River, but for the first time it spilled out across large sections of the lower Chesapeake. The outbreak, however, had no known toxic effects. Even among toxic algae, a bloom can be strongly toxic or scarcely harmful, again for reasons not well understood.

In 1999, in the Potomac River, which divides Maryland and Virginia, one of the biggest blooms on record occurred with *Prorocentrum,* another alga with toxic capability. It turned the water a rich, reddish brown, a "mahogany tide," killing fish and oysters. Like any big algal bloom, toxic or not, the *Prorocentrum* explosion lowered oxygen in the water to deadly levels as the algae's eventual decomposition rapidly used up oxygen.

Globally, scientists have documented an increase in the occurrence and extent of harmful algal blooms, or HABs. There are several reasons for the increase, including closer observation and better reporting of such events in recent decades, but the primary causes appear to be a gradual warming of the oceans and the widespread increase of nutrients in coastal waters around the world (the bay is not alone in this, its major problem). While the Chesapeake as yet shows no trend toward more toxic algal blooms, "there is evidence that concentrations of potential toxin producers now living in the bay are increasing and gradually becoming more common," says a recent report from Old Dominion University in Virginia.

FOREIGN INVADERS

Another source of toxic algae and other problems for the bay, overlooked until recently, is contamination that arrives by the billions of gallons each year in ballast water taken on by ships to stabilize themselves on sea voyages. Before taking on cargo, they discharge this ballast, releasing an array of potential problems: serious disease pathogens, algae, and small marine animals. The zebra mussel that is devastating the Great Lakes and slowly spreading down the Susquehanna River to the Chesapeake entered the country in ballast water. So did the rapa whelk from Japan, which is now threatening native shellfish in the lower Chesapeake. Cholera entering Mobile Bay, Alabama, in ballast water closed oyster reefs there.

Currently, bay researchers are carrying out a series of promising experiments to find the best way to decontaminate ballast water before it is discharged.

TOXICS IN THE BAY'S FUTURE

Substantial progress has come in the last decade or so from reducing toxics that enter the Chesapeake from traditional sources such as sewage and industrial discharge pipes. Industry has also made progress during the last decade in reducing the toxics it releases to the air, which rain later washes into the bay. The latest bay restoration agreement, *Chesapeake 2000,* contains commitments from government to continue this progress, including a 20 percent reduction goal. Unfortunately, the industry-reported toxics-release data for 2000 show increases in Virginia and Maryland. Fortunately, farmers' adoption of better pest management has reduced pesticide use on an estimated 61 percent of cropland in the watershed. Pesticide collection, disposal, and recycling programs have taken more than a million and a half pounds of these chemicals out of circulation since 1991.

Significant toxic impacts to the bay system, however, can still come from other sources:

• The worst toxic threats have not always been from wastes or by-products, but from products that were deliberately introduced widely into the environment because they were considered benefi-

cial. Examples are lead in gasoline (as an effective anti-knock ingredient); the "miracle pesticide," DDT; chlordane (about the only sure
thing to kill termites); TBT (the extremely effective boat anti-fouling
paint, now banned for many uses); and even PCBs, globally distributed for their superior insulating qualities in electrical transformers.
Another deliberately introduced product, the lead shot in shotgun
shells, has killed large numbers of ducks and geese, which consume it
when they feed on the bay bottoms where shot falls during hunting
season.

- Most of the above toxics are now banned or severely restricted, but
as chemical analyses of bay fish and crabs indicate, the sins of the
past keep coming back to haunt us, leaching from the watershed's
soils or recycling from bay bottom sediments. Virginia, where TBT is
a contaminant, has only begun to meet highly restrictive water quality standards for the chemical after fifteen years of effort to limit it.

- Pollutants from the air are undoubtedly having toxic impacts on the
bay. Mercury and PAHs come from auto and power plant emissions,
and neither source is regulated with an eye to reducing these troublesome contaminants. Air quality in general is still regulated more
from the standpoint of protecting human health, not aquatic health
(see also "Air," this chapter).

- Agriculture continues to use massive quantities of chemical pesticides that routinely turn up in surface and ground waters. Pesticide
use across the watershed—mainly for farming, but with a growing
share for lawns and golf courses—has more than tripled since the
1950s. Many of today's pesticides, which are used to kill weeds, insects, and soil fungus, are designed to break down in the environment far faster than chemicals such as DDT and chlordane. While
that breakdown reduces their long-term accumulation in the environment, their quickness to dissolve in rainwater means they are easily and quickly transported to waterways and into drinking water
aquifers.

U.S. Geological Survey sampling during 1987–1998 detected pesticides
in 90 percent of samples from 463 surface water sites across the mid-
Atlantic region, an area dominated by the bay's watershed. As with most

toxics in the bay, these pesticides weren't at levels high enough to pose a direct human health threat, but their impacts on the environment are not understood. Neither has anyone looked at the cumulative impacts, to see whether exposure to several contaminants at low levels adds up to a serious threat.

Most pesticides were found in levels below state and federal danger levels, but it was not uncommon to find places contaminated enough to violate drinking water levels. Similar sampling of groundwater, which is often a source of human drinking water, found pesticides in about half of all samples, though rarely at levels that exceeded human health standards. More troubling was the finding of nitrate, from fertilizer, in 75 percent of the samples. Though only 10 percent of all samples exceeded federal drinking water standards of 10 parts nitrate per million parts water, studies from the Midwest indicate links between nitrate and bladder cancer at levels well below 10 parts per million.

A toxics-free bay continues to be the goal of the federal-state restoration program for the Chesapeake, but it is clearly a long way off. Current commitments are focusing on continued reductions from industries and sewage treatment plants, with a particular emphasis on eliminating the current use of "mixing zones." These essentially allow the discharge of toxics in amounts that violate water quality standards as they come out of the pipe, but declare surrounding river and bay waters as "sacrifice" areas, using their dilution to meet standards at some point downstream. Mixing zones constitute an archaic "treatment" method and need to be phased out, especially for those toxics that persist in the environment for long periods, bioaccumulating in aquatic life and in humans.

BEYOND TOXICS

It seems likely that the revolution in chemicals that have both made our lives easier and caused many unintended environmental impacts will be repeated in coming decades with biotechnology, including the genetic engineering of many living organisms. Maryland clearly is pursuing this future, already experimenting with scientists transplanting cold-resistant genetic material into Chesapeake Bay striped bass, with unknown potential to alter the habits of that species and others with which it interacts in the environment. Elsewhere, genetically altered species of fish are being developed for aquaculture, with unknown risk to native species should the modified fish escape and interbreed.

Conclusions

- For the foreseeable future, wherever we look, we will continue to find low levels of toxics in the bay's water, sediments, and seafood; and it will be a long time before science can definitively evaluate their impacts on human and aquatic health. Therefore, with toxics more than with any other bay problem, it remains crucial to act conservatively, to do all we can to minimize what enters the bay and its rivers, and to not wait for subtle, long-term environmental effects to become apparent.

- Real progress with toxics has come in two areas during the last decade. Traditional sources such as industrial and sewage facilities have notably reduced toxic discharges to the bay. A strong effort has been made to identify where toxic contamination from all sources is occurring. This effort has revealed sections of eight bay rivers with more toxic pollutants than suspected. Some twenty additional sections of the bay system remain to be analyzed for contamination.

- While traditional sources of toxics decline, chemical contamination is growing from automobiles and urban runoff, and from largely unregulated contaminants such as mercury from coal-burning power plants.

- Fish tumors and the widening health advisories against eating fish and crabs from the bay are strong warning signs of the need to work for a toxics-free bay. Except for hot spots—Washington's Anacostia River, Baltimore's Harbor, and Norfolk's Elizabeth River—the Chesapeake has not seen the levels of degradation by toxics experienced in New England waters, the Great Lakes, the Hudson River estuary, and Puget Sound.

- Closures of shellfish harvesting areas due to bacterial contamination are fewer than a decade ago, and both Maryland and Virginia are significantly better than the nation as a whole in avoiding bacterial contamination from sewage, septic tanks, and other sources.

- Toxic chemicals do not seem a likely dominant cause of any down-turns in bay fish, oysters, and crabs. But scientific studies are showing that even very low levels of toxic chemicals can weaken the ability of oysters to fight disease.
- The potential for blooms of toxic algae in the bay appears to be growing, though actual toxic episodes from such events show no trend, up or down, in the last decade. *Pfiesteria,* an alga that can kill fish and cause severe memory loss in humans, made its first documented toxic appearance in the Chesapeake in 1997.
- Agricultural and lawn care chemicals continue to show up routinely at low levels in surface and underground water throughout the bay watershed. An exception is nitrate from fertilizer, which exceeds drinking water guidelines in a significant number of cases.
- Major toxic threats to the bay in the future will not necessarily come in the form of wastes or industrial by-products. They may well come from useful consumer products, such as batteries, or perhaps, in the future, from genetically engineered substances that are deliberately distributed in the environment.

Dissolved Oxygen—The Bay's Bottom Line

We don't pot the deep water anymore in summertime . . . the crabs just aren't there.

—Tangier Sound waterman

Dissolved oxygen, which tends to get scarcest in the deeper waters of the bay, is the literal bottom line of the Chesapeake's pollution problems. Oxygen is just as essential to bay creatures as it is to humans, though aquatic life needs lesser quantities than land dwellers. Fourteen parts of oxygen per million parts of water is about as much as the bay ever gets, while the air we breathe has more than 200,000 parts per million (ppm). Restoring more oxygen to the bay is one of the major driving forces behind the programs to reduce pollution from nutrients and sediments.

Dissolved oxygen levels decrease in summertime and increase in winter, because warm water can hold less of any dissolved gas than cold. Those low levels may have occurred naturally from time to time in the bay's deeps long before modern pollution became a problem. Scientists can find instances of this condition by analyzing several-foot-long cores of sediment, which tell what was happening on the bay bottom in centuries past. But the cores also indicate that low oxygen has gotten dramatically worse in recent decades—more severe, longer lasting, and covering greater areas of the bay.

Most creatures in the bay, for example, do well when dissolved oxygen in the water is above 5 parts per million. Since the 1950s, summertime bay water with less than 2 ppm, called *hypoxic*, has grown from a yearly average of 4 percent of the bay's volume to more than 13 percent of its water in the late 1990s. More alarming yet has been the increase in

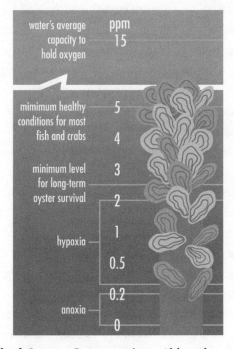

FIGURE 2.11. **Dissolved Oxygen Concentrations.** Although aquatic animals require much lower levels of oxygen than humans do, they nevertheless need it to live. Less than 5 ppm (parts per million) stresses most fish and crabs, and less than 2 ppm is lethal for them.

volumes of bay water that have virtually no oxygen at all. Such *anoxic* conditions (defined as having dissolved oxygen of 0.5 ppm or less) were quite rare before the 1950s, scientists think. But by the late 1990s, more than 7 percent of the bay's 50 billion cubic meters of water was anoxic. Put another way, the amount of truly lethal water that is commonly present in the bay today exceeds the amount of harmful water four decades ago. In truly bad years, nearly 25 percent of the bay's water is hypoxic, with about 12 percent anoxic.

During such times, the bay may look no different to the observer crossing it by bridge or boat; but to fish and crabs, huge sections of the estuary have become as hostile as a desert. The lack of oxygen in deeper waters can "squeeze" fish such as striped bass between near-surface water that has oxygen but is too warm for them and deeper water that is cool enough, but where they can't "breathe." Essentially, the fish are forced to survive in a dramatically shrunken habitat. Striped bass also have more deformed eggs and smaller hatches as dissolved oxygen begins to plummet. Crabs trapped in watermen's pots die when low-oxygen water spreads through the bay. Increasingly, watermen simply don't find the crabs in deep water during the summers anymore. Even waters that are above 2 ppm can cause subtler stresses, such as the changes in feeding behavior documented in some bottom-dwelling worms that make them more susceptible to being eliminated by predators. Low oxygen also slows chemical processes in the bay's bottom sediments that can convert nitrogen into harmless gas that rises back into the atmosphere.

Neither is the "bad" water, as bay watermen call it, confined always to the deep channels, though that is where the bulk of it occurs. Winds pressing on the surface can cause the bay to tilt from east to west, sloshing oxygen-poor water from the deeps across large acreages of the highly productive shallower areas, where it stresses oyster beds and other species. Such bad water from the bay's main channels may also intrude for miles up the mouths of rivers. And local versions of the main bay's oxygen losses have been documented in several of the bay's tidal rivers. The problem is spreading. Low oxygen was once rare in much of Virginia's portion of the Chesapeake, where being closer to the ocean assured that bottom waters were filled with oxygen. But during the late

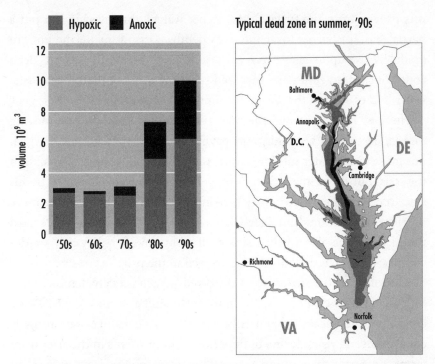

Figure 2.12. Increasing Hypoxia: Five Decades of Trends. A disturbingly increasing volume of the bay's deep water goes hypoxic or anoxic in summer, creating a "dead zone" for bay creatures. [Jim Hagy, Center for Environmental Studies, University of Maryland]

1990s, areas of anoxia were reaching as far south as the mouth of the Rappahannock River.

WET YEARS MAKE UNDERWATER DESERTS

Two forces, one mostly natural, the other human-caused, are the reasons for large sections of the Chesapeake becoming an underwater desert in recent decades. The worst years are associated with wet springs, which cause high flows down the bay's rivers, especially the Susquehanna, source of nearly half of the estuary's freshwater. These powerful flows of freshwater, running seaward atop the heavier, saltier ocean water that is always pushing up the bay's channels, cause stratification—strongly defined layers of fresh and salt. Combined with a lack of strong winds to mix oxygen from the surface into deeper waters, this layering can put a partial "lid," or barrier, over the bay's depths. Organisms on the bottom gradually use up available oxygen, resulting in an oxygen-starved "dead zone." Such dead zones are now seen regularly in more than fifty coastal water bodies around the world, on almost every continent.

Humans have worsened the high river flows somewhat by removing forests, destroying wetlands, and paving for development, all of which put more water faster into the rivers, rather than allowing it to soak into the soils. But the primary factors triggering the worsening oxygen trends since the 1950s have been nutrients—nitrogen and phosphorus. As more nutrients have poured into the Chesapeake, they have fueled more algal production. The algae, which sink to the bottom after they die, are decomposed by bacteria that suck up oxygen in the process.

The interplay of nutrients and dissolved oxygen is easily demonstrated by comparing two periods, the mid-1960s and the mid-1990s. Flows down the Chesapeake's major tributary, the Susquehanna, were roughly equal in several years during both periods. But nutrients in the river from farms, sewage, urban runoff, and fallout from polluted air more than doubled on average between the 1960s and the 1990s. As a result, deadly anoxia downstream in the bay was far more severe during the more recent period of the 1990s. In 1965, for example, no anoxia was present in the bay, whereas in 1995, a year with similar river flow, almost a quarter of the bay's volume was anoxic.

There is building evidence that just as the Susquehanna's springtime flows drive oxygen levels throughout much of the Chesapeake, so does its massive delivery of nutrients dwarf all other bay rivers in causing the oxygen problems of the estuary.

A primary goal of the current bay restoration is to return oxygen levels during the summer problem periods to something approximating those of the 1950s. But to date, despite limited success in reducing nutrients during the 1990s, there is no evidence of improvement. Scientists think we are still flooding the Chesapeake with so many nutrients that until we reduce them much more substantially, we won't see any response in oxygen levels. The ups and downs that we do see from year to year are probably driven by wet and dry springtimes (with high-flow years causing bigger oxygen problems). Think of the situation as adding salt to a glass of water until the water cannot absorb any more, then adding more and more even though the excess just settles out on the bottom. Now, begin removing salt from the glass. You can remove a good deal before the water begins to reflect your progress by actually getting less salty. So it may be with nitrogen and dissolved oxygen.

Conclusions

- Low oxygen levels in the bay have worsened dramatically since the 1950s, lasting longer, dropping lower, and spreading farther throughout the system. Increased human inputs of nutrients, particularly into the Susquehanna, the bay's biggest river, are responsible.
- Low oxygen now affects more than half the bay's entire volume in some summers, shrinking habitat for crabs, fish, and oysters, and stressing many organisms even at levels above what is technically defined as low oxygen.
- Nutrient pollution will likely have to be reduced far below current levels before we see much response in oxygen.

Oil Spills

It can't happen to me.

— Joseph Hazelwood, former captain of the *Exxon Valdez,*
quote with his yearbook picture, New York Maritime College

In 1976, an oil barge spilled 250,000 gallons of its cargo into the middle Chesapeake Bay, killing thousands of wintering waterfowl and contaminating areas of the bay bottom with hydrocarbons. In 1988, a similar spill, of similar size, occurred in almost the same location. There had been very little progress in the intervening twelve years in making oil transport on the bay safer. The 1990s, however, saw some progress in making oil transport safer on the nation's waterways, including the Chesapeake. Large spills (over 1,000 gallons) have declined dramatically, due in part to tougher federal laws enacted in 1990 following the multimillion-gallon

Exxon Valdez spill in Prince William Sound, Alaska. Double hulls, less likely to rupture and leak, are being phased in for both tanker vessels and oil barges—though more slowly for the smaller barges that transport most of the oil that moves around the bay and its rivers. Overflow alarm systems and automatic shutoffs are now required at fueling terminals along waterways. (The lack of these caused at least one large spill in Baltimore Harbor in recent years.)

While oil spills from ships and barges often get the lion's share of publicity, waterborne transport accounts for only about a third of the billions of gallons of petroleum products moving through the Chesapeake region each year, according to petroleum industry figures. As much or more moves through pipelines, many of which were built during the 1970s and are beginning to show their age. Indeed, the Chesapeake's two biggest petroleum spills of the past decade have come from pipeline failures— 400,000 gallons into the Potomac River at Fairfax, Virginia, in 1993 and 129,000 gallons into the Patuxent River marshes and tidal creeks near Chalk Point in Maryland in 2000. The latter spill came from a local pipeline that fell through the loopholes of a law requiring federal inspection and oversight of pipelines that move through more than one state. Attempts to let Maryland inspect pipelines that run within the state had been defeated by oil and pipeline industry lobbyists in the legislature in 1994 and 1995. Following the Patuxent River incident, a bill requiring such inspections passed quickly.

Another critical aspect of oil spills that often escapes public notice is that nearly 85 percent of the 29 million gallons of gas and oil spilled into the nation's waterways in a typical year does not come from large, or even very noticeable, spills. A National Academy of Sciences report, highlighted in the May 24, 2002, *New York Times*, concluded that it comes from the everyday runoff of petroleum from parking lots, highways, airport runways, pleasure boats, and other diffuse, or nonpoint, sources. About half that total runoff occurs within the East Coast, Boston-Washington corridor, which includes the Chesapeake watershed. Only about 8 percent of the nation's total of oil entering waterways comes from oil-carrying vessels and pipelines in an average year. Just the unburned oil and gas spewed out by two-stroke outboard motors—an estimated 1.6 million gallons a year—slightly surpass the annual average spills from oil tankers (see also "Recreational Pollution—Boats," this chapter). A Coast Guard official, speaking of the impacts of oil on water quality, calls this nonpoint runoff "death by a thousand cuts."

Of course, the impact of thousands or millions of gallons spilled suddenly in one place can far exceed the impact of the daily seepage of nonpoint runoff of oil. The bay is immensely vulnerable to pollution from a large spill on several counts. First, it is quite shallow, with an average depth of less than 22 feet. Anything spilled here doesn't have to move very far to contaminate the bottom. And much of the life in and around the bay either resides on the bottom or depends on it for food and habitat. Second, the bay's shorelines tend to be either marsh or beach, with huge acreages of shallow underwater grass beds and tidal mudflats adjoining them. Spilled oil, once it hits these shores, is almost impossible to clean up and can persist with damaging environmental effects for years. "A marsh is the worst place in the world to spill oil," says an expert on environmental effects of petroleum with the National Oceanic and Atmospheric Administration (NOAA). The Chesapeake Bay, the same official noted, has about as many miles of marsh as the entire west coast of the United States (excluding Alaska). Third, the bay's primary wintering and spawning area for blue crabs, its most valuable single seafood resource, lies in a high-traffic area for shipping, including oil transport, near Norfolk, Hampton Roads, and Virginia Beach. Coast Guard officials say that the tracking and collision-avoidance systems for vessels in that area have been significantly improved in the last decade.

Since the *Exxon Valdez* disaster in Alaska highlighted the inability of state and federal agencies to contain a large spill, oil-spill response capability is widely considered to have improved around the nation. It is hard to evaluate such capability, though, until a real test happens, and recent years have been relatively quiet in the bay region. The 2000 Chalk Point spill was not contained well because a strong storm hit the area, resulting in large-scale contamination of the marshes. Currently, it is clear that the U.S. Coast Guard, the agency primarily responsible for responding to spills to the water, is overburdened with intercepting drugs and with homeland defense. Virginia's oil response capabilities have been seriously weakened by eight years of governors hostile to environmental concerns during the last decade. The General Accounting Office (GAO) has raised serious concerns about federal oversight of interstate pipelines. A GAO report noted that nationally, the number of major pipeline accidents (including natural gas and other toxic materials transported by pipeline) increased by 4 percent a year from 1989 to 1998—growing from 190 accidents annually to 280.

David Kennedy, a NOAA official whose experience with oil spills covers several decades, notes that a predictable cycle occurs after a disaster such as the *Exxon Valdez* spill, beginning with a burst of concern, progress, and more vigilance, then followed by a period with no major incidents that produces a drop in attention and investment in preventing and responding to oil spills. Kennedy believes the country might currently be in a period where conditions are making the possibility of a large spill more likely.

Conclusions

- Overall, there has been real progress—and probably some luck—in avoiding disastrous oil spills from barges and tank vessels. Meanwhile, pipelines, which move more oil than vessels, have caused two major bay spills since 1993.
- The Chesapeake Bay is extremely vulnerable to a large oil spill, both because of its shallowness and marshy coastlines, and because large quantities of petroleum products are shipped on its waters daily.
- Around the bay and the nation, an estimated 85 percent of all the oil entering waterways comes from the daily runoff from parking lots and highways, from pleasure boats, and from hundreds of other nonpoint sources.
- Oil pollution has been moved well down the U.S. Coast Guard's priority list, as homeland defense and drug interdiction have become larger responsibilities.

Recreational Pollution—Boats

There is nothing—absolutely nothing—half so much worth doing as simply messing about in boats.

—Rat, introducing Mole to the river in Kenneth Grahame's
The Wind in the Willows

Every weekend from May to October, tens of thousands of recreational boaters cruise the Chesapeake Bay and its many tributaries. More than 400,000 such boats are now registered in Virginia and Maryland. Rising far faster than the number of people living in the bay region, the number of recreational boats has more than tripled from the 124,000 registered, baywide, in 1967. While boat-related pollution is relatively small in the overall scheme of bay water quality problems, it can cause severe local problems in areas of high use. Areas around marinas, for example, are routinely closed to shellfishing because of the threat of contamination. And ultimately, the question is not just the quantity of pollution but ethical behavior toward the environment. Pleasure boaters have no more right than midnight dumpers of toxic chemicals to put their wastes into public waters. Neither does such irresponsible behavior give boaters much moral authority to point fingers at industries, farmers, sewage treatment plants, and other sources of bay pollution.

HUMAN WASTES

It is illegal to discharge raw sewage within 3 miles of the U.S. coastline. But the reality is that by opening a valve from a marine toilet or dumping a bucket overboard, most recreational boats can release their wastes without detection. So the Coast Guard and state agencies responsible for enforcing the law have given the issue low priority. In 1990, when this book was first published, an EPA official termed recreational boating wastes "perhaps the single most embarrassing failure of all our [bay cleanup] commitments." Since then, both Maryland and Virginia have made progress in giving boaters sounder waste disposal options, though the fast growth in numbers of boats has surely offset some unknown amount of that progress.

Both states have passed laws or regulations requiring most marinas to have stations to pump out boaters' toilets. Efforts have been aided by federal Clean Vessel Act funds covering 75 percent of the cost of such pumpout stations. As of 2002, Maryland had around 300 pumpouts installed, out of about 600 marinas, while Virginia had 190 pumpouts and another 371 "dump stations" where boaters could empty portable toilets. These statistics represent an improvement over having had only a few dozen such facilities baywide in 1990. Maryland estimates a million gallons of human waste are now being taken from recreational boats and sent to sewage treatment plants, compared to 65,000 gallons in 1994. Still, no one knows just how much is still disposed of illegally. "Some marinas tell me if [their pumpout stations] get used once a week in the summer, it's a big deal," one Virginia official said. Stories still abound of malfunctioning pumpouts, waiting lines at the end of weekends, inconvenient locations, and poor accessibility to larger boats. Nearly 40 percent of owners of boats larger than 22 feet reported pumpout station problems in a Maryland survey in 2000.

While boat wastes are not a major bay problem, real problems can occur where boaters congregate in quiet coves and smaller rivers and creeks. The wastes can cause bacterial contamination, as well as nutrient pollution. Nitrogen and phosphorus are not affected by marine disinfection systems that kill only bacteria. In a largely symbolic move, Maryland has designated its first "no-discharge" zone at Herring Bay, south of Annapolis. The designation applies only to the small number of boats with on-board systems that treat and discharge human waste—about 5 percent of recreational boats larger than 22 feet. Nonetheless, proponents of no-discharge zones say they add pressure on marinas to step up the use of pumpout stations. Some believe no-discharge zones may offer local areas a marketing advantage: who wants to water-ski in feces-filled water?

Chesapeake 2000, the latest Chesapeake Bay restoration agreement, watered down draft language that would have declared the whole bay a no-discharge zone, calling instead for the states to establish them in "appropriate areas." Despite the increased emphasis given pumpouts and no-discharge zones, however, the gritty reality is that most boat use on the bay consists of day trips on small boats with no toilets. Also, use by canoeists and kayakers is increasing dramatically. When nature calls, those users have little access to permanent or portable restrooms at public access sites around the bay's shoreline.

DIRTY OUTBOARD ENGINES

The two-stroke outboard engine that has been the mainstay of recreational boat propulsion for decades may be the greatest source of boat pollution to the bay. EPA estimates that a typical two-stroke engine, running for about 20 miles, produces as much air pollution as a modern automobile driven 800 miles. The pollutants include nitrogen and unburned oil and gasoline, all discharged by two-strokes in large quantities. A National Academy of Sciences report estimates that 1.6 million gallons of oil and gasoline enter the nation's coastal waters unburned each year from two-stroke engines. That's slightly more than the 1.5 million gallons spilled by oil tankers in North American waters in an average year. Pollution from recreational boats is a particular concern because it often occurs near sensitive areas such as wetlands or shellfish beds, where it also introduces polycyclic aromatic hydrocarbons (PAHs), which are highly toxic even in minute amounts and accumulate in bottom-feeding fish.

Progress is coming, if slowly, on the outboard front. Newer direct-injected two-strokes and cleaner four-stroke outboards reduce air emissions 75 percent or more, burn 35–50 percent less gasoline, and use up to 50 percent less lubricating oil. The EPA is requiring that conventional two-stroke engines no longer be sold beginning in 2006, but it will take years before all the old engines are off the Chesapeake. They still account for about 75 percent of all recreational boat engine sales, nationwide, though Maryland and Virginia foresee sales of old-style engines falling rapidly as buyers realize how much cleaner, more efficient, and quieter the new-technology engines are. Some immediate solutions to the problem, meanwhile, include taking advantage of the many launch ramps around the bay to trailer one's boat behind a car wherever possible, rather than running the boat. This is less polluting and more fuel efficient than running the outboard. An automobile, even one hauling a boat, is far less polluting than the boat itself.

Two-stroke outboards certainly pose the most serious pollution problems, but there are also increasing efforts to clean up gas and diesel inboard engines. In both cases, electronic control of fuel delivery provides major improvements in efficiency. Marine manufacturers are also working with the EPA to develop exhaust system catalysts that reduce inboard emissions even further.

TOWARD CLEANER MARINAS

Roughly a thousand marinas are scattered around the Chesapeake Bay and its tidal tributaries. Each is a potential hot spot for boat pollution. Because they are located on the water's edge, marinas offer little opportunity to buffer runoff from parking lots and maintenance areas. Pollution from routine boat maintenance—sanding, painting, cleaning, and fuel pumping—can quickly send chemicals into sensitive shallow waters and wetlands. Most hull paints contain copper or other toxic chemicals to prevent the buildup of fouling organisms that can cut boat speeds dramatically. Gasoline and oil contain PAHs that accumulate in shellfish and bottom-feeding fish. Also, marinas are often located in areas of calm water with little tidal flushing, allowing easy buildup of pollutants. Tests of Virginia creeks with marinas have shown significantly elevated levels of PAHs, as well as high levels of bacteria from human wastes.

In 1996, the EPA developed guidelines to control marina pollution. Rather than adopt those as regulations, Maryland and Virginia developed voluntary "Clean Marina" programs that establish extensive checklists of actions marinas should take to reduce pollution—maintaining pumpouts, keeping toxic paints and solvents from running off, putting in stormwater runoff controls. Maryland aims to certify 125 marinas, a quarter of those in the state, by 2004. Virginia has a goal of 50 certified marinas by 2004. A number of marinas are beginning to use the Clean Marina designation as a marketing tool to lure boaters, and some studies suggest cleaner marinas are more profitable.

Conclusions

- Recreational boating is a small but significant source of bay pollution, with problems coming from the discharge of human waste, from outboard engine exhaust, and from runoff around marinas.

- Maryland, Virginia, and the federal government have made real efforts in the last decade to deal with all three problems, mostly on a voluntary basis. To an unknown extent, progress here has been offset by the rapid growth in recreational boats, whose use on the bay is increasing much faster than population is growing.

If Fish Made Clean Water Rules

What would the water quality goals and standards that guide the restoration of the bay look like if the creatures that live in the water wrote them? Three decades after the federal Clean Water Act of 1972 called for just such an approach, the states of the Chesapeake region are finally beginning to do it. In hindsight, it seems astounding that although nitrogen and phosphorus have been acknowledged as major bay pollutants for many years, there are still no legal limits on how much of either can go into the estuary. No one can violate the standard for either pollutant for bay waters, because there is no standard, no bottom line on how much a river can take before its creatures say "ouch."

That is not to say that the states and the EPA haven't been working for decades on reducing such pollution, but their approaches have focused most meaningfully on the discharge pipes from sewage treatment plants and industries. Largely ignored have been the nonpoint sources such as the polluted runoff and sediment from farms and urban areas. Also lost in the shuffle is any overall limit to guarantee the bay's health.

In contrast, the original concept of the Clean Water Act actually called for restoring and maintaining the "chemical, physical, and biological integrity" of the nation's waters by 1983. The act was vague on details of just how to set standards. As of 2003, about 300,000 miles of rivers, 5 million acres of lakes, and many coastal water bodies are still polluted, according to the EPA, which maintains a list of these "impaired waters." Only recently, forced by lawsuits filed by frustrated environmental groups, has the EPA turned to promising water quality standards based on a "fish-eye view" of the world, that is, standards based on how much pollution from all sources a river or bay can stand and still be healthy. "If you are a fish, and there's too much pollution, you don't care where it's coming from, you just want it stopped," says Michael Haire, an EPA water quality specialist.

So now, under *Chesapeake 2000,* the new bay agreement, the states are finally creating a water quality effort around what is known as Total Maximum Daily Loads (of pollution), or TMDLs, with the stated goal of improving the bay's health enough to get it off the impaired waters list by 2010. Though the name is lame, TMDLs represent a profound and welcome shift in cleanup, forcing places such as the Chesapeake to confront the fact that there must be ultimate limits on what can go into the water, no matter how many people (or farm animals) live in the watershed. A TMDL requires regulators to look beyond the discharges from pipes and examine all of the contributors to a pollution problem. When added up, the total amount of pollution allowed under a TMDL has to be low enough to ensure that water quality standards are met, with a margin of safety added in.

The setting of such overall limits on pollution will be no instant cure, and there are signs that new proposals from EPA will weaken the TMDL program to where it won't do the job. Agricultural interests have fiercely opposed the TMDL concept, fearing farm runoff (about 40 percent of the bay's nitrogen problem) will be regulated for the first time. Other industries have also opposed what they see as a move toward stricter regulation. Under fire, the EPA has been considering changes that might relax enforcement of the TMDLs once they are set. Court-ordered time frames for putting the new fish-eye concept into effect and removing the Chesapeake from the EPA list allow up to fifteen years, though nothing prevents states from moving faster. Figuring out the amounts of different pollutants each part of the bay can tolerate and stay healthy (it will differ from place to place) is a time-consuming and complicated process; and after completing that assignment, water quality managers must figure out how to divvy up the cleanup job among all polluters, not an easy task in the case of runoff and fallout from the air, whose sources are spread out and far-flung.

For the time being, the EPA has given the Chesapeake Bay region permission to continue its more voluntary "cooperative" approach, as outlined in *Chesapeake 2000,* to restoring healthy water, based on the bay states' promise to move quickly and effectively, and to look at all sources of pollution. The states have essentially voluntarily adopted the TMDL approach, without calling it that, by working to determine the maximum amount of nitrogen and phosphorus the bay can absorb and still support healthy communities of fish and underwater grasses. When the water quality criteria are completed, the cleanup task will be apportioned among the bay's major rivers, for which the states are developing cleanup plans that they call "tributary strategies."

The TMDL approach, if the EPA or lawsuits by opponents do not weaken it, will remain in the background as a legal safety net to the voluntary, cooperative approach of the bay states. Ideally, it will put pressure on them to succeed in the next decade or be found in violation of federal water quality laws. But to date, the EPA and the bay states have delayed issuing their promised new water quality criteria twice, citing "technical difficulties." There seems little likelihood that cleanup strategies will be in place until the decade is nearly half over, and the bay region has only until 2011 to make good on its goals.

Conclusions

- A new generation of legally enforceable water quality measures represents real progress toward restoring the bay's health. These measures will apply to all sources of pollution, including farm and urban runoff, rather than just what comes from pipes. They will establish the maximum pollution the bay's aquatic life can stand and remain healthy.
- However, the bay states and the EPA are already falling seriously behind on putting the measures into action, raising real concerns about meeting the year 2010 goals of *Chesapeake 2000* for restoring the bay's health. In addition, there are signs that the TMDL program emerging from EPA will be a weak one.

Harvests

There is a story told of Ed Ricketts, the eccentric marine biologist immortalized in John Steinbeck's Cannery Row. *After listening for days at a conference to theories of what caused the crash of the West Coast's sardine fishery, Ricketts stood up, a shiny object half concealed in one hand.*

"You want to know where all the sardines went?" he said. "I'll show you. We put them all in these little tins."

Water pollution, loss of habitats, disease, and natural cycles—all have played roles in the declines of the Chesapeake's fabled abundance of fish and shellfish. But the role played by both sport and commercial fishermen in taking seafood out of the bay faster than it can grow more is often underestimated. Without sound management of harvests, even the healthiest Chesapeake imaginable could not withstand the capacity of today's technology and large populations to overfish. In today's impaired bay environment, close attention to how much fishermen catch is more critical than ever before. Even the bay's greatest fish comeback story of the past decade, the resurgence of the striped bass, or rockfish, is raising

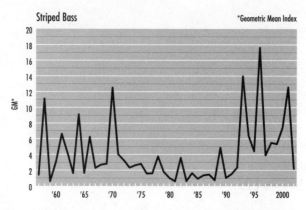

(a) Striped bass, called rockfish on the bay, were a prime sport and commercial fishery, but fishing pressure drove the stocks down to the point that in the early 1980s young of the year surveys showed few fish spawned in those years. Scientists predicted the stock would crash, and Maryland in 1985 and Virginia in 1989 placed moratoria on the fishery. As the numbers of mature fish increased, the numbers of the young of the year also climbed until fishery scientists felt the moratorium could be lifted in 1990. [Maryland Department of Natural Resources data]

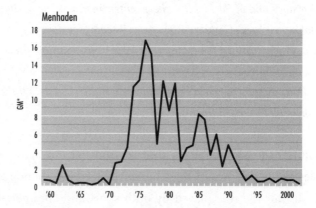

(b) The menhaden fishery is the largest commercial fishery in the bay and a vital piece of the bay's web of life. Young of the year surveys have shown variability in the past, but in the recent years, fishery scientists have warned that fishing pressure may be too great, and the young of the year survey is showing fewer fish. [Maryland Department of Natural Resources data]

FIGURE 3.1A–C. Trends in Three Major Bay Fisheries: Striped Bass (Rockfish), Menhaden, and Shad.

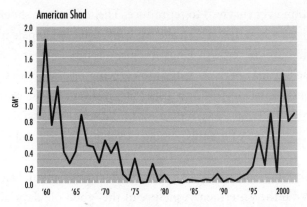

(c) Shad once were the symbol of the bay's productivity, but they were fished to the point that the fishery crashed. It was closed in Maryland in 1979 and Virginia followed. Since then, fishways and lifts on the dams have reopened the rivers to the spawning run, and restocking programs have been instituted. Numbers of shad are increasing. [Maryland Department of Natural Resources data]

unexpected challenges for fish management and posing questions about the modern estuary's ability to support all the life it once knew.

Lessons of the Rockfish

The story of the rockfish's decline and return—and the new issues it has raised—holds lessons that apply broadly to stewardship of the Chesapeake's natural resources. Ranging from the Carolinas to Maine, and growing to more than 4 feet long and 90 pounds, since colonial times the rock has been one of the bay's and the East Coast's premiere commercial and sport species. Of this entire coastal population, an estimated 90 percent are born in the Chesapeake and its tributary rivers.

Rockfish can live for thirty years, but by the 1970s, as fishing pressure soared coastwide, more than half of all those spawned in the Chesapeake each year were being harvested as soon as they reached legal size, at two to three years of age. This practice of cutting their numbers quickly in half, halving them again the next year, and so on, and carried out for several years before the females matured at age six or seven, meant that only a tiny fraction ever survived to reproduce. The toll it took shocked scientists years later when they did an age study of large, old female rockfish by counting the annual growth rings in their otoliths, or ear bones. They found these big spawners, so critical to carrying on the species, were virtually nonexistent from 1972 to 1981. Overfishing, before it was ended during the 1980s by a severe reduction in harvests, coastwide, had come within a year or two of literally wiping out the rockfish's ability to renew itself.

Sportfishermen on the bay during those times caught just as many rockfish as did the watermen. A picture of the "good ole days" that ran in an Eastern Shore newspaper showed two anglers squatting proudly in their boat, while the third grinned up from a pile of rockfish that had been arranged to completely cover him, head to toe, with plenty more spilling off the sides of the pile. They had made the catch in only three hours. No sportfisherman ever thought he was as much a threat as the few thousand commercial watermen who used up to 5 or 6 miles of nets and sometimes returned with daily harvests measured in tons. And, individually, the sportsman wasn't a threat—but there were close to a million of them.

Historically, there was ample precedent for fishing the Chesapeake beyond its capacity. From the time of Captain John Smith's journals, the bay had been framed as a place of incredible natural abundance—with a heavy-handed implication that it was a table set by nature especially for humans to exploit. The early settlers were too few to do serious damage to the bay, but that would change dramatically. Oyster harvests soared from fewer than a million bushels a year in 1840 to greater than 15 million bushels in 1884. That all-time peak of harvest, which dwarfs today's baywide harvests of as few as 80,000 bushels, did not represent anything that was sustainable, even in a perfectly healthy bay environment. Rather, it more resembled strip-mining of the bay's historical shellfish treasures.

Beginning in the early 1900s, the same fate befell shad, a fish that enjoyed status as a food and sport species the equal of the rockfish. Shad were netted and shipped by rail out of bay ports such as Crisfield, Maryland, in quantities up to several boxcar loads in a night. From the time of George Washington, who ran a major shad netting operation from

Mount Vernon on the Potomac, large sections of the bay were virtually closed off by nets during spring. One shad fishing operation in the early 1900s regularly strung a huge net across nearly half the upper Chesapeake in the rich spawning grounds just below the mouth of the Susquehanna River. Shad fishing has now been closed in Maryland's bay waters for some twenty years for lack of fish. Only recently has the species shown any signs of revival.

The rockfish was spared the long-term, dismal status of the oyster and the shad. One reason—a lesson for managing all species—was a scientific survey of the species' annual spawning success begun by Maryland biologists in 1954, when the fish was so abundant no one could conceive it would ever be in short supply. It would become one of the best sets of long-term data on any of the bay's species. Like most fish that spawn in bay rivers each spring, the rock's success in reproducing varies widely from year to year, depending on variations in climate and food supply, and probably to some extent on luck. Only by collecting data over long periods of time can we see trends that help sort out human impacts from the bay's considerable natural variability. Through the 1970s and 1980s, as arguments raged over whether rock were really being overfished, the humble spawning survey kept pointing out, more and more forcefully as the years went by, that for whatever reason the species was no longer reproducing well.

One of the arguments made by those who wanted to continue fishing as usual was that rockfish produced so many eggs, millions from a single large female, that as long as even a few were left to spawn, they could produce huge numbers of young, could "bring the species back," if environmental conditions were favorable. The flaw in the argument is that many of the bay's spawning fish are, in effect, gamblers who spread their bets. Environmental conditions are almost never uniformly right for success across hundreds of miles of spawning waters scattered throughout widely separated river systems, but if all those areas are flooded each year with spawning fish, some are bound to hit the jackpot. But if overfishing removes too many spawners from the action, their ability as a population to cover all their bets, or possibilities for success, goes down. And at some point, so does spawning success.

The importance of grind-it-out, long-term monitoring of the bay environment—such as the rockfish spawning survey, now approaching its fiftieth anniversary—cannot be overstated. It is always a tempting place for governments to cut budgets in tough economic times; like tree plant-ing in public parks, no one notices the impact for a while. But had similar monitoring of submerged grasses, dissolved oxygen, nutrient pollution, crabs, and other keystones of a healthy bay been kept meticulously since 1954, there is little doubt that restoration of the Chesapeake would be years farther down the road today.

Two other factors—both too often missing from attempts to manage the bay's fish—played a crucial role in bringing rockfish back from the brink. The first was a healthy investment of state and federal money in solid research that helped make sense of the debates that swirled: Was the problem natural cycles? Toxic chemicals? Was it really necessary to ban fishing when many catch restrictions had already been put in place?

It was this growing body of scientific evidence that gave Maryland's governor and its secretary of natural resources the confidence, in the clos-ing months of 1984, to make Maryland the first East Coast state to ban all taking of rockfish—a hugely controversial move with significant political risks. The ban stopped fishing just in time to save the fish hatched during a moderately good year of reproduction in 1982—they would have been catchable size by early 1985. No one could have known it then, but there would not be another good spawn until 1989. With the rock depleted by years of overfishing, if the 1982 fish had not been protected, it is quite possible the species could never have recovered.

The other critical factor in the rock's comeback was a law passed by Congress in 1984 that gave a coastwide fish commission the power and money to enforce conservation plans for rock in all the states through which they migrated. This federal oversight led to sharply reduced fishing throughout the rockfish's entire range, from Maine to the Carolinas. The law was extended to other species in 1993, though without adequate funding for developing management plans in many cases. But it recog-nized what Congress had concluded decades earlier when it regulated mi-gratory waterfowl (ducks, geese and swans): Without enforceable

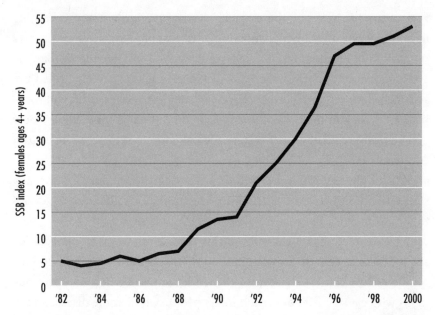

FIGURE 3.2. **Striped Bass (Rockfish) Spawning Stock.** Since the fishing moratoria in Maryland in 1985 and in Virginia in 1989, the numbers of mature female
rockfish have steadily increased, rebuilding the population. [Chesapeake Bay
Program data]

oversight, several states acting independently find it almost impossible to
decide who gets how much of a shared natural resource.

The inability of the states to act jointly to conserve the rock was costly.
Economic studies showed that the decline in rockfish in less than a
decade leading up to the ban cost 7,500 jobs in the fishing and tourism
industry and an estimated $220 million in lost commercial activity re-
lated to rockfishing.

A COMEBACK—AND NEW QUESTIONS

With virtually no fishing to eliminate them, the little rock born in 1982
grew into the largest population of the species in the modern history of
the bay. By 1989, they had become almost a nuisance to fishermen, who
could not keep the still illegal-to-possess rockfish out of their nets and off
their hooks. And when enough of the females born in 1982 finally matured enough to spawn in 1989, the result was the best hatch of young

rock in two decades, and the second best since 1954, when record keeping began. In 1990, after being banned for five years in Maryland and nearly two years in Virginia, rockfishing again opened in Chesapeake Bay. By 1995, as the results of several years of renewed good spawning piled up, scientists declared the species "fully recovered." But never again will rockfishing go back to the days of taking fish without any limits. Seasons now are carefully regulated, with states allotted annual quotas, or held to a conservative fishing rate.

So it might seem that the future of the rockfish is assured. But many scientists are not so sure. During the late 1990s, examinations of several thousand rockfish in both Maryland and Virginia showed that 50–70 percent are infected with a chronic wasting disease known as mycobacteriosis. It causes large ugly growths inside the fish, and in some cases lesions on the outer skin. Rarely seen in the wild, the disease doesn't affect humans who eat sick fish, but could infect people who handle diseased rock when they have open cuts or sores on their hands.

Currently, researchers say the findings raise more questions than answers. It's not known whether all infected fish eventually die, which might cause the population to crash again, or whether many eventually recover. Mycobacteria, like many of the bacteria that make humans get sick, are naturally present in the environment, though widespread infection usually occurs only in fish farms, where crowding and poor water quality are present. The question is, Why are so many rockfish in the Chesapeake becoming infected now? One answer may be the same reason that allows humans to get sick—stress weakens their immune systems. The bay to which the rock have come back in huge numbers may be an unhealthier place than the pre-1970s bay in which they flourished before overfishing took its toll. Rockfish now are "squeezed" each summer, scientists think, by low oxygen in the polluted bay's deeper, cooler waters. This forces them closer to the surface, where summer temperatures are hotter than the fish prefer. Sandwiched between layers of the bay that are too hot and those that are too low in oxygen, there may be too many fish competing in too little habitat.

The species may also be stressed by too little nutrition for its burgeoning numbers in today's bay. One of its most important food sources, a small, oily fish called menhaden, has declined dramatically in the Chesapeake since the 1980s. "All our best and most valued food fishes are only menhaden in another shape," wrote the bay scientist W. K. Brooks in 1903. He meant that the menhaden are a key food for many of the larger predator species—and by implication, that we cannot manage the bay for the top fish without also managing for their food supply. Although it has been a century since Brooks wrote that, it is only in the last year or so that we have begun to manage the menhaden as if bay life other than fish depended on it—ospreys, eagles, and loons also feed heavily on menhaden. A commercial fishing industry that catches menhaden by the thousands of tons to sell as fishmeal, oil, and bait until recently had undue influence in deciding management policies for the species. As a result of overfishing, a run of unfavorable natural environmental conditions for spawning, and perhaps pollution, numbers of spawning menhaden have fallen to near-historic lows. Studies indicate that menhaden during the 1990s fell from as much as two-thirds of the rockfish diet to as little as 12 percent.

ARE ROCKFISH EATING ALL THE CRABS?

The need to learn how to manage the bay's fish populations as a whole rather than species by species is further highlighted by concerns that the current large numbers of rockfish may be eating too many blue crabs. Commercial watermen have been particularly vocal in arguing this, as crabs have declined to historic lows and as both Maryland and Virginia have placed more restrictions on crabbers. A study by the Virginia Institute of Marine Science in 2000 estimated that rockfish were eating about 75 million small blue crabs a year from underwater grass beds in the middle Chesapeake that serve as a refuge for young crabs. That number, however, amounted to less than 5 percent of all the little crabs estimated to be hiding in the grass beds—some 1.6 billion.

Furthermore, the scientists said, natural mortality is huge for the tiny (the size of your thumbnail or less) crabs eaten by rockfish—that is, most of them get eaten by something anyhow (most frequently by other crabs). On the other hand, the size crabs caught by watermen, 3 inches across or larger, have survived to the point that natural mortality is quite low—not much but humans eat them at that size. The conclusion was that rockfish are not nearly as significant a factor in the scarcity of blue crabs as is human harvesting. However, scientists emphasize that much remains unknown: Did rockfish eat an even lower percentage of crabs in the past, when grass beds were more abundant in the bay, or when they had more menhaden to eat than now? How many little crabs are they eating outside of the diminished grass beds, where the crabs are less able to hide? How many do they eat in the spring (the scientists did their study in the fall)? In addition, there are suggestions that other species of fish currently in abundance, such as croakers, could be eating small crabs.

Managing Fish—The Big Picture

Currently, human ability to understand all the interactions among predators and prey in the bay is not good enough for management purposes. It is complicated by the growing realization that some species, including oysters and menhaden, are valuable in their own right for the "environmental services" they perform. Both oysters and menhaden, when they feed, filter tremendous amounts of polluting algae from bay waters (see Chapter 4, "Resilience").

But there are tantalizing clues to how we might someday be better able to tell fishermen what they can take each year and still sustain the overall health of the system. Consider the bay anchovy, which may be an even more important food for rockfish and other top predator fish than the menhaden. The anchovy (only distantly related to the ones on your pizza) seldom grows to more than a few inches and lives only about a year. It takes hundreds to weigh a pound, but in a good year there may be as many as 50 billion in the bay. They are incredible spawners, producing 150 times as many eggs, per pound of body weight, as do rockfish.

This critical food supply can vary in abundance as much as ninefold from year to year, and being able to forecast these huge, natural variations could have important implications for understanding interactions among the rockfish and other species that it eats. For example, it seems that wet spring weather can hamper reproduction of sea nettles, which boosts numbers of another gelatinous species known as ctenophores, or comb jellies, whose larvae are preyed upon by nettles. This, in turn, is bad news for anchovies, as comb jellies eat their eggs and larvae and compete with them for food (sea nettles also eat anchovies, but not as effectively as comb jellies). While there are other factors involved in anchovy abundance, a wet spring, with fewer nettles and more comb jellies, can mean billions fewer anchovies for rockfish to eat. A dry spring would bring the reverse scenario.

The future of managing the bay's seafood resources clearly lies in understanding and working with such interactions—the old ways of trying to optimize yields from numerous individual species at the same time is nearly impossible and, in fact, is unnatural. There are simply too many, complex interactions between prey and predators, and too many climate-driven variables. A new generation of managers—and fishermen—will have to be more flexible and opportunistic, using better knowledge of multispecies interactions to step up harvests of whatever is "winning" at any given time in the bay and to reduce pressure on what is currently "losing." A 1998 fisheries workshop on the bay that drew experts from around the world concluded that such multispecies management "is not rocket science . . . it is a lot harder."

Crabs—A Historic Opportunity Lost

The Chesapeake produces 40–50 percent of the national harvest of blue crab, a species that ranges abundantly from Maine to Mexico. Dockside values of the catch range as high as $100 million a year. With rockfish now managed more strictly, and with oysters in steep decline, the blue crab, *Callinectes sapidus* (literally, "most savory beautiful swimmer"), has become the Chesapeake's last, great commercial fishery—and an imperiled one, despite long-stated intentions to prevent that. "The blue crab is our test species for effective fisheries management," the late L. Eugene Cronin, an eminent bay biologist, was fond of saying. "It spends its entire life in the bay; it ranges the entire bay, it is of exceptional value, and every aspect of harvesting it is susceptible to our management—if we fall short of good management for this species, it is difficult to imagine real success for any species in the bay," Cronin explained.

Indeed, when *Turning the Tide* was first published a decade ago, it noted that crabs would soon provide "a test case of whether or not we have truly entered a new era of fishery management." Catches at the time were still fairly healthy, averaging 75 million pounds a year; but the scientific evidence pointed ominously to increasing pressure—watermen in both Maryland and Virginia were using more gear and fishing harder each year just to take the same amount of crabs. Crab pots, the gear used by commercial watermen to take the majority of bay crabs, had risen in use, baywide, from around 60,000 pots in 1948 to around 665,000 by 1987—and numbers continued to rise during the 1990s. Less quantifiable, but also clearly growing, were recreational catches, the ones made by you and me and our kids with chicken-neck baits on strings.

Federal and bay state governments pledged to make it a priority to limit crab harvests at levels that would sustain healthy catches. That would be, *Turning the Tide* said in 1991, "the first time measures have been taken to conserve a species *before* it was in decline."

It didn't happen. A major push for new crabbing limits by the CBF and the governor in Maryland in 1995 failed to overcome opposition by commercial fishing interests and legislators. Cooperation between Maryland and Virginia, critical to managing a species that migrates freely across the state line dividing the bay, never jelled. And scientific consensus on the extent of the problem and its solutions was lacking. Crabs can vary in number hugely, and naturally, from year to year, and probably also in longer cycles of a decade or more. The long-term monitoring to sort out human and natural roles in those variations did not prove convincing enough to halt business as usual in the crab industry.

The result was that the opportunity to act in advance of a decline for the first time in bay history was lost. Crab harvests declined steadily after the early 1990s, to around 60 percent of the long-term average harvest. Worse, the number of adult female spawners has been reduced to perhaps the lowest levels in the half century or so that records have been kept. As of 2002, crabs in the Chesapeake remained at these low levels.

Nonetheless, real progress finally seems to be occurring in the management of crabs. A joint effort by Maryland and Virginia and the federal government has made a compelling scientific case for the troubled state of the blue crab and has outlined solutions that should begin putting har-

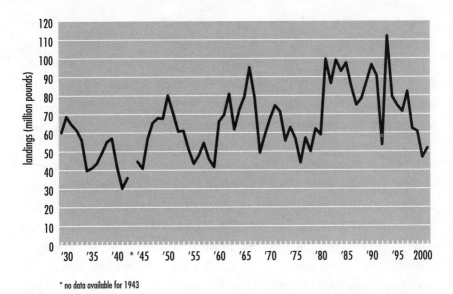

* no data available for 1943

FIGURE 3.3. **Trends in Blue Crab Catches: Maryland and Virginia.** Blue crabs are the best-known fishery and one of the last viable commercial fisheries in the bay. Recently, scientists have warned that blue crabs are overfished, and a commission has put regulations in place to decrease the catch. These landing data show a highly variable but slowly increasing catch. What they do not show is that during this period, the "unit of effort" expended to catch each crab has drastically increased. It now takes far more effort, with more gear and more hours spent, to catch the same numbers of crabs than it did in earlier decades. In addition, the size of crabs has been declining. [Chesapeake Bay Program data]

vests on a healthy and sustainable track. Both states have committed to reducing crabbing pressure by 15 percent by 2004 and are passing regulations to do that. The intent is that harvests will still fluctuate up and down, as environmental conditions produce more or fewer crabs from year to year. But regulations will be set to ensure that the number of adult spawning crabs never sinks below a "safe" level determined by scientists as sufficient to maintain a healthy reproduction. Although this is reason for optimism, the current harvest reductions are only a starting point, intended to stabilize the population. To rebuild a healthy fishery that will provide a dependable livelihood for watermen will require a long-term, comprehensive crab management plan—one that may well require further cutbacks in fishing in the near term.

With Chesapeake Bay watermen almost totally dependent on crabbing nowadays, one of the thorniest issues the states face is how to curtail fishing pressure equitably. The success of the current management efforts depends on this. Although the blue crab is a single species, and one that is spread throughout the entire bay, managers who would divvy it up in a time of scarcity could hardly find a more difficult task.

This is because the blue crab fishery of the Chesapeake is incredibly fragmented. Many different types of gear are used to catch the crab—hardcrab pots, peeler pots, trotlines, dip nets, scrapes, bank traps, dredges—and all are effective in different places at different times and at different stages of the crab's life cycle. The fishery is also split between those who crab the upper, fresh to brackish waters of the bay, mostly in Maryland, and those who crab the saltier waters of the lower bay, mostly in Virginia. Female crabs tend to stay in saltier waters, with males ranging farther up the bay and its Maryland tributaries. Regulations weighted toward preserving spawning females sound good to many Maryland crabbers, but Virginia's total harvest is 80 percent females.

Marylanders also tend to decry Virginia's harvesting of pregnant female crabs, egg "sponges" protruding visibly from their abdomens. Such fishing does look bad, and like every segment of crabbing, it needs to be better managed. But the fact is, crab potters in Maryland are catching mature, pregnant females every summer and fall as they swim south to bury for the winter. Visibly, these females—"sooks" as they are called—don't appear pregnant because they aren't yet showing any egg masses. But studies show that more than 99 percent of them have been impregnated.

Further splits exist between full-time and part-time crabbers—two-thirds of Virginia's are full time, but only a third of Maryland's are. Problems of perception are also rampant. Scientists, looking at the whole bay, see a dramatic decline in crabs. But depending on what part of the bay they traditionally crab, watermen during the last decade may have seen catches go up, plummet, or hold fairly steady.

Failure to deal with several other issues could also impede the current progress in managing the blue crab. While both Maryland and Virginia are moving rapidly to limit the overall number of crabbing licenses they issue, there remain huge numbers of crab pots that are already licensed, but not used. License holders thus have a giant, latent potential to increase fishing pressure by deploying all this unused gear if prices or crab numbers were to jump.

There is also a critical need to retain some sort of oversight, independent of the two states, to evaluate and compare the many different techniques each will employ to reduce crabbing pressure. The Chesapeake Bay Commission, representing the legislatures of the three bay watershed states, currently fills this role. But there is no assurance it will continue to be funded to do so.

The watermen's lament is that, to date, most of the focus has been on controlling their crabbing, while the real culprit is water quality and loss of habitat to pollution. Indeed, the bay's much diminished submerged grass beds, victim of too much sewage and polluted runoff from farms and pavements, were prime habitat for little crabs and refuge for crabs when they shed their shells to grow. Although major efforts are being made to bring habitat back, they will take years, and probably decades. In the short term, controlling fishing pressure is the only means of keeping the blue crab healthy. The states have also moved to limit recreational catches of crabs, which appear to be significant, but not nearly as large as commercial harvests.

The brightest hope may lie in the nature of the blue crab itself, a superbly resilient creature that is adapted to life in the Chesapeake Bay like few other species. The crab thrives even in Baltimore's polluted harbor and in Norfolk's Elizabeth River, both major bay hot spots for toxic chemicals. Baltimoreans catch them off the Patapsco sewage treatment plant and from heavily industrial shorelines. Pursued throughout the bay in every month of the year, caught in virtually every stage of its life cycle from spawning to mating, the crab miraculously has endured. It is, one biologist noted, "the only thing we catch in the bay that will try to bite us back."

The capacity of the crab to flourish in the bay can be glimpsed by this observation from W. K. Brooks, a Johns Hopkins marine biologist, who wrote in 1893: " . . . we were told, in 1884, by fishermen in the lower part of the Chesapeake Bay, that they were earning from $1.50 to $2.00 a day catching crabs to sell at one cent a dozen or ten cents a bushel; and these men seldom went to their work before sunrise or fished longer than til noon. In fact, most of them were home for the day at ten in the morning." Brooks's numbers work out to catching 1,800 to 2,400 crabs in a morning's work—and this was with relatively primitive gear (the crab pot would not be invented for another few decades). There is little doubt that if we give it half a chance, the blue crab will be with us as long as there is a Chesapeake.

Oysters: Rebuilding, Restoring

Chesapeake, or Chesepioc, is said to be an Indian word for Great Shellfish Bay. Certainly, the American oyster, *Crassostrea virginica,* is what the bay was all about for most of its history. "Oysters there be in whole banks and beds . . . some thirteen inches long," wrote William Strachey, a visitor to the bay in 1612. "The abundance of oysters is incredible . . . there are whole banks of them so that the ships must avoid them. I often cut them in two, before I could put them into my mouth," wrote a Swiss traveler, Francis Michel, a hundred years after Strachey.

And so it would continue to be for nearly another two centuries. It was not until the 1880s that gross overharvesting (see Figure 3.4) propelled the landings of oysters to a peak that crested, like a huge tidal wave, just before the twentieth century, then broke on an unrelenting downward trend that has left a harvest as thin as a lap of receding surf. Maryland and Virginia had the authority to better regulate harvests for virtually all this time, but failed to do so. From harvests that peaked at more than 15 million bushels a year, and still were counted in the millions of bushels as recently as the 1980s, oysters have fallen to a recent, pathetic annual harvest of 80,000 bushels baywide.

What overfishing and mismanagement began has been all but finished off by a combination of diseases and pollution that has ganged up on the oyster in recent decades. The decline has meant the annual loss of thousands of jobs and tens of millions of dollars, as well as the destruction of a hugely important natural filter for cleansing the water and an efficient mechanism for ordering the flows of food energy through the bay. In addition, oyster bottoms are in effect hard underwater platforms, or reefs,

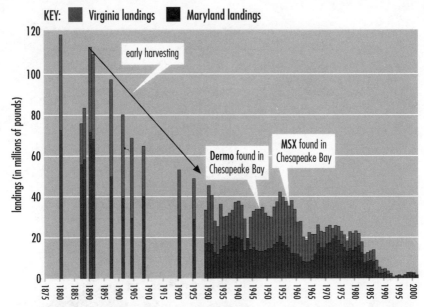

FIGURE 3.4. The Bay's Dwindling Oyster Harvest. Large-scale oyster harvesting using dredge boats began in the 1870s. Over the next century the numbers of pounds of oyster meat landed steadily declined because of fishing pressure. In the 1960s the disease MSX was introduced to the bay and the native disease, Dermo, began to take a heavier toll on the depleted oyster stocks. [National Research Council data]

forming a base for larger communities of life. Sponges, worms, minnows, and the young of crabs and dozens of other species inhabit the millions of protective nooks and crannies provided by the shelly surface of the reef (see Figure 3.5). All these in turn attract larger fish. Moreover, other filtering creatures settle atop oyster bars, amplifying their cleansing effects on the water.

"It is beyond our ability to imagine what it was like when the bay's oyster reefs were all intact," says James Wesson, Virginia's chief oyster restoration scientist. These great "rocks," as the oyster reefs were also known, once stretched for as much as 15 miles in places along rivers such as Virginia's James. The breakup of the reefs began in the first few decades of the nineteenth century as New England dredge vessels invaded the Chesapeake, having exhausted the oyster troves of their own region (see Box

FIGURE 3.5. The Oyster Reef: A Hospitable Home.

3.1). By 1900, when more than a thousand boats dragged the bay bottom with their heavy, toothed iron dredges, it is likely that virgin reefs beneath the water were as scarce as old-growth forest is in Virginia and Maryland today. This leveling of the bay's oystery, hilly bottom was a dramatic change to the region's geography across hundreds of square miles—as if the Shenandoah Valley's rolling landscape had been bulldozed and flattened to resemble the Eastern Shore. But occurring underwater, out of sight and out of mind, it attracted scant notice.

Box 3.1. The Age of Exploitation

This account, drawn from old oyster journals, tells of the opening of an oyster season in Connecticut during the early 1800s. The beds there were exhausted and the businessmen, in search of new beds, sent their large fleets of ships south to the Chesapeake. The age of exploitation of the Chesapeake oyster had begun.

"It was a time of great excitement, and nowhere greater than along the Quinepiac [river] . . . as midnight approached, men dressed in oilskin and carrying oars, paddles, rakes and tongs, collected all along the shore, where a crowd of women and children assembled to see the fun.

"No eye could see the face of the great church clock on the hill, but lanterns glimmered upon a hundred watch-dials and then were set down, as only a coveted minute remained . . . it was like an electric shock as the great bell struck a deep-toned peal. Backs bent to oars and paddles churned the water. From opposite banks, waves of boats leaped out and advanced towards one another in the darkness, as though bent on mutual annihilation.

"Before the twelve blows upon the loud bell had ceased their reverberations, the oyster beds had been reached, tongs were scraping the long-rested bottom and the season's campaign upon the Quinepiac had begun.

" . . . a week of this sort of attack, however, usually sufficed to clean the bottom so thoroughly that subsequent raking was of small account. . . . at the present time the bed does not yield marketable oysters . . . "

The year 2000 commitment of the federal-state bay restoration program to begin restoring and rebuilding oyster reefs is the most positive news about oysters in many years. The commitment calls for increasing the bay's oysters by tenfold by 2010.

Virginia and Maryland are both spending millions of dollars, and seeking tens of millions more in federal money, to construct hundreds of oyster reefs around the bay and its rivers. Experiments have shown the value of reefs: Oysters spawn more efficiently when clumped together in their natural reef formations, as opposed to scattered about on the bay bottom; the protective crevices of the reef allow better survival of little oysters; and oysters raised off the bottom are less prone to being smothered with sediment.

Related restoration activities explore new techniques. Buying watermen's harvests from areas with larger, older oysters and using them as the spawning stock on reconstructed reefs is a technique pioneered by the Chesapeake Bay Foundation. It is hoped that these older oysters have developed some natural resistance to the oyster diseases Dermo and MSX that are rampant in the bay. Experiments are also under way to find alternatives to scarce oyster shells with which to create new reefs. Baltimore's famous old Memorial Stadium, once home to the Orioles baseball team and football's Baltimore Colts, was demolished in 2002 and given new life as an oyster reef in 7 to 13 feet of water near Baltimore. And state and private investment in oyster hatcheries is providing record numbers of young oysters, or *spat*, for planting on reefs.

A CLOUDED FUTURE

Activity to restore oysters has never been more encouraging. And appreciation of oysters as natural filterers of the bay has gripped the public and politicians as never before. Yet, the odds seem long for achieving great progress within the next decade in restoring a bright future for the native oyster, now at 1 or 2 percent of its historic numbers. It is even remotely possible that *Crassostrea virginica*'s very future as a species in the bay could be in question. As it did a decade ago, the specter of disease nearly obscures everything else. MSX, which first appeared in the 1950s, and Dermo, both caused by microscopic parasites, continue to kill *C. virginica*.

Research budgets aimed at the disease problem, and at breeding disease-resistant oysters, are relatively modest considering the importance of the oyster. Four decades of study have not yielded a solution to the oyster diseases. Breeders have developed oysters with increased tolerance to MSX, and oysters resistant to Dermo, but not oysters tolerant of both diseases. And it is unclear whether disease-resistant oysters are able to pass on their resistance to successive generations. Yet, as research continues, large-scale planting of disease-tolerant strains of baby oysters demonstrates encouraging results with increasing spat sets and longer-lived oysters.

Researchers note that the disease problem is not directly related to pollution; however, it is possible that stresses from oxygen-poor water and from low levels of toxic chemicals common throughout the bay have made oysters more vulnerable to disease.

NEW OYSTER ON THE BLOCK

The disease dilemma has for several years fanned interest in finding alternatives to the native oyster, other oyster species that would survive in the bay and that are naturally tolerant of the diseases. Experiments with an oyster originally from Asia and grown on the West Coast, *Crassostrea gigas,* found that it did not survive well in the Chesapeake. The *C. gigas* experiment, however, illustrates the perils of introducing a species to an ecosystem. Scientists using DNA comparisons recently proved that MSX, whose origins had always been mysterious, almost certainly came from *C. gigas* oysters that were put into the Chesapeake and Delaware Bays decades ago as unauthorized experiments. While the oysters themselves didn't survive, the MSX parasite, which evolved with *C. gigas* and is relatively harmless to it, survived and went on to devastate the entire oyster industry.

In 2002, interest was building to a high pitch for another exotic oyster from Asia, *Crassostrea ariakensis.* Virginia has been experimenting with *C. ariakensis* since 1996 under controlled conditions to prevent releasing its spawn or any disease into the bay. This latest oyster on the block presents a tempting scenario. It looks like the native oyster and tastes good. At least during experiments, it grew a lot faster and survived better than the native in the presence of MSX and Dermo. At best, employing *C. ariakensis* in Chesapeake oyster restoration programs could revitalize the oyster industry and bring back a critical natural filter to the algae-clogged bay. It would not be a quick fix; it would take decades to regain the numbers of oysters found in the 1970s and 1980s, let alone anything like the bay's original shellfish stocks. At worst, such a bold experiment might unleash some new, MSX-like disease, perhaps affecting other species such as blue crabs. There is also evidence that *C. ariakensis* doesn't form reefs, where small oysters can grow among the shells of older oysters, protected from hungry blue crabs and other predators. In any case, assuming the new oyster survived as well in the bay as early experiments indicate, its release to the wild would likely be irreversible, and we would have to be prepared for the possibility of saying goodbye to the native *C. virginica*, the product of thousands of years of evolution as an integral piece of the bay's natural system.

There might be a middle ground. The technology exists to mass-produce the new oysters in sterile versions to be used solely as a basis for oyster farming. Even that could have social consequences. What would happen to the market for wild, native oysters harvested by watermen? Virginia, which has virtually no oyster industry left to lose, is pushing ahead with experimentation with *C. ariakensis*. Maryland has been more cautious and is just beginning to study the new oyster's possibilities. The CBF has called for stepped-up research and evaluation of *C. ariakensis* so that consequences of releasing it can be thoroughly understood. In the meantime, it would be a mistake to slow the considerable momentum that has been painstakingly built during the last decade for restoration of the native oyster. North Carolina is also experimenting with the new oyster, and many experts fear it is only a matter of time before someone puts it, authorized or not, into Chesapeake waters. It is impossible to predict now which is the oyster of the bay's future; it is possible only to know that oysters, lots of them, are one of the keys to a healthy bay.

Shad: Welcome Home

It did not take a fisheries scientist to see how the nets of commercial fishermen virtually sealed off the bay rivers to which spawning American shad returned each spring from the ocean. Recreational fishermen also lined the banks, though they took a far smaller toll. In addition to being caught as they spawned, the shad were netted at sea as they moved close to the coasts on their journeys to and from the spawning rivers. Catches in the bay, once registered in the millions of pounds annually, were almost nonexistent when Maryland, under threat of a lawsuit by recreational fishermen, closed its shad season in 1979. Virginia eventually followed suit, though not until the 1990s. Taking American shad, and its smaller cousin, the hickory shad, has been illegal ever since in Chesapeake waters. Yet even after fishery managers sharply reduced fishing pressure in the bay, Maryland, Virginia, and other coastal states unwisely continued to allow fishing for the species as it migrated along their ocean coasts. We overfished the American shad well past anything we did to the rockfish. A prized sport and eating fish that grows to 8 pounds or more, the shad reached the point where it was unable to rebound on its own.

The last decade has been marked by the first real progress in the shad's modern history in the bay. Maryland, Pennsylvania, Virginia, and the federal government have stocked tens of millions of baby shad in bay rivers. Salmon-like, shad somehow "imprint" to the waters where they are born or are released as fry and return there each year from the oceans to spawn. The states have also been reconnecting the bay's amputated tributaries—removing dams or installing fish passages through or over them, reopening some 1,200 miles of historic shad and herring spawning habitat. Plans are on schedule to reopen another 400 miles soon.

The greatest success has come on the mighty Susquehanna River, which enters the main bay at its head above Havre de Grace and extends inland more than 440 miles into New York State. Fish passages have been constructed there over four big hydro dams, including the 110-foot-high Conowingo near the Maryland-Pennsylvania line. For the first time in more than a century, shad can run all the way to Binghamton, New York.

In 2001, nearly 200,000 returning American shad were passed over the dam at Conowingo, up from 80,000 in 1999. Surveys show reproduction rates in the upper bay at levels not seen since the 1950s. Shad returning to the upper bay and Susquehanna are estimated now at close to a million fish, compared to a few thousand when the season was closed in 1979. Even more significant, most of the young shad being taken in surveys now are wild fish (those released from hatcheries are specially marked to differentiate them). That means natural reproduction is taking over from the states' fish-stocking efforts.

The return of the shad means more than can be measured in pounds or dollars, although Pennsylvania projects more than $30 million in economic benefits from returning a sportfishery for shad to the river. Historically, the shad, thronging virtually every Chesapeake tributary between March and May, formed a link between the bay and the people of its drainage basin as far inland as Cooperstown, New York, the foothills of Virginia's Blue Ridge Mountains, and nearly the eastern edge of the Eastern Shore. "Never was the coming of the shad looked for with more anxiety or hailed with more cordial delight," recounts a history of Pennsylvania's Wyoming County from 1773: "The fishing season dissipated all fears, and the dim eye was soon exchanged for the glance of joy and the dry, sunken cheek of want assumed the plump appearance of health and plenty." "Their coming was the principal food for all the inhabitants . . . no farmer or man with a family was without his barrels of shad," wrote the *Berwick* (Pennsylvania) *Independent* in 1881. "Just as the sacred cod of Massachusetts is the accepted emblem of [that] state, so the shad may rightly be considered the piscatorial representative of the states bordering the Chesapeake," wrote Rachel Carson in 1936.

Shad are also just beginning comebacks in other rivers where stocking from hatcheries followed the success of the Susquehanna; the Patuxent, the Choptank, the Potomac, and the James are all showing an upward trend of returns, and the start of natural reproduction. The smaller hickory shad are also making dramatic comebacks in both the upper bay and some Virginia rivers. Despite the encouraging trends, the shad still has a long way back. The long-term restoration goal is to pass 4 million shad over Conowingo Dam and 2 million over York Haven, the last dam before Binghamton. To date, about 12,000 shad a year are making it past York Haven. Power turbines in the dams will also undoubtedly kill some of the little fish on their first trip back downstream to the ocean. Adult shad that ran far up the Susquehanna may have expended so much energy that they didn't survive the return trip even in the pre-dam era, although on shorter runs up other bay rivers, shad do return to spawn several years in a row.

The final piece of the shad restoration puzzle is the phasing out, by 2005, of commercial fishing for the species as it migrates along the ocean coasts of Maryland and Virginia. This is critical, given the expansion of the "ocean intercept" fishery as fishing for shad in the bay was curtailed. It remains to be seen whether looming court challenges to the ocean phase-out materialize. If the phase-out proceeds on schedule, it seems likely that future generations will be able to enjoy the sport and taste of a healthy population of Chesapeake shad. Meanwhile, overfishing has already meant an entire generation, twenty years, grew up scarcely knowing this premiere bay species; and almost another generation may pass before the bay enjoys healthy shad runs throughout its tributaries.

Management of Other Species

Progressive state, baywide, or coastwide management plans now cover most major bay fish species, and this marks real progress from a decade ago. The state of these plans, and the state of each species, varies considerably (see Figure 3.6). For example, some of the states through which striped bass migrate are spending on the order of several million dollars a year for the research and monitoring needed to manage the fish sustainably. Spending on the management of blue crabs in Maryland and Virginia is less than a quarter of the spending on striped bass, and the management of most other species gets considerably less funding than crabs. Where good management, backed by good science, monitoring, and adequate funding, is employed, it gets results. Weakfish, or yellowfin trout, is one popular bay sport and commercial species to which considerable attention has been paid in the last decade; and its numbers are rebounding nicely now that fishing pressure has been reduced.

It is important to realize why good management takes money. It is not enough to know how many of a species are being caught—in fact, that may be the last thing managers need to know. Harvests often just represent fishing effort, which in turn is influenced by the price fishermen get, by the weather, by what else is available to catch instead, by how many hours watermen are fishing and how much gear (miles of net, numbers of crab pots) they use. In order to understand a fishery, its managers also

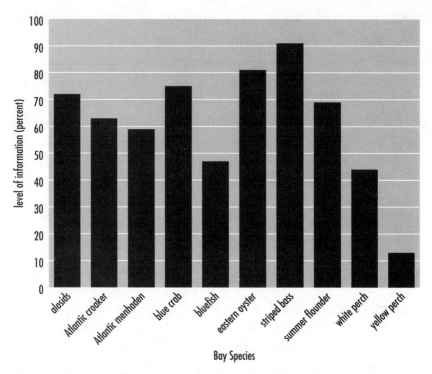

FIGURE 3.6. **State of Knowledge for Managing Selected Fisheries.** Scientists must understand far more than how many of a species are caught in order to effectively manage a fishery. They also must understand such things as the species' life cycles, age distributions, habitat needs, and spawning habits. [*Plans and Practices for CBSAC Research,* Miller and Stone]

need to know roughly how many fish there are, the age structure of the population (a wide spread of ages is a good indicator that fish population is in good health), the number of spawning-age fish, the health of species on which the fish in question prey, the migration patterns, the annual spawning success, and the survival rates. All this, and perhaps other information, must be gathered independently from just looking at how many fish are being caught. Most such data become useful only after they have been gathered long enough to see trends developing. Yet there is a tendency to fund the gathering of such information only when a species is in trouble.

Collecting data only when a fishery is in trouble is not good management, but it is not unusual. Consider what is known about the status of several major bay species:

- *American eel.* Numbers decreasing, possibly overfished, but too little information to say for sure.
- *Croaker, or hardhead.* Abundant in the last decade, after decades of depressed numbers. Upsurge is due largely to better management of a class of fishing boats known as trawlers, whose large nets took huge numbers of hardheads and other species as they migrated out of the bay each fall. Virginia banned trawling in 1989. Coastal restrictions to reduce the incidental, or "bycatch," of juvenile weakfish by trawl boats operating south of Virginia also helped croakers. Favorable climate has helped, too.
- *White perch.* Reproducing well. Being managed sustainably in Maryland, which has the bulk of the bay's population. More information needed to say accurately how healthy.
- *Yellow perch.* Moratoriums on fishing for them in some bay tributaries, and more limits on catches in others. Spawning appears to be improving, and harvests, though still very low, are increasing.
- *River herring.* Numbers severely depleted, but improving. Should benefit from being included in management plans for shad.
- *Horseshoe crabs.* Numbers have been decreasing sharply during the last decade. A recent management plan that reined in overharvest of the crabs for eel and conch bait should improve the situation. The crabs are important to migrating shorebirds, which depend on plucking their eggs from spawning beaches to fuel their northward flights in the spring. The crabs and their eggs are also food for a variety of fish.
- *Hard clams.* A gradual but noticeable decline in catches in recent years raises concerns. Too little information to assess.
- *Soft clams.* Low and consistently declining catches during the past decade. Too little information to assess.
- *Summer flounder.* Coming back slowly but steadily after curtailment of fishing pressure.
- *Red drum.* Likely that overfishing is occurring, but fishing limits in place may rebuild the population.

Watermen

The beleaguered state of the Chesapeake Bay waterman may provide the ultimate indication of the state of the bay's fisheries. There are fewer than 7,000 licensed commercial watermen in Maryland, down from 9,000 a decade ago. Virginia reports about 3,000 now, down from an estimated 5,000. The very term, waterman, recognizes that bay seafood harvesters have traditionally specialized in no single fishery, instead relying for a living on shifting frequently among catching everything from crabs and oysters to clams, rockfish, terrapins, eels, conchs, and even bloodworms. But in the last decade or two, watermen have seen their world shrink dramatically—oysters almost lost, the boom days of rockfishing gone. The picturesque oyster dredge boats, or skipjacks, that once plied the bay by the hundreds have all but vanished as working watercraft. Watermen nowadays are mostly crabbers, and here, too, they face increasing restrictions on how many crabs they can harvest. In the last decade, both Maryland and Virginia have moved toward limiting the number of watermen, freezing the number of licenses available for entering various bay fisheries.

Watermen are a paradox. On the one hand, they are a powerful symbol of the bay we want to preserve, and their preservation is a major motivation for the current bay restoration programs. Marylanders and Virginians (and vacationing Pennsylvanians) love the images of the men and the boats and their independent lifestyle. As most of us punch clocks and live lives increasingly disconnected from nature, watermen are still attuned to natural forces. Bay residents have a luxury that few developed regions enjoy—not just eating oysters on the half shell, but oysters caught by salty captains under full sail in century-old wooden skipjacks; not just rockfish stuffed with crab meat, but rock and crab that come from little communities along the bay's edge where quaint language persists and the harbors are the stuff of picture postcards.

On the other hand, having watermen around can be like having a large predator in your aquarium. It is their nature to be very, very good at exploiting any and all fishery resources. Working as they traditionally have in a *commons*—that is, public waters that are open to all citizens—it is not in the interest of any individual waterman to catch less than he can, for whatever he leaves would just be fair game for someone else. Thus, although the need for conservation is recognized by many watermen today, the practice of conservation is not fostered by the highly competitive arena in which they have to work. Both commercial and sport fishermen now use a range of modern electronics, mechanized gear, and abler, faster boats that make them far more effective than even a couple decades ago. In the absence of strong fisheries management, watermen are capable of quickly overwhelming the natural resource.

With more than a million sportfishermen using the bay, in contrast to fewer than 10,000 watermen, there is pressure to reserve species such as shad and rockfish for recreational catching alone and to manage crabs and other species to ensure an abundant catch for sportfishing interests. The money from a maximized sportfishing and tourism industry outstrips by far the economic value of commercial harvests.

Watermen meanwhile face other problems. Throughout the bay, their communities and lifestyles are either crumbling or under severe stress. There are many forces behind this besides the state of the bay's water quality, including modern expectations and college opportunities for their youth, and competition with condominium builders for their waterfront space.

On remote Smith Island, Maryland, 12 miles out in the bay, perhaps half of the homes that once belonged solely to watermen now are owned by New Yorkers, Washingtonians, and other "foreigners" from Norfolk, Richmond, Baltimore, and Pittsburgh. In Annapolis, Rock Hall, Solomons, and St. Michaels, all bay ports, dock space traditionally used for watermen's workboats shifts more every year to space for pleasure boats. The most recent round of restrictions on bay crabbers, designed to reduce harvest pressure by 15 percent, seems likely to reduce significantly the incomes of many crabbers, at least in the short term.

Several thousand watermen have left the water in recent decades, drawn to jobs with more security. Some have turned to aquaculture, especially in Virginia, where farming clams has become a highly successful, $40-million-a-year industry. A few are trying ecotourism, guiding birdwatchers in the marshes or taking the public "sport oystering" aboard their skipjacks. A 1999 sampling of full-time crabbers in Maryland and Virginia showed that 32 percent in Maryland and 27 percent in Virginia were age sixty or older. Only 3.3 percent in Maryland and 7.8 percent in Virginia were under thirty. It is enough to raise concerns about who will harvest seafood in the bay in the future. On the other hand, given the high demand for crabmeat, rockfish, and other Chesapeake bounty, it is hard to imagine that someone will not be working the bay's waters, as long as they remain productive.

Watermen and environmentalists will not always see eye to eye, despite sharing a natural alliance in wanting a high-quality, sustainable Chesapeake. Differences often arise from environmentalists' legitimate focus on the big picture and the long run, while watermen are just as legitimately focused on making a living in the here and now. Despite this, both groups in the last decade have begun to work together on restoration projects, from building oyster reefs and monitoring water quality, to replanting submerged grasses. A bay without the independent and outspoken waterman would undoubtedly be easier to manage; but a unique part of the region's human spirit would be missing, as well as one of its most powerful symbols for engaging the public in preserving the place.

Waterfowl

The twenty-two species of waterfowl—geese, ducks, and swans—commonly inhabiting Chesapeake Bay are among the most visible signals of natural abundance or decline. In their feeding and breeding, they depend on a range of bay habitats, from upland fields and stream banks to the marshes, to the shallow grass beds and to the shellfish in deeper bottom waters.

Still, caution must be taken in using waterfowl as indicators of bay health. Green-winged teal, for example, have increased markedly in the last decade. But like most waterfowl, they are highly migratory, spending only part of their year (wintertime) in the Chesapeake. Their recent increase in the bay is largely due to more favorable conditions where they breed in the midwestern prairies. Canada geese in the last several decades more than tripled their population, then fell so sharply that hunting for them was closed throughout the Chesapeake from 1995 to 2001. A key reason for the increase was the ability of the Canadas to adapt to feeding in tidewater grainfields, a "habitat" that was increasing even as pollution (partly from such grain farms) was killing underwater sea grasses, the goose's traditional food. The subsequent drop in geese that closed the hunting season was similarly less a failure of bay habitat than it was years of bad weather for breeding on the Canadas' northern tundra nesting grounds.

Overall, the number of waterfowl wintering on the Chesapeake has remained fairly consistent during several decades—around a million birds—as measured by a midwinter aerial survey conducted by federal and state biologists. That survey does not measure the total number of waterfowl using the bay, but it is a good index for determining trends in abundance. The seeming stability of the overall numbers, however, masks a number of shifts occurring in individual species (see Figure 3.7). Of the twenty-two varieties of waterfowl using the bay, fourteen meet the year 2000 goals of the bay restoration program—populations equal or better than in the mid-1970s (note that these are modest goals, since large declines had already occurred in many waterfowl between the 1940s and 1970s).

Eight species are below the goal, including some whose declines relate directly to declines in the Chesapeake environment. Redhead ducks, which numbered some 80,000 fifty years ago, feed almost exclusively on sea grasses. As the grasses declined by 90 percent during the 1970s and 1980s, redhead numbers crashed to fewer than 2,000 ducks counted in the late '80s (heavy hunting pressure was also a factor). Unable to adapt to feeding on land like Canada geese and some other species, redheads remain scarce, with fewer than 10,000 on the Chesapeake, despite a major upsurge in numbers nationwide.

Another prized duck of the Chesapeake in serious decline is the black duck, down from 100,000 in 1960 to around 25,000 nowadays. Black ducks are one of the few waterfowl that nest in the bay watershed, but breeding success continues to plummet. Black ducks have suffered from the widespread destruction of habitat by development and by changes in agriculture from hayfields, where they nested, to grain. It is also likely that

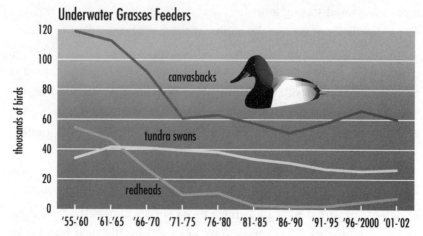

Underwater Grasses Feeders

(a) Canvasbacks, tundra swans, and redheads all fed primarily on underwater grasses. As the bay's grasses declined, canvasbacks switched to small snails; tundra swans adapted to eating grain in farm fields; but redheads, unable to switch their diet, have, for the most part, left the bay. [U.S. National Fish and Wildlife Service, Midwinter Survey data]

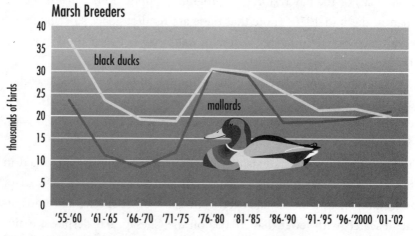

Marsh Breeders

(b) Black ducks and mallards breed in the Chesapeake's marshes as well as the prairie potholes of the northern plains. The secretive black ducks, faced with a decrease in habitat and an influx of people, have declined in numbers. The gregarious and adaptable mallards have become ubiquitous. [U.S. National Fish and Wildlife Service, Midwinter Survey data]

FIGURE 3.7A–C. **Chesapeake Bay Waterfowl Trends: Underwater Grass Feeders, Marsh Breeders, and Geese.**

Geese

(c) Canada and snow geese were both originally underwater grass feeders, but they have adapted to feeding in grainfields as the grasses declined. The numbers of both Canada and snow geese have been increasing. [U.S. National Fish and Wildlife Service, Midwinter Survey data]

rising sea levels are degrading the high marshes where they once nested into wetter areas, where nesting is difficult.

A counterpoint to the black duck decline is the rise of the mallard, which competes directly with the black duck for food and nesting areas and whose numbers have risen steadily around the bay in recent decades. The mallard is more adaptable, often nesting adjacent to human development, becoming semi-domesticated. A common sight these days waddling along docks and lawns edging the bay, mallards are often taken as a sign of environmental health—but they, and the habitat they require, are pale shades of the vanishing black duck.

Canvasbacks, another premiere bay duck whose numbers are just barely meeting current goals, have done so partly by making a remarkable adaptation. The species, like the redhead, can hardly walk to feed on land. But it was able to shift from eating about 90 percent sea grasses to about 90 percent hard-shelled clams and snails on the bay bottom. Canvasbacks have declined sharply since the 1950s, but appear to have stabilized in recent years at around 45,000–50,000 ducks. Some biologists think humans may be helping prop up the canvasback, as it has become widely popular among waterfront communities to feed tons of corn each winter to large flocks of the photogenic "cans."

To complicate the waterfowl situation further, some of the species that are doing the best are actually causing problems for the environment. Mute swans are a prime example. These huge, graceful white birds are not native to the bay. Introduced from Europe, their populations have risen from 6 birds to more than 4,000 in the last four decades—and climbing fast. Mute swans don't migrate north in spring like the native tundra swans. Instead, they consume large quantities of sea grasses, already scarce habitat for crabs and fish. There is evidence, too, that mutes are competing for nesting habitat with smaller species such as terns and black skimmers. Maryland, where most mute swans live, has begun a program to reduce their numbers and keep them low. Similarly, a nonmigratory variety of Canada goose has also been gaining population rapidly around the Chesapeake. These geese now number more than 300,000 in the bay watershed and soon may exceed the populations of migratory Canadas. They are becoming a nuisance, fouling lawns and golf courses with their feces and polluting ponds, lakes, and streams. The states are hoping that hunting seasons will control their numbers, but so far the trend continues upward.

In general, the last decade has seen modest progress with waterfowl, though attributing that to improvements in the Chesapeake is tricky. More aggressive programs to protect and restore bay wetlands have helped some species, but others, dependent on bay sea grasses, have shown little progress. Even the "success" story of the Canada goose's adaptation to cornfields is not guaranteed in the long run. Dependence on a human agricultural system that could change quickly to growing other products at the whim of markets is no substitute for the goose's diminished natural food supply, the sea grasses. And even if corn remains a staple of agriculture in this area, the amount of farm acreage is heading steadily downward.

The declines in waterfowl that feed on the bay's sea grasses provide a small, but fascinating, illustration of the complicated way in which human activities become intertwined with the natural world. The decline of redheads and canvasbacks caused a decline in the number of offshore duck blinds—essentially wooden boxes mounted on poles and covered with pine boughs for camouflage. Wildlife managers say those blinds provided not only wintertime hunting, but in spring and summer were fine nesting places for ospreys, owls, black ducks, and green herons, and sometimes for all four species at the same time.

Conclusions

- Although pollution and habitat destruction have contributed to the declines in many important bay fish, an equal or greater culprit has been overfishing. Both commercial and sport fishermen have played substantial roles.

- The comeback of the striped bass, or rockfish, shows the importance of good science, continuous monitoring, adequate funding, and regulatory oversight. It also has made clear the need to move beyond managing for one species at a time to managing for the whole ecosystem.

- Blue crabs, the bay's last great commercial fishery, have become an imperiled species despite pledges by Maryland, Virginia, and the federal government a decade ago to manage them sustainably. Consequently, the first-ever opportunity for managers to protect a species before it declined was lost.

  Just in the last few years, real progress with crabs seems to be occurring, with both Maryland and Virginia implementing meaningful harvest restrictions designed to boost populations. But it is too early to tell for sure.

- The huge loss of oysters from the bay has meant far more than a lost seafood industry. It removed 98 percent of a keystone species, one that cleansed the water as it fed and whose reefs supported a stunning assemblage of marine life.

  Efforts to restore oysters have never been better organized or better funded than in recent years; but oyster diseases continue to be a major challenge, raising questions about whether goals can be met to increase oysters in the bay tenfold by 2010. Meanwhile, debate rages over whether to introduce a new species of oyster from Asia that is disease resistant but could cause unforeseen harm if released. Better information is needed to weigh the potential damage from such a release against the potential benefits.

- American shad, fished into commercial extinction by the early 1980s, are making real progress. Years of stocking hatchery fish have revitalized spawning runs on some bay rivers, and natural reproduction is taking over. Hundreds of miles of historic spawning habitat have been reopened by providing fish passage over or around dams and other obstructions on bay rivers. The reopening of a full-fledged fishing season, closed now for more than twenty years, is still years away.

- Most major bay species are now covered by improved management plans, representing real progress from a decade ago. The body of scientific knowledge about many species and the money allocated to make these plans work varies widely, however.

- The future of bay seafood harvesting lies in multispecies management, which recognizes that optimal yields from all species, all the time, are impossible and would never occur in nature. Such management attempts to sustain a healthy food web and to recognize the numerous interdependencies among various species.

- The number of watermen working the Chesapeake continues to decline, and few young people are entering the occupation. Watermen, whose preservation is a major thrust of the bay cleanup efforts, have become dangerously dependent on a single species, the blue crab.

- Overall numbers of waterfowl have remained stable. But within that, species dependent on the bay's diminished sea grasses are doing poorly. Mute swans and resident Canada geese, two species that are doing the best, are actually harming the environment.

Resilience

If we were to present a citation to nature for a near-victory in her struggle of resistance against the works of man, I hope this Conference would vote unanimously the Chesapeake as the recipient. The valiant way in which the vast ecology in the waters, in the marshes, on the land, and even in the sky, has fought against the poison of pollution and man's rank disregard for the living values makes one stand in awe of the power of nature.

—Rogers C. B. Morton, Secretary of the Interior,
September 1968 speech

We have always put a lot of faith in the bay's resilience—in its ability to bounce back from environmental insults. The history of the estuary is full of examples of this species or that being knocked back by natural events or pollution, only to resurge to record levels. It was partly our expectations of this resilience that delayed recognition during the 1970s that the bay had dropped to a lower plateau of environmental quality.

In June 1972, Mother Nature delivered the bay a fierce blow—the worst rain and flooding in perhaps two centuries. Across the vast watershed, the floods blasted the bay for days on end with unheard-of volumes of choking silt, farm chemicals, sewage from ruptured lines, and freshwater—too much of the latter being just as deadly as any other pollutant to many bay creatures.

That tropical storm, Agnes, combined with several more unusually wet years that characterized the decade of the 1970s, would have stressed the bay's system in any era. But coming at a time when much of the bay's historic resilience was depleted, it sent the estuary into a tailspin from which it still has not recovered. It was as if an aging prizefighter had suddenly found that he could no longer take a punch and come back.

In retrospect, it was not so surprising. A major system of resilience, the forest that once covered most of the watershed, was 40 percent gone, and much more was gone of the forests closest to the bay. This represented the loss of a superb filter and regulator of the bay's environment. Rainstorms trickling through a forest canopy soak into the deep organic matter of the forest floor. Less rain runs immediately off the land, and in dry times there is plenty stored in the forest water table to feed rivers by seeping in from underground. And far less pollution, from sediment to nutrients to toxic chemicals, escapes from each acre of forest than from any land use that usually replaces it. As a result, flows of water to the bay from forest-land are cleaner and less subject to wild fluctuations in storms than with any other land cover, from pastures to pavement.

Gone, too, were more than half of the watershed's original inland and coastal wetlands. These not only harbored rich wildlife, they also played a role at least as great as forests (per acre) in filtering pollutants running from the land and in buffering the bay against the extremes of flood and drought.

Yet another system of resilience lay along the shallow edges of the bay and its rivers, where as much as half a million acres of submerged grasses once grew. But by the time of Agnes, the grasses were severely stressed and in decline. Pollutants that clouded the water, cutting off light needed for optimal grass growth, had been picking up sharply since the 1950s. The grasses, like the wetlands and the forest, were most obviously vital habitat for a variety of bay species; but they played an equally important role in trapping sediments and absorbing nutrients to clarify and cleanse the bay's waters.

In slightly deeper water lay what little was left—perhaps less than 10 percent in 1972—of the bay's fabled oyster beds, which once grew in reefs thick enough to pose navigational hazards to shipping. We had valued them as hors d'oeuvres and as an economic mainstay for watermen; but by filtering water through their gills to feed, the bay's original oyster populations could remove polluting sediment and algae every few days from a volume of water equal to the whole bay, thereby cleansing and clearing the water.

Altogether, the forests, the wetlands, the grasses, and the oysters once constituted a marvelous system of buffers and filters, stabilizers and regulators. They lent the bay a tremendous resilience, a capacity to absorb environmental insult and recover. Even today, people will sometimes remark of this or that aspect of the bay's decline that "things haven't been the same since Agnes." But the problem wasn't just Agnes, or even the record wet decade of the 1970s, marked by high river flows into the estuary. It was the extent to which humans had reduced the modern bay's ability to take the punches. Since Agnes some of the bay's vital filters and buffers have been reduced still more, while others have increased. Only about 2 percent of its oyster beds remain; the rest became victims of harvest and disease. Yet 200 miles of its streamside woodlands have been replanted (as of 2002).

The following sections set out the ways we must measure progress in restoring and maintaining these systems of resilience, which help the bay help itself. It will never be possible to argue to a scientific certainty that paving this patch of forest will kill so many rockfish or that building a highway that fills that little marsh will stress submerged grasses a hundred miles downstream. But if the bay continues to lose resilience, when the next heavy blows land, we may find that the fight has all but ended.

Forests

Forests, coral reefs, ocean depths . . . are not separate and independent entities; they are interrelated parts of the total system of the world of life, of the biosphere.

—Marston Bates, *The Forest and the Sea*

It is a beautiful and delightsome land with clear rivers and brooks running into a faire Bay . . . there is little grass, but for that which grows in the marshes, for this country is completely overgrown with trees.

—Captain John Smith, 1607

To the modern timberman, an oak tree is in its prime at around 60 to 80 years. Beyond that time, it is no longer adding wood as rapidly, and delaying its harvest will only risk disease or injury from lightning or wind.

To the squirrel, the same oak is just coming into its own after about 150–170 years, when its acorn production begins to peak—a peak it may sustain for another century.

To woodland birds, a forest studded with oaks two, three, and even four centuries old is living at its finest. The remarkable habitat afforded by the canopy and structure and height of the old-growth forest provides the maximum amount of niches for nesting and feeding.

The forest itself might say that the most productive oak is the dead one—the old giant that has spanned half a millennium, nourished hundreds of generations of squirrels, cradled millions of songbirds, died, rotted, and, at long last, crashed to the ground. The sizable pit created by the oak's uprooting and the carcass of the fallen tree create unevenness on the forest floor, trapping and filtering water, damming up leaves that will rot into rich piles of compost, regenerating forest soils. The "dead" bulk of the oak bristles with new communities—mosses, fungi, lichens, beetles, ants, microbes; a whole new ecosystem has been created, further enriching the diversity of life, strengthening the food web, benefiting everything from salamanders to black bears.

And the bay, which ultimately depends on the quality and quantity of the rainwater that runs from the lands of its watershed, would say that no other land use—pasture, cornfield, suburban lawn, or urban street—consistently delivers the clear, pure water it receives from the forest.

THE GREAT GREEN FILTER

We can only speculate about the quality of freshwater flows to the pristine bay that existed when the old-growth forest covered almost all of the bay's watershed from New York State to Norfolk. Forests that have not been logged and otherwise altered by humans are so rare and scattered nowadays that even most professional foresters have never studied their workings. Our whole concept of a healthy and mature forest now applies to something that once would have been considered inferior and scraggly. Nonetheless, study after study confirms that even today, forested lands of the watershed result in cleaner, clearer water flowing down the bay's tributaries than any other use to which we put land.

This very much includes well-managed commercial forestlands. Nothing looks less natural than the wreckage of a recently clear-cut tract of timber; but if replanted, or allowed to regenerate on its own, such lands quickly resume fulfilling most of the water quality functions of an untouched forest (though not most of their wildlife functions). Excellent commercial forestry, from the bay's standpoint, is a healthy alternative to both development and agriculture.

We can get a tantalizing hint of what the original, mostly forested bay was like from federal and state studies of pollution sources in the Susquehanna River's huge watershed, which delivers nearly half the bay's freshwater and is a dominant source of polluting nitrogen and phosphorus. Forests there cover more than two-thirds of the watershed, but they contribute less than one-twentieth of the river's phosphorus and less than one-sixth of its nitrogen. On one of the river's largest subwatersheds, the West Branch, phosphorus is estimated to come equally from urban areas, which are 2 percent of the watershed, and from forests, which are 81 percent of the land there. Nitrogen is estimated to flow about equally down the West Branch from forests and from agriculture, even though the former is 81 percent of the landscape and the latter only 15 percent.

THE REAL WORTH OF TREES

Just by growing, forests in the bay's watershed today are sopping up an estimated 184 million pounds of nitrogen from polluted air each year that would all wash into waterways if it fell on paved lands. The forests are thus accomplishing about three times the annual reduction of nitrogen achieved by all the technological pollution control efforts of the last two decades. And the trees do it for free, while manufactured controls cost billions. Every acre of trees also removes 40 tons of carbon a year, offsetting the buildup of carbon dioxide responsible for global warming and climate change.

A study by the conservation group American Forests estimated that increasing forests in the Baltimore metropolitan area from 32 percent to 40 percent of the land's surface would achieve benefits equal to spending

$100 million on stormwater controls to protect streams and to spending $3 million a year on air pollution control equipment for smokestacks and auto exhausts. Often overlooked, and seldom accounted for by traditional economics, these are prime examples of what are sometimes called *ecosystem services*. They include everything nature provides, from recreation and genetic resources to raw materials for industry, soil formation, and water quality protection. Ecologists from around the world, in a 1997 issue of *Nature* magazine, estimated the worth of global ecosystem services at around $33 trillion a year. By comparison, the world's gross total of goods and services from the human economy is around $18 trillion a year.

FOREST PROTECTION IN DECLINE

While there is no doubt that the modern bay's forests have lost some of their ability to protect the bay, drawing a picture of why must be done with care. Just as important as how much forest covers the watershed is its location and the quantity of pollution it must filter.

Until the time of colonization in the 1600s, forests covered 95 percent of the 41-million-acre watershed. Clearing for agriculture, firewood, and building materials reduced the historical forest to 70 percent by the 1700s. By the mid-1800s, increasing demand for timber had reduced forest cover to 50 percent; and by the start of the twentieth century, the watershed was dramatically more denuded of its trees than at any time before or since, with forest covering as low as 30 percent. By 1970, as many fields and clear-cuts regrew trees, forest cover reached an estimated 60 percent, approximately 24.5 million acres—more extensive than at any time in nearly two centuries.

Considering all this, you might ask: If forests are so important to water quality, why wasn't the bay's health far worse a hundred years ago at the historic peak of tree clearing?

One big reason is that the increased pollution in past centuries was largely limited to sediment. It was not until modern times that farmland was routinely saturated with the nitrogen and phosphorus fertilizers that are the primary source of the bay's decline. Even animal manure, a major source of fertilizer in earlier times, was sparsely used around much of the

Chesapeake, according to historical accounts. Until recent decades, the air was not raining down huge quantities of nitrogen, nor was there factory farming of poultry, hogs, and dairy cows, which now concentrates mountains of manure near waterways in many parts of the watershed.

In addition, the watershed's population has grown from an estimated 45,000 Native Americans when forest clearing began, to more than 16 million residents—headed for 19 million by 2030. Thus it was not until modern times that the forest was replaced to such a large extent by paved surfaces, from streets and parking lots to rooftops and driveways. The hard surfaces dramatically increase runoff, which nowadays sends a potent range of chemicals—pesticides and concentrated fertilizers from farms and lawns, pollutants from septic tanks, toxic metals and compounds from polluted air—all directly into waterways.

In other words, the forest filters are smaller, polluting land uses are larger, and the pollutants are far nastier than simple dirt.

A second big reason bay pollution wasn't as severe a century ago when there was less forest cover than there is now is the forests' location. Since the 1970s, it seems that forests are again disappearing from the bay watershed at a slow rate—but this big picture is misleading. Forests are gaining or stable in the far western and northern parts of the watershed, in the mountains of New York, West Virginia, and Pennsylvania. That masks significant declines in the areas closest to the bay—precisely where the pollution-filtering capabilities of forests are needed most. These areas, the Piedmont and Coastal Plain of Virginia, Maryland, and Pennsylvania, are where most of the people and the farming are located. This is where the forest filter needs to be thickest, but is thinnest. Thus, more than two-thirds of the watershed's forest is farthest from the bay, while less than a third occurs where the bay needs it most (see Figure 4.1).

During the 1980s and 1990s, losses of forest, mostly in these regions nearest the bay, totaled around 100,000 acres in Maryland, 200,000 acres in Virginia, and 85,000 acres in southern Pennsylvania (whose bay watershed forests, overall, were stable). Forests also declined by 4,000 acres in Delaware, which has a small but important part of the Chesapeake watershed, containing the headwaters of five bay rivers.

These are estimates by the U.S. EPA's Chesapeake Bay Program. Even

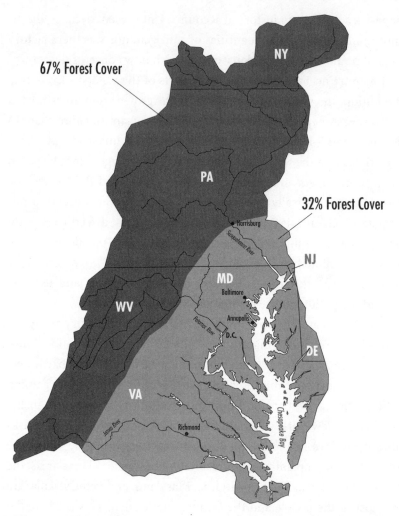

FIGURE 4.1. Percent of Forest Cover in the Chesapeake Bay Watershed. The Chesapeake Bay watershed has more forest overall now than it did a century ago, but most of the gains have come in the headwater areas of the system. Forests continue to be lost from the densely populated lands closest to tidal waters, where the bay needs them most to absorb and filter runoff. [EPA Chesapeake Bay Program]

within regions that are clearly losing trees, estimates of how much will vary depending on whether "loss" is defined as total clearing or as a thinning of tree cover. "The quality of a forest matters as much, or perhaps more, than the total forest area," says a recent Chesapeake Bay Program report.

In that light, a study by the private conservation group American Forests is revealing. It compared satellite photos from the 1970s through the 1990s to examine not only outright loss of forest, but also acreage where development had replaced enough trees that the areas, while still "green," had lost a significant part of their ability to cleanse the environment and support wildlife. Not too surprisingly, in the bustling, 1.5-million-acre Baltimore-Washington metro corridor, American Forests found forests had declined by nearly 280,000 acres, going from 55 percent to 37 percent of the landscape, as development went from 31 percent to 49 percent. A turning point of sorts was reached in 1985, when developed land for the first time exceeded forested land.

More surprising was a look at the satellite study of a larger region, the one-quarter, or 11.5 million acres, of the watershed closest to the bay, an area ranging from Delaware to the Pennsylvania border, including Hagerstown, Maryland, and Norfolk, Virginia. Losses there were 2 million acres during the twenty-four-year study period. Fully functioning forests declined from 55 percent of the landscape to 38 percent—as bad as in the smaller metro corridor.

RESTORING FORESTS

In a nutshell, we can expect to accomplish more in the next decade to maintain the bay's resilience through forests than in the last decade or two—but still not nearly enough to call it real progress by the standards of this book. Formal goals have been set for increasing other major parts of the bay's resilience—wetlands, oysters, and submerged grasses. For forests, there is still not even a goal of halting the decline. Even as programs are formulated across the watershed to decrease pollution from farms, urban pavements, sewage, and industrial plants, there is no program to increase the quantity and quality of the "least-polluting" land use, the forest.

There are encouraging signs, nonetheless.

All three principal watershed states and the federal government should easily exceed a goal of planting a total of 2,010 miles of streams with forest buffers by 2010. As of the fall of 2002, Maryland had buffered 1,980 miles, Pennsylvania 400, and Virginia 312. Such buffers are at least 35 feet wide and can provide extraordinary benefits by keeping sediment, nutrients, and other pollutants from bay tributaries. Recent research has shown that streams lined with forest buffers can process as much nitrogen as the buffers themselves.

The concept of targeting forest restoration where it is most needed—close to waterways and largely in parts of the watershed closest to the bay—is an excellent one. Such watershed forests also cool the water for aquatic life and provide corridors for the movements and migrations of wildlife.

But the 2,010-mile goal pales in the context of the 45,000 or so miles of streams in the bay watershed that are not adequately buffered by forest on both sides. Counting each stream mile as 2 miles needing buffers (both sides) means that the current goal is restoring less than 2 percent of all the miles that need to be buffered.

Another caveat: Do not assume that one newly created streamside forest will remove pollutants equally as well as another, whether new or existing. Many existing forest buffers are there because the soils underlying them were too wet to farm or develop. Such "hydric" soils are particularly good at cleansing polluted runoff. Where new buffers are created on different soils, the water quality benefit, while positive, may not be as large. The effectiveness of the buffer is also highly dependent on whether the buffer intercepts the polluted water. Therefore, even buffers with hydric soils may be bypassed in areas with deep groundwater flow paths, such as can occur on the lower Eastern Shore. Conversely, forest buffers on non-hydric soils can remove tremendous amounts of pollution where there are steep, erosive slopes or shallow groundwater flows.

Forests will also gain modest protection if the bay restoration program adheres to its new land preservation goals that call for 20 percent of the entire watershed to be protected in open space by 2010. Meeting this goal means protecting another 1.1 million acres. However, much of this land, probably the majority, will be farmland or other open space that is not specifically forested.

Maryland is one of only six states nationwide—and the only bay watershed state—to have a tree protection law. The law has achieved its goals, based on a recent five-year evaluation, but it was intended only to slow, not stop, forest losses. Out of a total of 36,000 acres of forests that fell under the law, 12,000 acres were cut and 4,000 acres were planted in partial mitigation. That represents progress, but it also represents a loss of 8,000 acres.

Both Maryland and Virginia have laws aimed at retaining forest and other natural vegetation around the tidal shoreline of the Chesapeake and its rivers (see "Edges of the Bay," this chapter, for more detail). Maryland's Critical Area Act, despite a number of loopholes, has been fairly successful at limiting the loss of waterfront forest in many areas. Virginia's Chesapeake Bay Preservation Act is considered quite weak and badly flawed, and has not tracked shoreline forest losses.

No matter how successful, the states' protection of forest buffers within the tidal zone will do nothing to buffer the estimated 90 percent of pollutants in runoff that enters the bay from lands above these coastal zones.

A KINDER CUT FOR TREES

Despite forests being the watershed's least-polluting land use, the harvesting of trees may cause serious pollution. New roads may have to be constructed to reach remote cuts. Cutting may occur without leaving adequate forested buffers next to waterways, and heavy equipment can cause erosion and compaction of forest soils, degrading their capacity to remove pollution for a time even if they are replanted. However, under proper management, timber harvesting has a large net benefit to the bay by virtue of the fact that trees are allowed to grow for many years at a time and is far preferred to agriculture or development from the bay's perspective.

To their credit, forestry agencies and commercial timber companies in much of the watershed are putting more emphasis on harvesting with an eye to maintaining water quality. Commercial timber firms, who own large acreages across the watershed, generally replant after harvesting, as do managers in state and national forests. But the great bulk of the watershed's forests, particularly in the regions closest to the bay, is on private land, where tens of thousands of owners harvest under largely voluntary guidelines and often find more rapid economic returns than replanting trees and waiting decades for another harvest.

Promising programs under way now would create an international standard of excellence for commercially harvested wood. "Certified" wood that was harvested in accordance with high environmental standards, including water quality, would be labeled accordingly. Forest product suppliers and their customers would then be able to reward companies and landowners who did right by the environment.

FRAGMENTING THE FORESTS

The loss of forests represents more than a loss of pollution filters. Forests are home to wildlife, from black bears to warblers. They are at the base of a huge hunting and outdoor recreation industry, and are key to maintaining cool temperatures in the thousands of miles of prime trout streams in Maryland, Pennsylvania, and Virginia.

Here, too, gross forest acreage statistics sometimes miss the real story of impacts on wildlife. More rapidly than they are being cleared, forests are being "fragmented," crisscrossed and isolated by roads, power-line corridors, interstate highway fencing, and housing developments.

Many species of songbirds need the deep forest interior for successful breeding. If they are too close to a forest edge, their nests are easier prey to raccoons, blue jays, opossums, and cowbirds. A study by the Wilderness Society that compared such "edge" losses on deep-woods nesters found impacts on 70 percent of all nests in suburban Maryland, but only 2 percent of nests in the intact forests of the Great Smoky Mountains. Forest fragmentation, along with the loss of wintering habitat in the tropics, is thought to be a factor in declines among many eastern songbirds since the 1940s.

FOREST HEALTH AND WATER QUALITY

Much is made of the forests' capacity to absorb pollution, particularly nitrogen from the air and from runoff, before it can enter the bay. But sometimes forests can release nitrogen in startlingly large quantities. A University of Maryland study of streams in forests defoliated by gypsy moths found that the highly stressed trees were releasing up to fifty times more nitrogen than normal into waterways. This was a relatively isolated incident. But studies increasingly indicate that forests will not be able to absorb forever all the acidic compounds of nitrogen and other air pollutants that currently bombard them.

The risk is that forests could begin to "leak" their stored nitrogen, in amounts that overwhelm all the other attempts to control pollution of the bay. Conversely, reducing air pollution and its offspring could improve forest health, and that could actually increase the ability of forests to absorb pollution. The bottom line is that we cannot rely on forests to keep the bay resilient without also paying attention to the rest of the environment.

Conclusions

- The bay watershed's forests are its least-polluting land use. They are a basis for much of the bay's wildlife, a renewable economic resource, a major source of recreation and tourism, an air pollution filter, and a carbon bank working to reduce global warming. They are vital to maintaining clear, clean water and to maintaining stability and resilience in the bay ecosystem.
- Nearly half the forests have disappeared since colonial settlement, and they are still declining. The situation may be worse than gross forest acreages indicate, because high-pollution areas nearest the bay, which need the forest buffer most, tend to have the least forest acreage and are losing it the fastest. Distribution of forest is equally as critical as the total amount.
- Improved programs to restore and protect forests, particularly in streamside buffers, are in place. But there are still no goals or policies to increase overall forest acreage or to halt overall declines. Forests are the only major element of bay resilience for which no such comprehensive goals or policies exist. There is a goal for forest buffers, but it needs to be increased significantly to improve the bay's health.
- With forest ownership spread among tens of thousands of private landowners, the ability to ensure environmentally sound harvesting

techniques and provide guidance on stewardship to forest owners is limited.

- Forests absorb huge quantities of pollution from the air before it can run off into the bay. But there are indications they cannot continue to perform such functions indefinitely, unless air pollution is reduced and forest health maintained.

Nontidal Wetlands

What would the world be, once bereft,
of wet and of wildness? Let them be left.

—Gerard Manley Hopkins, *Poems,* no. 56

Although they cover only a few percent of the bay's 41-million-acre watershed, nontidal wetlands, acre for acre, have all the forest's values for bay resilience, and then some. They are, like the forest, a least-polluting land use. They filter and cleanse and improve the quality of water flowing through them. Whenever a nontidal wetland is turned into pasture or cornfield or homesite, the pollution runoff to the bay is certain to increase.

The word *wetlands* conjures for most people images of the broad expanses of tidal marshes and forests that extend, often spectacularly, along the edges of the bay and lower parts of its rivers. Recognized by science and in state and federal law for their extraordinary environmental values, tidal wetlands in the bay region have enjoyed substantial legal protection for more than two decades (see "Edges of the Bay," this chapter).

A HISTORY OF LOSS

Nontidal wetlands, though just as valuable as tidal wetlands, have been until very recently their poor cousins, routinely destroyed or degraded by development and agriculture, or flooded for reservoirs. Scattered from coastal plain to mountaintop, they comprise about 1.4 million acres. Bogs, glades, sloughs, potholes, pocosins, vernal ponds, and wet woods and swamp are just a few of the names they go by. Such wetlands range from peat bogs to towering cypress forests; to cattails fringing a pond in a highway median strip; to slight depressions in the middle of farm fields that are not even distinguishable to the layperson until they become saturated periodically with rainwater, instantly attracting life ranging from spring peepers to breeding ducks and great blue herons and muskrats.

Nontidal wetlands, despite their relatively small coverage of the bay's watershed, are home to an extraordinary number of the bay region's rare plants and animals, species unable to exist outside of these isolated pockets of "wet and wildness." These wetlands also afford flood protection and recharge areas to replenish belowground water supplies (think of them as sponges). And they add diversity, interest, and character to the landscape.

The community of Sherwood Forest on Maryland's Severn River is among a growing number of places discovering the remarkable capabilities of nontidal wetlands. Adults and schoolchildren there have transformed a deep, eroded ravine that funneled pollution from septic tanks and golf course runoff into the Severn. Landscaped into a staircase of terraced pools, each planted with native wetland plants, the ravine now filters out most of the pollution and doubles as a nursery for rare and endangered plants. A project nearby has planted a thousand Atlantic white cedars, a beautiful wetlands tree whose fallen needles build a thick, acidic peat that acts like an activated charcoal filter, trapping and neutralizing toxic airborne mercury and nutrient-laden runoff.

Not all nontidal wetlands are much to look at, however. "Is This a Wetland?" asks a recent flyer published by environmentalists to aid in identifying these important areas. "Are the bases of the trees swollen? Do the leaves on the ground look matted, washed with silt, grayer than those on adjacent sites? Are bottles and cans lying on the site filled with mud . . . are there leaves or trashy debris that look like they've been washed up against roots . . . ?"

The U.S. EPA estimates that more than 60,000 acres of nontidal wetlands were lost from the Chesapeake watershed between the 1950s and the 1980s (see Figure 4.2). Losses probably were greater than these numbers indicate, given the lack of required reporting and the difficulty in identifying seasonally saturated areas that qualify as nontidal wetlands (year-round, standing water is not necessarily required for lands to perform as nontidal wetlands). Virginia alone, for example, estimated losses (57,000 acres) nearly equal to the official estimates for the entire

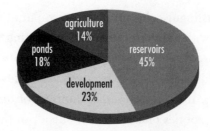

FIGURE 4.2. Causes of Nontidal Wetlands Loss, 1950s–1980s. Scientists estimate that the Chesapeake watershed has lost 58 percent of its wetlands over the past 400 years, with attendant losses of "ecosystem services" such as water treatment, flood control, groundwater recharge, and wildlife habitat. [EPA Chesapeake Bay Program]

watershed. The bay watershed has historically followed a national trend that saw more than half of all wetlands across the lower forty-eight states destroyed or degraded since colonial times.

A HISTORIC TURNAROUND

In the last decade or two, for the first time in history, gains in nontidal wetlands acres appear to be outpacing losses in the bay watershed (see Figure 4.3). The turnaround comes from a combination of better protection—all three states now have comprehensive nontidal wetlands laws—and a multitude of federal, state, and private programs aimed at creating and restoring wetlands, often with healthy financial incentives for landowners.

The official federal-state bay restoration goal of "no net loss" for wetlands and a long-term "net gain" is under way in a much fuller sense than a decade ago, when the first edition of *Turning the Tide* concluded that "continued losses seem assured." To be sure, wetlands recovery remains very much a work in progress, with many caveats that are discussed below. But the trends are encouraging.

Virginia, for example, reported a net gain of 132 acres of wetlands, mostly nontidal, for the year 2000. "Net gain" here means a loss of 142 acres whose filling or draining was permitted by the state and the federal government—but offset by 275 acres whose creation or restoration the state required in compensation. In 2001, Virginia's net gain rose to 354

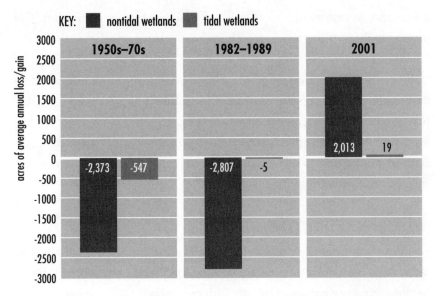

KEY: ■ nontidal wetlands ■ tidal wetlands

FIGURE 4.3. **A Historic Turnaround.** Until the early 1990s, the Chesapeake watershed saw destruction of tens of thousands of acres of wetlands. However, protection for tidal wetlands in the 1970s and for nontidal wetlands in the 1990s is beginning to make a difference. Recent years, such as 2001, exemplify this historic turnaround, though there is a long way to go to restore these "lungs and kidneys of the bay." [EPA Chesapeake Bay Program]

acres, and another 311 acres of nontidal wetlands was added under voluntary restoration programs.

Some cautions: The actual wetlands losses used to calculate these net gains may well be greater than reported, since they don't include illegal activity or some types of wetlands destruction that fall outside the jurisdiction of the U.S. Army Corps of Engineers. Also, there has been little follow-up to the wetlands created in compensation to see how successful they have been.

In Maryland, which has an independent, long-term goal of adding 60,000 acres of wetlands, regulatory permit programs showed net wetlands gains of about 20 acres in 2000 and 73 in 2001. Voluntary programs added more than 300 acres in 2000 and 1,350 in 2001. Maryland also claimed another 2,300 acres during those two years as wetlands "enhancements." Such enhancement doesn't actually make more wetlands; rather, it attempts to restore quality to existing wetlands by eliminating invasive plants, such as phragmites, which can crowd out species with higher wildlife values.

Pennsylvania has not reported wetlands data in the same form as its bay neighbors, but appears to be adding around 400 acres a year in nontidal wetlands. Its "Growing Greener" initiative, which includes money for a variety of open space protection, is projected to add an extra 4,200 acres of nontidal wetlands in coming years, much of it in the bay watershed portion of the state.

CAUTIONS AND FUTURE DIRECTIONS

Scientists unanimously caution that it is misleading to look only at how many "net" acres of wetlands are being added to the watershed. That is because replacing natural wetlands with created ones is still more art than science, particularly when it comes to the complex, underground hydrology that makes wetlands wet. A recent National Academy of Sciences study concluded as much, warning that there is no assurance all new wetlands will last or that they will ever perform all the wildlife and water quality functions of the wetlands whose loss they are supposed to compensate for. There is little provision for the long-term monitoring of created wetlands to see how well they perform.

Even the best wetlands laws focus mainly on preventing direct destruction, but indirect impacts can and do damage wetlands—overloading with sediment running from a nearby construction site or alterations of above- and belowground drainage patterns, sometimes by a ditching or quarrying or pumping project some distance removed.

Virginia, with the largest share of nontidal wetlands in the watershed, did not pass a wetlands protection law until 2001, and it is still too soon to know how well it will be enforced by the state's department of environmental quality. Its passage, however, is a major change for the good since Turning the Tide was first published. Aggressive state wetlands laws are more critical than ever in light of sizable loopholes in federal wetlands protections, coupled with recent moves by the Bush administration—over the objections of the EPA and the U.S. Fish and Wildlife Service—to ease protections further. Recent court rulings have also clouded the future of federal wetlands protection.

A case in point is Virginia's recent, chilling experience, which saw the quick draining of some 2,600 acres of wetlands, many inside the bay watershed portions of the state (because they fell outside federal jurisdiction, they were not reported in "no net loss" calculations). Developers found a way to exploit a legal loophole in federal wetlands laws, putting more than half a million acres of wetlands across the state at risk of destruction. This so-called Tulloch Ditching was stopped only after the state passed its own, more protective law.

Massive losses of wetlands are still quite possible. At this writing in 2003 a proposal to build a reservoir on the Mattaponi River has been approved by the Army Corps of Engineers, despite a recommendation against it by the local Corps office, several other agencies, and the Mattaponi tribe and despite strong local opposition. If built, this reservoir, the King William Reservoir, would drown over 400 acres of wetlands.

Wetlands scientists have a cautionary saying: "Avoid, minimize—mitigate only as a last resort." They mean that given the uncertainties about how well new wetlands will work, we should always put our highest priority on avoiding or minimizing destruction of the wetlands we already have. If we end up merely counting net gains in acreage as our measure of success, we may look back in another decade or two and realize progress with wetlands was far less than assumed.

Similarly, we must be careful about how much projects that merely "enhance" or "protect" (through purchase or easement) existing wetlands get counted into net gains.

Other caveats: Wetlands laws only weakly regulate agriculture and forestry, activities that occur across huge portions of the watershed. In addition, home building that destroys less than about a tenth of an acre of nontidal wetlands is not required to make up for the loss by creating new wetlands nearby.

One more long-term uncertainty—and another reason to protect all possible existing wetlands—is that significant amounts of new wetlands are being created under ten- to fifteen-year contracts that pay landowners annually for helping the environment. The federal or state government may renew the contracts once they have expired or protect the project with an easement, but landowners will have a five-year window to destroy the restored wetlands without penalty before such permanent protection could be exercised. So there is no guarantee that all the gains being made now will be permanent.

OPPORTUNITY LOST

Long term, the single biggest opportunity to regain big wetlands acreages may come on farmlands, where hundreds of thousands of acres of hydric, or poorly drained, soils that once underlay natural wetlands still exist. There is evidence that such soils, even if they have been drained and plowed for hundreds of years, will revert to wetlands if the original drainage is restored.

In the late 1980s the Army Corps of Engineers, which administers federal wetlands regulations, proposed to extend its jurisdiction to these "prior-converted" lands. The move would not have interrupted agriculture where it was already going on. However, if a farm went up for sale for development, those potential wetlands areas would have then been protected. The impacts fell only on land speculation, not on agricultural operations; but the idea created such a firestorm of protest that the Corps backtracked. Since then, none of the watershed states have tried to embrace this opportunity with their own laws. As tens of thousands of acres of farmlands are developed during the coming decades, we are missing out on a considerable opportunity to restore wetlands on their hydric soils.

Conclusions

- Nontidal wetlands are a vital part of the bay's resilience with their ability to filter and improve the quality of water flowing through them and to cushion the extremes of drought and flood. They help the bay rebound from both natural and human disturbances. In addition, they are a haven for wildlife; and despite covering only a few percent of the watershed's lands, they harbor an extraordinary proportion of its rare plants and animals.

- Although hundreds of thousands of acres of nontidal wetlands have been lost since colonial times, and at least 60,000 acres in recent decades, nontidal wetlands acreage now appears to be gaining for the first time in history. This is a result of better protections and programs that offer private landowners incentives and technical help in creating and restoring wetlands.
- There are many caveats to the above turnaround. Chief among them is that creation of new wetlands to replace those destroyed by development is still more art than science. It is not yet known how well new wetlands will perform, compared to those whose loss they are supposed to compensate for.
- Avoiding and minimizing destruction of existing wetlands must be firm priorities. Wetlands creation to compensate for losses must be seen as a last resort, not a license to destroy wetlands.
- Restoration efforts have increased substantially over the past ten years, but need to be taken to another order of magnitude to show an impact on the bay.

Edges of the Bay

We feel the greatest personal freedom is to be able to walk all the way down the waterline. Freedom for you is buying land all the way down the waterline.

—Bengt-Owe Jansson, Swedish scientist visiting the Chesapeake Bay

Edges have always been among the most interesting and vital phenomena in nature. Many scientists think humankind evolved along the intersection of the African jungle and savanna, a friendly edge that allowed tree-dwelling apes the safety of the forest and access to the abundant game of the plains. Modern-day hunters, human and animal, frequently find the edges where one type of vegetation gives way to another, like forest and field, the most abundant with game—just as fishermen often find drop-offs and channel edges highly productive.

The edge seems to create an abundance and diversity of life that add up to more than the sum of the habitats on either side of it. Scientists

from around the world, in a book called *Nature's Services*, recently calculated the value of the natural planet—services ranging from pollination
of plants to production of seafood—at $16–$54 trillion a year. Close to
half of all that natural value came from less than a tenth of the planet's
surface—the coastal edges, including sea grasses, coral reefs, and rich
fishing grounds of continental shelf waters. Nowhere do these extraordinary qualities of land–water edges come together more gloriously than
where the bay's watershed slopes down to the beaches and marshes and
shallows of the estuary (see Figure 4.4). And nowhere more than along
the bay's edges do human pressures and pollution clash more directly
with prime habitat for the bay's plant and animal life.

One of the bay's most striking features is the way in which land and
water intertwine, forming a shoreline that wanders an estimated
6,000–9,000 miles (including islands and tidal rivers), down and back the
195-mile length of the estuary. No other bay on Earth has so much shoreline for its size. Try this experiment during the summer months from any
marsh or beach along the bay or river shoreline: Pull a small seine net—

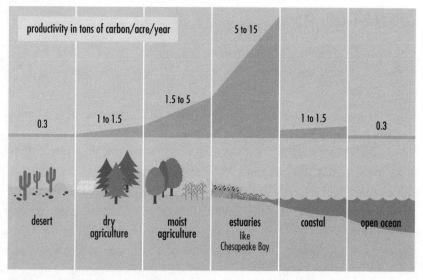

FIGURE 4.4. **Productivity of the Land–Water Edge.** Estuaries like the Chesapeake
are among the most productive ecosystems on Earth, outstripping even intensive
forms of modern agriculture.

say, 25 feet long—through the shallows. If you do it properly, you will likely come up with a wriggling mass of minnows, crabs, jellyfish, hog-chokers, baby spot, menhaden, perch, and perhaps several other species—all this harvested in minutes from a patch of water no bigger than a room in your home. Multiply it by the times that room would fit along several thousand miles of shoreline and you will begin to get an appreciation for life at the bay's edge.

It is not in the middle of the bay, or at its mouth or in its depths, that the most life lies. It is in these warm, food-rich, protective seams of marsh and tide flat where land and water knit together, where crabs shed their shells and the young of fish reside and the eagles and ospreys and great blue herons feed (see Figure 4.5). A study of 367 longtime eagle nests in the bay watershed showed 95 percent were within 2 miles of the bay or its tidal tributaries and 60 percent were within half a mile. The natural habitats of the tidal river edges, the marsh and the forest, also lend the bay a measure of resilience by absorbing pollution, helping the estuary rebound from both natural and human environmental insults.

But from the modern human perspective, this long, fertile edge is better known as waterfront real estate, and it is every bit as attractive to growing numbers of people as it is to crabs and ducks and rockfish. Nearly two-thirds of all Americans live in the narrow, 50-mile ribbon of land that borders the Atlantic, Pacific, Gulf of Mexico, and Great Lakes coasts. In the Chesapeake Bay region, power plants seek the edge of the bay and its tributary rivers for cooling water; sewage plants locate there for a ready avenue of dilution for treated wastes (Figure 4.6); marinas want expansion to accommodate a growing demand for boat access. The competition for use of the edge—all along the nation's and the world's coasts—is immense. And in this conflict, the Chesapeake Bay's long, desirable edges are second to none.

In recent years Maryland and Virginia have increasingly recognized the special importance and special vulnerability of their Chesapeake edges. The rest of this section looks at whether any real progress is being made in preserving this unique subset of the bay ecosystem.

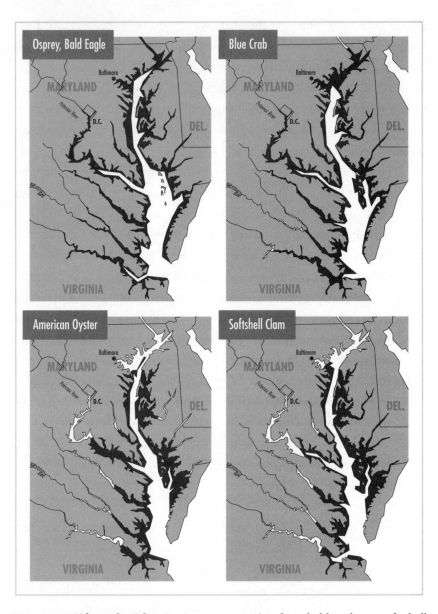

FIGURE 4.5. **Life on the Edge.** For creatures ranging from bald eagles to soft-shell clams ("mannoes"), the richest concentrations of life in the Chesapeake lie in the bay's "edges," its marshes, tide flats, and underwater grass beds. [U.S. Army Corps of Engineers, U.S. Fish and Wildlife Service]

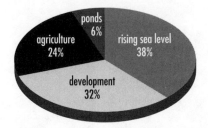

FIGURE 4.6. Causes of Tidal Wetlands Loss. Note that rising sea level is now the largest single cause of tidal wetlands loss in the Chesapeake. [EPA Chesapeake Bay Program]

TIDAL WETLANDS—THE BAY'S MOST ENDANGERED LANDSCAPE

Despite the marked progress of recent decades in stopping the filling and draining of the bay's rich tidal marshes, these may well be the watershed's most endangered landscape. The problem, a rapid rise in sea level from both human and natural causes, has little remedy in the near term.

Only since the turn of the twenty-first century have the dimensions of the threat facing tidal marshes been clearly exposed. University of Maryland scientists compared satellite photos of Chesapeake wetlands from the 1970s, '80s, and '90s. This allowed them to measure significant shifts from high-marsh vegetation to lower, wetter plant types and from low-marsh to open water. Based on these shifts, which occur as sea level rises too fast for normal marsh-building processes to keep up, the scientists compiled an index of marsh health, with startling results: Out of an estimated 290,000 acres of tidal marsh around the Chesapeake, only 85,000 acres, about 30 percent, is healthy. Another 145,000 acres, 50 percent, are mildly degraded. And 60,000 acres, a fifth of all the bay's tidal marsh, are severely degraded, raising the prospect of massive losses in this critical part of the bay's resilience and habitat for fish and wildlife within the next few to several decades.

In the well-studied Blackwater National Wildlife Refuge on Maryland's Eastern Shore (Figure 4.7), more than 5,000 acres of tidal marsh have disappeared during the last several decades—turned into open water, turbid with sediment from the old marsh peats. Similar declines, averaging more

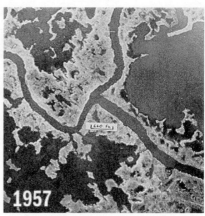

FIGURE 4.7. Marsh Losses in the Blackwater National Wildlife Refuge, Near Cambridge, Maryland, 1939–1989. Rising sea level and sinking land, aided by heavy consumption of plants by nutria (large, invasive rodents), have combined to destroy thousands of acres of marsh in the Blackwater National Wildlife Refuge on the Eastern Shore. Note that the junction of the Little Blackwater River and the main Blackwater (to left) is obvious in 1939 but nearly invisible from the air in 1989. [Blackwater National Wildlife Refuge, U.S. Fish and Wildlife Service]

than 120 acres per year for the last sixty years, have been documented in the tidal marsh along Maryland's Nanticoke River at the head of Tangier Sound.

Tidal marsh has been lost naturally to erosion by wind and waves since the bay was formed, but something new and ominous appears to be operating in recent times. By studying cores extracted by boring several feet deep into marshes, scientists can look back through time at how fast the wetlands were accumulating sediment and organic matter on which to build, to stay ahead of a rising sea level.

For most of the last thousand years, the marshes could keep up pretty easily. Sea level, which has been rising since the last ice age began receding, rose an average of 0.02 inch a year, about 2 inches a century. But the study of sediment cores from the marshes shows that beginning around 1850, sea level began to rise at a hugely accelerated rate. Since then, it has been coming up in the Chesapeake at 12–16 inches a century, depending on the part of the bay. In more recent decades there have been periods in which the rate of rise was as much as 2 inches a year—100 times the thousand-year average!

Sea level has been rising considerably faster in the Chesapeake than it has been globally. The reason is that the land around the bay's edges is also sinking—half or more of the "rise" in sea level that is threatening the marshes is actually the land subsiding. The causes of this are not well understood. A lot of it probably involves "postglacial rebound," a term geologists use to describe how the land just south of the glaciers' farthest advance during the last ice age (which includes the bay region) bulged up from the weight of the glaciers pressing down. Though the glaciers are long in retreat, this bulge, including the bay's edges, is still subsiding back to its original shape. It is also possible that increased modern withdrawals of groundwater for agriculture, drinking, and industrial uses are causing some of the subsidence in some parts of the bay.

As for the increasing rise in the level of the sea itself, only a small part comes from melting glacial ice as worldwide temperatures have increased in recent decades. More important is the simple fact that water, when warmed, expands. And the oceans are well documented to be warming, at least partly as a result of humans putting more carbon dioxide into the atmosphere, trapping more solar radiation—the greenhouse effect. The EPA projects this warming will markedly increase sea level rise again during this century, increasing risks of flooding and storms to low-lying coastal communities, as well as destroying wetlands.

There are no obvious quick fixes for most of this degradation, which if it keeps up could dramatically change the Chesapeake edges as early as mid-century (see Figure 4.8). One technique that is being tested now is the pumping of extra sediment into marshes to give them enough material on which to build new vegetation faster, keeping up with the increased rise of sea level. A pilot project has begun at the Blackwater National Wildlife Refuge as of 2002. This might actually prove to be a use for the spoil dredged from shipping channels, whose disposal is an ongoing problem (see "Dredging," Chapter 2). But sediment pumping is expensive—estimated at $100 million just to meet total marsh-building needs at the Blackwater Refuge.

As marshes lose out to rising water levels and begin to dissolve, they may be releasing large quantities of sediment that was bound up in their roots, adding to the bay's already considerable lack of water clarity, shading out light needed for growth by the estuary's underwater vegetation. The well-studied Blackwater marshes are estimated to be releasing an average of 20,000 tons of sediment a year (still a small fraction of the 5 million tons of sediment a year that enter the bay). The decaying organic matter dissolving from the Blackwater marshes has at times forced dissolved oxygen in the waters there to about one-fifth of healthy levels.

In the face of such huge projected marsh loss to forces that are largely beyond short-term control, it is all the more imperative to eliminate the losses of tidal wetlands to development and other factors that can be controlled. And in this, progress has been made during the last decade or two. Filling and draining by humans was largely responsible for historic losses that cost Virginia an estimated 42 percent of its original wetlands, tidal and nontidal, and an astounding 73 percent in Maryland. Tidal wetlands around the bay were still being destroyed by development at the rate of more than 1,000 acres a year until the last two decades.

That trend represented the decline of some of the richest habitat on Earth and also marked a significant decline in the bay's ability to cleanse

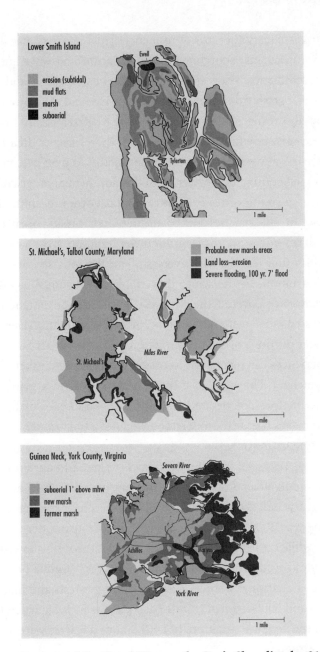

FIGURE 4.8. Impacts of Sea Level Rise on the Bay's Shoreline by 2100. At the most conservative estimate, the level of the bay relative to the land will be 3 feet higher within the next century—with dramatic impacts on many areas of the bay's shoreline. Some bay islands will be left with almost no land above water (subaerial). [J. Court Stevenson and M. Kearney, University of Maryland]

and stabilize itself, another loss of resilience. Tidal marshes provide excellent protection against shoreline erosion by absorbing wave energy and stabilizing sediments. They are also capable of absorbing and filtering pollutants that wash from farms and urban areas, and they provide flood control by absorbing excess runoff in storms. Research in Maryland's Patuxent River is showing that tidal wetlands there, despite their relatively limited acreage, appear to be capturing an astounding 50 percent of polluting nitrogen coming downriver from development and agriculture, effectively keeping a ton or more of nitrogen a day from reaching the bay.

Not least of all, marshes are beautiful. Their broad, open expanses along the bay's edges are a playground for light, an artist's canvas that changes color and texture with every shift in the intensity and angle of the sun and moon. In the wind, they ripple as sensuously as the great prairies that once covered the Midwest before the advent of the steel plow. Forested tidal wetlands that occur farther up the rivers and in fresher-water portions of the bay provide some of the most haunting and lovely experiences the region has to offer for canoeists, kayakers, hunters, and birdwatchers. The sight of a bald eagle roosting in a giant bald cypress along the forested wetland edges of Virginia's James or Maryland's Pocomoke makes it easy to understand why the words *raptor* and *rapture* have the same Latin root.

During the 1970s, state and federal laws designed to curtail tidal wetlands losses took effect. Losses before the law were estimated at 948 acres a year in Maryland. By the early 1990s, losses were averaging 13 acres a year. By the year 2000, Maryland gave permits for just under 1 acre to be destroyed, while creating nearly 9 acres. In 2001, the state allowed half an acre to be destroyed, while creating about 23 acres. Virginia has averaged losses (or degradation) of about 7.5 acres of tidal forests and marshes between 1993 and 2000—down from 18 acres a year in 1988, when the state first began tracking the situation. In 2001, about 3.5 acres were lost or degraded in Virginia.

The actual losses of tidal wetlands by human activities are almost certainly somewhat larger than the state numbers show. Data collection is still not as good as it should be, and some wetlands are damaged or destroyed without a permit. Agricultural drainage, for example, is exempt from permits. The same cautions apply to tidal wetlands as to nontidal ones: There is no way to know how created or restored wetlands will perform relative to existing wetlands that are lost, but most likely they will not work as well. Maryland also includes substantial acreages of "enhanced" wetlands in its official restoration numbers (not included in the numbers above). Enhancement often means replacing lower-grade wetlands vegetation, such as the phragmites reed, with vegetation more beneficial to wildlife; but the longevity of such enhancements and their added value for water quality, if any, are difficult to calculate.

One source of this much-reduced but continuing wetland loss is the desire of waterfront property owners to "harden" their shoreline against erosion with vertical steel or wooden walls, or bulkheads. This stops erosion behind the bulkhead, but destroys any wetlands there. It also reflects wave energy hitting the bulkhead downward, causing rapid scouring and erosion of productive shallow-water habitats in front of the bulkhead. A somewhat better solution is large rocks, or riprap, which break wave energy, but leave better shallow-water habitat than do the bulkheads. Better still, where possible, are "soft" shoreline enhancement measures, protecting shorelines from erosion by planting wetlands along the edge.

The states are making some progress here, though they need to do more. Between 1996 and 2000, Maryland issued permits for about 34 miles of bulkhead (new and replacement), 104 miles of riprap, and 24 miles of "soft" shoreline protection, including planting wetlands. State regulations encourage the latter two approaches now. Virginia, between 1993 and 2000, allowed an average of 4.8 miles a year of bulkheads and 12.7 miles a year of riprap. Virginia estimates that about 500 miles of its bay shoreline has been hardened with bulkheads and riprap. But incentives for soft shoreline protection remain slight compared to generous, low-interest state financing of hard measures such as riprap. And states continue to grant permits for shoreline armoring almost as a guaranteed right, which leads to projects in areas where erosion is slight. One recent project in Maryland, where there was little evidence of erosion (perhaps 50 feet over the last few hundred years), resulted in 3,000 feet of stone, piled 5 feet high. The Chesapeake Bay Foundation and others are now leading an effort to develop and encourage new "living shoreline" approaches that utilize more natural, softer materials, such as coconut fiber logs, to stabilize shorelines and wetlands instead of rock.

Another way human activities can accelerate the losses of tidal marshes is by ditching them—a technique developed to control mosquitoes by opening the marshes to small fish that eat mosquito larvae. But studies at Blackwater and along the Nanticoke River show marsh loss proceeds as small patches of open water are expanded by wind and wave erosion into larger areas. Anything that creates open water, or expands the existing drainage network within such marshes, has the potential to hasten their demise.

One way we can act now to counter the looming losses of tidal wetlands from sea level rise is to preserve as much of the bay's remaining natural edges as possible. That way, in the long run, a rising sea will have room to create new wetlands from what are now uplands along the shore. Preserving this natural edge, valued for reasons ranging from wildlife and scenery to water quality, has been the object of programs in both Maryland and Virginia, discussed below.

VIRGINIA'S CHESAPEAKE BAY PRESERVATION ACT

In 1988, with pomp and promise, Virginia enacted a law that required towns and counties in the state's coastal areas to manage land use to protect water quality. The Chesapeake Bay Preservation Act applied only to the twenty-nine counties and more than fifty cities and towns, although nothing prohibited other places from adopting it.

The law's passage represented a herculean effort on the part of environmentalists and their allies in the legislature; and given the weakness of protection for the coastal environment at the local level, it was a sweeping breakthrough. Regulations specified that a 100-foot buffer of natural vegetation be kept along the water's edge to filter pollutants from runoff. The concept of the new law—linking land use to water quality—seemed almost radical in Virginia at the time.

But a decade and a half later, reviews of the law's performance are decidedly mixed. Parts of northern Virginia and jurisdictions west of Richmond have aggressively utilized the law; other places—particularly Hampton Roads—have fought it. Moreover, the administrations of Governors George Allen and James Gilmore sought to systematically mis-manage how the law was carried out. "Flawed Law Fails the Bay" head-lined an in-depth series on the act in Norfolk's *Virginian-Pilot* in 2002. The law, the report noted, has been funded inadequately and has been impaired by a high rate of turnover in staff assigned to it. This has been exacerbated by a number of loopholes, variances, and exceptions, and by the vague wording of its regulations.

In practice, some local jurisdictions have felt free to continue business as usual with coastal development. In Hampton Roads, hundreds of de-velopment projects have been exempted from the act, and Virginia Beach approved 806 of 868 requests to bypass restrictions of the 100-foot buffer nearest the water. Portsmouth has been essentially rubber-stamping flawed projects for years. Buffer exemptions often hinge on developers' promises to install more effective antipollution controls, but there is no system for checking to see whether these pledges are ever kept or whether their controls are working effectively. Most compliance with the act has been up to citizens to check and report on their own.

To the good, the Chesapeake Bay Preservation Act has brought more modern planning to many small towns and rural counties—and it has es-tablished a clear link in the minds of many Virginians between land use and bay water quality. However, unless enforcement of the law is dramat-ically strengthened, and political commitment from the state is stepped up, the preservation act will fall well short of its goals.

MARYLAND'S CRITICAL AREA ACT

Maryland's attempt to protect the bay's edge, the Critical Area Act of 1984, amounted to a sweeping rezoning by the state to restrict develop-ment in a zone 1,000 feet back from the water around the entire bay and its tidal rivers—about 10 percent of the state's 5.2 million land acres.

The act gave the state a strong role in land use powers that traditionally had belonged to the counties. It limited building to one home per 20 acres in the bulk of the new critical area and forbid most development and clearing of natural vegetation in a 100-foot buffer (up to 300 feet in some cases) nearest the water. It also recognized for the first time that protecting undeveloped shorelines for wildlife habitat was a legitimate reason to limit development. Perhaps its most far-reaching premise was that the sheer "number, movement and activities of people" can cause environmental degradation even if traditional pollution sources are controlled. This foreshadowed Maryland's current attempts at statewide growth management, or Smart Growth, which makes it state policy to steer development out of the countryside and into existing or planned developed areas.

Opponents claimed the critical area law would end all growth along the state's highly valuable waterfront. Supporters hailed it as keystone legislation, without whose passage a wide-ranging package of other measures to clean up the bay would ultimately fail. In practice now for more than a decade, the Critical Area Act has become an accepted part of the Maryland zoning landscape, though it is not without controversies. Far from shutting down development as opponents claimed, it allows more than its supporters hoped—enough to spawn an oft-heard citizen complaint: "I thought they couldn't develop along the water like that anymore."

Though it is plagued by far fewer loopholes and weaknesses than Virginia's Chesapeake Bay Preservation Act, Maryland's shoreline protection law has its share. More than 10,000 undeveloped waterfront lots, for example, were legally recorded before the law took effect in 1985 and are exempted, or "grandfathered," from its provisions. These lots account for much of the surprise people express when waterfront building occurs along shoreline they had assumed was protected.

Another loophole is an "intrafamily transfer" provision, intended to let landowners living in the critical area when it was created split off extra lots for their immediate children. Unfortunately, in some cases, the state Critical Area Commission has allowed this exemption to continue after the original owner has sold the land.

Recent attacks on the critical area law by some of Maryland's judiciary also appear to have muted the state's readiness to take challenges to the law to court.

Still, the Critical Area Act has made a major, positive impact overall on Maryland's tidal bay and river edges. At the time of its passage, close to 20 percent of Maryland's development was going on in the 10 percent of the state along tidal shorelines. With the law in place, development in the tidewater zone has in most places fallen below 10 percent of state development.

Where the law has worked best is where it has the most teeth—in the resource conservation area, or RCA, where a strict one-home-per-20-acres is enforced. The RCA covers 363,000 acres, most of it still in a natural state, out of a total of half a million or so acres in the critical area. Compared to most attempts at conservation zoning in the 90 percent of Maryland outside the critical area, the RCA appears to be doing a better job at protecting farms, forests, and other open spaces. This assessment comes from a report done for the private Abell Foundation, in Baltimore, one of the first thorough attempts to assess how well the critical area law is performing.

While the RCA zone seems a reasonable success, other parts of the Critical Area Act could well undermine shoreline protection in Maryland in the long run, according to the Abell report. To allow the state's sixteen counties with tidal bay shoreline more flexibility in development and to ease passage in the legislature, the law allowed a "growth allocation." Each county can shift 5 percent of its most protective RCA zone into less protective zones, the limited development area (LDA) or the intensive development area (IDA). The spirit, though not the letter, of the law was that counties would treat this one-time allocation of prime waterfront as a precious resource, to be doled out sparingly for maximum economic and environmental benefit. A county, for example, would make sure most of its 5 percent growth allocation acres went into well-planned communities that maximized the number of dwelling units per acre, rather than letting unplanned, low-density sprawl fragment the open space along miles of waterfront.

It is still too early to say for sure how this is going to play out. As of 2000, more than a decade after the law took effect, about 14,000 acres—77 percent—of the counties' total growth allocation potential remained unused. Fast-developing Anne Arundel County was an exception, having used 85 percent of its allocation. Some counties are treating this acreage as special, to be used wisely, while others are dispensing it with little regard for wise planning, driven more by the desires of developers and builders.

However, the overall trend is worrisome, according to the Abell assessment. The bulk of growth allocation lands is being shifted to LDA instead of IDA—the difference being that the limited development designation allows much more scattered, low-density sprawl, versus the more compact, town and city concept of the intensive development part of the critical area. Continuing this trend would develop another 12,600 acres of unspoiled bay shoreline before all the growth allocation is used up.

Furthermore, the LDA itself, which includes 95,000 acres of shoreline in the sixteen counties, has become an outdated concept, badly out of step with modern Smart Growth planning that emphasizes clustered, compact development and large tracts of open space. Worse yet, a provision in the original act that half of all growth allocation had to go into IDA, or intensive development, has been waived for twelve of the sixteen counties.

Compounding the problem, the original law stated that for every home built as part of a growth allocation, 20 acres had to be deducted from a county's allocation, based on the one-home-per-20-acres zoning in the RCA area from which the growth allocation comes. But this has been liberalized to allow significantly smaller deductions. The bottom line: If the substantial remaining growth allocation is used poorly, and if the LDA zone remains out of step with land use planning in the rest of the state, the protections of the critical area could be severely eroded over time.

Another exemption in the law allows farmers to plow and plant well within the 100-foot buffer nearest the water's edge. All that is necessary for the exemption is for a farmer to have best management practices, or BMPs, in effect on his or her land. Although practices such as winter cover crops and plantings of natural vegetation on the edges of croplands can buffer waterways from polluted farm runoff, many farms still don't include these; nor do they work well unless they extend substantially farther than 25 feet from water's edge.

Conclusions

TIDAL WETLANDS

- The edges of Chesapeake Bay reflect the wider fight to reconcile the region's natural resources with a growing human impact on them. In the marshes and the shallows of the edges lies the bay's greatest productivity, while along the waterfront is where most of us are drawn to live and to site power plants, marinas, and sewage treatment discharges.

- The bay is likely to lose tens of thousands of acres from its 290,000 acres of tidal wetlands in the next several decades. The forces causing · this—a rapid increase in sea level rise and subsidence of land along the bay's edges—have no short-term remedy. One well-studied area, Blackwater National Wildlife Refuge, already has lost more than 5,000 acres in the last half century.

- Human impacts on tidal wetlands have slowed in the last decade or two, and creation of new marshes is probably exceeding losses. As with nontidal wetlands, it is likely that many created wetlands will not last as long, or perform as well, as the existing wetlands they replace. Minimizing losses is key, as opposed to simply creating more wetlands than we destroy.

- Maryland has lost 73 percent of its original wetlands, tidal and nontidal, while Virginia has lost an estimated 42 percent.

- Both Maryland and Virginia routinely approve hardening of their shorelines with erosion control devices that can degrade and destroy wetlands and shallow-water habitat. Both states have moved toward soft alternatives, such as planting wetlands, but they need to push such alternatives much more and do more to discourage shoreline armoring where evidence of erosion is slight.

CHESAPEAKE BAY PRESERVATION ACT

- Virginia's attempt to extend statewide protection to its environmentally critical bay shoreline was considered a bold step in 1988, but in retrospect was badly flawed. It has been largely a failure, lacking mechanisms for enforcement, adequate funding and staffing, and aggressive political support from state and county governments.

MARYLAND'S CRITICAL AREA ACT

- Maryland's attempt to protect its bay shoreline from development and pollution is tougher and more mature than Virginia's, although it applies in a narrower area, 1,000 feet back from the shoreline.

In 363,000 of the critical area's half a million or so acres, where strict, protective zoning applies, the law has been relatively successful in protecting open space along hundreds of thousands of acres of shoreline. A number of loopholes and exemptions and a lack of strong enforcement make the law less effective than it could be.

• A larger threat is the trend in many counties to develop in a substantial portion (95,000 acres) of the critical area that allows low-density sprawl, out of step with modern Smart Growth strategies. A part of the law lets counties transfer thousands of acres of land from the most protected shoreline into this area.

• What seemed a radical step in controlling growth in 1985 now seems increasingly like a solid but modest first step in what is needed across the watershed if the bay is to be healthy in coming decades.

Bottom of the Bay

Men who never wrote a line
Are the greatest poets ever.
Verses of love inscribed upon
The bottom of the cove.

—Gilbert Byron

It is not surprising that the Chesapeake poet Gilbert Byron would write these lines about oystermen who came to tong the little cove where he lived. The most important thing about the bay's bottom is how very close to the surface most of it is. Water that extends horizontally about 1 million feet (200 miles) and more than 100,000 feet (20 miles) across averages only about 21 feet deep. If we were to represent the whole estuary on the scale of a regulation football field and fill it to scale with water, the deepest spot in its main shipping channels would be a little over 1 inch and its average depth would be the thickness of three dimes—scarcely enough to dampen the field's turf.

What this means for the health of the Chesapeake is that its bottom—the sediments and also the grasses, oysters, and abundant other life there—is very much influenced by its water quality. And the state of these bottom communities in turn exerts huge influences on water quality. These two-way "conversations" between the bay's watery domain and its bottom communities are constant and loud . . . and all because the bottom is so extraordinarily close to the top.

As discussed earlier, the bay's resilience, its ability to handle environmental insult, has suffered from changes in its watershed—clearing and paving the forests, saturating the soils that drain to its rivers with excess agricultural fertilizers and manure, laying bare the soil to erosion through development and poor farming techniques, destroying the wetlands. In the same fashion, the estuary's degraded condition also reflects changes humans have caused to its bottom, where resilience also lies.

This section assesses the state of the bay by measuring three parts of the bay's bottom that are especially significant to the estuary's health—the grasses that grow in its shallows; the "benthos," the oysters and clams and worms and other creatures that inhabit the bottom muds and clays; and the sediments themselves.

UNDERWATER GRASSES—AN ECOLOGICAL DISASTER

It is hard to summon comparisons on land to the ecological disaster that swept the Chesapeake Bay's shallows a few decades ago. Imagine a great wind across the land that blew down most of the forests but, unlike a natural wind, never died down. This wind created an atmosphere so thick with dust, a climate so inhospitable, that trees could not regenerate. Woodland life that could not adapt to the new desert decreased or vanished. Some years the storm would relax its grip and the land would start to re-green, only to wither with renewed blasts. After a few decades, people almost regarded the desert as the natural state of things.

It sounds like science fiction. But it is a well-documented story—the 90 percent decline of the bay's estimated 600,000 acres (or more) of underwater meadows—rich habitat for everything from baby blue crabs to wintering tundra swans from Alaska's North Slope. Scientists call the meadows SAV, short for submerged aquatic vegetation, but that is like identifying the forest on land only as "woods." The SAV includes some sixteen varieties of plants, from the elegant, slim-bladed eelgrass of the salty lower bay, to the fluffy coontail grass, the horned pondweed, and the wild celery of the brackish and freshwater sections of the bay and its tidal rivers. Other varieties, like widgeon grass and redhead grass, are named for the waterfowl that fed on them. Indeed, the grass decline is one reason those and several other species of duck are below healthy population levels on the Chesapeake. The same goes for the troubled blue crab, whose young find the grassy bottoms a superb refuge in which to shed their shells as they grow.

The disappearance of SAV, which first began to be noticed during the 1960s and 1970s, was perhaps the strongest indication that a systemwide failure was occurring in the bay. Even so, it was ignored for years. Had a similar catastrophe occurred on the forests of the watershed, it would have drawn immediate attention from all over the world; but even the shallow water of the bay keeps problems out of sight and out of mind. The grasses are sensitive to changes in water quality. Analyses of old SAV pollen grains in the bay's deep sediments showed they had existed successfully throughout the estuary for hundreds and probably thousands of years until the early 1970s. Scientists think a big reemergence of the grasses would be one of the best indicators that the bay as a whole is coming back.

The grass beds are critical to bay health in several ways. They lend resilience to the system by interacting with the bay's waters—sopping up polluting nutrients such as nitrogen and phosphorus when the grasses are abundant, then releasing them as the grasses die back each year. Springtime storage of nutrients by the grasses, occurring when high river flows are delivering great pulses of nitrogen and phosphorus to the estuary, reduced growth of today's massively polluting levels of algae, which also feed on nutrients. Later in the year, the dieback of grasses released nutrients when river flows were lower, making nutrients available to the food chain when they were otherwise relatively scarce. The EPA has estimated that the underwater vegetation in a healthy Chesapeake Bay could have absorbed about half of all the nitrogen and phosphorus in modern sewage discharges to the bay.

The grass beds also filtered large quantities of sediment suspended in the water flowing into the bay, settling it out and stabilizing it around their roots. The net impact of all this was to clarify the water, which in turn allowed sunlight to penetrate, creating better growth conditions for the grasses. Thick beds of SAV also dampened wave energy before it hit shorelines, reducing erosion and sediment even further. A dramatic demonstration of this occurred one night during a kayak trip, when paddlers were mystified as they traveled through waters that grew uncomfortably choppy, then smooth, then back—several times in the course of a half mile or so. The next morning revealed they had been crossing a series of SAV beds and barren bottoms.

In effect, the bottom of the bay, when it was lush with grasses, was actively regulating the environment of the water above and around it, helping to keep it clear and clean, much as a large forest can create a microclimate of moist conditions that favor its continued survival. Nowadays, with most of that natural resilience gone, an endless "storm" of fertilizers and sediment assaults the bay. Sometimes, after a dry year or two reduces polluting runoff from the land, the storm abates a little and the grasses begin to spring back; but every time it becomes wet again, most of the gains vanish quickly. This now seems almost normal to a whole generation that has grown up since the 1970s.

That is a pity, because the grasses, wherever they still exist, are alive! If you had ever seen a Smith or Tangier Island soft-crabber pull up a huge roll of grass in the "scrape" (or dredge) dragged behind his boat— watched it vibrate and wriggle with shrimp, little fishes, soft crabs, sea horses, terrapins, baby hardcrabs—you would never again think of the grasses as just so many green plants. Losing grasses in the bay is as devastating for the estuary's life as clearing the jungle is for life in the Amazon rain forest. The grasses are also food for ducks and geese and swans, and an indirect source of food for many other creatures, such as egrets and herons and striped bass and speckled trout, that feed on crabs and shrimp and other small creatures that inhabit the grass beds.

LOSING THE LIGHT

The grasses died primarily from a lack of light, which they needed to grow. Too many nutrients—from human sewage and from agricultural chemicals, urban runoff, and air pollution—are entering the bay, causing so much growth of floating plankton that it clouds the water. Sediment flowing from farms and construction sites and from eroded shorelines and marshes adds to the problem. Algal growths directly coating the grasses' leaves provide the coup de grâce. As the grasses weakened, their very decline led to a loss of the bay bottom's capacity to absorb and filter the pollution, which in turn weakened the grasses further . . . and so the vicious cycle went. Indeed, declines in sea grasses are increasingly reported around the world in recent decades and frequently are linked to nutrient pollution similar to the bay's.

Rock bottom for the bay's grasses occurred in 1984, when the EPA estimated their acreage in the bay and its tributaries at about 37,000 acres. Since then, comebacks in a few areas where nutrient controls have worked—mostly downstream of upgraded sewage plants or where development has taken farms out of production—has raised the acreage to around 60,000–75,000, varying from wet years to dry ones. No one knows for sure how much SAV carpeted the bay bottom in healthy times, because scientific measurements didn't begin until the decline was well under way. The short-term restoration goal is 110,000 acres, with a long-term goal of around 600,000 acres—eight to ten times present levels of SAV.

Even that goal is probably no overestimate of what used to be. It assumes that enough light for healthy grass growth never existed below depths of 2 meters (about 6.5 feet). But there is tantalizing anecdotal evidence from old watermen who made catches of seafood from bay grass beds that the grasses were once thick in some places as deep as 10–15 feet. And recent reviews of 1938 and 1950s aerial photographs of Maryland are revealing huge, unbroken stretches of grasses around parts of the bay that have been barren for decades. In many areas grasses appear to be growing to depths of at least 12 feet—nearly 4 meters. Even today, in special places such as Dundee Creek of the Gunpowder River, grasses can be found growing 10 to 15 feet deep, offering a window into the past.

PROSPECTS FOR RECOVERY

If the bay's grasses remain far from healthy, there is solid, if scattered, evidence that the prospects of a major rebound are far from hopeless. Since 1984 the bay has seen substantial returns of grasses in a few places. In the Potomac, the river where reductions of nutrients from sewage have been most dramatic in the last decade, underwater vegetation went from al-

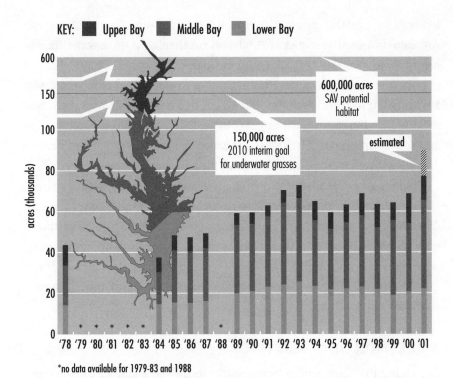

KEY: ■ Upper Bay ■ Middle Bay ■ Lower Bay

600,000 acres
SAV potential
habitat

150,000 acres
2010 interim goal
for underwater grasses

estimated

*no data available for 1979-83 and 1988

FIGURE 4.9. **Trends in Underwater Grasses.** Since the low points of the 1980s, the trend for underwater grasses has been upward, with strongest growth in dry years when the bay receives less runoff pollution (nitrogen, phosphorus, and sediment). The recovered areas give rich glimpses of what a recovered bay would be like, but key parts of the system are rebounding slowly or not at all. [EPA Chesapeake Bay Program, Virginia Institute of Marine Science]

most nothing to covering several thousand acres. As the grass beds proliferated, water clarity improved, as did the fishing and the populations of waterfowl observed on the river. (See Figure 4.9.)

One lesson from this is that reducing nutrients in the water, a major goal of the Chesapeake Bay cleanup program, is on the right track, although sediment reductions will likely be required in addition for a true restoration of SAV. Another lesson is that grasses can rebound quickly once conditions become favorable—and once established, they can further clear the water, creating even more favorable conditions for more grasses, and so forth. Just as environmental declines, once pollution worsens to a certain point, sometimes accelerate out of control, so may some environmental comebacks take off on their own once water quality improves to a certain level. The upper tidal Potomac had been so bare of grasses for more than a decade that many wondered whether there was anything left to come back; but like weeds in a field, the grasses seem able to reside, dormant, in what appears to be barren bottom for many years and still spring forth. The tides also can spread grass seeds from healthy areas to barren ones, as can waterfowl, in their feces.

There is also a small, but growing, movement in the last decade in both Maryland and Virginia to actively restore grasses by planting them. To date, this has involved only small acreages, more for educational purposes with schoolchildren than for true restoration. But techniques for planting larger acreages are coming into their own and may, in places where water quality can be improved enough, become an important tool in jump-starting a comeback.

A QUESTION OF QUALITY

In judging the success of any comebacks in the bay's grasses during coming years, we must be careful to look at more than just acreage. Are the grasses that evolved during centuries to do best in a given part of the bay the varieties that are coming back? Are we regaining the same diversity, or mix of species, that was there previously, or just one variety? Is the growth sparse, or thick and lush? Even in parts of the bay that have retained substantial grass beds, much of the acreage has shifted from the more stable eelgrass to widgeon grass, a more pioneering species that is prone to surging when conditions are good, but declining just as rapidly when they deteriorate. And significant portions of the SAV counted in today's acreage totals are characterized by sparse growth.

Finally, while the state of the grasses is one of the very best indicators of the state of the bay, we need to realize that like everything else about the estuary, any single year's observation will not tell us much. In the Choptank River on Maryland's Eastern Shore, for example, the grasses have made numerous comebacks, only to die back dramatically in a succeeding year. How do we interpret such confusing messages of success followed by failure? Scientists say the resurgence and subsequent flop were mostly responses to climate rather than to effects of pollution control programs. The increase in nutrients and sediment entering the bay from land runoff in a wet year, versus a normal or dry year, is enormous (Chapter 1)—more than enough to cause grass diebacks, or in dry years to cause comebacks. A long drought that lasted through the fall of 2002 boosted SAV to its best level in more than a decade. The true test will be whether those grasses hold up after several wet years—a test they cannot yet pass.

"MEMORY" OF THE BOTTOM

The bottom of the bay is often thought of as where the buck stops, where the soils and toxic chemicals and nutrients from sewage and farms and city streets all over the watershed finally come to rest. But they do not simply rest there.

Consider, for example, one of the bay's largest problems, the excessive amounts of nutrients—nitrogen and phosphorus—that it receives each year from sewage and from runoff from farms and developed areas. These nutrients grow too much algae, which in turn leads to oxygen depletion. In 1972, during Tropical Storm Agnes, the Chesapeake received some of the most intense rainfall in more than a century. The rivers delivered extraordinary volumes of nutrients during that time—more in days than the bay ordinarily gets in years. As expected, the bay experienced high growth of algae, or plankton, that year; but the next year, when much lower amounts of nutrients were flowing down the rivers, algae production surged even higher than in 1972. Apparently, nutrients from the year before were released from the bay's bottom to fuel the excessive growth. The bay was, in effect, remembering Agnes. It may seem odd to associate "memory" with something so unthinking as the mud at the bottom of the bay, but the question of how long pollutants in the bottom will keep coming back to haunt us is of major importance—because we have been insulting the estuary for a long time now.

Scientific thinking in the early 1980s held that the bay was a literal "sink" for virtually everything that entered it, including nitrogen and phosphorus. What came into the system never left it. Even if we were to succeed in drastically reducing the flows of sewage and farm fertilizers into the bay, the thinking went, there was enough nutrient buried in the bottom to keep causing problems with algae and oxygen for many, many years (lower summertime oxygen levels trigger the release of nutrients from bottom sediments).

But now a scientific consensus seems to be building that says the sediments are not the ultimate storage place for nutrients. Preliminary research is indicating that, far from being a total sink for nitrogen and phosphorus, the bay retains less than 20 percent of its nitrogen and related compounds and less than 70 percent of its phosphorus—and those numbers may drop as more is learned about the variety of physical, chemical, and biological processes that appear to transport them from the sediments into the atmosphere or out to sea. The implication for the bay cleanup is positive: The sediment memory for nutrients now appears to be short-term—on the order of months or perhaps a year or two at most. If we ever succeed in reducing the runoff to the bay of those pollutants to levels compatible with good water quality, then we should see a comeback sooner rather than later.

There may even be a better comeback scenario. Scientists who have looked at healthy estuaries comparable to the Chesapeake find they are up to twice as efficient at converting nitrogen buried in their sediments to harmless nitrogen gas (which goes back into the atmosphere). This is called denitrification. It means that as we reduce nitrogen and the bay's bottom begins to recover, it should increasingly help things along, ridding itself of more and more nitrogen. The healthier it gets, the faster it will help itself.

For many toxic chemicals and industrial metals, which bind permanently to sediments, the bay's bottom does appear to be more of a final sink. This long memory for toxics is all the more reason to be zealous in reducing what gets into the bay. Even with toxics, however, there is hope for recovery as we cut pollution. The normal processes of new sediment settling atop the old will bury the contaminated bottom layers. In fact, this has happened to the poisonous Kepone lodged in the bottom of the James. A decade after the dumping of this pesticide was halted, the river was declared open to fishing again. A cautionary note is that dredging places where old toxics are buried can stir up those poisonous substances.

BENTHOS—THE BOTTOM DWELLERS

Like the underwater grasses, the teeming assortment of clams, worms, sponges, corals, and other benthos lodged in the muds and sands and clays of the bay bottom interact constantly with the water above them. Many species filter huge quantities of algae and sediment from the waters of the bay as they feed. Most notable is—or was—the American oyster. Scientists estimate this most famous member of the Chesapeake's benthic communities once had the capacity, as it fed by straining water through its gills, to filter and clarify large portions of the bay every few days. Today's depleted oyster populations take nearly a year to cleanse that much bay water.

Until recent decades, the decline of bay oysters was regarded only as the loss of an economic and food resource. But the loss to the bay's resilience is an equal or even more serious impact of the great oyster decline. As discussed in Chapter 3, oysters have been reduced by pollution, overfishing, mismanagement, and disease to about 1 percent of the original population, and even the current goal of restoring them to 10 percent of earlier numbers is highly ambitious, given the continued presence of diseases.

Like the underwater grasses, the oyster also functions as a "banker" and recycler of the huge pulses of nutrients that surge off the watershed in the wet springtime. It filters the lush, nutrient-fertilized spring plankton bloom through its gills, using some of it for growth, but also depositing nutrient-rich packets of feces and sediment on the bay's bottom—a bottom that is seldom far from the top; thus these nutrient packages gift-wrapped by the oyster's excretory system can be recycled into production again. Some scientists think this same process also rids the bay of significant amounts of polluting nitrogen, converting it to harmless nitrogen gas, which rises into the atmosphere.

In addition to its stabilizing and cleansing functions, a healthy oyster bed is also the bay's equivalent of the tropical coral reef. Its hard surfaces and millions of crevices provide habitat for more than 300 different bay organisms. These, in turn, attract feeding fish in warmer months and sea ducks and possibly loons in the winters. Young crabs also seem to prefer oystery bottoms as wintertime habitat. Indeed, all the benthos form a vast reservoir of food and habitat for fish and blue crabs and diving ducks, providing the majority of their diet. The benthos are especially central to the diet of many fish during their juvenile stages. A decline in the benthos may thus have every bit as much impact on fish populations as filling wetlands or damming a spawning river.

That makes the benthos one of the more valuable indicators of bay health. Because they have little ability to move, and spend their whole adult lives in the same place, their health is an accurate reflection of water quality. Healthy benthic communities have a wide mix of long- and short-lived creatures, and also of species that range from tolerant to intolerant of pollution. Using these and other measurements of health, scientists in the last decade have developed an Index of Biological Integrity, which in effect describes how the living is along the bottom of the estuary. They rank different areas of the bottom on a scale of 1 (very bad) to 5 (very good). Any bottom with a benthic scorecard of 3 or higher is considered healthy. Anything lower than 2 is considered severely degraded. In recent years, about half the bay bottom has scored lower than 3, and about a quarter has been ranked severely degraded. In 1998, a year with especially terrible drops in oxygen throughout the bay's deeps, nearly 60 percent of the whole bay bottom was below 3, and almost a third was below 2. In Maryland, where oxygen problems are typically worse than farther down the bay, 69 percent of the bottom was unhealthy that year.

The trends have been upward in some places. The abundance and diversity of benthos in recent decades have increased significantly in the middle and outer portions of Baltimore Harbor, apparently a response to reduced levels of toxic chemicals discharged there.

There is also some suggestion from recent scientific studies that several pollution-tolerant species of benthos are capable of filtering and cleansing volumes of water on the scale of the bay's original populations of oysters. These filterers include varieties of small clams, sea squirts, and hydroids (which resemble underwater tumbleweeds), as well as barnacles, sea anemones, and sponges. What is not known is the extent to which these organisms occurred when oysters were in their heyday—were they doing their job in addition to all those oysters, or have they expanded since the oyster declined? Unlike the long-lived oyster, many of these organisms may vary tremendously in numbers (and filtering) from year to year.

Scientists have not been keeping an index of benthic health long enough to show trends, up or down, in the health of bottom communities for the bay as a whole. But by counting the tiny fossils of certain types of algae taken from sediment cores drilled several feet into the bay bottom—sediments going back several centuries—they have been able to reconstruct a profound change that has occurred over time. In pre-European times, the bay appears to have been dominated by types of algae known as "pinnate," which dwelled in the bottom layers of bay water, indicating healthier conditions there. Bottom algae outnumbered floating algae three to one. This balance began to shift as early as 1800, but galloped out of control during the last half century as the bay grew more polluted, favoring floating algae. Today, surface algae dominate bottom algae five to one, an underwater shift as profound as replacing the pre-European prairies with cornfields or the great forests of the mid-Atlantic with urban corridors.

ALGAE—A BAY OUT OF BALANCE

The bay's tiny floating plant life, known as algae or phytoplankton, is the base of the food web for all higher forms of seafood. The menhaden is the only bay fish able to get its nourishment directly from grazing the algae. The vast majority of algae is consumed by the zooplankton, small floating animals, which in turn are eaten by the bay anchovies, silversides, and other small fish that support rockfish, weakfish, and other larger species.

One might suppose that the overfertilized bay's huge excesses of algae would mean great eating all the way up the food web—the more the better. But scientists increasingly think that the varieties of algae typical in the modern, polluted bay do not form a balanced meal for their zooplankton consumers. Like humans, the zooplankton need a mix of amino acids, carbohydrates, and proteins to thrive. But the variety of algal species they need for that is lacking in the modern, polluted bay, which is more single entrée than smorgasbord and includes algae the zooplankton find hard to ingest, or even toxic. Instead of being transformed into fish food, a lot of today's algae sinks to the bottom, decomposing and robbing the waters of life-giving oxygen.

Conclusions

- The bottom of the bay, from its grass beds to its oysters and worms and muddy sediments, is intimately and continuously influencing— and being influenced by—the water. The water, of course, is in large part a product of what rain carries off, and what percolates through, the lands of the watershed.

  It is all connected. It may never be possible to link, with legal pre-ciseness, the destruction of a forest acre at the head of some bay river with the decline of an underwater grass bed downstream or to con-nect directly the poor management of manure in a specific dairy barnyard with the loss of oxygen where fish once fed in the bay. But the general connection is all too clear. As humans have eliminated and overloaded the buffering and filtering capacities of forest and soil on the land, so they have also eliminated and overloaded similar systems such as the grasses and the benthos on the bay bottom. And the thin film of water in the middle—what is (too narrowly) defined as the Chesapeake Bay—has suffered, and will continue to suffer, until both watershed and water's bottom are restored to a greater de-gree of natural functioning.

- The underwater vegetation that carpeted the bay's bottom for thou-sands of years has been reduced by pollution to about 12 percent of the area it once covered. To date, it has shown no strong trend to-ward baywide recovery, though there are signs in a few rivers it can rebound rapidly when water conditions improve.

- The grasses' sensitivity to improvement in water quality, along with their vital roles as habitat and resilience, make them one of the best indicators of environmental success or failure in restoring the bay.

- The current strategies to bring back the grasses—reducing sediments and nutrients—appear to be the proper courses to follow. Attempts to reestablish them by replanting don't yet have much promise on a large scale because efforts are so labor intensive and water quality is not good enough.

- The benthos, the assortment of shellfish, worms, and other bottom dwellers, are also excellent indicators of improving or declining water quality and should be monitored. Virginia especially needs to improve its database.

- Monitoring of the benthos indicates a worsening in oxygen levels in some parts of the bay between the 1970s and the 1980s, a modest environmental improvement in Baltimore Harbor in recent years, and a possible improvement in water quality coming down the Susquehanna River.

- The loss of most of the bay's oysters has meant much more than a loss of an economic and food resource. It has meant the loss of a vital part of the bay's resilience, its ability to rebound from environmental insult. Healthy populations of oysters, with their immense filtering capacity, can play as large a role in maintaining bay water quality as the multibillion-dollar human technology of sewage treatment.

- The bay's bottom is less of a final resting place, or "sink," for key pollutants nitrogen and phosphorus than was thought a decade ago. (For other pollutants, such as sediment and the toxic chemicals that cling to it, the bay still appears pretty much a sink.) In general, the fact that the bay is less a sink for nutrients than thought is good news. It means pollutants from years and decades past should not come seeping back out the sediments, degrading water quality for lengthy periods of time after current pollution is reduced. In sum, if pollution is reduced enough, the bay should respond faster than was once thought.

CLEARING THE WATERS

How clear were the bay's waters when its rivers ran cleaner, when grasses grew lushly across half a million acres or more of its bottom and hundreds of millions of oysters filtered a volume equal to the whole bay every few days? It's a vital question now that water clarity has been added to the water quality standards deemed necessary for the estuary's restoration. In fact, no one measured clarity scientifically in the days before cloudy, algae- and sediment-clogged water became a permanent fixture and the source of systemwide bay declines.

But there are some tantalizing anecdotal accounts.

Frank Leslie's Illustrated Newspaper, in its February 10, 1866, issue, tells of canvasback ducks feeding on wild celery that grew on shoals "eight or nine feet deep" in the upper Chesapeake, where the water now is some of the bay's most turbid, and where wild celery—and canvasbacks—are scarce these days.

Old watermen who were catching soft crabs from the bay's bottom during the 1920s and 1930s have shown the author places where they worked in thick grass, which needs good light to grow, in 15–16 feet of water.

Bernie Fowler, a former Maryland state senator from the Patuxent River in southern Maryland, holds an annual "wade in" every June to commemorate when he could walk out, crabbing, during the 1940s, shoulder deep, and see his feet. Bernie says crab nets then used handles as long as 10–12 feet to dip crabs from the grassy bottoms. Average underwater visibility there now is often less than 2 feet.

One of the most compelling accounts of a clearer bay comes from the late Donald Heinle, a noted bay scientist. He was aloft in a National Guard aircraft on a clear, windless day in 1963, flying the length of the estuary for several hours. Heinle, then a Ph.D. student in marine science, said he was able to see virtually the entire bay bottom except for the deep channels—see to depths approaching 40 feet. It made a strong and lasting impression on him, Heinle recalled, "because I grew up around Puget Sound, which is hundreds of feet deep. To be able to see the bottom in such a huge body of water was just amazing."

Heinle did have optimal conditions. It was late fall or early winter, and colder water is generally clearer, as algae production slows down. And 1963 was a dry year, with little runoff of sediment and nutrients to cloud the water. Still, his observations are remarkable, compared to today's limited visibilities in bay waters—and remarkable also because they indicate the bulk of the change in clarity has come quite recently in the bay's history.

The late Dixie Buck would have agreed with that. She made a living for decades peering into the waters of the lower Patuxent River to dip soft crabs. She told the author that it was around the mid-1960s that she was certain the water clarity had taken a permanent shift for the worse.

Upstream and Down

. . . for the savory shad is seen no more
above Columbia's smoke-wrapt shore.
Through centuries we'll sing the psalm,
O dam Columbia! Columbia dam!

—Anonymous poem, 1899, on the first dam cutting off
fish passage up the Susquehanna River

Water quality is the aspect of the bay's rivers that gets the most environmental concern, but the physical flows of those rivers are critical to the bay's health, too.

DAMS

The bay's resilience has been lost in varying degrees from the forests and wetlands of its watershed, from its marshy edges, and from its bottom. But nowhere has the loss been more complete—or more clearly reversible—than on its blockaded rivers. We think of the bay's vast drainage system as flowing always downstream to the estuary; but moving upstream are the great springtime tides of migratory fish, surging in from the oceans and lower rivers, driven by a spawning urge to penetrate the watershed to its farthest edges. These include the herring and shad and rockfish, and to a lesser extent the white and yellow perch.

For the fish, spawning is a gamble, highly dependent for success on coinciding with just the right water temperature, and with just the right streamflows to wash food downstream at the right time to nourish the hatching larvae. In most places and in most years, the result is more bust than boom. The fish have evolved to cope with such difficulties in two ways. They lay a lot of eggs (millions in the case of big female rockfish), and they spawn over hundreds and even thousands of miles of water—in effect, placing their bets at many different windows, covering all the options. This strategy ensures that at least some of their species in some places each year will make a go of it.

As we built dams during the last few centuries to harness the rivers for power, or to pool them in lakes for drinking water, flood control, and recreation, we began to close windows for the upstream spawners, to make them dependent on ever smaller portions of their historic habitat—a loss of resilience as certain as destroying the forests in which upland game roamed.

Herring and shad were the real long-distance runners. They originally swam and leaped up the rocky, shallow, Susquehanna River as far as New York State, more than 300 miles from the river's mouth. Farmers in the Amish country of Lancaster County, Pennsylvania, in the early years of the twentieth century, filled their wagons with as much as 400,000 pounds of shad annually, netted from the Susquehanna. Similarly, shad and herring reached upriver on Virginia's mighty James and its tributaries to the foothills of the Blue Ridge Mountains.

The greatest river migrations vanished as hydroelectric and water supply dams built from the 1820s through the 1930s closed off hundreds of miles of major spawning rivers and thousands of miles of lesser streams. The era of the automobile also took its toll, as thousands of smaller tributaries were blocked to fish passage where earthen berms carried roads across streams. The pipes, or culverts, that carried the stream beneath the road were often elevated too far above the stream on one end to allow fish passage. Plenty of spawning areas lower down the rivers, and in parts of the bay proper, remained open—enough to sustain large harvests until overfishing and pollution brought catches down to a shadow of their potential by the 1980s.

In the last decade, for the first time in nearly two centuries, bay restoration efforts have begun to reverse this loss of resilience, showing dramatic progress. Between 1989 and 2002, the three principal watershed states have built more than a hundred fish passages over and around dams, including a giant lift that takes fish over 110-foot-high Conowingo Dam near the mouth of the Susquehanna. Nearly forty dams have been removed, and another thirty have been breached or notched to allow fish passage. Nearly 850 miles of "amputated" spawning habitat has had its circulation restored. By 2003, the states expect to meet their ten-year goal of restoring 1,357 river and stream miles to spawning. Reopening a stretch of river or stream does not guarantee an automatic explosion of spawning fish; in some cases, it will take years of effort to restock waters

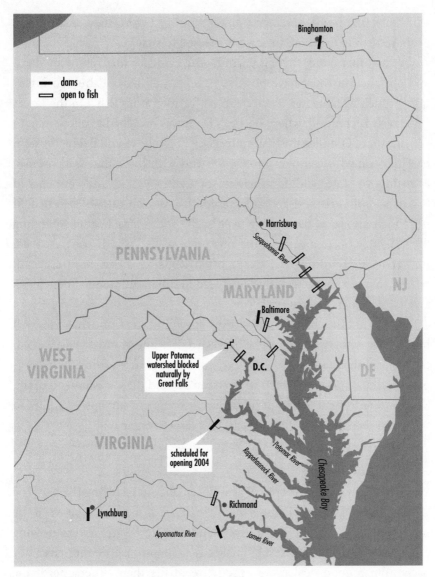

FIGURE 4.10. The Amputated Bay. Thousands of miles of rivers and streams that used to serve as spawning grounds for bay fish such as shad and herring were cut off by dams in the late nineteenth and twentieth centuries. In the past ten years, however, there has been significant progress in opening up effective fish passageways, notably on the Susquehanna and the James, and the only major dam on the Rappahannock is scheduled for removal in 2004.

with baby shad and herring, and years more before they mature and begin returning to where they were released to spawn.

On the other hand, there is encouraging evidence that removing dams and obstructions may have positive benefits well beyond human intentions, which were just to restore habitat for migratory fish. On the James River near Richmond, where Bosher's Dam was breached to allow shad to run another 200 miles upstream, the river both above and below the dam has "blossomed" with new aquatic life and with birds that feed on fish, according to state wildlife officials. Apparently, year-round residents of the river, from eels and gar to largemouth bass and catfish, also benefit from the removal of dams. Seventeen such species have begun expanding their habitat upstream since the obstruction at Bosher's was removed. Just as one environmental insult often leads to other, unforeseen ill effects, so also can one positive deed lead to other, unintended benefits—a vicious cycle in reverse.

There is another benefit of restoring spawning runs, one that goes well beyond the extra fish that can be harvested. It is one of most vivid ways to reconnect inhabitants of the watershed who dwell far from the Chesapeake with the place to which their streams—and their wastes—all drain. Shad and herring arriving far inland each spring are a happy reminder to upstream dwellers that they are part of a larger system.

LOW FLOWS

Water quantity can be as critical as water quality in restoring the bay. The very essence of the bay is the dynamic balance it maintains between the salt ocean pushing up its channels and the freshwater rivers flowing down. The mixture that results makes the Chesapeake neither river nor ocean, but a good deal more productive of life than either one. If the flows of the rivers were to diminish permanently, the bay, of course, would not dry out; the ocean would just push up further, maintaining the same volume as always. But the balance of fresh and salt would be altered, with dramatic impacts on aquatic life. A panel of experts several years ago evaluated the impacts of a saltier bay, given trends toward increasing human use of the freshwater flowing into the estuary. The panel conceded that making such projections stretched the limits of science, but nevertheless believed that many more bay species would be harmed than helped. Some of those projected to suffer most were striped bass, oysters, shad, and redhead and canvasback ducks. Moderately favored by the change were sea nettles, hard clams, barnacles, spot, and menhaden.

Not all freshwater use harms the bay. A large percentage of what humans consume for drinking, flushing toilets, showering, and cooling industrial machinery is returned fairly efficiently to the bay through sewage flows and industrial discharge pipes. The key is "consumptive loss." This is often evaporation, such as from watering lawns and crops and golf courses on hot days. By far the largest consumptive losses come from the cooling towers used by power plants and some industries. On the Susquehanna River, where water is monitored more carefully than on any other bay tributary, consumptive losses have been heading steadily toward a critical point that is not many years away (see "Susquehanna" in Chapter 2, "Pollution").

Another potential loss of freshwater to the bay is the proposed widening and deepening of the Chesapeake and Delaware Canal, the shipping link between the upper Chesapeake and Delaware Bays. The canal shuttles massive flows of water in and out of the upper Chesapeake through its 45-foot-deep channel. At peak tidal flow, oceanographers must use 1,100-pound locomotive wheels to anchor their current meters in place. Of course, the tides run equally in both directions—from the Chesapeake and back to it. However, the net flow, because of the canal's slope, is out of the Chesapeake. Currently, it is a small loss of freshwater, but the impacts of widening and deepening the canal will need to take into consideration whether the net freshwater outflows from the Chesapeake would be altered.

Despite the real potential for a saltier bay in the long term, there has been little action among the bay states and the EPA to form a coherent, long-term plan to avoid changes to the bay's essential balance of freshwater and salt. Water conservation is usually pursued on a short-term basis during severe droughts. Energy conservation, which could cut consumptive losses of water by cutting the growth of power plants, is not nearly as high as it should be on state and national agendas.

Conclusions

- The current baywide goal of reopening all historical spawning rivers and streams by removing dams that have cut off thousands of miles is an excellent one, and real progress was made in the last decade, restoring nearly a thousand miles of habitat. Its value is both economic—increased commercial and recreational fishing opportunities—and political: What better way to convince Pennsylvanians near the New York border and Virginians in Albemarle County they are part of the bay's watershed than to send them a gift of shad and herring every spring?

- Humans are using the freshwater of the bay watershed in quantities that will eventually shift its salinity in ways that will harm more creatures than it will benefit. On the Susquehanna, freshwater consumption is already at the point where a severe drought would compromise the amount of river flow needed to sustain good fisheries habitat below Conowingo Dam.

- A proposal in the decision process in 2002 to widen and deepen the canal linking the Chesapeake and Delaware Bays has potential to cause additional leakage of freshwater from the upper Chesapeake.

- Water conservation and energy conservation to cut losses of freshwater are not getting the consideration they deserve.

The Ultimate Issue: People

We end at what might be called the standard paradox of the twentieth century. Our tools are better than we are, and grow faster than we do. They suffice to crack the atom, to command the tides. But they do not suffice for the oldest task in human history: to live on a piece of land without spoiling it.

—Aldo Leopold

More than sixty years have passed since the conservationist and author Leopold wrote those words. Our technology has continued to grow, and it is clearer than ever that, as vital as good technology is to environmental progress, our best tools will never restore systems like the Chesapeake Bay unless we also retool ourselves.

A conference held along the Patuxent River in the spring of 1977 touched on the heart of what such a retooling would mean. Maryland and Virginia were concluding their first-ever joint meeting on the health of the Chesapeake Bay. They called the estuary "fairly healthy," but identified several worrisome trends that in retrospect were warnings of a widespread and worsening systemwide decline. The speaker chosen to summarize the conference, Dr. J. L. McHugh, of the Marine Sciences

Research Center of the State University of New York-Albany, ended on a prophetic note—as true today as it was then:

> One theme has run like a thread through all the papers and discussions in this conference, as it does in all discussions of environmental management. It is an issue that is almost always evaded, and certainly never addressed seriously. Yet this is the root problem of the environment, the basic cause of all the other problems—the human population explosion . . . if we cannot cope with it, maybe everything else will be in vain.

Assuming that we eventually reduced population growth, Dr. McHugh said, another set of problems might also do us in: "That is our preoccupation with what we call 'progress,' which promises to add a growing load, per capita, of contamination to the environment."

He thus proposed the two core issues fundamental to protecting the health of the Chesapeake Bay: How many people can ultimately coexist with the rest of the natural system; and at what level of consumption—that is, how much demand can their lifestyles make on the natural resources of the region? The two—how many people, and what impact each makes—are obviously linked. The entire population of Earth, some 6 billion souls, could fit into a couple of the metro counties surrounding Baltimore; and a few good-sized Pennsylvania or Virginia farms could accommodate all 16 million or so people who live in the bay's watershed. Of course, they would be packed like poultry in a coop, shoulder to shoulder, about 4 square feet apiece. And before long, someone would raise a hand, wanting to go to the bathroom, and another would decide he or she wanted a house—on a little land, and while you're at it, how about a water view, even if it did mean cutting a couple trees and filling a smidgen of wetlands. Then someone would get hungry and plow up some extra land to feed them; and consumer goods, heat, air conditioning, transportation—here would come the factories and the power plants and the highways; also pollution and loss of open space, and regulations to limit the impacts of both. The scenario is absurd, but the point is not. The more people there are in a place, the less each one can afford to live in ways that degrade its air, landscape, and water. As a result, we make rules that govern how we live; and it is likely that as our numbers grow, so will the numbers of laws and regulations that restrict what we can do. Better technology, such as breakthroughs in sewage treatment and cleaner-running cars, has helped hold the line on pollution without much limiting population growth or lifestyles, but clearly there have been limits to this. Nearly two decades of concerted bay restoration efforts, including more and tougher rules on pollution and on use of private property, have only modestly improved the estuary's poor health. A lot of prime farmland and wildlife habitat has been lost forever, and traffic congestion degrades the quality of life more every year in suburban regions throughout the bay.

In large part, this is because around a million new people have been added to the watershed every decade, doubling population in the bay region since 1950 and heading toward doubling it again in this century. To reach the goals of dramatic reductions in key bay pollutants, we must offset *all* the pollution caused by a million new people each decade before we can even get started—like rowing 4 knots upstream against a current running at 3. You expend a lot of effort and all in the right direction. But are you ever going to get there?

Adding to the difficulty of making progress against population growth, today's new residents of the watershed are very different from those who were moving in fifty years ago. In recent decades, most of us have cast a much larger "ecological footprint"—each of us uses more open space, per capita, to house ourselves; we drive more cars more miles, use more energy, and produce more waste. Scientists who have calculated a modern American's consumption of energy for transportation, food, housing, heating, cooling, and the like find that each is equivalent to a full-grown sperm whale in the calories of energy he or she requires each day for support. So there are more of us, each grown large as whales in our demands on the environment, and there is little sign of either population growth or individual consumption slowing. We are still very much trying to figure how, in Leopold's words, to "live on a piece of land without spoiling it."

FOCUSING ON ONE SIDE OF THE PROBLEM

Around the Chesapeake and around the nation, virtually all the considerable energy put into environmental protection has focused on half of the problems outlined a quarter century ago by Dr. McHugh. Despite generous lip service paid to local and national population growth as a root of environmental problems, the overwhelming emphasis of our actions remains on trying to "accommodate growth" by moderating our per capita impacts on the environment. There are certainly huge gains for the Chesapeake to be had from modifying how we live, from making "progress" less polluting. We have only scratched the surface of what is possible, and it is critical to continue working this side of the equation no matter what happens with population growth. If no more people moved to the bay region after today, for example, the current, degraded state of the bay means we would still need to continue working hard to reduce the polluting impacts of the population already living here. Also, any actions to limit population will require decades to take effect, leaving reduction of our per capita impacts nearly the whole ball game in the shorter term.

But for the long run, is it realistic to assume that population growth, without any regard to limit or pace, can be "accommodated" by relying solely on technology, pollution control, and land use restrictions, critical as all those will continue to be? Will the job of restoring the Chesapeake to the health it enjoyed when population was one-half current levels, and sustaining that health as population doubles yet again, succeed if we keep ignoring a significant force that drives environmental degradation? These are urgent questions for the nation's and the bay region's policymakers to address. Some new studies discussed later in this chapter are beginning to question whether our best current efforts at limiting environmental impacts will only delay the inevitable if numbers of people mount without limit. Certainly, technology and smarter land use can go a long way to improve environmental conditions even as population grows. But the time is past due, around the Chesapeake and around the world, to move from just talking about population to considering actions that would stabilize or even reduce it.

It is beyond the scope of this book, and beyond the Chesapeake Bay Foundation acting alone, to offer precise strategies for limiting population. Yet the CBF challenges others to join it in what ultimately must be a national and global debate on the topic. This chapter lays out, while not endorsing, some current points of view about how population stability might be achieved and touches on the social and economic ramifications of such a policy.

Taking on the issue of population growth and its impact on the environment is a daunting task, but one that has been in the offing for decades. Consider these conclusions of the bipartisan Congressional Commission on Population Growth and the American Future, convened by President Richard Nixon and chaired by John D. Rockefeller III in 1972:

> *In the long run, no substantial benefits will result from further growth of the nation's population. Rather, the gradual stabilization of our population would contribute significantly to the nation's ability to solve its problems.*
>
> *We have looked for, and have not found, any convincing economic argument for continued population growth. The health of our country does not depend on it, nor does the vitality of business nor the welfare of the average person. . . .*

In a similar vein, alternatives to the current, high-consumption, high-pollution notion of progress do not mean a lesser standard of existence. They do mean giving serious thought and encouragement to achieving a quality, sustainable existence for our descendants and for ourselves. The antidote to gluttony, whether it involves appetites for food or natural resources, is not starvation, but eating well and wisely.

The rest of this chapter is divided into two major sections. The first looks at how we live, at the environmental impacts of our current lifestyles. The second part examines the need for limiting how many people live here.

How We Live

We have met the enemy and he is us.

—Pogo

If the enemy is us, the solution is near at hand. For those who wonder how many more people can ultimately live around the Chesapeake Bay without degrading it, the short answer is this: Too many are here already—given the way we live today. The bay is already degraded, its capacity to remain healthy already exceeded. The real point, of course, is that population numbers can never be divorced from population impacts. As important as how many of us live here is *how* we live. What is our per capita consumption of land and other natural resources? What are our per capita production of wastes and the disposal of those wastes? Americans comprise about 6 percent of Earth's people but consume more than 25 percent of Earth's petroleum, industrial metals, and other nonrenewable natural resources. If global trade someday enabled the other 94 percent of the world to live the American way, we'd need a few more Earths to support it.

To simply assign the blame for bay pollution to "industry" or "agriculture" or "developers" is to ignore a critical fact: Many of the problems with the Chesapeake Bay are the cumulative impact of fulfilling the wants and needs of every one of the nearly 16 million people who live in its watershed. Consider one of the leading answers to a bay-region survey that asked people if they "scooped up" after their pets defecated on urban pavements (this can significantly cut pollution in stormwater runoff): "It's only a small dog." The answer is a small example of how people often multiply their individual actions by a factor of one, when they should be multiplying by the 16 million who inhabit the bay's watershed.

A classic example of the power of millions of individual actions was the change in home laundry detergents brought about more than a decade ago by phosphate bans in Maryland, Virginia, and Pennsylvania. It was painless and virtually without cost to consumers (though it was bitterly opposed by industry lobbyists who predicted people would leave the region in despair at the lack of "whiter whites"). Almost overnight the ban accounted for a 30 to 50 percent reduction in phosphorus from sewage plants, a major pollutant of the Chesapeake Bay. Achieving similar reductions through technological changes to the plants would have cost hundreds of millions of dollars and taken years for construction. Make no mistake, environmental protection measures that do not consider moderating the habits and lifestyles of individuals will always undershoot their target, or fail outright. Consider the following examples.

- To accommodate the meat-heavy American diet, we concentrate animals in factory-like farms, where manure becomes a major source of polluted runoff. We use nitrogen fertilizer, another large source of water pollution, in amounts up to 40 percent greater than required by a less meat-intensive diet (the reason: feeding grain to farm animals takes several times the fertilized acreage to produce a given amount of nutrition as feeding it directly to people in pastas, vegetables, breads, and cereals).

- Manufacturers have dramatically reduced emissions from individual vehicles, but we now own more cars, drive them more than ever, and increasingly favor gas-guzzling SUVs and pickup trucks that are exempt from the most stringent tailpipe controls, sending air pollution from cars ever upward. Since 1970, total vehicle miles driven in the bay watershed have increased nearly four times as fast as population.

  Vehicles also take up more open space than just highways—an estimated seven paved parking spaces exist for every automobile in the United States. "Car habitat," the sum total of driveways, streets, garages, and parking lots, accounts for 55–75 percent of all paving of open space in the towns and subdivisions around the Chesapeake watershed.

- We have expanded landfills and built waste incinerators, but we continue to generate more and more trash per capita than in the past. Residents in the watershed a few decades ago generated 2.2 pounds of garbage a day. This has risen more than 50 percent, to 3.3 pounds a day. (See Figure 5.1.)

- Around the bay, we plan and zone and lobby for Smart Growth more than ever in history, but we average using around twice the open space to live on, per capita, as we did fifty years ago—and each new resident uses more than three times as much open space. This galloping sprawl means that of all the land development in the bay watershed since the Jamestown colony almost 400 years ago, nearly a third (1.3 million acres) has happened in the last 20 years (USDA Natural Resources Inventory statistics). It means that the Washington–Baltimore metropolitan area's geographic spread has increased substantially faster than its population.

- Energy consumption in the watershed has followed a course similar to waste—energy consumption is up twice as fast as population.

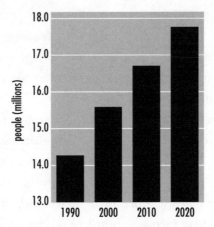

FIGURE 5.1. **Population Trends.** Population growth in the Chesapeake Bay watershed has doubled since 1950. It is expected to increase by more than 2 million people during the period 2000–2020, an increase of 15 percent to the "people pressures" already affecting the system. To make net progress in restoring the bay, we must deal with these additional stresses as well as existing ones. [EPA Chesapeake Bay Program]

BOX 5.1. Why Farms?

Open space, as opposed to development, generally is taken to be an unquestioned good in terms of environmental impacts to the Chesapeake Bay. But in preserving open space that happens to be on farms, the issue is more complicated. As discussed in the section on agriculture in Chapter 2, farms constitute a major source of pollution to the bay. Indeed, they have been among the most difficult sources to control, although the problems are as much political and financial as technical. Developers sometimes argue compellingly that a development with excellent controls on sediment and stormwater pollution can equal or surpass the water quality running to the bay from even the best-managed farm. Increasingly, too, modern farming techniques have destroyed the hedgerows and windbreaks and forested streamsides that promoted wildlife. So why fight development on farmland?

One obvious argument for preserving farmland is food production. Locally grown produce and feed and meat result in a better and more economic diet for the citizens of a state. Eating locally produced food also reduces transportation needs and thus energy use. Moreover, agriculture is still very much part of our heritage, a vital part of the "working landscape" discussed in this chapter. There is more to maintaining a pleasing landscape than maximizing pollution control.

Keeping land in agriculture also keeps open options for land use in two ways. First, the nature of agriculture has gone through many changes in the last century; on Maryland's Eastern Shore, for example, it has gone from orchards to truck farming to dairying to corn and soybeans. The present-day intensive grain and animal cultures that dominate the watershed are among the most polluting forms of agriculture we have experienced; but there is ample historical precedent to make us think this is not a permanent state.

Second, if it becomes necessary for preserving water quality or natural habitat, a farm (or parts of it) can be fairly easily taken out of production and returned to less-polluting land uses such forest or hayfields or nontidal wetlands. Once the land becomes a strip mall, most other options are forever precluded. If our aim is to contain sprawl development, which is harmful both economically and environmentally, most farms are the worst place to allow more development, because most of them are not near existing growth centers where we want to encourage additional development.

Development also has many impacts on the environment and the economy that extend beyond the borders of the farm it supplants. Commercial and residential areas require a multitude of new public services, from road improvements to utilities to police and fire protection to schools. They also add cars, air pollution from driving and home heating, and more demand for recreational amenities. Farmland, by contrast, puts a very low demand on public services.

There is also good reason to think that farming can be carried out with minimal pollution if we get serious about both pollution control and changing the way we farm to create less pollution to control in the first place. Finally, "working landscapes"—those that contain farms and watermen's villages and towns and open space in a diverse mix—are what give each region of the bay its uniqueness and character, an essential part of what some have called the "spirit of place." For all these reasons a policy of replacing farms with development would be the most shortsighted of solutions to the bay's problems.

And these numbers only hint at the ripple effects of an increasingly consumptive lifestyle—the added trees that were felled for the added pavement needed for the added cars, reducing the natural resilience of the landscape to cleanse polluted runoff; the destruction of bay and river shoreline to site the added power plants needed to meet the added electrical demands; and the air pollution from generating more power. Even if the population were not growing rapidly, the bay could not stand having its present population continue to live as it does now. We bay dwellers and our fellow Americans are the hungriest and most destructive resource users ever to inhabit the earth. The greatest of the dinosaurs by comparison were nibbling mice.

CONSPICUOUS CONSUMPTION AND HAPPINESS

Fortunately, the alternatives leading to a restored bay do not mean an impoverished existence; rather, they may lead to a higher quality of life. One example: Western Europeans, with a high standard of living, use about half the energy we do to generate each dollar of economic activity. Similarly, reducing waste means recycling and reuse, emphasizing quality products over disposables, not doing without material goods. Reducing the runaway consumption of open space can lower property taxes and breathe new life into small-town and village patterns of development, and into enhancing the livability of existing cities. Limiting sprawl also limits time spent in traffic jams and on long commutes, and increases time for family and fun. Using fewer pesticides is turning out to increase profitability for more and more farmers. They hire "scouts" who track insect populations and tell them when they need to spray (and when not), saving substantial money in most years.

And just as increasing individual consumption can have adverse ripple effects far beyond the direct impact, so can reducing it, or shifting it to cleaner alternatives, send out beneficial ripples. Thus, channeling growth into more compact population centers not only saves open space, but it makes mass transit, biking, and walking more viable, reducing air pollution from cars and environmental degradation from highway building. Recycling plastics not only saves energy, it helps attack the problem of throwaway plastic waste, which now accounts for more than 60 percent of the billions of pounds a year of garbage humans throw into the world's oceans. Marine life and seabirds become entangled in floating plastic products, or eat them, clogging their digestive tracts.

Commercial interests and supporters of "business as usual" will argue that Americans live and consume as they do because that is precisely the way they wish to live, and pity the politician who tries to tamper with this American dream. But pursuing our dreams this way inevitably ruins other dreams. There is compelling evidence that our sense of well-being is not at all linked to environmentally destructive consumption. Economist Robert H. Franks in his book *Luxury Fever* marshals a host of studies going back half a century that all reach the same conclusion: Past a certain point, which the great majority of Americans reached decades ago, "more material increases produce virtually no measurable gains in our psychological or physical well-being. As national income has soared in recent decades, about the same percentage of us say we are as happy as fifty years ago."

But we could be happier, or at least have a better society with no loss of happiness, Frank argues. He points to other polls and studies that show we would like less traffic congestion, cleaner air, more affordable health care, more time with families, better schools, and more protected open space near where we live. All of this is eminently achievable and affordable if we were to shift spending away from levels of consumption that scarcely relate to our happiness. Indeed, it is the endless pursuit of bigger, more, and grander that causes or worsens many of our environmental problems. It's all relative, Frank concludes—wealth and luxury, a sense of well-being, all have little to do with what one possesses, but everything to do with how we perceive our possessions relative to the rest of our society. Thus, today's high levels of conspicuous consumption (a phrase invented in 1899 to describe American lifestyles) are literally contagious, a "luxury fever," he writes. It follows that scaling back or shifting consumption patterns—if this were done across our society—would not be perceived as cause for great unhappiness.

The author's interviews with older women on Smith Island, a watermen's community in the Chesapeake Bay, echo this concept. Their lives, growing up, would have appeared materially sparse, even hard, to outsiders. When asked whether they were happy, most answered that they were "content"—life had gone according to the expectations they had been raised with, similar to the lives of their peers. Calvin B. DeWitt, co-founder of the National Evangelical-Environmental Network, who has visited the bay island communities, thinks contentment may be a better goal for American society than the pursuit of happiness. He also thinks that happiness, defined by the dictionary as "the fulfillment of wishes," is too open-ended, too easily warped by modern advertising into never-ending chasing after more and more. In contrast, contentment (from the Latin, *continere*) means restraint, connotes satisfaction with what one has, and is a whole lot easier on the environment.

"In our culture, having money is not novel; having time is," says Betsy Taylor, director of the Center for a New American Dream, a group dedicated to changing Americans' consumption habits. Its motto is "More Fun, Less Stuff!" "Our dream," Taylor says, "is that there are limits, and that limits do not have to be bad. Having no limits has left us financially and spiritually exhausted and is damaging our natural surroundings."

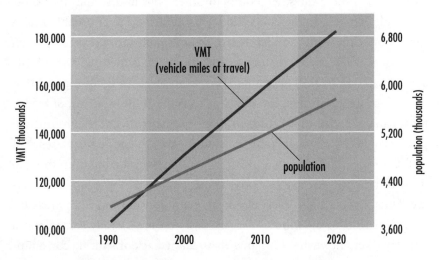

FIGURE 5.2. **Vehicle Miles Driven versus Population Growth.** As fast as the bay region's population is increasing, the total number of miles we drive is increasing even faster. This growth in VMT (vehicle miles of travel) means more traffic, more congestion, more construction of roadways, and more polluting runoff from them, especially nitrogen from vehicle tailpipes. [EPA Chesapeake Bay Program]

American business interests might seem to run counter to such a philosophy, but there are more ways than the present one to run an advanced, prosperous economy. William McDonough, an architect who has worked successfully with industries to dramatically reduce their environmental impact, sees pollution regulations as "evidence of a design flaw"; that is, the way to avoid more regulation, a Holy Grail of business, is to design products and processes that don't generate any pollution to regulate. Paul Hawken, a successful businessman (cofounder of Smith and Hawken) and the author of *The Ecology of Commerce,* notes, "Business now only has two words for profit, gross and net. It makes no distinctions as to how profit was made, does not factor in whether people or places were exploited, resources depleted, communities enhanced, does not discern whether profit is one of quality or quantity." Clearly, we have just scratched the surface of reducing the impacts to the environment from how we live.

WHAT CAN YOU DO?

Close to 3 million more people will move into the bay's watershed by 2025. If the bay is to be restored, the impacts each person makes on the air, land, and water must be reduced and then capped, so that to the bay, it is as if the coming millions did not even show up. This need not be left up to government. Taking personal responsibility for your actions can make a huge difference (remember to multiply by 16 million). It has been fashionable to offer lists of "one hundred things you can do for the environment" or even one thousand things. But authors and scientists Michael Brower and Warren Leon (*The Consumers Guide to Effective Environmental Choices*) make a good case that we can get more result from focusing on a few things that make real differences. An across-the-board, 10-percent cutback in Americans' consumption of all goods and services would not do much to stop current environmental problems, they conclude. But a few areas of consumer behavior, seven out of fifty categories examined in their book, would make a big and positive difference.

These include, in descending order of importance, the vehicles we drive and how much we drive them, what we eat, and how we choose and operate our homes. It is in these three areas that individuals can make the most difference for the Chesapeake Bay.

Transportation

The air pollution from burning gasoline and diesel fuel to get from one place to another is one of the largest categories of pollution for the bay (see "Air" in Chapter 2, "Pollution"). Nationally, individual transportation needs generate more than 30 percent of the greenhouse gases implicated in global warming and climate change, some 50 percent of all toxic air pollutants, more than 20 percent of toxic water pollution, and half or more of our paved lands (for roads and parking). The cars and light trucks and SUVs most of us use daily generate by far the greater source of pollutants in each of the above categories, with air, rail, bus, and off-road travel contributing relatively tiny amounts.

What can you do? Choose a place to live that reduces the need for long commutes to work and to shop. And if you can, locate your business near homes, schools, and shopping, again reducing travel and improving connections with customers and employees. Roughly 47 percent of Maryland residents now commute out of their home counties to work, according to census data.

Choose the "greenest" vehicles that fit your needs. The huge difference to the environment in what we drive is admirably detailed by the annual *Green Book—The Environmental Guide to Cars & Trucks*, available from the American Council for an Energy Efficient Economy (ACEEE) in Washington, D.C. Just as the *Kelley Blue Book* is the definitive guide to auto prices, the *Green Book* gives each vehicle made a comprehensive rating number, so its impact on the environment can be compared. The lowest-polluting Honda Accord, for example, which gets a green rating of 34 (2002 model), produces about one-twentieth of the bay-polluting nitrogen oxides as a typical, big SUV with a green rating of 12–15. Even for those who must have four-wheel drive, a Subaru station wagon produces less than half the nitrogen oxides of a Ford Expedition. Choosing the most fuel efficient, lowest-polluting vehicle, combined with planning ways to drive it less frequently, is a potent bay-saver.

Diet

Eat less meat and dairy products. Increasingly, health and nutrition advocates are advising Americans to moderate their consumption of meat, cheese, and milk. There is significant environmental harm associated with the way these products are currently produced. Nationally, agriculture is responsible for about 60 percent of all polluted waterways. In the Chesapeake, it is among the leading sources of nitrogen and phosphorus, both primary bay pollutants. Nationally, raising meat and poultry accounts for the bulk of water pollution from agriculture, with red meat production, including pork, the worst. The reasons are the huge amounts of manure generated by modern, concentrated animal facilities as well as the large amounts of land that must be cleared and fertilized just to grow feed for animals.

Marina Bleken, a Norwegian agricultural economist, has shown that changing from a typical, meat-rich American diet to the so-called Mediterranean diet, a widely recommended diet based on what Italians were eating in the 1960s, would require at least 40 percent less nitrogen fertilizer than is used today. The Mediterranean diet, praised by nutritionists as balanced, tasty, and healthy, is far from meatless but is heavier on grains and vegetables. Producing a pound of pasta (growing wheat) according to Brower and Leon, generates about 6.5 percent the water pollution of producing a pound of red meat and about 10 percent as much as producing a pound of chicken. In the bay watershed, however, poultry is a larger part of the problem than beef and pigs; and dairy farming, though a small part of the pollution problem nationally, is a big part in the bay. This is because both are so dominant in the region.

Buying organic foods and those that are locally produced is good for reducing pesticides and good for your health. And supporting local farms is good for the economy of your community and for preserving the look and heritage of agriculture in the local landscape. But it is still farming in general that has the greatest impact on the bay's water quality problems.

It is worth noting that farmers around the bay, whatever they are raising, are working as hard as anywhere in the nation to reduce pollution. There is plenty of scope for producers of meat and dairy products to reduce their impact on the land, water, and air. Another complication to altering your diet to help the bay is that you have no easy way to know whether many food items you choose are grown within the bay watershed. Except for a few small-scale efforts, no one has figured out how to make a dollar by certifying, or labeling, a particular brand of chicken or milk as "bay-friendly" or "Chesapeake-safe."

And what about eating fish? The growing aquaculture industry, where it concentrates large numbers of fish in pens or nets in poorly flushed waters, can cause huge pollution problems. And escapees from aquaculture operations can spread diseases among wild populations and introduce undesirable genetic traits. To date, there is no evidence that aquaculture is causing these problems in the Chesapeake Bay. If you want to abstain from eating species that are being overharvested or poorly managed for environmental impacts, the National Audubon Society publishes an up-to-date list of seafood, including some Chesapeake species, to be avoided on those grounds.

Home and Household

Choosing a home in an existing city, town, or suburb, and choosing one built on less land rather than more, is the strongest message consumers can send about the rampant sprawl development that is consuming more than 100,000 acres of open space each year across the bay watershed. As far as running a house, two areas place by far the greatest burden on the environment, primarily through burning fossil fuels: heating and cooling (including hot water, appliances, and lighting), and sewage. Among appliances, the refrigerator is the biggest energy consumer, averaging 1,383 kilowatt-hours per year, per household; it is followed by lighting (940 kWh/yr), television (739), and electric dryers (495). Other appliances may use more energy, but they aren't as commonly used in most households. Essentially, anything you can do to reduce home energy consumption will directly help the bay by reducing air pollution, which is a leading source of water pollution. Buy the most energy efficient appliances available, and buy the most energy efficient home, or insulate an existing house. Planting trees to shade a home is a great way to reduce air conditioning. Fluorescent lights can dramatically cut the use of energy. Increasingly, consumers can choose their electricity supplier, including some that generate energy from wind, solar, or other environmentally friendly sources.

As for sewage, human waste coming from homes connected to the public sewers that usually serve densely populated areas is generally freer of pollutants than waste flowing from the too often failing septic tanks that serve most homes on the suburban fringes.

Keeping on top of local land use plans and being engaged as a citizen in the process of determining your community's future are equally vital.

The Most Important Choice

There is one other personal choice with profound impacts on the environment. It is the largest choice most people make—how many children to have. Long term, stabilizing or reducing the human population will be essential in restoring ecosystems like the Chesapeake Bay.

RESTORATION AND REGULATION

While this chapter has focused on a few changes in individual behavior that will make the greatest difference to the bay, that does not mean other changes, such as recycling, are not worth doing. And there may be other problems that are most important in a particular locality. There is also a wide range of restoration actions individuals around the bay can participate in to counterbalance the impacts of our lifestyles on the environment. The Chesapeake Bay Foundation and other organizations now sponsor a host of restoration projects: planting oyster reefs to filter and cleanse the water; planting aquatic grasses to replace lost habitat for waterfowl, crabs, and fish; hatching baby terrapins and shad for release to help rebuild stocks in the wild. Other projects include planting wetlands and streamside trees, both of which help restore the landscape's natural resilience (see Chapter 4), helping the bay help itself.

Important as they are, individual actions to restore the bay must be reinforced by regulation and other government actions. In guiding where such actions will be most effective, a few overarching themes stand out. First, these actions must attack the fundamental sources of pollution and degradation. There is nothing wrong with continuing to rely on "fixes" in the interim such as more benign pesticides, cleaner automobile exhausts, and new sewage treatment technologies. Indeed, this is where the bulk of progress may be made in the next few years. But these fixes must be seen as means to ends (less automobile use, for example, and more mass transit, and communities designed to be walkable and bikeable). Second, some of the most notable environmental successes have resulted from outright banning of the polluting substance or activity rather than from merely regulating to lessen its impact. Examples include getting the lead out of gasoline, ridding the environment of the DDT that was killing eagles and ospreys, stopping all harvest of striped bass, outlawing production of PCBs that destroyed Earth's protective ozone layer, and switching to nonphosphate detergents throughout the watershed.

SPRAWL—A CURABLE DISEASE

Sprawl is inhuman, it is antihuman, the vast formless sprawl of housing, pierced by the unrelated spotting of schools, churches and stores, creates areas so huge and irrational they are out of scale with people . . . too big to feel a part of, responsible for, important in.

—James W. Rouse, developer of Columbia, Maryland

One of the few human rights that aren't officially guaranteed in this country is an agreement that the place you grow up caring about will be there for you when you're ready to start a family of your own.

—Robert Yaro, Regional Plan Association, New York, New York (1989)

Sprawl development of land is occurring throughout the Chesapeake Bay watershed, harming water quality, air quality, the economy, and the quality of life. It takes many shapes and fits no single category. Land use planners use four overall categories to evaluate sprawl: housing compactness, or density; neighborhood mix of homes, jobs, and services; how well downtowns and town centers are flourishing; and connectedness of the transportation network. In layperson terms these translate to how much housing and people there are per acre; the degree to which a place integrates people's daily needs, from workplaces to schools to shopping; whether an area has strong and vibrant downtowns and other central locations; and how easily people can get around in a variety of ways, from roads to mass transit to walking and biking.

To the extent these are lacking, sprawl exists. The easiest way to think of sprawl is as far-flung, low-density housing, associated with miles of poorly connected roadways, served by—and distant from—auto-oriented employment and retail centers such as strip malls and "office parks" with giant parking lots.

Sprawl, in sum, is the best way ever invented to waste a shrinking resource—open land—and the rural, agricultural heritage rooted in such landscapes. Sprawl's impacts run the gamut. Because it develops so much land per capita, it destroys extraordinary amounts of forest and other natural vegetation that buffer waterways against polluted runoff. Rainfall sheeting off roads, parking lots, and other paved surfaces worsens erosion and wrecks the natural channels of small streams. Sprawl is synonymous with more driving, because it spreads everything out and increases dependence on automobiles. This translates into significantly increased air pollution from driving. In addition to destroying forests, fields, and wetlands, sprawl fragments natural habitats with its mishmash of roads, buildings, and parking lots. Wildlife loses not only space but also the critical ability to move freely from one place to another.

Sprawl is also hard on human habitat, drawing people and tax money out of existing towns and cities where expensive infrastructure—sewers, roads, schools, water systems—is already built. By essentially duplicating this effort, requiring new schools, roadways, utilities, health and safety services, and the like, sprawl generally costs a county or township more money than it brings in through new taxes.

THE LAND INDUSTRY

Arguably, the industry with greatest environmental impact across the bay's watershed is neither manufacturing or agriculture or chemicals. It is what might be called the "land industry," the development, sale, resale, surveying, landscaping, lawn cutting, homebuilding, subdividing, speculating, zoning, planning, rezoning, real estate, and other activities that all relate to turning open space into where people live and work. It is an industry whose raw materials are nothing mined from distant caverns, such as coal or oil, nor chemicals delivered in tank trucks and railcars. The feedstock of the land industry is our natural environment, our forests and fields, our views and vistas and wildlife, and the communities where we were born. Though not classed as a single industry, all the above occupations frequently act with one mind and great effectiveness in opposing more environmentally sound approaches to land use (see also "Growing Smarter," later in this chapter).

Vital as the land industry is to providing shelter, in recent decades it has been as wasteful of its basic resource as the automobile industry was of petroleum in the heyday of the 400-horsepower gas guzzler. Even as the rate of population increase held fairly steady during recent decades, the rate of land conversion from rural open space to development surged wildly. To accommodate housing needs in the bay watershed during the five-year period from 1982 to 1987, the land industry converted 60,000 acres of open space a year. During the next five years, for about the same amount of growth, it used 80,000 acres. And in the five years that followed, 1992–1997, it used an astounding 128,000 acres. In less than two decades, developed land in the bay watershed leaped from 3 million acres—8 percent of the watershed—to 4.3 million acres, or 12 percent of the watershed.

This does not mean that every bit of 1.3 million acres was wiped clean of natural vegetation or converted to city-like density. The U.S. Department of Agriculture's Natural Resources Inventory, the source of the development numbers above and the most widely used source in the watershed, takes a broad view of what constitutes "conversion" of open space—five or more new, nonfarm buildings in half a mile along one side of a road, or five, counting both sides, along both sides of the road in a quarter mile. Experience shows that the low-level density used by the USDA to determine "conversion" is a good predictor of the eventual demise of an area's rural and natural character.

Put another way, of all the land developed in the bay watershed since Captain John Smith founded Jamestown Colony in 1607, about a third has been converted in just the last two decades. The trend is a result of smaller families choosing larger houses on larger lots, opting to leave the more compact environments of cities and towns. The massive building of far-flung highway networks, bypasses, and beltways that open access to land has fueled that trend. People buying homes in the bay's watershed now may not look much different than people in the 1950s, but they are, on average, much larger, hungrier animals in their appetite for land. Although the average family size has fallen from 3.6 to 2.7 in the last fifty years, homes are built on lots a full 60 percent larger, on average, according to Maryland planning officials. In the Washington, D.C., region the population grew 35.5 percent between 1970 and 1990; during the same period, the land converted from open spaces such as farms, woods, and wetlands increased 95.7 percent, according to *A Region Divided*, a Brookings Institute study published in 1999.

Thus, exploitation of land in the bay region now is in a phase comparable to the exploitation of bay oysters during the unsustainable heights of harvest in the 1870s. With oysters, we realized more than a century later that we had destroyed more than an economic resource—we had destroyed a major part of the bay's habitat and capacity to filter and clarify the water. With the rapid and wasteful conversion of open space to developed lands, we are likewise degrading the watershed's capacities to buffer the bay against pollution washing off the land (see Chapter 4, "Resilience")—and just beginning to realize how expensive it is to replace the "free" pollution control work done by wetlands and forests with human technologies such as sewage treatment.

Developing these natural filters is a largely irreversible process; we may be on the way to learning how to rebuild oyster reefs, but we are not nearly so capable of turning a parking lot back into a fully functioning freshwater wetland. That does not mean we cannot reduce pollution from such paved and developed lands. Reusing old industrial sites or run-down neighborhoods is an opportunity to install stormwater control methods that are far better than those used in the past (see "Stormwater Pollution" in Chapter 2, "Pollution"). For this reason, turning old urban land to new uses can reduce pollution.

SPIRITS OF PLACE

But the damage from the modern land industry goes well beyond what can be measured in added pollutants or acreage of open space lost. We are frittering away the heritage of the places we live—the character of our traditional landscapes, the community of our small towns, and the vitality of our urban areas. Consider the following:

"I am only twenty-two years old, but I am already sick and tired of seeing the places I loved as a child 'improved' in the name of progress," writes Virginia resident Helen Woods. And from Maryland, Pamela Tanton writes of the thrill of watching plovers, herons, and other birds feeding at a nearby stream, but "I am terrified that they are going to do something to ruin it—'they' being whoever it is who decides to widen roads, pave waterways, wreck nature. . . . I fear it's only a matter of time."

Such sentiments are common in letters to me over the years, reflecting a deep anguish about what is being done to the landscape. The current approach to the farms and forests, wetlands and meadows that make up open space is largely a landscape equivalent of "guilty until proven innocent." Unless specifically protected by easement or purchase, virtually every acre of the watershed is zoned for development. Most of the "agriculture" zones, "forest conservation" zones, and "resource protection" zones differ from residential or commercial zoning only in the amount of development permitted—merely a way to lose open space somewhat more slowly. In a very few places, such as parts of Maryland's Baltimore County, there is open space zoning strict enough—one home per 50 acres—to actually preserve the landscape. But this is the rare exception.

Our society's approaches to preventing air and water pollution, while imperfect, work in large part because air and water are largely accepted as public trusts. No one has a right to despoil OUR air, OUR water. By contrast, much of the land is not so much ours, but MINE and HERs, a farmer's retirement nest egg, and a speculator's proposed subdivision. But as surely as water runs downhill, whatever happens to alter the landscape ends up draining to OUR Chesapeake Bay. The issue is not just pollution. The literature of Native Americans and other aboriginal peoples of the world is full of references to the land as "sacred," to spirits of place, to a common heritage. There is no reason to think that a few centuries of industrialization, of pavement and air travel and road maps, have bred out of us the old, genetic attachments to spirits of place, to sacredness in the landscape. And the idea that these connections are spiritual implies that their all-too-frequent disruption by thoughtless development is on some level profane, leaving us literally dis-spirited.

Having society set stricter limits, as with zoning, on what private individuals can do with their land is sometimes painted as radical action. But what seems really radical is pursuing a course that guarantees bay residents will live amid increasing ugliness on the lands of the region, even as we spend hundreds of millions to clean up the bay itself. Radical is the thought that unique regions such as Lancaster County, in Pennsylvania, the Eastern Shore of Maryland and Virginia, and the Northern Neck of Virginia are on a path to losing their essence. Radical is the thinking that dictates a Wal-Mart, if not several Wal-Marts, for every county of the land, also the notion that larger building lots are the only way to a higher quality of life.

SUBSIDIZING SPRAWL

Some would argue that the bay's watershed remains a vast open place—even by 2020 its 40 million acres will still be more than 80 percent in undeveloped forest and farmland, with developed lands approaching 20 percent. But 2020 is only the end of the current statistical projections, not the end of time. The longer sprawling development goes on, the more the whole watershed becomes unfit for other uses. And 20 percent developed is enough to make many smaller streams and creeks of the bay watershed thoroughly unfit for aquatic life. Indeed, degradation of water quality often begins long before that, when development reaches around 10 percent of a stream's watershed.

Just a few hundred homes, scattered like pellets from a shotgun blast across thousands of acres, can effectively preclude the commerce of farming and forestry, as well as the large, unbroken areas of habitat many species of wildlife need to thrive.

Patterns of subdivision and land speculation often precede actual development by decades. A lot of what still looks like open space around the bay is in fact as good as gone. We have to ask now where we are headed in 2040, 2060, even 2120. Future generations will pay dearly for our inattention to today's trends, just as today's bay pays dearly for the rapacious oyster overharvesting of more than a century ago.

But sprawl causes plenty of more immediate problems, such as higher taxes and lost worker productivity. Patterns of sprawl development, almost across the board, tend to be more costly and polluting than the more compact settlement patterns of decades past. Today's sprawl requires more road building, more energy use (for commuting and for heating and cooling big, single homes), more driving time, more air pollution, and more sediment flowing into waterways from cleared land.

Maryland calculates it could save nearly a billion dollars in the next twenty years on extending roads and sewers if it repatterned its sprawl development into growth closer to existing population centers. A similar study in New Jersey puts savings there at $1.2 billion. In Virginia, fast-growing Stafford County figures each new home built under current sprawl trends ends up costing $16,000 more than it brings the county in taxes and other revenues. In Pennsylvania, 10,000 Friends of Pennsylvania has estimated local governments alone could save $120 million a year with more compact development. Planners in Oregon calculate that the added services, from roads to fire departments, needed to serve sprawl development amount to a $400 annual subsidy to such growth from every taxpayer.

Local governments initially may see revenues rise from rapid development as building creates more properties to tax. But under current sprawl conditions, that is a fleeting gain. Municipal debt for Howard County, Maryland, and Loudon County, Virginia, two of the watershed's fastest-growing localities, shows a steady rise during the last decade or so. Debt more than doubled in Howard; in Loudon, debt as a percentage of the county's total budget rose from less than 4 percent to more than 10 percent. In Montgomery County, Maryland, to accommodate the shifting needs of unplanned growth, sixty-eight schools in older communities were closed and seventy new ones built to serve sprawling new suburbs in a single decade (1980–1990). Sprawl development, which initially appears to gain homeowners freedom from traffic jams, inevitably ends up causing at least as much congestion, spread over much wider areas. Around the Chesapeake and much of the nation, the miles we drive have risen three to four times as fast as population in recent decades. Our freedom to drive anywhere, a freedom unparalleled in the rest of the world, is ironically beginning to limit our mobility. The average speed on Washington's Beltway has dropped in recent years from 47 mph to 23 mph. California's average rush hour speeds are projected to fall from 35 to 18 mph. The Baltimore metro area transportation plan envisions spending $16 billion in the next two decades—not in any hope of improving congestion—just to make sure congestion worsens at a slower rate. The Texas Traffic Institute says that nationwide traffic congestion now costs major cities a total $53 billion annually in lost work time. Polls in the Washington metro area show traffic congestion is the number-one quality-of-life issue.

The national Centers for Disease Control (CDC) in Atlanta links sprawl development to health. The spread-out, car-oriented nature of modern communities means less walking and biking and more obesity. And heavy auto dependence means dirtier air. During the Atlanta Olympics, for which the city's mass transit system was upgraded significantly, the CDC noted a striking correlation between less auto use (down 22 percent) and a decline in asthma admissions to hospitals (down 41 percent). By contrast, one recent study (Abt Associates, *Adverse Health Effects Associated with Ozone in the Eastern United States,* October 1999) pegged air pollution during an average "ozone season" in 1997 as the cause of some 6,700 hospital visits in the Baltimore–Washington area and almost 1,000 such visits in Richmond.

GROWING SMARTER

If continued sprawl seems increasingly a dumb way to grow, then why do we continue to do it, and what is the smart alternative? In the last few years, around the turn of the twenty-first century, the concept of Smart Growth has taken root as a national movement, with Maryland one of the states in the forefront. It is the best hope to arise for making real progress in countering sprawl since this book was first published in 1991.

At its heart, Smart Growth means keeping growth and development out of the countryside and focusing it around existing towns and cities, or other areas where adequate roads, sewers, schools, and other facilities to support growth are already planned. It means employing the best urban design principles to create appealing communities with mixed uses—homes, stores, and businesses located in areas that are not heavily vehicle oriented but are easily accessible through local transit, walking, or bicycling. While it means more compact development patterns than sprawl, that doesn't mean Manhattan-type density everywhere, but a mix of housing choices, from single-family homes on smaller lots, to town-homes and high-rise apartments. A compact and attractively designed development might not be "smart" if it were plunked in the middle of a rural region, a long drive from anywhere. The smartest growth is redevel-opment of existing cities and towns, strengthening them and knitting them together with new economic activity and housing. The second order of preference is a location immediately adjacent to an existing com-munity. Both of these should take advantage of existing or planned sew-ers, roads, and transit services. In sum, Smart Growth is using the landscape efficiently, in a less-polluting, fiscally prudent way, just as we should use any valuable, nonrenewable resource. On paper, a great many local governments in counties and townships throughout the Chesapeake region have had that as their stated goal for a long time. But with few ex-ceptions, reality has mocked their best plans. The reasons are many. Al-though we often think of sprawl as a random development pattern, in fact it is meticulously planned through local county and township zoning codes and the land use decisions local governments make. The land in-dustry has proved to be a powerful and effective opponent of smarter growth, easily coopting local plans. And even good local land use plans often have no legal basis in local zoning, leaving growth free to expand into the countryside. In fairness to developers, outdated and cumbersome rules on development in existing towns and cities often make expanding into rural areas and building single-family houses on large lots the path of least resistance. Other incentives for business as usual in land use in-clude heavy government subsidies to road building and auto use; tax poli-cies that favor building new, large houses; and lack of public investment in sewers, schools, mass transit, public safety, and other features vital to attracting people back into older communities.

Smart Growth, passed into law in Maryland in 1997, is one of the best examples in the nation of how a state can begin to reverse these trends. The aim of the new legislation is that the state will redirect its multibillion-dollar annual spending to promote growth where it already exists or is planned, and to send a clear signal that the state will no longer bail local governments out once their poorly planned growth creates pressure for additional schools, roads, and other services. The second critical component of Maryland's plan has been the creation of Rural Legacy and other open space programs aimed at preserving large tracts of remaining countryside from development. Accordingly, in the late 1990s and early 2000s, Maryland under Governor Parris N. Glendening moved aggressively on several fronts:

- The state construction budget that pays the costs of new schools was shifted from 62 percent on new construction to 83 percent on the renovating of existing buildings.
- Five planned highway bypasses around Maryland towns were identified as likely to promote sprawl into the surrounding countryside and were canceled or scaled back.
- Several state facilities, from a new state police laboratory to a new University of Maryland campus, were kept or shifted to existing communities instead of being built outside of towns.
- All the state's counties were required to identify Priority Funding Areas, lands around existing communities or where growth was planned. These will be where new state spending to serve growth is directed.
- The legislature authorized tens of millions in bonds for Rural Legacy, a program whose goal is to preserve 250,000 acres of farms and forestland over fifteen years.
- When one local jurisdiction, Carroll County, proposed land use legislation that would have promoted more sprawl development, the governor threatened the loss of state funding until the county backed down.
- The legislature passed a suite of "smart codes," changes in subdivision regulations to make it easier to redevelop in existing cities and towns.
- The governor halted a huge new highway project, the ICC, or intercounty connector, in the D.C. metro area.

Smart Growth, in just the last few years, has become a national movement. Its promise casts a broad net: "Home values rise, cars take less of our money and traffic less of our time; property taxes are down, schools are better, green space is nearby . . . clean water and air and healthy rural economies complement an uncluttered landscape," says Robert Liberty, president of 1000 Friends of Oregon, a group helping to shape perhaps the country's strongest state land use plan.

To developer Christopher Leinberger, managing partner of Robert Charles Lesser & Company, there is not just cleaner water and air, but pure gold in Smart Growth's ability to reduce American auto dependence through more compact patterns of growth. "We spend three times more than Europeans on transportation. Every car you get out of your household, you save enough, if you put it into a mortgage, to buy another $100,000 worth of home. As a real estate developer, I want my share of that hundred thousand," Leinberger said at a 1998 national Smart Growth conference in Austin, Texas.

And to Maryland's Governor Glendening it was economic sense of another sort: "Maryland would go bankrupt building the roads, schools and other facilities needed to accommodate more of the sprawling suburban growth of the last few decades," Glendening told the Austin conference.

Box 5.2. Atlanta and Portland: A Tale of Two Cities

America is all about freedom, which is sometimes best preserved by setting limits. Those who would preserve the option to develop every available acre of farmland and forest often invoke one version of freedom—the right of every individual to an affordable house on a grassy plot in a suburbia that knows no outer limits.

But where does unlimited freedom to do that lead? Atlanta, Georgia, has seen the future and is backtracking hard. For more than a decade, the Georgia metropolis pursued the right to live and build how and where anyone wanted with unmatched zeal. The city sprawled during the 1990s from a metro area about 60 miles long to one about 120 miles long. Job growth boomed, up 37 percent, and incomes rose a healthy 60 percent.

But property taxes, driven by the high costs of supporting ill-planned sprawl development, rose 22 percent. The miles an average citizen drove to work and shop rose 17 percent. And all that driving caused air quality to deteriorate—enough that the EPA suspended about $500 million a year in federal highway money for Georgia. It caused enough gridlock that Hewlett-Packard delayed a twenty-story office building project, saying it was getting hard to attract to Atlanta the high-tech talent it needed. Such workers were picky about the quality of life where they settled, and Atlanta's was becoming questionable.

Now look at the future in Oregon, the leading example of a state that limits where growth occurs. Portland and other Oregon cities have urban growth boundaries that strictly limit sprawling suburbs. They do expand over time, to make room for population growth, but very slowly. "You can tell when you leave town," is a common observation by visitors there.

Oregon zones about 40,000 square miles of farmland and forests to stay just that, as opposed to the "conservation" zoning common on such lands around the Chesapeake Bay—zoning that often leads to little more than large-lot residential development. Since 1987, just 4,070 acres, or 0.2 percent, of Oregon's total farmland has been rezoned for development.

Metropolitan Portland, where about 45 percent of Oregonians live, has had population growth, job growth, and income growth roughly comparable to Atlanta's. But unlike Atlanta, the city that limits freedom to sprawl has seen property taxes fall 29 percent, commute times for motorists decrease 9 percent, and the number of days that violate federal clean air standards fall 86 percent. Perceptions of neighborhood quality of life rose 20 percent in Portland and fell by 10 percent in Atlanta. Housing prices in Portland did jump 62 percent versus about 20 percent in Atlanta, in absolute dollar terms. But as a percentage of residents' incomes, housing prices in the two areas rose about the same. Housing in Portland is relatively inexpensive for West Coast cities.

Often overlooked, too, is the fairness Oregon has brought to development, says Robert Liberty, director of 1000 Friends of Oregon, one of the nation's original watchdog groups for better land use (there are spin-offs in thirty states, including Maryland and Pennsylvania). Zoning within Oregon's growth boundaries, Liberty explains, must include the full range of housing, from mobile homes and multifamily dwellings to

upscale mansions. It offers people a far wider range of choice than the il-
lusory freedom of choice that results mostly in single-family homes on
large lots. With the traditional nuclear American family of parents and
kids making up only 26 percent of American households now, the demand for alternatives to single homes is growing fast.

As for Georgia, it is now heading toward a sweeping reform in its any-
thing-goes tradition of development. The state has created a new regional
level of government with veto power over land use and transportation
decisions in Atlanta and surrounding counties. The aim is to halt the rapidly growing number of acres consumed by development, yet officials say
they do not consider their action antigrowth. Indeed, "if we don't do
something, growth is going to stop," then governor Roy Barnes said. The
statistics above, including those for Portland, come from an analysis by
Georgia Tech researcher Arthur C. Nelson, reported in "Growing Pains," a
special report by the National Governors Association.

IS SMART GROWTH WORKING?

While Smart Growth is currently the best thing going in Chesapeake region land use, it is far from certain whether the bay will see real progress
in land use during the next decade. Maryland is by far the leader of all the
bay states in addressing land conservation, yet the Maryland legislature
significantly weakened the state's ability to intervene in local land use decisions when it passed the Smart Growth law in 1997. And a 2001 analysis by environmental groups showed that most local jurisdictions are only
partly on board, despite concerted action at the state level to control
sprawl. The analysis looked at how much development continued to
occur outside the Priority Funding Areas (PFAs) that the Smart Growth
law required each county to designate. The PFAs are where growth already exists, or is planned for, and are where the state intends to direct future expenditures to support development.

Only one of the jurisdictions analyzed, Baltimore County, had anything approaching an exemplary Smart Growth trend. Development outside its funding area is projected to drop to just 9 percent in coming
decades, down from 15 percent. By contrast, neighboring Carroll County
projects 58 percent of all new development still sprawling outside its pri-

ority areas, up from 39 percent. Harford County projected development outside its priority growth boundaries going up from 17 percent to 25 percent, while Anne Arundel County projected a rise from 21 percent to 30 percent. Howard County, the worst, has lost more than half its farmland since 1982 and is projected to lose virtually all its rural lands except those that have been expressly protected through conservation easements or outright purchase.

One fundamental problem is that most counties continue to zone their rural lands to allow plenty of sprawl development—this despite having more than twice the land needed for the next twenty years within their planned growth areas. Equally important is that focusing lots more growth in and around existing towns, suburbs, and cities is often as controversial as letting it continue overrunning the countryside. In addition, county governments have not uniformly followed state Smart Growth policies of redirecting investments away from unplanned growth. At the state level, sprawl-inducing highways stopped by one administration have every chance of being revived by the next, it is not clear that the political courage will survive to resist building new roads and extending water and sewage lines outside the PFAs, and local response to implementing most growth continues to be tepid.

Even when one county does manage to enact strict zoning, such as Baltimore County's one lot per 50 acres on much of its remaining farmland, the lack of regional coordination means growth just leapfrogs to the next, less-prepared jurisdiction. Thus, ads for real estate just across the line from Baltimore County in Pennsylvania tout new, sprawl development: "New Freedom (PA), Baltimore's newest suburb." Also, one county's designated growth area often abuts another county's designated open space lands. Without better regional planning, without better local zoning of the rural landscape—and without more creativity by the counties in denser development—Smart Growth is unlikely to deliver on its full promise.

Virginia and Pennsylvania, with the great bulk of the watershed's 40 million acres, lag far behind Maryland's effort. Pennsylvania is especially hampered—authority for zoning and other land use is fragmented among 56 cities and towns, 964 boroughs, and 1,500 townships. In Maryland and Virginia most land use authority is at the county level. Until recently, if any local jurisdiction tried to be restrictive of growth, it was wide open to lawsuits from developers for not providing a full range of land use opportunities. It was a classic divide-and-conquer situation, a fertile ground for rampant sprawl.

Now Pennsylvania has passed its own Growing Smarter legislation. For the first time, the state has given local jurisdictions the power to work together regionally to shape a joint land use agenda. They are no longer so vulnerable to developers' lawsuits if they zone land more restrictively. This has great potential for controlling sprawl—if jurisdictions take advantage of it. One county, Lancaster, has established growth boundaries, but has not yet passed the zoning to make them work. In addition, the Department of Environmental Protection has begun checking to make sure new developments conform with local land use plans before it issues them any environmental permits.

Virginia appears little more prepared than Pennsylvania to meet the commitments in the latest Chesapeake Bay agreement: to reduce the rate of sprawl development in the watershed by 30 percent in the next ten years. Coupled with a commitment to preserve from development some 1.1 million acres watershed-wide, that would bring preservation ahead of losses to development for the first time in modern history.

Finally, some new studies, discussed later in this chapter, are showing that even with exemplary Smart Growth, the bay region may experience substantial losses of open space from the sheer, continued increase in numbers of people who inevitably take up more space, even if they do live more compactly. For the long term, the studies caution that Smart Growth, if population does not stabilize, only delays many impacts of sprawl.

Box 5.3. Keeping Our Commitment: Protecting Open Space

"Keeping Our Commitment—Preserving Land in the Chesapeake Bay Watershed" is a report by the Chesapeake Bay Commission that lays out what it will take to meet the three bay states' ambitious new goal—protecting 20 percent of the watershed by the end of 2010. It means preserving at least an additional 1.1 million acres, with an estimated price tag of $1.8 billion in new spending by all levels of government (the report assumes private spending by local land trusts and groups such as The Nature Conservancy will remain at present levels). The report is a good first cut. But differing definitions of "protected" among the state and outdated data mean that the 1.1-million-acre goal is probably a significant underestimate.

Even protecting another 1.1 million acres, while "very achievable," will take a fuller range of financing and preservation techniques than any government in the Chesapeake region now employs, the report says. Currently, protected lands cover 17.2 percent of the bay's 40-million-acre watershed, the report says. Much of that land is public parks and forests created decades ago. A companion goal of the *Chesapeake 2000* restoration plan, signed by the three bay states and the federal government, is to rein in sprawl development, bringing losses of farms and forest down to 90,000 acres annually from the current 128,000. A third related goal aims to increase public access points to the bay's thousands of miles of shoreline by 30 percent. If sprawl is checked and watershed protection meets its goal, which translates to preserving 110,000 acres a year, then preservation could pull ahead of losses to development for the first time in modern history. Again, this carries the caveat that the states may be using very liberal definitions of what is protected. Virginia includes all military lands, for example.

The three states vary widely in land protection. The report shows that between 1992 and 1997, Virginia spent only $23 million in state funds, compared to $305 million in Maryland (where land is more expensive) and $138 million in Pennsylvania. On the other hand, Virginia was creative in protecting land through the private sector, largely by creating the Virginia Outdoors Foundation (VOF), which encourages donations and easements from landowners. A whopping 81 percent of the 92,000 acres Virginia preserved during 1992–1997 came from private actions, according to "Keeping Our Commitment." Private sources accounted for less than 20 percent of Maryland's 152,000 acres protected and less than 5 percent of the 153,000 preserved by Pennsylvania.

"Keeping Our Commitment" details a number of areas where the bay states must improve, and learn from one another, if they are to double current rates of land protection to achieve a 20 percent preserved watershed by 2010. Maryland, a national leader in state land preservation programs, could do more at the county level. Some of its counties have preservation programs, but many are used to letting the state do the work of open-space protection.

Virginia needs to raise its state spending dramatically. In 2002 Virginians passed by nearly 70 percent a $119 million bond referendum for parks and natural areas that could preserve thousands of acres of land in Virginia's portion of the bay watershed and provide increased public access to the bay and its tributaries. As an illustration of how important this kind of dedicated funding can be, consider the case of "Chesapeake Forest."

The John Hancock Insurance Company put tens of thousands of acres of woods and wetlands on the market in 1999. Maryland, with its Program Open Space, a large funding source drawn from land recordation taxes and dedicated to buying natural lands, was able to acquire more than 50,000 acres, including miles of scenic riverfront. The state's new bond issues will help, but Virginia's local governments need broader taxing and bonding authority from the state to allow them to start their own land protection programs. Virginia has seen a surge of interest since it enacted a tax credit in 1999 that gives donors of land or easements up to 50 percent of the land's fair market value.

Pennsylvania's state government makes virtually no use of federal funds for land acquisition in its portion of the bay watershed.

But checking unplanned growth anytime soon will be hard in Virginia. Counties there have less power to restrict growth without express state permission than in Maryland and Pennsylvania, though they could still do a lot more than most are doing now. A few are trying. Loudon County recently elected a board of supervisors committed to slower growth and adopted a land use plan that wiped 83,000 potential homes off the drawing boards. The plan calls for a Smart Growth–like approach to preservation in rural areas. But like so many places, Loudon has yet to enact the zoning that must provide a legal basis for its admirable plans and may face considerable litigation once it does so.

VISIONS VERSUS WISHES

Large numbers of Americans will not likely give up their desire for single-family homes on large lots on the suburban fringes until they are convinced there are compelling alternatives. Too many citizens take it on faith that the American Dream demands the kind of sprawling development that uses whole farms for a few dozen homes. An urban planner once said, looking at our decades of attention to improving water quality while we squandered our open land: "Visitors from outer space would immediately ask each other, Are these creatures really terrestrial beings?"

Selling the public on more compact patterns of living, or higher-density development, has a long way to go. "People tend to hear 'density' and just think 'crowded,'" says Randall Arendt, a landscape architect who has researched many of America's most desirable older communities. Most of them, he has documented, are built very compactly, on very little land, but they are well designed and include attractive green spaces. "We suffer from almost a national amnesia," Arendt said in an interview. "We've forgotten how to build. What if we only put the effort into our developments—where we live our whole lives—as we do our 'signature' golf courses, where we spend just a few hours a weekend?" he asks.

A new generation of landscape planners like Arendt is showing how we can accommodate high levels of population in an area while preserving the vistas and diversity and all other features of the landscape that are important to us (see Figure 5.3). While the kind of development Arendt promotes is far better than most, it is not without critics, who note that where such development goes into rural areas, it still encourages more car travel and the extension of public services into the countryside.

Fulfilling true land use vision will absolutely require planning and zoning on a regional or state basis, as well as locally, because landscapes and their unique qualities may transgress county or city borders. It further requires zoning that is innovative enough to allow high densities and nonstandard street widths, tree placements, and the like. "People don't realize how much fire chiefs plan our towns and cities," developer Chris Leinberger says. "American fire trucks are the largest in the world, and city building codes often require 70-foot streets so they can turn around,

Site before development.

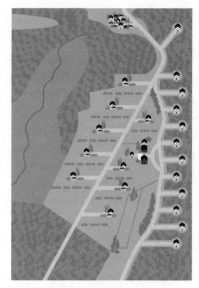

Site after conventional development.

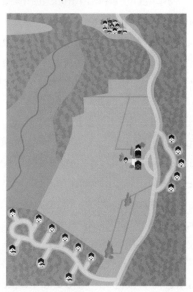

Site after better development.

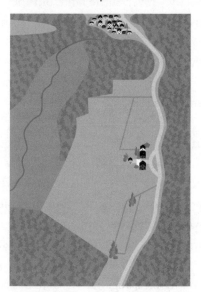

Site after best development.

FIGURE 5.3. Developing Land without Destroying the Landscape. These four illustrations show that growth need not be synonymous with destroying the characteristics of the natural landscape. Traditional suburban sprawl often occurs where open space should remain to preserve the integrity of the landscape. By clustering development, the same amount of growth is achieved, but the scene retains its natural beauty and ecological integrity. [Adapted from *New England Manual of Design,* Center for Rural Massachusetts)

when a denser, innovative, pedestrian-oriented development might mean only 24-foot streets." Impetus for sprawl development comes from many sources, Leinberger said, adding that in most cases it is easier to obtain financing for sprawl development than for more compact and innovative projects.

Realistically, the watershed's larger urban areas have problems bigger than just refocusing of development can easily solve—crime, drugs, poverty, and a declining quality of public education, to name a few. But without a refocused effort to improve cities, the problems may never be solved. The next decade and a half presents an opportunity: Aging baby boomers who are "empty nesters," smaller family size, and a growth of young, single people create a market for smaller, more compact homes on less land. Proponents of urban redevelopment note that with redevelopment, cities would reap more tax revenue and be able to invest more in services and education, starting an upward spiral that may draw in more new homeowners.

The environmental movement will have to become more involved in the struggling environments of the cities if it expects them to ever recapture their historic role as vibrant population centers. Bay watershed cities such as Baltimore, Washington, and Richmond have the infrastructure already built to accommodate significant percentages of all growth expected in the next twenty years—but the fact is, all now continue to lose population to the suburbs. (Washington, D.C., and Baltimore showed small up-ticks in population since 2000. Whether this will continue is uncertain.) Preserving the environment cannot afford to be only about maintaining a diverse and pleasant natural world for the wealthy and the middle-class suburbanite in the bay's watershed. There is every reason for linking preservation of the landscape in Virginia's Northern Neck or the farmland for Lancaster County's Amish with a better life for the less-privileged inhabitants of Richmond and Harrisburg and Baltimore.

A "DESIGNER BAY"?

And if that smacks too much of trying to engineer the shape of our society, then consider that human impacts in the watershed have already grown to the point where, one way or another, we are inevitably creating what might be called a "designer bay." The question is no longer whether we should actively determine the future shape of the region—only whether we should continue to abandon it to the unthinking forces of supply and demand for land and land use policies that encourage sprawling development and piecemeal, tunnel-vision projects. We face the challenge of melding economically sound growth with preservation of what is most attractive about living here.

Box 5.4. Tom Hylton: One American's Dream

After his father's death during the 1950s left the family in reduced circumstances, Tom Hylton grew up in an apartment in the declining downtown of Reading, Pennsylvania. As an adult, his wish for his own children was "that they grow up in a place just like I did."

"It was a wonderful place to grow up. I could walk to [schools], where I had a range of friends, from the son of a janitor to daughter of a neurosurgeon. I could walk to all my friends' houses . . . to the public library . . . to downtown department stores . . . to choir practice after school; to my grandmother's apartment. She was always home and ready to give me lots of love and attention, and I'd run errands for her at the store, stopping to visit adult friends at Sally's Luncheonette."

It was a life, Hylton recalls "that was inexpensive and fostered a sense of community . . . elderly people served as neighborhood watchdogs; poor and working class patronized the same schools, stores and public places as the middle class . . . children could be independent, but still be observed by adults who knew our parents."

Hylton, an author, public speaker, and tree commissioner of Pottstown, Pennsylvania, dwells on such mundane themes because, he says, "there is a whole generation now who have no idea what a wonderful and enriching place a city or town can be." About half of Berks County lived in Reading during the 1950s, occupying about 1 percent of the county's land area. Humans have mostly settled in just such patterns for 6,000 years, he explains. But in the United States in the last 50 years, we have begun to grow up with an American Dream defined by sterile, sprawling suburban and exurban development.

Hylton has written a book about this: *Save Our Land, Save Our*

Towns: A Plan for Pennsylvania. But it's a plan for Maryland and Virginia, too; a plan for anyplace where citizens wonder if there isn't an alternative to more traffic and less open space, if there is any way to recapture the community that existed in places like Reading in the '50s and '60s. The book captures the tragic connection between sprawl development's uglification of the landscape and the decline of cities and towns. But mostly it is a positive and hopeful message, with compelling, real-life examples of people living and working in vibrant centers of community, leaving prime farm soils and rural heritage intact for all to enjoy.

It is no armchair philosophy Hylton brings to bear on the subject. He and his wife live on a tenth of an acre in a low- to moderate-income part of Pottstown, Pennsylvania, population 22,000. Both can walk to work, which explains how he has driven the same car for twenty-one years. They figure living close to work has saved 10,000 hours of drive time and $85,000 in transportation costs. She is a teacher. He helped found Preservation Pottstown and also organized Trees, Inc., a nonprofit that maintains 3,100 shade trees on Pottstown's streets.

How Many of Us?

It has brought us exponential growth, and I think that's been good for Maryland.

—Jim Mathias

Jim Mathias was mayor of Ocean City, Maryland, in 2002, on the fiftieth anniversary of the Bay Bridge that connected Maryland's sleepy Eastern Shore to the Baltimore-Washington metropolis. You might discount his hyperbole as just the rhetoric of a boosterish leader of a tourist town, but the truth is that continuing population growth, for all the problems it may cause, is widely accepted in America as not only inevitable but necessary. A reading of any newspaper will show the built-in bias: the Baltimore-Washington region is "growing nicely," an economics professor tells the *Baltimore Sun*; Maryland's rapid growth shows "Maryland is still an attractive place to live," says an economic development official; and

Baltimore City's "shrinking population causes budget woes," says a headline. One county is said to grow at "an anemic pace," while another, with high growth, is said to be "booming." Even an environmental coalition's pamphlet on limiting sprawl development is entitled, presumably, to present an image of reasonableness: "Where do we GROW from here?" Growth is going to happen; growth is good, or at least necessary; lack of growth is a problem; growth must be accommodated. This is the vocabulary that we have come to accept—unthinkingly, perhaps—which defines our future. This virtually unquestioned assumption in America that if an area's population isn't growing, its prosperity and economic well-being are headed for trouble is coupled with another prevalent belief that we can solve all our environmental problems without attention to how many of us there are. These assumptions are implicit in the decision making throughout our political and economic system, from county commissioners to Congress. More than any other single factor, the idea that growth is necessary to prosperity needs resolution, a thorough and high-priority national debate, before a consensus on whether, and how, to stabilize growth can be reached.

At the same time most of us think that growth is vital to economic progress, we usually acknowledge there must be some limit to how many people we can add to places like Chesapeake Bay and still preserve the environment—but no one, including most of the nation's and region's leading environmental groups, has wanted to talk about where that limit might be. So we end up with paradoxical conclusions such as one from the recent *Chesapeake 2000*, the state-federal agreement governing the restoration of the bay: "There is a clear correlation between population growth and . . . environmental degradation." It adds that the 3 million new people expected to move into the watershed by 2020 "could potentially eclipse" all past environmental gains. But what can be done about that? The agreement, the guiding document to the bay's future, says nothing more about population growth except that there is a need to "accommodate" it.

Two separate studies that have recently looked at attempts to control sprawl with Smart Growth provide examples of where accommodating growth will land us in the bay region. Smart Growth means refocusing government spending and policies to channel growth out of the country-side and back into, or around, existing towns and cities. It is based on the perfectly valid assumption that Americans in recent decades have been consuming far more open space, per capita, as they move to single-family homes on large lots in suburbia. It has become a popular national move-ment, and it is considered the best thing going in the bay region to protect open spaces from development. But is it a solution or a delaying tactic?

Numbers USA, a Washington-based nonprofit that works to stabilize population by reducing immigration, looked at 100 urbanized areas around the nation, including the Baltimore-Washington area. It deter-mined that people's increased demand in recent decades for larger lots, further from existing towns and cities (the larger "ecological footprint" discussed earlier), was responsible for only about half of a region's annual consumption of farms, forests, and fields. The other half was due to the growing numbers of people, who, even if they can be persuaded to live more compactly, still take up space. Particularly striking was Simi Valley, California, where per capita land use actually shrank by 16 percent be-tween 1970 and 1990. Nonetheless, the region's developed lands nearly doubled, because population soared by 125 percent.

Another analysis, by Edwin Stennett's Growth Education Movement in Gaithersburg, Maryland, found that population growth per se in the booming Washington, D.C., region accounts for nearly two-thirds of all conversion of open space. Increased per capita use of land—the primary target of Smart Growth–type policies, was about a third of the problem. Stennett looked at what would happen if D.C. region governments, through the aggressive use of Smart Growth strategies, could convince all newcomers and people already living there to adopt much more compact living patterns—each person taking up nearly 40 percent less open space than today's norm. By 2025 this would save a whopping 480 square miles, or 307,000 acres, of open space over continuing business as usual. But as the population continued growing, even assuming it grew "smartly," it would consume that 480 square miles in another three to four decades. "The only thing we could honestly celebrate is delaying the loss," Stennett concluded.

Studies such as Numbers USA's and Stennett's, which look at population growth as a component of sprawl, are relatively new. Traditional studies of sprawl have simply not included population increase. But some of these calculate that Smart Growth might achieve even more compact living patterns than Stennett thinks likely. These could offset the impacts of population growth on open space for a few more decades.

Stennett, whose results are published in an analysis of the bay region's population growth, *In Growth We Trust*, also contends that the huge leap in the region in automobile use—it has risen more than three times as fast as population—is also partly driven by sheer population growth as well as by sprawl development. Smart Growth or no, he argues, increasing population means more driving, which adds to the horrible congestion that is degrading the quality of life in metropolitan Maryland and Virginia.

His point, and that of Numbers USA's director, Roy Beck, is not that Smart Growth and similar strategies to conserve land aren't worthwhile and an essential part of the solution (the only part in the next few decades, given the long time lags in changing population growth). But both argue that only working to moderate how people live will not be enough if population grows without limit. Smart Growth, with its socially progressive emphasis on revitalizing older towns and urban cores, is a true advance; but it is a delaying action, not a solution, to protecting significant amounts of open space. Herman Daly, a nationally known economist who has written widely on alternatives to progress as usual in America, compares Smart Growth to redistributing the load in a boat. It will do some good in keeping the boat afloat by balancing the load, but if the load keeps increasing without limit, the boat eventually sinks no matter how well the burden is distributed.

POPULATION—THE PROSPECTS

The environmental problems that arise from population growth are very much the stuff of our news and interests, but few want to speak about population itself. In 2002, the population of the United States was about 281 million, up from just over 200 million in 1970. The U.S. Census Bureau projects population will rise to around 400 million in 2050 and to 571 million—more than double today's numbers—by century's end. The Chesapeake region, currently adding close to a million people each

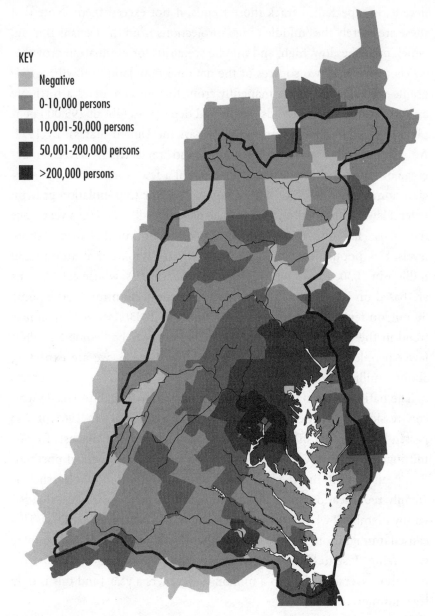

KEY

Negative

0-10,000 persons

10,001-50,000 persons

50,001-200,000 persons

>200,000 persons

FIGURE 5.4. Where the Watershed's Population Is Increasing. The watershed's population has grown fastest in the areas bordering the bay, putting great pressure on the bay's natural filters. [EPA Chesapeake Bay Program]

decade, is expected to track those trends, if not exceed them. Note that these are merely the "middle range" projections from the Census Bureau, which publishes low, high, and middle scenarios for population growth.

There are only two sources of the national population growth: immigrants who move here permanently from foreign lands and a birthrate among residents that exceeds deaths and departures (about 195,000 people a year, on average, permanently depart the United States). By 1972, American fertility rates had fallen to around "replacement" levels, an average of about 2 children per woman. Until a few years before that, foreign immigration had not been a big contributor to population growth; federal law had limited it to an average of well under 200,000 a year since the 1920s. Had immigration and fertility rates continued at around those levels, U.S. population would have peaked and stabilized at around 230 million in 2030, according to Beck of Numbers USA, whose calculations are based on U.S. Census Bureau data. That projection for 2030 is some 50 million fewer citizens than we have now in 2003. Assuming a similar trend in the Chesapeake watershed, we would have had some 2 million fewer people here in 2030 than we do now. Instead, we are expecting about 3 million more.

The nation's expectations of population stability began to recede with congressional enactment of an immigration reform act in 1965. It was passed with the best of intentions, to make racially fairer the tests for admitting immigrants, which up to then had favored foreigners of northern European descent. But the law passed with inadvertent loopholes, such as "family reunification" that allows immigrants to later bring in extended family members, who in turn could bring in their extended families. This caused immigration to surge beyond all expectation. By 1968, the country was taking close to half a million immigrants, and during the 1990s, immigration averaged close to a million newcomers a year (and this is only legal immigration).

The other change ratcheting population upward has been a swing back to fertility rates that are higher than replacement levels. In part this has also come from the larger numbers of immigrants who came during the last few decades. They tend to have more children than Americans whose families have been here for generations.

What's the solution? A number of organizations working to stabilize or reduce population favor reductions in immigration, which could be accomplished by a single act of Congress. Others stress making a high national priority of voluntarily reducing fertility rates among all Americans. Education on the need to reduce population, better family planning services, reducing poverty, increasing educational levels—all are proven ways to lower fertility rates. Stennett argues we might realistically expect to stabilize population at around 400 million people by 2070 through voluntary reductions in fertility. Beck says, based on Census Bureau data, that returning immigration rates to their historical average, around 250,000 per year, would stabilize population at around 320 million people by 2050 (currently there are 281 million Americans). A third view is represented by Negative Population Growth, a national nonprofit, which says the optimum population for the nation is around 150 million people. It argues that level, based on surveys of scientists and researchers across a range of disciplines, would optimize the nation's environmental, social, and economic well-being in the long term. With a combination of reductions in both immigration and fertility rates, the United States might reach that level in three to four generations.

It is critical to understand that none of the above approaches, even if they were begun today, will have full effect for several decades. That is because of both "population momentum," which continues as generations of Americans already here move through their reproductive years, and "population echo," which occurs as their children have children. This means two things: If the nation wants population stability, we must begin working immediately to see results in any meaningful time frame; and in the next couple decades, no matter what we do to reduce how many of us there are, the whole ball game for the environment will continue to be in working the "how each of us lives" side of the equation.

WHO'S AFRAID OF POPULATION STABILITY?

As noted earlier, perhaps the biggest roadblocks to a discussion about stabilizing population are the prevalent assumptions that if an area's population isn't growing, its prosperity and economic well-being are headed for trouble, and that we can solve all our environmental problems without attention to how many of us there are. But is the "grow or die" assumption true?

On the broadest scale, it is obvious that many healthy economies exist without population growth. Examples include much of Western Europe and Scandinavia; citizens in many of those countries enjoy a quality of life at least equal to that in the United States. In the bay watershed there are places like rural Kent County on Maryland's Eastern Shore. One of the state's least populous jurisdictions, Kent is no boomtown, but it is considered a good place to live by residents, despite, or because of, decades of little population growth (19,000 people in the most recent census). Kent has a reasonably vibrant and charming town center in Chestertown, the county seat, and is one of the few counties in the region to have emphatically rejected a Wal-Mart.

It is also important to differentiate between development and growth. A healthy nation must have continuing economic development. And while some economies, such as the United States, may have evolved large sectors like the land development industry that depend on population growth for profits, there are obviously many other ways to make a buck. Any shift toward a stable population would occur slowly, over decades, giving the economy time to adjust. And even sectors like new home building would find equal opportunities in redevelopment of existing cities and town and in reclaiming hollowed-out cities such as Baltimore. But the present economy contains powerful interests in favor of continued high population growth.

Indeed, American's historical tendency to accept unlimited population growth uncritically has left the field to what has been called the "Growth Machine," which is really just an extension of the "land industry" discussed earlier. It includes many of the same players—developers, lands speculators, real estate agents—but also includes mortgage bankers, highway builders, the construction and building supplies industry, and others. These interests advance their pro-growth agenda through local and regional Boards of Trade, Chambers of Commerce, and local and state economic development agencies. The business community at large supports the Growth Machine, because the prevailing wisdom is that growth is essential to increase prosperity. The target of the pro-growth lobby is typically local government, which is always hungry for the added tax revenues it believes flow from continued population growth. Indeed, a fair number of local officeholders come from Growth Machine backgrounds or are actively employed in such occupations. During 1998 and 1999, industries that are all major players in the Growth Machine outspent environmental groups by about $6 million to $6,000 in contributions to candidates for state office in Maryland and Virginia, according to the National Institute on Money in State Politics. It would be surprising if the imbalances were not also large in contributions to candidates for local office.

While there is little doubt that continued population growth benefits the Growth Machine and its allies, there are serious questions about how much it benefits society at large. As noted earlier, there is mounting evidence that sprawl development—in part a product of unending population growth—costs government and taxpayers far more in the long run than it brings in. In fact, taxpayers end up subsidizing the Growth Machine, whose profits would not be nearly so healthy if growth paid its way. Often overlooked as a public subsidy to continued growth are the hundreds of millions of dollars in public funds spent to preserve farms and other open spaces in the path of development. Nature itself takes a major hit from never-ending growth. Because current economics doesn't assign value to the work done by forests and wetlands in cleansing and filtering polluted runoff, these losses are never counted against any increased revenues from growth. They are, unfortunately, reflected both in the huge costs of extra water-pollution-control technology necessary to make up for the loss of natural cleansing and in the lost value of damaged recreational and commercial fisheries.

Box 5.5. GDP: Accounting for Nature

Accounting sleights of hand that land private corporations in court are small change compared to how the U.S. government carries both nature and human welfare "off the books" to falsely boost the economy's value. This is the conclusion of Robert Costanza, a University of Vermont professor and director of the Gund Institute for Ecological Economics. The target of his criticism is the GDP, or Gross Domestic Product, the government's broadest gauge of how the economy is doing. GDP measures total national spending for goods and services, but it makes no distinction between good spending and bad spending, Costanza notes. Spending on crime, divorce, pollution, sickness, car wrecks—it all adds to GDP just the same as purchases of barbecue grills, new cars, and day care for children and the elderly.

But the real problem is what GDP doesn't measure. People who cut back on paid work to care for their own children or elderly parents are not valued at all; in fact, their lower paychecks decrease GDP. Marshes and forests and oysters, with their well-documented abilities to filter and absorb massive quantities of air and water pollutants, count for nothing in GDP. Why? Since no one actually pays for their ecological services, they have no value as GDP sees it, Costanza explains. But draining a marsh to build a shopping mall, or bulldozing a forest for new housing, would move GDP upward. Similarly, the cleanup spending required by a big oil spill calamity like the *Exxon Valdez* gives GDP a boost.

Maybe if we understood GDP for what it is and isn't, it wouldn't be so harmful; but Costanza says it has become a widely accepted and simplistic indicator of economic health: GDP up = good; GDP down = bad. Indeed, a sustained decline in GDP is a key factor in the government declaring that the country has officially entered a recession.

Some economists, including Herman Daly, a professor at the University of Maryland, have for years been refining alternatives to GDP—keeping the nation's accounts as if nature and human well-being mattered. The latest version, the GPI, or Genuine Progress Indicator, is maintained by the nonprofit group, Redefining Progress (www.rprogress.org/projects/gpi). The GPI shows a more sobering, but more accurate, picture of how the United States has been doing in preserving *all* its assets—material, natural, and social: While the government's GDP shows a steady upward trend since 1950, GPI climbed more modestly until about 1975 and has gradually drifted downward ever since. In a sense, Costanza says, the United States has been in a recession for the last twenty-seven years.

We're driving more cars more miles, living in bigger homes on larger lots, enjoying a host of material luxuries undreamed of in 1950. But we've lost, off the books, gobs of natural capital, from old-growth forests to oyster reefs. And survey after survey show that since the 1970s, about when "genuine progress" peaked, there's been little change in the percent of people who consider themselves "happy" and "satisfied," despite soaring material well-being. For the Chesapeake Bay, the implications of GDP's accounting would be criminal if the bay were a corporation. We protect what we value, and we aren't valuing nature in ways that are reflected in the bottom line. The remedy lies in learning that our portfolios contain wetlands and oyster reefs as well as stocks and bonds.

A detailed study in Oregon by Fodor & Associates of Eugene documented that subsidies to growth now amount to $18,000 for each new person moving into the state—and Oregon is a leader in growing in an environmentally and economically sound way. While we often hear that "we couldn't stop growth if we tried," attempts to make growth pay its fair share, such as the (very limited) "impact" fees assessed by some counties on new development, are usually met by cries that "it will kill our growth."

In fact, even the economic Holy Grail of new job creation, in which states and counties around the bay watershed spend huge sums in incentives to attract industries, is often less than meets the eye. Reported economic benefits never take into account the downsides of more traffic congestion, loss of open space, added pollution, and costs of serving new residents who move from other areas to take the jobs.

Where the preponderance of new jobs created goes to people already living in an area, recruiting new business would make more sense, but frequently the jobs go to new arrivals, who add to population demands on natural resources but not necessarily to the overall well-being of the region. It is not uncommon to find unemployment remaining about the same in areas that are creating lots of new jobs as in those that are not. Another way of looking at it: Population growth does not appear to be related at all to growth in per-capita incomes in the Washington area, according to a Brookings Institution analysis. Other studies show the same lack of relationship nationally between adding more people and increasing per-capita economic benefit.

This is not to say that recruiting new business is always wrong or that population growth is always a negative for every area of the bay watershed. Rather, the problem is that we currently assume, with little critical analysis, that these things are always right.

Meanwhile, the thought of slowing growth remains an unsettling prospect to most of our political leaders and economic decision makers. It is worth briefly discussing a few of the most common objections to stabilizing population.

Restricting immigration is unfair, given the world's needs and America's plenty. We are a nation of immigrants, from the *Mayflower* on, and immigration continues to offer our country both a healthy diversity and at least partial discharge of our social responsibility to the less-advantaged of the world.

But this country has always limited immigration. The historical annual average from the 1770s through the 1960s was around 250,000, nearly a quarter of what it is nowadays. Those most in need of humanitarian aid make up only about 3 percent of immigrants to the United States. And whatever number of immigrants the country takes, it will make only a tiny dent in world needs. The United Nations estimates there are close to a billion people in dire straits economically and nutritionally.

It is true that when U.S. population was smaller, the country took more immigrants as a percentage of total population. The environment, however, does not see percentages. It sees gallons of sewage, acres of forest felled for housing, pounds of pollution put into the air. These increase just the same with every new person, regardless of whether that person is a smaller percentage of total population than the ones who came before and regardless of whether that person was born here or immigrated here.

There is still plenty of space in the United States to accommodate more population. Indeed, there are tens of millions of acres left in our country with extremely low numbers of people. But many of those acres are desert and mountain, or they form our most productive farm soils, our national forests, our military reservations. Some two-thirds of all Americans now live within a few hours' drive of the coastlines, a trend seen in spades around Chesapeake Bay. The coasts are already overstressed by population growth.

Without immigrants, who will do the jobs Americans no longer are willing to do? And who but immigrants will repopulate our ailing inner cities? This argument has some merit. Historically, immigrants have assumed both of the above roles. The recent revival of New York's blighted Bronx has been attributed to a boom in immigrants who've moved there. Many older, struggling cities now see hope of revitalization in attracting immigrants.

But the jobs argument and the city revitalization one are to an extent chicken-or-egg arguments. Would Americans refuse to do jobs now held by immigrants if pay and working conditions were better? Would pay and working conditions be so bad were it not for a steady stream of immigrants with few options?

Similarly, to look at immigration as the major solution for our ailing urban cores is to ignore the reasons they have lost population in the first place, from crime and drugs and underperforming schools to massive government subsidies favoring the growth of sprawling suburbs.

TOWARD A SOLUTION

Ultimately, nothing we can do in the Chesapeake Bay region alone will bring population stability. Even if we could achieve it here, no one could stop the rest of the country from moving in (though rethinking our land use and business recruitment policies might slow things significantly). But a national debate on population limits has to start somewhere, and perhaps there is no better place than the watershed of the Chesapeake, where members of Congress and the president live, and where international attention is focused on the massive effort to restore the bay environment.

It is no longer a case of wait and see. The pollution load on the bay is many times what it was when Captain John Smith explored it in 1607. Nitrogen alone is estimated to be seven times greater, and the best science indicates we need to cut that nearly in half. Before we can even begin, however, we must reduce pollution enough to completely offset the million new people who move here every decade. All the work we currently do to reduce pollution from the ways we live must continue. In the next decade or two it is possible that pursuing this course alone might restore the bay's water quality. But could we maintain it as population continued to grow? And even if the water meets legal standards, what will happen to the quality of life, from traffic jams to the loss of wildlife and open space? It is irresponsible to continue acting as if the numbers of us who live here are of no consequence. National environmental groups, along with businesses that want cheap labor and humanitarian groups dedicated to maintaining high immigration numbers, all assume that growth will be "accommodated."

We need to develop consensus in three areas: (1) to test the premise that our overall prosperity and well-being are somehow linked to a never-ending increase in our numbers; (2) to examine the assumption that population growth, unchecked, is likely at some point to overwhelm even our best technology and pollution control efforts; and (3) to find the best and fairest ways of reducing fertility rates, immigration, or some mix of both to achieve the desired population number.

Who should take the lead to begin this debate? Two groups come to mind: the nation's environmental groups and its business community. Both have much to gain in resolving the issues raised by continued population growth. The benefit to environmental groups in addressing the questions seems obvious. Many in the leadership of environmental groups agree that population is perhaps the leading root cause for environmental decline. The benefits to the businesspeople, farmers, and watermen may be no less real. The ultimate form of pollution from increasing population may be rigorous regulation. As more people live in a place, rules multiply to keep them from bumping into nature and into one another. The longer we wait, the less space and fewer good options we will have.

Conclusions

- Restoring the Chesapeake Bay and sustaining it for the long term will most likely mean limiting both the environmental impacts people make and the numbers of people who live in the watershed. The environmental movement has focused largely on the first part of that equation—how we live with regard to nature. That must remain a critical concern, but it is vital to begin a debate on the necessity of stabilizing population. This must happen nationally, but there is no better forum in which to begin than around the Chesapeake Bay.

- The ecological footprint of a person moving to the bay region today—the demands each person makes on the region's natural resources—is substantially larger than it was fifty years ago.

- Reducing our environmental impacts is absolutely consistent with a high quality of life. So is shifting from never-ending growth to a stable population, but currently the philosophy of "grow or die" is widely and uncritically accepted.

- While we cannot restore the bay without government actions and regulation, the individual choices of 16 million people living in the watershed can have huge impacts. Changing our lifestyles in a few areas—transportation, diet, and home choice and operation—will have more impact than any across-the-board reduction in consumption.

- Sprawl development, which is devastating environmentally, economically, and socially, remains as rampant a problem as it was on the first issue of *Turning the Tide* more than a decade ago. We continue to use open space and unique parts of our natural heritage with the same wastefulness we have historically shown for other nonrenewable resources, such as coal and oil. Nearly a third of the land development in the bay watershed in four centuries of European settlement has occurred in just the last twenty years.

- Smart Growth, a significant new strategy for checking sprawl, has taken hold in Maryland state government in the last few years. Smart Growth directs state spending away from projects and incentives that favor growth in the countryside and focuses it on revitalizing cities and towns and on promoting growth in areas where roads and sewers are planned to serve it. Smart Growth in Maryland also provides money to preserve large acreages of open space. It is too early to call Smart Growth a success or a failure, but few Maryland counties, where much of the power over land use resides, have wholeheartedly bought into the strategy. Pennsylvania and Virginia, while showing some progress in the last decade, remain in the dark ages of land use.

- While few people love sprawl development, few are eager to accept more compact, denser settlement patterns around where they live. There is a need for more working models of denser development that incorporate attractive, desirable, mixed-use housing, pedestrian- and bike-friendly access, and a sense of community.
- The benefits of unchecked population growth are greatly overstated. Society hugely subsidizes new growth when its real costs, from new roads and schools to pollution control, are taken into account. Losses to nature are scarcely even counted against the benefits associated with increasing population.
- Reducing foreign immigration or reducing the U.S. fertility rate, or a combination of both, could stabilize national population in the next fifty years or so. Powerful interest groups that benefit from a high-growth economy—often at considerable cost to taxpayers—are generally opposed to any attempt at stabilizing numbers.

PART III

LESSONS *and* RECOMMENDATIONS

Recommendations

The beginning of this book discussed how to measure the cleanup and restoration of the troubled Chesapeake: If we measure progress by the money and manpower expended on bay restoration, and by the increasing sophistication of environmental regulations and scientific knowledge, then we have been making progress fairly steadily since the first Earth Day in 1970. But if we measure it by the current responses in the bay's water quality, in its fisheries and in its resilience, then progress is more muddled.

The challenge facing us is this: We must not only reduce the present level of human impacts enough to restore the bay; we must also reduce those impacts enough to offset another few million people who are

projected to move into the watershed by around 2020, and we must reduce pollution almost twice as much in this decade as in the last
decade and a half. This challenge, as the preceding chapters have made
clear, is not being met now. And despite some notable efforts and
successes, there are far too many areas where it does not have much
likelihood of being met in the foreseeable future. Serious, focused
restoration efforts have been under way now for fifteen years, managing mostly to hold the line. This achievement is not restoration, which
will require doing twice as much in the next decade or so as we have
done to date.

Doing less is unacceptable. If the wealthiest, most powerful and technologically advanced nation in the history of the planet cannot live in a
place without ruining it, what message does that send to the rest of the
world? What does that say about the future of nature—including
humans—on the planet?

It does not have to be this way. There is no reason to accept that, as the
"price of progress," the best we can hope for is slowing the inevitable decline of natural resources or holding the line at some tolerable level of environmental degradation. The brighter vision articulated in this final
section will not happen without fundamental change, however. Sixteen
million of us, and counting, cannot go on behaving as if there were still
only a few million of us.

The first conference on the Chesapeake Bay, in 1968, concluded with
a challenge to define "how many acres of wetlands should we preserve;
how many pleasure boats will we be operating; how many people do we
wish to house; how many tons of seafood do we want to harvest; how
big a ship do we wish to accommodate?" Decades have passed, and with
the exception of wetlands and, to some extent, seafood harvests, we
continue to shy from acknowledging any limits. The endpoint of such
restraint can actually be a higher quality of life. The alternative to a
mob's disjointed shouting need not be enforced silence; it can be the vibrant harmonies of a choir. We need more than a reinvigorated commitment to fighting for the environment. We must redefine the nature
of the struggle.

What Kind of Bay Do We Want?

Before setting out detailed recommendations based on the issues and conclusions presented throughout the book, let us articulate where the bay region should be heading. How will we know success when we see it? What kind of bay do we want?

A CLEARER BAY

We want a cleaner bay, too, but clean enough for what? Shipping? Swimming? Fishing? For what kinds of fish? Clear water is relatively easy to comprehend and to measure; and in the bay's case, clearer water means licking two of our biggest pollution problems: sediment and nutrients. Doing so, in turn, will mean we are improving conditions for the return of underwater grasses and improving oxygen in the water.

How clear is clear enough? It will vary, of course, from one part of the bay to another. Based on abundant anecdotal information, we want water clear enough that we can see bottom 4 feet down where now we can see it only 2 feet down; clear enough that places 10–15 feet deep at Smith Island and Solomons, where old-timers recall spying crabs on the bottom in summer and catching them with a dip-net, are visible again. And certainly clear enough for Bernie Fowler to see his toes in the Patuxent River some fine June day soon. Bernie is a former legislator who led the fight to clean up his native river, which drains central and southern Maryland. His story of wading out, shoulder deep, as a youth fifty years ago chasing soft crabs and looking down and seeing his feet on the bottom has become a local legend. Every second Sunday in June, on Bernie Fowler Day, the old senator and supporters of the cleanup of the river dress up in their best and wade out shoulder deep to look for their toes. (They're still looking, but still hopeful, and resolute in this annual renewal of faith in the river.)

The point is that science alone may never be able to provide all the standards needed for judging success or failure in maintaining the Chesapeake Bay and its watershed—though new, developing regulations will soon attempt to define standards for clarity. But no amount of standards can substitute fully for respect for the bay's natural integrity. All citizens of the watershed, whether they live by a river, a forest, a marsh, or a tiny creek, should feel encouraged and supported to set their own personal standards, or ones gathered from their elders, to help scientists and regulators judge whether or not we are doing right by nature. Judge with your head, most certainly, but also with your heart (and your toes).

A RESILIENT BAY

Chapter 1 showed how estuaries like the Chesapeake Bay are, by nature, among the most variable, dynamic, and disorderly of environments, as the flow of forty-seven rivers collides with the intruding ocean in the mixing bowl that is the estuary. Creatures there are well adapted to a measure of chaos. But in cutting nearly half the watershed's forests, filling more than half its marshes, polluting nearly 90 percent of its underwater grasses to death, and destroying more than 90 percent of its oysters, humans have severely degraded key natural mechanisms that acted to buffer and filter the bay against floods and drought and pollution, and fundamentally disrupted the pathways by which food and energy historically moved through the estuary.

We want to regain this natural resilience, the natural systems that help the bay help itself. At a bare minimum, the watershed must not lose any more of its ability to soak up the rain that falls, as the original forest and wetlands did across all the land. This capability reduced floods and replenished the underground water table to maintain the flows of rivers and streams in drought. Wetlands and forest also filter pollutants from the water and clarify it before it runs downstream to the bay. Resilience aplenty also lies in the bay's bottom, where lush meadows of underwater grasses and vast shoals of oysters soaked up and filtered and evened out the pulses of nutrients and sediment that enter the bay, further enabling it to rebound from both natural and human disruptions.

Human structures, from stormwater detention ponds to agricultural manure pits, can be useful tools to supplement natural resilience, but as the preceding chapters point out, they are far from perfect substitutes, and society puts too much faith in them now. We want, in sum, maintenance and restoration of a natural ecosystem that could take a beating from natural and human disturbances and come back, and that with favorable environmental conditions could nurture seafood and wildlife like few other water bodies on the planet.

A DIVERSE BAY

Nature seldom declines as much as it simply shifts; thus the bay's total production of plants and fish and birds has not been reduced so much as it has been concentrated into larger numbers of fewer species, from algae to fish and ducks, favoring the ones that can adapt to polluted and stressful conditions. We want a bay with self-sustaining populations of the fish and fowl and other species that traditionally have lived in the watershed. A return to such natural diversity would be a prime indicator of a healthy system.

This diversity extends to human occupations. On the water, we want a bay with working watermen, a group whose survival is tied inextricably to maintenance of the highest environmental quality. Similarly, on the lands of the watershed we want to ensure the long-term health of natural resources–based economies such as agriculture and forestry. Both watermen and farmers are also implicated, as are all of the bay's residents, in many of the bay's problems. But it would be shortsighted and impoverishing to both the food supply and our cultural heritage to think the answers to bay pollution lie with forcing either group out of the picture.

A LIVABLE BAY

However much we may love and enjoy the water, it is on the lands of the watershed that we live most of our lives. If we cannot preserve extensive natural green spaces, accessible to all, if our transportation systems are congested and our air is not fit to breathe, then all the rockfish and canvasback ducks and clear, clean water we could imagine will not make this the "Land of Pleasant Living." We want a watershed that retains its sense of regional heritage, rather than melting entirely into a homogenized suburbia. The requirements for all forms of life, writes John A. Hostetler, the Pennsylvania scholar on the Amish, include not only soil, water, air, and sunlight, but also community. Fifty years from now, the mention of "Eastern Shore," "Northern Neck," and "Lancaster County" must continue to evoke rich and unique identities. The compact patterns of growth that best preserve and assist all the above will tend to be those that also maximize the resilient capacities of forest and wetlands and all natural open spaces to reduce polluted runoff to the water.

A PEOPLE'S BAY

The day when farmers in Charlottesville, Virginia, and Lancaster County, Pennsylvania, take the afternoon off to fish for sea-run shad and kids in the foothills of the Blue Ridge and the Appalachians dip silver herring from their home streams need not be far off. The value in reconnecting these fishermen to a distant bay has value far in excess of what can be measured in pounds of fish.

Removing dams and other obstructions that have amputated thousands of miles of tributaries from annual fish migrations can also bring the bay to many citizens who cannot easily go to it. Systems of hiking and biking trails on land, canoe and kayak and small boat trails through the marshes, and public access along the edges of every river system should ensure that no citizen of the watershed is far from water-based recreational contact with the bay or a tributary.

Environmental education systems, which have evolved significantly if unevenly across the watershed, are still just scratching the surface. They are not yet changing values on a broad scale to create a constituency for the environment that goes well beyond the membership in environmental organizations. Environmental awareness and nature education need to pervade school curriculums much as English, math, and civics do now, from kindergarten through high school graduation. One extremely hopeful model is CBF's "Bay Schools" pilot program, which enlists willing schools to teach the traditional curriculum through the lens of Chesapeake Bay.

A BAY SEEN WHOLE

A good doctor, Aristotle said, treats the patient, not the disease. Environmental preservation too often has fought specific pollution and development threats while the environment as a whole deteriorated. Ecological science provides the framework for comprehending the "patient"—the bay and its watershed and its airshed, and the creatures therein—as an interrelated system, rather than responding to environmental problems as a series of unrelated "symptoms."

It should be a high priority of research to refine this image. We know, for example, that in altering the landscape on a wide scale we have changed dramatically how water and energy and food flow from forested mountain to the bay's waters and bottom sediments, and from there into creatures that inhabit the system. To the extent we can understand the implications of such alterations we will be more successful environmental healers.

Just as critical is our ability to take the bay's pulse—monitor it— through long periods of time. In a system as turbulent and naturally variable as the bay, development of long-term trends is vital to knowing whether it is getting sick or well and whether nature or humans are causing a change. Such long-term, comprehensive monitoring—only recently begun when this book was first issued in 1991—is coming into its own. The lack of it a few decades ago undoubtedly delayed our recognition of and response to the bay's decline. Even well-meaning people during the 1960s and 1970s could not say for sure what was human impact and what was natural cycle.

Monitoring is still often an endangered program—the type that, like tree planting in cities, is most easily cut back when economies sag, because in the short term no one misses it. We must never let that happen. Additionally, we have to improve similar monitoring of changes in the land, using satellite photography and other modern, cost-effective tools to track trends in the resilience of the watershed as well as the health of the water. Prime areas for land monitoring are forested stream buffers, wetlands, fragmentation patterns in forest, and environmentally unsound agricultural practices.

Finally, while we should always seek out and monitor good indicators of bay health, from eagles to submerged grasses, we should also recognize the limitations of our present ability to take the pulse of large, complex ecosystems like the Chesapeake. Natural systems often don't decline in neat and predictable increments; rather, they may approach a threshold without our knowing it—even seem to be coming back—then fail quickly and massively. This is why, in the absence of perfect understanding, we must act conservatively.

THE NEED TO ACT NOW

Changes to the bay's water quality were mostly gradual until fifty or sixty years ago. But since then there have been unprecedented explosions in population growth, in wasteful land use patterns and energy consumption, in the use of agricultural and industrial chemicals, and in continued and higher-tech overfishing. As a result, natural systems have been overwhelmed.

The specific recommendations that follow are keyed to the preceding chapters. They are not meant as detailed blueprints but rather as guidelines for political, scientific, and citizen action that will vary from region to region. Some can be implemented quickly, while others are much more ambitious. All of them, however, are urgent if we are serious about saving the bay. One reason is the tremendous lag time between recognizing a problem and actually turning it around in a big, complex system like the bay and its watershed. While we huddle on the sidelines plotting cleanup strategies, pollution and other impacts from relentless population growth take no time-outs.

Recognition of the problem with the bay's environmentally critical underwater grasses, for example, began in the late 1960s, as they began a decline that eventually reduced them below 10 percent of their historic acreage. Now, nearly forty years later, at the beginning of the twenty-first century, we are still trying to bring them back, and a big comeback still seems years away.

The "2020 report" on population growth and development in the watershed, issued in the late 1980s, explained the consequences of delaying action this way: the households established in the watershed between the 1980s and 1999 will contribute a greatly disproportionate amount of all the pollution from development through 2020. This situation occurs simply because they are the ones that will be here the longest. In other words, if we wait until halfway to 2020 to begin dealing with development impacts, far more than half of the impact already will be guaranteed to happen.

Two further factors compel us to act now. Population continues to increase. Modifying our impacts on the environment, even assuming better technology will give us some boost, does not get any easier when we are adding a million people a decade to the watershed. And memories of the bay we want, roughly equivalent to the bay that existed in the 1950s and early 1960s, are growing dimmer. There is a difference in motivation between generations that experienced that bay and generations for whom that bay is a history lesson, no matter how compelling the lesson.

Pollution

Chapter 2 discussed the major pathways—air, land, and water—by which pollutants enter the bay. The following is a concise listing of those problems along with specific recommendations that could help save the bay.

AGRICULTURE

Problem: The runoff of nutrients—nitrogen and phosphorus—from chemical fertilizers and manure is a major pollutant of the bay. Soil eroding from farm fields and streams frequented by livestock is a problem in some areas. Runoff of pesticides is an unquantified but potential threat.

Recommendations: To have any hope of sharply reducing agriculture's pollution loads to the bay, we must vigorously pursue three broad approaches:

- *Reduce and better manage the fertilizer farmers apply to the land.* Every farm must be accountable for a nutrient management plan that matches its use of nitrogen and phosphorus, including manure, to no more than needed to grow crops. A "yield reserve" program is needed to give farmers financial incentives and safeguards against the risk of poor harvests if they agree to experiment with using less fertilizer.

    The spreading of manure (and municipal sewage sludge applied to farms), in many areas, must be based on how much phosphorus crops need, instead of just supplying nitrogen. Many soils are already dangerously saturated with phosphorus. This local saturation will mean shipping manure out of some farms and regions, to soils that need its nutrients; or burning it for energy or making it into pellets and compost for sale wherever more nutrients are needed.

- *Capture and cleanse polluted runoff before it reaches waterways.* Holding nutrients on the land or filtering them out before they enter local waterways must become universal. Planting winter cover crops like rye and oats must become a standard tool around the bay watershed. These can absorb large quantities of nitrogen that inevitably "leak" from even the best-managed farm fields. Planting buffer strips of forest, wetlands, and other natural vegetation between farm fields and waterways is a proven technique to intercept polluted runoff before it reaches the bay. It has many other benefits for wildlife and stream health. Streams, particularly small headwater portions, should be buffered with forest along their edges to maximize their ability to keep nutrients from running downstream.

  Manure must be spread only at times of year when crops are growing and can absorb its nitrogen and phosphorus. Manure from large, concentrated animal operations must be strictly regulated as a "point" discharge of pollution, much like sewage and industrial discharges. Fencing farm animals from streams keeps their manure out of the water, stops them from eroding stream banks, and results in healthy streams whose natural biological processes can significantly reduce polluting nutrients.

- *Modify what we eat and how we grow it.* Turn significant farm acreage back to forests and wetlands. Develop crops that require less fertilizer. Change farm animal nutrition to produce manures with less nitrogen and phosphorus. Limiting farm animal populations in some regions may be required. Restructure current public farm subsidies to give incentives for environmentally sound practices rather than overproduction of crops.

Shifting our diets to ones that are moderately, rather than heavily, meat intensive would significantly reduce fertilizer use and manure production. Allowing livestock to graze on grass instead of feeding them grain in barns would shift cropland toward pastures, with a significant reduction in runoff.

Many of the above recommendations are being employed already, but not widely for the most part. Doing what is right for the bay with agriculture will cost more, and it will almost certainly require more accountability than the largely voluntary approach taken with agriculture to date. Farmers must have better technological assistance and the necessary flexibility to cope with these added tasks.

The costs must be borne by all of us. We must make good stewardship of the environment the most profitable form of farming. Farmers are part of a national food system geared to produce abundant, cheap food, which has often ignored the costs to the environment. Similarly, individual farms cannot deal with regulations the same as large industries. They will need flexible approaches and substantial technical support.

SUSQUEHANNA RIVER

Problem: Source of half the bay's freshwater, the Susquehanna, whose degraded water quality is mostly influenced by Pennsylvania, in turn influences much of the water quality downstream in Maryland and parts of Virginia. Despite this problem, Pennsylvania would benefit relatively little from a restored Chesapeake.

Recommendations:

- Pennsylvania needs both additional resources and additional pushing from the downstream states and the federal government to do its share for bay water quality, a task in which it has lagged behind during the last decade. The major problems are with nitrogen from its agriculture and its sewage treatment plants. The Susquehanna is so dominant in bay water quality that it may make sense to shift cleanup dollars upstream from Maryland and Virginia.

- Decisions must be made now to dredge out the sediment and phosphorus that have been accumulating behind Susquehanna dams for decades. In a couple of decades, the dams will be bypassing large quantities of these pollutants downstream, offsetting today's expensive cleanup efforts.

- Pennsylvania and other states that share the Susquehanna's freshwater for drinking, industry, and irrigation must clamp down now on the growing consumption of the river's flow during dry years.

SEWAGE

Problem: Nutrients—nitrogen and phosphorus—in discharges of human sewage to the bay are a major factor in the decline of underwater grasses and low oxygen levels in the water.

Recommendations:

- Sewage treatment plants that serve about 75 percent of the people in the bay watershed are where proven technology can make the large water quality gains the soonest. Based on past experience, it may well be the only large source of pollution where rapid cleanup happens in the next decade. Accordingly, every major treatment plant in the watershed must upgrade as soon as possible to the best available technology. Currently that means removing all but 3 parts nitrogen per million parts of sewage. If going to 1 part per million appears achievable, that should become the goal.
- At a bare minimum, whenever sewage treatment plants expand their capacity to serve more people, regulators must hold them to current or reduced levels of total nitrogen and phosphorus, even as overall gallons of sewage discharge rise.
- The cost of sewage upgrades should be paid with federal and state help. But the large numbers of people hooked into treatment plants must also bear a fair share of the burden through increased water and sewer fees. Cleanups should not be postponed, even if federal grants fall short.
- The states must immediately begin to require new, less polluting technology for the 25 percent of the watershed's citizens who use backyard septic tanks. These have the potential to pollute more, per capita, than up-to-date sewage treatment. Allowing septic users to continue getting by on the cheap, polluting side is also unfair. It effectively subsidizes sprawl development, which is mostly on septic tanks, favoring it over existing cities and towns that have been upgrading their sewage treatment plants.
- To the extent that we remove pollutants from sewage discharges to the water, we increase the amounts of sludge, the semisolid residues from sewage treatment, that must be disposed of somewhere. Plans to incinerate sludge as a means of disposal should be rejected. This

practice wastes energy, contributes to air pollution, and runs counter to the concept that sludge, which is rich in nutrients, is a valuable resource.

TOXICS

Problem: While toxic chemicals and metals do not appear to be dominant causes of the bay's declines or a major threat to human health, their impacts are more widespread than we thought in both seafood and bottom sediments, and their effects can be extremely long lasting.

Recommendations:

- The long-term goal must be the elimination of toxics in discharges to the bay—particularly those that persist in the environment. There has been real progress here from traditional sources—sewage and industry. This can improve by phasing out "mixing zones," where toxics from discharge pipes are allowed at certain levels for a specified distance from the pipe. No new mixing zones should be approved. Meanwhile automobile exhausts, urban stormwater runoff, and mercury from coal-burning power plants are in need of tighter controls from the standpoint of toxics.
- Testing bay seafood for mercury, PCBs, and other persistent toxics must become routine and widespread. To date, wherever we have looked, we have usually found cause for concern.

OIL AND OIL SPILLS

Problem: The bay, with its long, shallow, productive edge of land and water, is extremely vulnerable to oil spills and is a major artery for oil transport.

Recommendations:

- Real progress in making oil transport in barges and tankers safer has been offset by two major spills from oil pipelines into bay waters in the last decade. Pipeline safety, now under federal and state scrutiny, must be made more spillproof.
- Attention to oil spill prevention and cleanup appears to have entered a period of reduced attention as Coast Guard priorities have shifted

to drug interdiction and homeland security. Declining vigilance produces just the environment in which another spill could occur.

SEDIMENT AND STORMWATER RUNOFF

Problem: The fastest-growing source of polluted runoff to the bay is from urban stormwater runoff, which carries sediment, chemicals, and nitrogen and phosphorus from developed lands. Such runoff is also the leading cause of degradation of the bay region's nontidal tributary streams. Sediment from shoreline erosion and bay rivers may need to be reduced by millions of tons a year to meet bay water quality goals.

Recommendations:

- All new development in the watershed must move rapidly toward producing runoff once building is completed that closely mimics the quality, quantity, and timing of rainwater running from the land before development. A range of techniques exists now that, if used in concert, can move us much closer to this goal.
- With present development, "hardening" more than a few percent of a stream's watershed by paving streets and building homes begins to degrade water quality. Limits on such impervious surfaces should be a major factor in new development. New technologies may allow more development without impacts on water quality, but this possibility has yet to be proven.
- Retrofitting older, densely developed areas to reduce stormwater impacts is quite expensive. Practices such as regular urban street sweeping can help. Longer term, reducing the fallout of a range of pollutants in modern air could help make runoff from paved areas cleaner.
- We do not know yet how to reduce the sediment reaching the main bay from rivers and shoreline erosion by as much as needed (40–60 percent) to meet water quality goals. Armoring the bay's edges with bulkheads and stone is not a preferred solution to this in most cases. The states should restrict armoring to cases where there is actually significant erosion and where alternatives like planting marshes are not possible.

AIR

Problem: Air pollution is the source of nearly a third of the bay's primary pollutant, nitrogen; it is also the source of toxic chemicals that accumulate in bay seafood.

Recommendations:

- Reduce the three main sources of air pollution: require less polluting, more fuel efficient vehicles; continue progress under current federal air quality laws in reducing emissions from power plants throughout the bay's airshed (six times as large as the watershed); and control airborne emissions from agricultural manures, which are now wholly unregulated. Push for a national energy policy that moves strongly toward conservation and energy sources other than coal and oil.
- Preserve and increase forests, wetlands, and other natural vegetation that absorb much of the airborne pollution wherever it falls on them.

BOATS

Problem: Recreational boating is a small but significant source of bay pollution. It is a fast-growing bay use, with impacts that range from habitat destruction (building and expanding marinas) to toxic pollution from bottom paints, motor oil, and discharges of human waste.

Recommendations:

- The bay and its rivers must be made a "no discharge" zone for all boat toilets. Every marina must have facilities or arrangements to pump out and properly dispose of such wastes. While there has been real progress with boat-related pollution in the last decade, this is being offset by boating use that is growing faster than population.
- Programs to educate boaters to voluntarily reduce their environmental impacts should be expanded.

DISSOLVED OXYGEN

Problem: Low oxygen in the bay's deep waters now affects more than half the estuary's total volume in some summers. Oxygen losses in shallow headwaters and coves are more widely spread and more routine than previously thought and are implicated in numerous fish kills.

Recommendations: Reducing nitrogen and phosphorus flowing down the bay's major rivers by as much as 40–50 percent will be necessary to re-store dissolved oxygen in the bay's deeps. Shallow-water losses of oxygen are linked to local pollution, such as from septic tanks and runoff from yards, golf courses, farmland, and urban pavement. Monitoring of shallow-water oxygen conditions must be stepped up significantly, taking advantage of new monitoring technologies.

DREDGING

Problem: Where we place the huge quantities of spoil dredged to keep the bay's shipping channels open can have large impacts on the bay's bottom and shoreline habitat.

Recommendations:

- Using the spoil to create or re-create islands that have eroded away can be a win-win solution. The possibility of using spoil to rebuild marshes that can't keep up with sea level rise is also worth exploring.
- There are limits to both of these approaches, but there is no limit as yet to dredging needs. The time has come for Maryland to give seri-ous consideration to doing less dredging of its northern bay ap-proaches, if use by large vessels continues to decline.

FISH-EYE VIEW OF WATER QUALITY—NEW STANDARDS

Problem: The bay states and the U.S. EPA are falling seriously behind schedule in finalizing a new generation of water quality standards to bet-ter guide the Chesapeake's cleanup.

Recommendations: Waiting to move forward with pollution reductions until every last standard has been issued should not be an option. The sizes of the reductions needed, in every part of the watershed and from every source, are so large that there is no risk of overdoing them before new standards are finalized.

Harvests

Problem: Blue crabs, the bay's last great commercial fishery, have reached historic low levels in the last decade. Oysters and American shad remain severely depressed. Bay watermen, dangerously dependent now on a single species, the crab, face tough times. Waterfowl dependent on the bay's diminished underwater grasses continue to do poorly.

Recommendations:

- Maryland and Virginia must continue to build on their recent, encouraging progress to restore blue crab stocks. It will mean achieving an honest 15 percent reduction in catches to start, followed by a long-term management plan that lets harvests move up and down, always with a margin of safety to protect enough spawning females, as notoriously cyclical crab stocks rise and fall. Attention to bay watermen and their communities should be an integral part of management plans, which may require further cuts in crabbing.

- Programs to restore the bay's native oysters should be scaled up to levels that have a better chance of meeting goals to increase populations tenfold. It is too soon to give up on restoring the native oysters, even though disease, pollution, and the effects of historic overfishing continue to depress any significant comeback. Meanwhile, carefully controlled experiments and other research to learn more about the prospects of introducing a promising nonnative oyster, *Crassostrea ariakensis,* should proceed. Rebuilding historic oyster reefs throughout the bay not only boosts oysters, but also creates a vital and much-diminished habitat for a variety of fish, crabs, and other marine organisms.

- The handful of successful efforts to restock American shad and their smaller cousins, hickory shad, should expand to other historic shad spawning rivers throughout the bay. The phase-out of commercial fishing for shad in the ocean, on their way to and from the Chesapeake to spawn, must be kept on track (concluding in 2004).

- The effort that restored striped bass throughout the bay during the last decade should become the model for management plans covering all other bay species—a combination of good science, adequate funding, and strong regulatory oversight. Additionally, management plans must account for—as quickly as scientific understanding permits—interactions between multiple species. Such a plan means managing a species in the context of what it preys on, and what preys on it, based on how predators and prey respond to cycles of climate, drought, and other variables. Trying to maximize the numbers of all species simultaneously is not something that would ever occur in nature.

- Fisheries management plans must put more emphasis on maintaining healthy populations of important forage species such as menhaden, whose abundance is critical to many of the bay's most desirable sport and commercial species of fish.
- While several species of waterfowl in the bay are doing poorly, two are doing all too well—nonmigratory Canada geese and mute swans. Both have undesirable environmental impacts, and their present numbers should be reduced.

Resilience

FORESTS

Problem: The watershed has lost nearly half its least-polluting land use, the forest. Worse, about two-thirds of the forest is gone in the heavily farmed and developed regions closest to the bay, precisely where forest is most needed to buffer polluted runoff. Declines in these regions are continuing, making it difficult to maintain the bay's natural resilience, or ability to rebound from environmental insults.

Recommendations:
- We need to set a no-net-loss goal (or net gain) for forests, as we have for wetlands, submerged grasses, and oysters, the other major elements of the bay's resilience. Lands near the bay and along the edges of all streams and rivers and the bay itself are the most critical places for increasing both wildlife habitat and pollution control.
- Reducing the rate of sprawl development is one of the most effective ways to stop forest loss. With forest ownership spread among tens of thousands of private landowners, we must also expand incentives and technical help to promote keeping trees on the land.
- Air pollution, already an acknowledged threat to human health and bay water quality, also needs to be reduced with regard for the long-term health of forests.
- We must prevent further fragmentation of existing forest, as several species of wildlife depend on unbroken blocks of forest. Where

forests are distributed and how their patterns (i.e., unbroken blocks) lie are often as important as total forest acreage in the watershed.

- Forests, so vital for wildlife, clean water, and clean air, must be treated as our green infrastructure, just as essential to our quality of life as the traditional infrastructure of highways, sewers, water mains, and electric lines.

NONTIDAL WETLANDS

Problem: The bay region has lost hundreds of thousands of wetland acres since colonial times and at least 60,000 acres in recent decades. We are now gaining acreage back for the first time in history by creating new wetlands and enhancing degraded ones, as well as providing better protection to existing ones in all three bay states.

Recommendations:

- Avoiding and minimizing destruction of existing, natural wetlands must be the highest priority. Creating wetlands to achieve goals of no net loss is still as much art as science, and it's unlikely all such new wetlands will perform as well as existing ones being destroyed. Wetland creation to compensate for losses must be a last resort, not a license to destroy natural wetlands.
- All three states can make their nontidal wetlands protection laws stronger and must do so, as federal laws do not provide an adequate safety net. Goals for regaining wetland acreage must also be set higher.
- A golden opportunity to reclaim large acreages of wetlands so vital to the bay's resilience occurs when farms with hydric soils are sold for development. Such soils originally underlay wetlands, and though farmed for decades, even centuries, they can revert quickly to high-quality wetlands. It should be a priority to identify such opportunities and work with developers to incorporate such soils back to their natural wetland functions.

TIDAL WETLANDS

Problem: While human destruction of tidal wetlands has slowed considerably, the bay stands to lose tens of thousands of acres from its 290,000 acres of such wetlands in the next several decades. Sea level rise coupled with a sinking of the land are the reasons, and neither is susceptible to short-term remedy.

Recommendations:

- Maryland and Virginia must halt virtually all destruction of natural tidal wetlands, which appear to be one of the most effective mechanisms for removing pollutants such as nitrogen from rivers before they can reach the bay. Both states should revise the almost routine granting of permits to harden shorelines against erosion with bulkheads and riprap, which can destroy wetlands. They should strongly encourage alternatives such as planting wetlands.
- Two long-term solutions to the loss of tidal wetlands to sea level rise are to keep as much shoreline as possible in an undeveloped state to leave room for new wetlands to form over time and to decrease fossil fuel use to reduce global warming, a cause of sea level rise.
- Innovative programs to rebuild sinking wetlands by spraying them with sediment from dredging projects may hold promise.
- Activities that create open water in tidal marshes, such as mosquito control ditching projects, should be discontinued if there is any chance they may worsen the marsh's susceptibility to rising sea level.

VIRGINIA'S CHESAPEAKE BAY PRESERVATION ACT

Problem: The edges of the bay and its rivers get the most pressure from development, but they are simultaneously critical habitat for a range of wildlife and aquatic life.

Recommendation:

- Virginia's 1988 attempt to extend broad environmental protection to the bay's shoreline needs a complete overhaul. It needs enforcement mechanisms, adequate funding and staffing, and aggressive political support at the state and county levels.

MARYLAND CRITICAL AREA ACT

Problem: The edges of the bay and its rivers get the most pressure from development, but they are simultaneously critical habitat for a range of wildlife and aquatic life.

Recommendations:

- Maryland's attempt to protect its tidal edges has been fairly success-ful on some 363,000 acres in the act's Resource Conservation Area (RCA), where strict, protective zoning applies. But it could work sig-nificantly better with stronger oversight and enforcement by the state Critical Area Commission.
- The act's Limited Development Area (LDA), 95,000 acres of shoreline where outdated, sprawl-inducing development can occur, is in need of immediate overhaul. A provision in the act that allows transfers of land from RCA to less-stringent LDA classification also needs reform.

BOTTOM OF THE BAY

Problem: Out of sight and out of mind, the bay's bottom has been devas-tated over the past several decades, more than most people can compre-hend. Oysters, submerged grasses, the whole assemblage of benthos, or bottom-dwelling worms and clams and snails, range from mostly gone to highly stressed. There is evidence that the composition of algal species has shifted toward forms not palatable to higher organisms that feed on them. All this change represents a huge loss of resilience and habitat.

Recommendations:

- With the great majority of benthic organisms, including the under-water grasses that are now 85 percent gone, the only real solution is reducing nutrients and sediment enough to bring back healthy oxy-gen levels and clear enough water that the grasses can get sunlight needed for growth.
- With oysters, now at perhaps 2 percent of historic levels, aggressive programs of reef building to restore lost habitat and research to solve the bay's deadly oyster diseases are the only solutions. It is too early to give up on the native oyster, but carefully controlled experiments with a promising Asian oyster should continue in the event the deci-sion is made to stock the bay with it.

UPSTREAM AND DOWN

Problem: In addition to water quality, the quantity of freshwater flows and the obstructions to flows, such as dams, have important environmen-tal consequences for the bay.

Recommendations:

- Programs in all three bay states to reopen historic spawning rivers to shad, striped bass, herring, and other fish are making real progress and should be expanded to smaller tributaries.
- We need to rethink water conservation in all three bay states, with a goal of using freshwater on a sustainable basis. Current overuse eventually could shift the bay's salinity higher, which will harm more creatures than it will benefit. The Susquehanna River especially needs stronger controls on the freshwater that may be removed in dry years.
- Proposed widening and deepening of the C&D Canal at the head of the bay should be thoroughly evaluated to make sure it does not increase the net loss of freshwater from the Chesapeake Bay to Delaware Bay.

The Ultimate Issue: People

Restoring the Chesapeake Bay and sustaining it will mean limiting both the per capita environmental impacts and the numbers of people living in the watershed.

HOW WE LIVE

Problem: The ecological footprint of a person living in the bay region today—the demands each person's lifestyle makes on the region's natural resources—is substantially larger than it was fifty years ago.

Recommendations:

- Moderating the individual choices of 16 million people living in the bay's watershed can have huge impacts. Changes in a few areas—transportation, diet, home choice, and household operation—will have more impact than across-the-board cutbacks in consumption.
- Reducing the rate of sprawl development remains a huge priority. Nearly a third of all development of farms and natural lands in the bay watershed during the last four centuries has occurred in just the last twenty years. Sprawl costs us all—environmentally, economically, and socially. Smart Growth, as practiced in Maryland in recent

years, is a significant new strategy for checking sprawl, employing the budgetary power of the state to steer growth into areas where it exists, or where it is planned, and away from the countryside. While each state will do it differently, Virginia and Pennsylvania need to put into practice the concepts of Smart Growth. In Maryland, many counties continue working counter to the state's Smart Growth goals.

- The toughest part of the Smart Growth equation may not be preserving the countryside, but convincing people to accept denser, more compact growth around existing developed areas. There is a need not only to make it easy and profitable for developers to build in such patterns, but also for working models of denser development that incorporate desirable housing, pedestrian- and bike-friendly access to services, and a sense of community.
- Open space acquisition in the bay watershed must be stepped up at all levels, local, state, federal, and private alike. At a minimum, 20 percent of the bay's watershed should be preserved by 2010.

HOW MANY OF US?

Problem: Our society, including the environmental movement, has focused largely on only one side of the equation—*how* we live with regard to nature—and it must remain a critical concern. But it is past time to begin a debate on *how many* of us live here, on the necessity of stabilizing population.

Recommendations:

- Ultimately, a stable population must happen as national policy. But any movement has to start somewhere, and there is no place more in need of it than the Chesapeake Bay, where we are trying to reduce pollution to levels that existed when the population was half what it is today—even as we head toward doubling the population again.
- There are only limited realistic ways to stabilize population: reduce foreign immigration by an act of Congress, convince Americans to have fewer children, or use a combination of both. A return to historic rates of immigration and a modest lowering of the fertility rate could stabilize population within fifty years.

- It is beyond the scope of this book, or the Chesapeake Bay Foundation's agenda, to prescribe the proper path to stabilizing population (or reducing it). But we challenge environmental groups everywhere to join us in putting this vital issue on the national agenda.
- A likely precursor to any debate on stabilizing or reducing population is a thorough discussion of how the United States could enjoy a prosperous economy without unending growth of its population. Many countries already do, but powerful economic interests are opposed to slower growth of population. The benefits of never-ending population growth are greatly overstated, ignoring society's many and large subsidies to growth—from roads to schools to pollution control and the expenditures of large sums to preserve natural landscapes from being overwhelmed. It is essential to keep in mind that a stable population need not mean stagnant economic development.

Toward an Environmental Ethic

What must we do then, to save the bay, to give substance to the outlined recommendations of this chapter? We must learn to see the bay whole, as water and watershed and airshed inseparably linked; to see it as a system whose forests and oysters and underwater grasses and marshes are every bit as much components of pollution control and environmental health as sewage treatment plants, automotive emissions controls, and sediment fences. We easily accept spending $50 million or more on sewage treatment, but the filtering, cleansing forest may not be allowed to stand because it is "uneconomic" not to develop it. Likewise, we will haul sewage sludge and municipal trash halfway across the country for environmentally sound disposal; but to haul excess farm manure halfway across Lancaster County to soils that can use it is "not cost effective."

We must articulate and demonstrate visions to replace the "grow or die," "economics versus environment," and "pollution is the price of progress" myths that underlie so much current development of the watershed. What is needed to save the bay can and must be linked to a better quality of life, not simply to sacrifice—saving open space by revitalizing existing towns is an example; protecting forests for water quality also benefits hunters and hikers and decreases air pollution.

Just as introducing a pollutant or altering a river's flow may have unforeseeable domino effects that reverberate throughout the environment, so can introducing one environmentally sound behavior have unexpected multiple effects for the good. Driving less to cut air pollution means, ultimately, fewer oil spills and less toxic rainwater running from parking lots and driveways as well as cities designed more for humans than for the cars whose use currently requires about half of all urban space.

Cleansing the water enough for bay grasses to rebound will, in turn, cleanse the water more as the grasses absorb pollutants, bringing back even more grasses—a vicious cycle in reverse. Once pollutants such as nitrogen are reduced enough to raise the levels of oxygen in the bay's deep waters, the sediments there will, in turn, convert more nitrogen to harmless forms, which will raise oxygen levels, which will. . . . The bay, damaged though it is, remains a system capable of enormous and rapid comebacks if we will just give it some breathing space.

But there are deeper reasons for cleaning up our act in the watershed of the Chesapeake. Everywhere in the world, environmental pressures are growing most severe along the edges of land and water. At least half of all the people on Earth live on about 5 percent of its land, and much of that 5 percent is around highly productive coastal edges and estuaries. The Chesapeake, with its thousands of miles of edges so attractive to humans and the rest of nature, is at the heart of the heart of this statistic. The problems of the bay are happening globally (see Figure 6.1). What will it say to the rest of humanity if the nation that considers itself a world leader cannot figure out how to stop fouling its own nest?

The world can learn vital lessons from environmental success on the Chesapeake. They range from the technical to the spiritual. Love for the Chesapeake Bay is the closest we come in this region of the world to having an environmental ethic. Something about it stirs us instinctively, apart from the quantity and the succulence of seafood. This love can be built on, extended to the watershed as a whole. If you love the bird, then you must learn to love and keep the forests in which it lives—and think about learning to live with less clearing and paving.

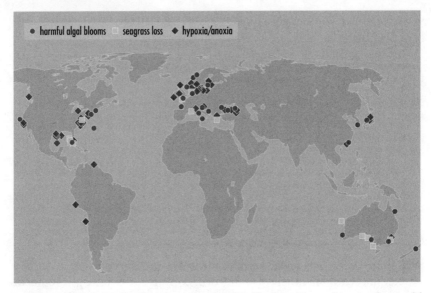

FIGURE 6.1. **Global Distribution of Coastal Pollution.** Everywhere in the world, environmental pressures are growing most severe along the edges of land and water. The problems of the bay are happening globally. What will it say to the rest of humanity if the nation that considers itself a world leader cannot figure out how to stop fouling its own nest? [Data compiled by W. M. Kemp, University of Maryland, Horn Point Laboratory]

The environmental crisis is also a moral crisis. Squandering natural riches that are collectively inherited, not one iota earned, is particularly irresponsible. We cannot justify continuing to take from future generations. Instead, we must choose stewardship, the care of what we have been given, rather than an economy built overmuch on the unending acquisition of material goods and on treating natural resources as if they had no real value.

Although we cannot preserve the Chesapeake Bay for future generations without laws and regulations, all the legislation we could imagine will not be enough without an ethic that defines an enduring and nurturing relationship between humans and the environment. Nor are we likely to get to such a point without a massive commitment to environmental education of the sort defined by the late Jacques Cousteau: "Education has nothing to do with learning how to compress acetylene without an explosion or how to make an atom bomb. That's instruction. A person is well educated when they know how to act or to behave in difficult situations."

Indeed, we who would save our environment are in difficult times. We need to learn how to behave, and quickly. We have already ensured that a generation has grown up in parts of the watershed without the ability to catch shad and with diminished chances to catch rockfish. We have also raised a generation or two with little opportunity to wade in grassy, clear shallows in pursuit of soft-shell crabs and consigned generations to come in many regions to accepting congested highways, polluted air, ugly strip development, and sprawling suburbia as normal parts of their environment.

We are not far from consigning a coming generation of children to seeing oyster skipjacks only in museums and books, to traveling ever further for a glimpse of natural landscape, to savoring the regional uniqueness attached to so many parts of the bay watershed only from books and pictures or from the reminiscences of their elders.

On the odds of avoiding such a future, it is something hard to be *optimistic* (a Latin word that means, literally, "feeling good"). Trends of the last decade and trends so far in this decade often don't merit feeling good. We remain, however, steadfastly and immensely *hopeful,* a word traceable to the Old English "hop." The writer Scott Russell Sanders tells of his small dog that kept getting lost in tall grass, but could hop high enough to see the way out, thereby keeping its hopes up. Just so, even as we slog through tall grass, struggling to restore this Chesapeake, we can clearly see better and achievable ways to live in keeping with the nature of the place.

Despite the damage we have done, the parts and plants and creatures of the bay of half a century ago still survive to a heartening degree. That so much has been lost is a tragedy. That so much remains is our hope of saving the bay.

APPENDIX A:
CBF'S STATE OF THE BAY
REPORT

People constantly ask CBF staffers, "How's the bay doing?" To answer that question in a meaningful way, we began in 1998 to issue an annual State of the Bay Report. In it, CBF scientists each year examine the best available current and historical information for thirteen indicators in three categories: pollution, habitat, and fisheries. Although we seek advice from other bay scientists, ultimately the best professional judgment of our own scientists determines the value assigned to each factor in this bay health index.

The current state of the bay is measured against the healthiest Chesapeake we can describe—the rich and balanced bay that Captain John Smith described in his exploration narratives of the early 1600s, supplemented by accounts of other early-seventeenth-century visitors and some sophisticated scientific detective work. Smith explored the Chesapeake when clear water revealed meadows of underwater grasses, oyster reefs so prodigious they posed threats to navigation, and abundant fish. The bay that John Smith saw, which was minimally influenced by human actions, rates 100 and is our benchmark.

The State of the Bay Report tells us how far we have fallen from Smith's bay and how great our challenge is to create a "saved" bay. We believe that the Chesapeake's health bottomed out at a score of 23—less than a quarter of its ecological potential—in the early 1980s. Since then, there have been modest improvements, to 27 in 1998 and 28 in 1999 and 2000.

Rather than continuing to rise, however, the index dropped back to 27 in 2001 and 2002, even when helped by reductions in runoff pollution due to drought. Despite this discouraging lack of progress, we believe that, with your help and strong leadership from our political leaders, we can make significant progress in the next eight years.

Our analysis indicates that meeting the commitments of *Chesapeake 2000,* the new interjurisdictional Bay Agreement, will bring the bay to a score of 40. That is our immediate goal and the overriding focus of all our programs throughout this decade. With such a large human population, the bay will never again score 100, but we believe firmly that together, we can reach 40 by 2010 and 70 by 2050.

Here, then, is a summary of our 2002 State of the Bay Report, with comments on the past and future of each indicator below.

2002 Chesapeake Bay Health Index

Habitat		Pollution		Fisheries	
Wetlands	42	Toxics	28	Crabs	40
Forested Buffers	54	Dissolved Oxygen	15	Rockfish	75
Underwater Grasses	12	Water Clarity	16	Oysters	2
Resource Lands	30	Nitrogen	16	Shad	7
		Phosphorus	16		
				Average	**27**

HABITAT

Wetlands 42 [−1 since 1998]

According to an authoritative review of historical wetlands losses, the three bay states have lost roughly 58 percent of their wetlands since colonial times. Despite stepped-up wetlands restoration efforts in recent years, the wetlands index has fallen a point since 1998, due to continued threats from sea level rise and from development, particularly in Virginia where the new nontidal wetlands law has been hampered by bad court decisions. The science and art of wetlands restoration are making progress, but regulatory programs still do not protect wetlands adequately against loss.

Forested Buffers 54 [+1 since 1998]

Riparian forests buffer roughly 54 percent of the basin's 110,000 miles of streams and shorelines. Restoration efforts have succeeded in reaching the Chesapeake Bay Program's initial 2010 goal for streamside forests, but the pace must be increased to see substantial progress in this index and benefits to the bay, especially along its heavily settled tidal shorelines. The extent of already established forest buffers lost to development or land clearing remains unknown and of much concern.

Underwater Grasses 12 [no change since 1998]

The index value of 12 indicates that 12 percent of the bay's historical acreage is currently covered by underwater grass. The severe drought of 2001–2002 reduced runoff, improved water clarity, and produced strong underwater grass growth in several areas of the bay, such as the Severn River and Mobjack Bay, which may cause the index to rise by as much as 20 percent in the next couple of years. The apparent increase is encouraging in that it shows us the Chesapeake will respond to reduced pollution, but even at a score around 15, these keystone communities are still minuscule relative to historic levels.

Resource Lands 30 [-3 since 1998]

Estimates suggest that the loss of resource lands in the watershed is continuing at the fastest rate in history. Consequently, land that used to filter pollution is now funneling it into waterways and the bay. In the *Chesapeake 2000* agreement, Pennsylvania, Maryland, and Virginia agreed to reduce the annual loss of forest and farmland to harmful sprawl by 30 percent by 2012. Programs and policies to accomplish this goal have yet to be developed, adopted, or implemented bay-wide, and the funding to permanently preserve 20 percent of the watershed from development by 2010 is endangered by budget shortfalls.

POLLUTION

Toxics 28 [-2 since 1998]

Among all threats to the bay, toxic chemicals are the most difficult to measure. The index has dropped because of substantial increases in actual releases of chemicals to waterways in Virginia and Maryland (as reported by the EPA's *Toxics Release Inventory*) and the increased number of health advisories limiting fish consumption throughout the watershed due to toxic contaminants. The index value of 28 indicates that the bay is deeply degraded due to chemical contaminants and is far from our goal of a toxics-free bay.

Dissolved Oxygen 15 [no change since 1998]

The levels of anoxia (no oxygen) and hypoxia (extremely low levels of oxygen) we see today reflect both nutrient pollution and consequences of river flows that were probably changed forever following land clearing in the watershed. The index of 15 reflects the severely degraded levels of dissolved oxygen in the bay watershed. Despite drought-driven nutrient improvements in 2001–2002, the bay's overall dissolved oxygen levels have not improved, and the bay's "dead zone" may in fact be growing. It will not improve until we reduce the inputs of nitrogen and phosphorus, particularly from the Susquehanna River.

Water Clarity 16 [+1 since 1998]

The index of 16 indicates seriously degraded water quality when compared to the bay of 400 years ago. Reliable reports of widespread underwater grasses that grew in 9 feet of water only half a century ago are a sign of this deterioration. Since 1998, the score has been 15 in wet years and 16 in drought, an increase for which we can take no credit. Experts agree that in 2002 the bay's water was as clear as it has been in recent years, but as soon as the rains come, nitrogen, phosphorus, and sediment will run off and adversely affect water clarity. It will not improve until we reduce all three pollutants significantly.

Nitrogen 16   Phosphorus 16   [both +1 since 2001]

CBF's original health index score of 15 for nitrogen and phosphorus was based on estimates that placed nitrogen loading to the bay at seven times what it was in pre-colonial times. As a result of drought, nutrient pollution loads to the bay decreased slightly in 2001–2002. Pollutants continued, however, to be deposited on the land, ready to enter the bay when the rains returned. Based on USGS trend analysis of nitrogen and phosphorus loads to the bay between 1985 and 1999, there is a downward trend in total nutrient loads. Nonetheless, the bay still suffers from extreme nitrogen pollution, and baywide nitrogen reduction efforts have yet to produce new reduction goals that point to a long-term solution. The best short-term opportunity for substantive improvements lies in upgraded sewage treatment, and longer-term in improved agricultural practices.

FISHERIES

Crabs 40 [-10 since 1998, the most ominous drop in the index]

The bay's blue crab fishery has suffered through consecutive years of poor harvest levels. With the crab spawning stock near a historic low and reproductive success continuing to decline, the crab population continues to be stressed by extremely heavy fishing and low levels of the underwater grass habitat critical to the species' life cycle. The scientific consensus is that the risk to the population is high and increasing. The poor status is tempered somewhat by optimism that the continuing implementation of the Bi-state Blue Crab Advisory

Committee recovery strategy and an upturn in underwater grasses will start to boost the stock.

Rockfish 75 [+5 since 1998]

Rockfish (striped bass) numbers and spawning stock biomass are higher than they've been since relatively good records started being kept in the 1960s. With each passing year, more older, mature fish broaden the population. A good year class in 2001 reinforced the positive assessment that the stock continues in a re-covered condition. Still, there are few fish more than fifteen years old (rockfish can live for thirty years), meaning the stock is not fully stabilized. And a limited abundance of menhaden, a favorite food, appears to hamper fish growth. Lack of food and poor water quality are both factors in a troublingly persistent outbreak of *mycobacteriosis* in the population.

Oysters 2 [+1 since 1998]

Although no definitive data exist, it has been estimated that oyster biomass in the late 1980s was only 1 percent of what it was before the heavy oyster harvest in the late 1800s. Numbers of oysters in the bay, at least as indicated by harvest, have declined since the late 1980s. Today's index of 2 represents an oyster population of less than 2 percent of its abundance in John Smith's time. Continuing restora-tion progress in some areas has been encouraging, but in others it has been ham-pered by disease mortality. The 2001–2002 drought's elevated salinity levels caused oyster parasites to move farther up the bay and its tributaries, so even modest survival in disease-plagued areas is encouraging. And the higher salinity promises to stimulate good reproduction in some areas. Although progress is being made on a baywide oyster assessment, no reliable measure of the total pop-ulation is yet in hand.

Shad 7 [+5 since 1998]

In the past five years, encouraging spawning runs in several bay tributaries have reinforced optimism for continued recovery of Chesapeake shad stocks. Contin-uation of stocking efforts, achievement of the goal to reopen more than 1,300 miles of bay tributaries to migratory fish passage, and plans to open another 400 miles by 2010 all bode well for the future. The ongoing phase-out of the coastal intercept fishery is an important complement to restoration. Despite these posi-tive trends, however, the bay's shad population remains severely depleted.

APPENDIX B:
CHESAPEAKE 2000

Chesapeake Bay Program
A Watershed Partnership

PREAMBLE

The Chesapeake Bay is North America's largest and most biologically diverse estuary, home to more than 3,600 species of plants, fish and animals. For more than 300 years, the Bay and its tributaries have sustained the region's economy and defined its traditions and culture. It is a resource of extraordinary productivity, worthy of the highest levels of protection and restoration.

Accordingly, in 1983 and 1987, the states of Virginia, Maryland, Pennsylvania, the District of Columbia, the Chesapeake Bay Commission and the U.S. Environmental Protection Agency, representing the federal government, signed historic agreements that established the Chesapeake Bay Program partnership to protect and restore the Chesapeake Bay's ecosystem.

For almost two decades, we, the signatories to these agreements, have worked together as stewards to ensure the public's right to clean water and a healthy and productive resource. We have sought to protect the health of the public that uses the Bay and consumes its bounty. The initiatives we have pursued have been deliberate and have produced significant results in the health and productivity of the Bay's main stem, the tributaries, and the natural land and water ecosystems that compose the Chesapeake Bay watershed.

While the individual and collective accomplishments of our efforts have been significant, even greater effort will be required to address the enormous challenges that lie ahead. Increased population and development within the watershed have created ever-greater challenges for us in the Bay's restoration. These challenges are further complicated by the dynamic nature of the Bay and the ever-changing global ecosystem with which it interacts.

In order to achieve our existing goals and meet the challenges that lie ahead, we must reaffirm our partnership and recommit to fulfilling the public responsibility we undertook almost two decades ago. We must manage for the future. We must have a vision for our desired destiny and put programs into place that will secure it.

To do this, there can be no greater goal in this recommitment than to engage everyone—individuals, businesses, schools and universities, communities and governments—in our effort. We must encourage all citizens of the Chesapeake Bay watershed to work toward a shared vision—a system with abundant, diverse populations of living resources, fed by healthy streams and rivers, sustaining strong local and regional economies, and our unique quality of life.

In affirming our recommitment through this new *Chesapeake 2000,* we recognize the importance of viewing this document in its entirety with no single part taken in isolation of the others. This Agreement reflects the Bay's complexity in that each action we take, like the elements of the Bay itself, is connected to all the others. This Agreement responds to the problems facing this magnificent ecosystem in a comprehensive, multifaceted way.

By this Agreement, we commit ourselves to nurture and sustain a Chesapeake Bay Watershed Partnership and to achieve the goals set forth in the subsequent sections. Without such a partnership, future challenges will not be met. With it, the restoration and protection of the Chesapeake Bay will be ensured for generations to come.

We commit to:

LIVING RESOURCE PROTECTION AND RESTORATION

The health and vitality of the Chesapeake Bay's living resources provide the ultimate indicator of our success in the restoration and protection effort. The Bay's fisheries and the other living resources that sustain them and provide habitat for them are central to the initiatives we undertake in this Agreement.

We recognize the interconnectedness of the Bay's living resources and the importance of protecting the entire natural system. Therefore, we commit to identify the essential elements of habitat and environmental quality necessary to support the living resources of the Bay. In protecting commercially valuable species, we will manage harvest levels with precaution to maintain their health and stability and protect the ecosystem as a whole. We will restore passage for migratory fish and work to ensure that suitable water quality conditions exist in the upstream spawning habitats upon which they depend.

Our actions must be conducted in an integrated and coordinated manner. They must be continually monitored, evaluated and revised to adjust to the dynamic nature and complexities of the Chesapeake Bay and changes in global ecosystems. To advance this ecosystem approach, we will broaden our management prospective from single-system to ecosystem functions and will expand our protection efforts by shifting from single-species to multi-species management. We will also undertake efforts to determine how future conditions and changes in the chemical, physical and biological attributes of the Bay will affect living resources over time.

GOAL

Restore, enhance and protect the finfish, shellfish and other living resources, their habitats and ecological relationships to sustain all fisheries and provide for a balanced ecosystem.

Oysters

• By 2010, achieve, at a minimum, a tenfold increase in native oysters in the Chesapeake Bay, based upon a 1994 baseline. By 2002, develop and implement a strategy to achieve this increase by using sanctuaries sufficient in size and distribution, aquaculture, continued disease research and disease-resistant management strategies, and other management approaches.

Exotic Species

• In 2000, establish a Chesapeake Bay Program Task Force to:
   1. Work cooperatively with the U.S. Coast Guard, the ports, the shipping industry, environmental interests and others at the national level to help establish and implement a national program designed to substantially reduce and, where possible, eliminate the introduction of non-native species carried in ballast water; and
   2. By 2002, develop and implement an interim voluntary ballast water management program for the waters of the Bay and its tributaries.
• By 2001, identify and rank non-native, invasive aquatic and terrestrial species which are causing or have the potential to cause significant negative impacts to the Bay's aquatic ecosystem. By 2003, develop and implement management plans for those species deemed problematic to the restoration and integrity of the Bay's ecosystem.

Fish Passage and Migratory and Resident Fish

• By June 2002, identify the final initiatives necessary to achieve our existing goal of restoring fish passage for migratory fish to more than 1,357 miles of currently blocked river habitat by 2003 and establish a monitoring program to assess outcomes.
• By 2002, set a new goal with implementation schedules for additional migratory and resident fish passages that addresses the removal of physical blockages. In addition, the goal will address the removal of chemical

blockages caused by acid mine drainage. Projects should be selected for maximum habitat and stock benefit.

• By 2002, assess trends in populations for priority migratory fish species. Determine tributary-specific target population sizes based upon projected fish passage, and current and projected habitat available, and provide recommendations to achieve those targets.

• By 2003, revise fish management plans to include strategies to achieve target population sizes of tributary-specific migratory fish.

Multi-species Management

• By 2004, assess the effects of different population levels of filter feeders such as menhaden, oysters and clams on Bay water quality and habitat.

• By 2005, develop ecosystem-based multi-species management plans for targeted species.

• By 2007, revise and implement existing fisheries management plans to incorporate ecological, social and economic considerations, multi-species fisheries management and ecosystem approaches.

Crabs

• By 2001, establish harvest targets for the blue crab fishery and begin implementing complementary state fisheries management strategies Baywide. Manage the blue crab fishery to restore a healthy spawning biomass, size and age structure.

VITAL HABITAT PROTECTION AND RESTORATION

The Chesapeake Bay's natural infrastructure is an intricate system of terrestrial and aquatic habitats, linked to the landscapes and the environmental quality of the watershed. It is composed of the thousands of miles of river and stream habitat that interconnect the land, water, living resources and human communities of the Bay watershed. These vital habitats—including open water, underwater grasses, marshes, wetlands, streams and forests—support living resource abundance by providing key food and habitat for a variety of species. Submerged aquatic vegetation reduces shoreline erosion while forests and wetlands protect water quality by naturally processing the pollutants before they enter the water. Long-term protection of this natural infrastructure is essential.

In managing the Bay ecosystem as a whole, we recognize the need to focus on the individuality of each river, stream and creek, and to secure their protection in concert with the communities and individuals that reside within these small watersheds. We also recognize that we must continue to refine and share information regarding the importance of these vital habitats to the Bay's fish, shellfish and waterfowl. Our efforts to preserve the integrity of this natural infrastructure will protect the Bay's waters and living resources and will ensure the viability of human economies and communities that are dependent upon those resources for sustenance, reverence and posterity.

GOAL

Preserve, protect and restore those habitats and natural areas that are vital to the survival and diversity of the living resources of the Bay and its rivers.

Submerged Aquatic Vegetation

- Recommit to the existing goal of protecting and restoring 114,000 acres of submerged aquatic vegetation (SAV).
- By 2002, revise SAV restoration goals and strategies to reflect historic abundance, measured as acreage and density from the 1930s to the present. The revised goals will include specific levels of water clarity which are to be met in 2010. Strategies to achieve these goals will address water clarity, water quality and bottom disturbance.
- By 2002, implement a strategy to accelerate protection and restoration of SAV beds in areas of critical importance to the Bay's living resources.

Watersheds

- By 2010, work with local governments, community groups and watershed organizations to develop and implement locally supported watershed management plans in two-thirds of the Bay watershed covered by this Agreement. These plans would address the protection, conservation and restoration of stream corridors, riparian forest buffers and wetlands for the purposes of improving habitat and water quality, with collateral benefits for optimizing stream flow and water supply.
- By 2001, each jurisdiction will develop guidelines to ensure the aquatic health of stream corridors. Guidelines should consider optimal surface and groundwater flows.
- By 2002, each jurisdiction will work with local governments and communities that have watershed management plans to select pilot projects that promote stream corridor protection and restoration.
- By 2003, include in the "State of the Bay Report," and make available to the public, local governments and others, information concerning the aquatic health of stream corridors based on adopted regional guidelines.
- By 2004, each jurisdiction, working with local governments, community

groups and watershed organizations, will develop stream corridor restoration goals based on local watershed management planning.

Wetlands

- Achieve a no-net loss of existing wetlands acreage and function in the signatories' regulatory programs.
- By 2010, achieve a net resource gain by restoring 25,000 acres of tidal and non-tidal wetlands. To do this, we commit to achieve and maintain an average restoration rate of 2,500 acres per year basin wide by 2005 and beyond. We will evaluate our success in 2005.
- Provide information and assistance to local governments and community groups for the development and implementation of wetlands preservation plans as a component of a locally based integrated watershed management plan. Establish a goal of implementing the wetlands plan component in 25 percent of the land area of each state's Bay watershed by 2010. The plans would preserve key wetlands while addressing surrounding land use so as to preserve wetland functions.
- Evaluate the potential impact of climate change on the Chesapeake Bay watershed, particularly with respect to its wetlands, and consider potential management options.

Forests

- By 2002, ensure that measures are in place to meet our riparian forest buffer restoration goal of 2,010 miles by 2010. By 2003, establish a new goal to expand buffer mileage.
- Conserve existing forests along all streams and shorelines.
- Promote the expansion and connection of contiguous forests through conservation easements, greenways, purchase and other land conservation mechanisms.

WATER QUALITY PROTECTION AND RESTORATION

Improving water quality is the most critical element in the overall protection and restoration of the Chesapeake Bay and its tributaries. In 1987, we committed to achieving a 40 percent reduction in controllable nutrient loads to the Bay. In 1992, we committed to tributary-specific reduction strategies to achieve this reduction and agreed to stay at or below these nutrient loads once attained. We have made measurable reductions in pollution loading despite continuing growth and development. Still, we must do more.

Recent actions taken under the Clean Water Act resulted in listing portions of the Chesapeake Bay and its tidal rivers as "impaired waters." These actions have emphasized the regulatory framework of the Act along with the ongoing cooperative efforts of the Chesapeake Bay Program as the means to address the nutrient enrichment problems within the Bay and its rivers. In response, we have developed, and are implementing, a process for integrating the cooperative and statutory programs of the Chesapeake Bay and its tributaries. We have agreed to the goal of improving water quality in the Bay and its tributaries so that these waters may be removed from the impaired waters list prior to the time when regulatory mechanisms under Section 303(d) of the Clean Water Act would be applied.

We commit to achieve and maintain water quality conditions necessary to support living resources throughout the Chesapeake Bay ecosystem. Where we have failed to achieve established water quality goals, we will take actions necessary to reach and maintain those goals. We will make pollution prevention a central theme in the protection of water quality. And we will take actions that protect freshwater flow regimes for riverine and estuarine habitats. In pursuing the restoration of vital habitats throughout the watershed, we will continue efforts to improve water clarity in order to meet light requirements necessary to support SAV. We will expand our efforts to reduce sediments and airborne pollution, and ensure that the Bay is free from toxic effects on living resources and human health. We will continue our cooperative intergovernmental approach to achieve and maintain water quality goals through cost-effective and equitable means within the framework of federal and state law. We will evaluate the potential impacts of emerging issues, including, among others, airborne ammonia and nonpoint sources of chemical contaminants. Finally, we will continue to monitor water quality conditions and adjust our strategies accordingly.

GOAL

Achieve and maintain the water quality necessary to support the aquatic living resources of the Bay and its tributaries and to protect human health.

Nutrients and Sediments

- Continue efforts to achieve and maintain the 40 percent nutrient reduction goal agreed to in 1987, as well as the goals being adopted for the tributaries south of the Potomac River.
- By 2010, correct the nutrient- and sediment-related problems in the Chesapeake Bay and its tidal tributaries sufficiently to remove the Bay and the tidal portions of its tributaries from the list of impaired waters under the Clean Water Act. In order to achieve this:
  1. By 2001, define the water quality conditions necessary to protect

aquatic living resources and then assign load reductions for nitrogen and phosphorus to each major tributary;

2. Using a process parallel to that established for nutrients, determine the sediment load reductions necessary to achieve the water quality conditions that protect aquatic living resources, and assign load reductions for sediment to each major tributary by 2001;

3. By 2002, complete a public process to develop and begin implementation of revised Tributary Strategies to achieve and maintain the assigned loading goals;

4. By 2003, the jurisdictions with tidal waters will use their best efforts to adopt new or revised water quality standards consistent with the defined water quality conditions. Once adopted by the jurisdictions, the Environmental Protection Agency will work expeditiously to review the new or revised standards, which will then be used as the basis for removing the Bay and its tidal rivers from the list of impaired waters; and

5. By 2003, work with the Susquehanna River Basin Commission and others to adopt and begin implementing strategies that prevent the loss of the sediment retention capabilities of the lower Susquehanna River dams.

Chemical Contaminants

• We commit to fulfilling the 1994 goal of a Chesapeake Bay free of toxics by reducing or eliminating the input of chemical contaminants from all controllable sources to levels that result in no toxic or bioaccumulative impact on the living resources that inhabit the Bay or on human health.

• By Fall of 2000, reevaluate and revise, as necessary, the "Chesapeake Bay Basinwide Toxics Reduction and Prevention Strategy" focusing on:

1. Complementing state and federal regulatory programs to go beyond traditional point source controls, including nonpoint sources such as groundwater discharge and atmospheric deposition, by using a watershed-based approach; and

2. Understanding the effects and impacts of chemical contaminants to increase the effectiveness of management actions.

• Through continual improvement of pollution prevention measures and other voluntary means, strive for zero release of chemical contaminants from point sources, including air sources. Particular emphasis shall be placed on achieving, by 2010, elimination of mixing zones for persistent or bioaccumulative toxics.

• Reduce the potential risk of pesticides to the Bay by targeting education, outreach and implementation of Integrated Pest Management and specific Best Management Practices on those lands that have higher potential for contributing pesticide loads to the Bay.

Priority Urban Waters

- Support the restoration of the Anacostia River, Baltimore Harbor, and Elizabeth River and their watersheds as models for urban river restoration in the Bay basin.
- By 2010, the District of Columbia, working with its watershed partners, will reduce pollution loads to the Anacostia River in order to eliminate public health concerns and achieve the living resource, water quality and habitat goals of this and past Agreements.

Air Pollution

- By 2003, assess the effects of airborne nitrogen compounds and chemical contaminants on the Bay ecosystem and help establish reduction goals for these contaminants.

Boat Discharge

- By 2003, establish appropriate areas within the Chesapeake Bay and its tributaries as "no discharge zones" for human waste from boats. By 2010, expand by 50 percent the number and availability of waste pump-out facilities.
- By 2006, reassess our progress in reducing the impact of boat waste on the Bay and its tributaries. This assessment will include evaluating the benefits of further expanding no discharge zones, as well as increasing the number of pump-out facilities.

SOUND LAND USE

In 1987, the signatories agreed that "there is a clear correlation between population growth and associated development and environmental degradation in the Chesapeake Bay system." This Agreement reaffirms that concept and recognizes that more must be done.

An additional three million people are expected to settle in the watershed by 2020. This growth could potentially eclipse the nutrient reduction and habitat protection gains of the past. Therefore it is critical that we consider our approaches to land use in order to ensure progress in protecting the Bay and its local watersheds.

Enhancing, or even maintaining, the quality of the Bay while accommodating growth will frequently involve difficult choices. It will require a renewed commitment to appropriate development standards. The signatories will assert the full measure of their authority to limit and mitigate the potential adverse effects of continued growth; each, however, will pursue this objective within the framework of its own historic, existing or future land use practices or processes. Local jurisdictions have been delegated authority over many decisions regarding growth and development which have both direct and indirect effects on the Chesapeake Bay system and its living resources. The role of local governments in the Bay's restoration and protection effort will be given proper recognition and support through state and federal resources. States will also engage in active partnerships with local governments in managing growth and development in ways that support the following goal.

We acknowledge that future development will be sustainable only if we protect our natural and rural resource land, limit impervious surfaces and concentrate new growth in existing population centers or suitable areas served by appropriate infrastructure. We will work to integrate environmental, community and economic goals by promoting more environmentally sensitive forms of development. We will also strive to coordinate land use, transportation, water and sewer and other infrastructure planning so that funding and policies at all levels of government do not contribute to poorly planned growth and development or degrade local water quality and habitat. We will advance these policies by creating partnerships with local governments to protect our communities and to discharge our duties as trustees in the stewardship of the Chesapeake Bay. Finally, we will report every two years on our progress in achieving our commitments to promote sound land use.

GOAL

Develop, promote and achieve sound land use practices which protect and restore watershed resources and water quality, maintain reduced pollutant loadings for the Bay and its tributaries, and restore and preserve aquatic living resources.

Land Conservation

- By 2001, complete an assessment of the Bay's resource lands including forests and farms, emphasizing their role in the protection of water quality and critical habitats, as well as cultural and economic viability.
- Provide financial assistance or new revenue sources to expand the use of voluntary and market-based mechanisms such as easements, purchase or transfer of development rights and other approaches to protect and preserve natural resource lands.

- Strengthen programs for land acquisition and preservation within each state that are supported by funding and target the most valued lands for protection. Permanently preserve from development 20 percent of the land area in the watershed by 2010.
- Provide technical and financial assistance to local governments to plan for or revise plans, ordinances and subdivision regulations to provide for the conservation and sustainable use of the forest and agricultural lands.
- In cooperation with local governments, develop and maintain in each juris-diction a strong GIS system to track the preservation of resource lands and support the implementation of sound land use practices.

Development, Redevelopment and Revitalization

- By 2012, reduce the rate of harmful sprawl development of forest and agri-cultural land in the Chesapeake Bay watershed by 30 percent measured as an average over five years from the baseline of 1992–1997, with measures and progress reported regularly to the Chesapeake Executive Council.
- By 2005, in cooperation with local government, identify and remove state and local impediments to low impact development designs to encourage the use of such approaches and minimize water quality impacts.
- Work with communities and local governments to encourage sound land use planning and practices that address the impacts of growth, development and transportation on the watershed.
- By 2002, review tax policies to identify elements which discourage sustain-able development practices or encourage undesirable growth patterns. Pro-mote the modification of such policies and the creation of tax incentives which promote the conservation of resource lands and encourage invest-ments consistent with sound growth management principles.
- The jurisdictions will promote redevelopment and remove barriers to in-vestment in underutilized urban, suburban and rural communities by working with localities and development interests.
- By 2002, develop analytical tools that will allow local governments and communities to conduct watershed-based assessment of the impacts of growth, development and transportation decisions.
- By 2002, compile information and guidelines to assist local governments and communities to promote ecologically-based designs in order to limit impervious cover in undeveloped and moderately developed watersheds and reduce the impact of impervious cover in highly developed watersheds.
- Provide information to the development community and others so they may champion the application of sound land use practices.

- By 2003, work with local governments and communities to develop land use management and water resource protection approaches that encourage the concentration of new residential development in areas supported by adequate water resources and infrastructure to minimize impacts on water quality.
- By 2004, the jurisdictions will evaluate local implementation of stormwater, erosion control and other locally-implemented water quality protection programs that affect the Bay system and ensure that these programs are being coordinated and applied effectively in order to minimize the impacts of development.
- Working with local governments and others, develop and promote wastewater treatment options, such as nutrient reducing septic systems, which protect public health and minimize impacts to the Bay's resources.
- Strengthen brownfield redevelopment. By 2010, rehabilitate and restore 1,050 brownfield sites to productive use.
- Working with local governments, encourage the development and implementation of emerging urban storm water retrofit practices to improve their water quantity and quality function.

Transportation

- By 2002, the signatory jurisdictions will promote coordination of transportation and land use planning to encourage compact, mixed use development patterns, revitalization in existing communities and transportation strategies that minimize adverse effects on the Bay and its tributaries.
- By 2002, each state will coordinate its transportation policies and programs to reduce the dependence on automobiles by incorporating travel alternatives such as telework, pedestrian, bicycle and transit options, as appropriate, in the design of projects so as to increase the availability of alternative modes of travel as measured by increased use of those alternatives.
- Consider the provisions of the federal transportation statutes for opportunities to purchase easements to preserve resource lands adjacent to rights of way and special efforts for stormwater management on both new and rehabilitation projects.
- Establish policies and incentives which encourage the use of clean vehicle and other transportation technologies that reduce emissions.

Public Access

- By 2010, expand by 30 percent the system of public access points to the Bay, its tributaries and related resource sites in an environmentally sensitive manner by working with state and federal agencies, local governments and stakeholder organizations.

- By 2005, increase the number of designated water trails in the Chesapeake Bay region by 500 miles.
- Enhance interpretation materials that promote stewardship at natural, recreational, historical and cultural public access points within the Chesapeake Bay watershed.
- By 2003, develop partnerships with at least 30 sites to enhance place-based interpretation of Bay-related resources and themes and stimulate volunteer involvement in resource restoration and conservation.

STEWARDSHIP AND COMMUNITY ENGAGEMENT

The Chesapeake Bay is dependent upon the actions of every citizen in the watershed, both today and in the future. We recognize that the cumulative benefit derived from community-based watershed programs is essential for continued progress toward a healthier Chesapeake Bay. Therefore, we commit ourselves to engage our citizens by promoting a broad conservation ethic throughout the fabric of community life, and foster within all citizens a deeper understanding of their roles as trustees of their own local environments. Through their actions, each individual can contribute to the health and well-being of their neighborhood streams, rivers and the land that surrounds them, not only as ecological stewards of the Bay but also as members of watershed-wide communities. By focusing individuals on local resources, we will advance Baywide restoration as well.

We recognize that the future of the Bay also depends on the actions of generations to follow. Therefore, we commit to provide opportunities for cooperative learning and action so that communities can promote local environmental quality for the benefit and enjoyment of residents and visitors. We will assist communities throughout the watershed in improving quality of life, thereby strengthening local economies and connecting individuals to the Bay through their shared sense of responsibility. We will seek to increase the financial and human resources available to localities to meet the challenges of restoring the Chesapeake Bay.

GOAL

Promote individual stewardship and assist individuals, community-based organizations, businesses, local governments and schools to undertake initiatives to achieve the goals and commitments of this agreement.

Education and Outreach

- Make education and outreach a priority in order to achieve public awareness and personal involvement on behalf of the Bay and local watersheds.
- Provide information to enhance the ability of citizen and community groups to participate in Bay restoration activities on their property and in their local watershed.
- Expand the use of new communications technologies to provide a comprehensive and interactive source of information on the Chesapeake Bay and its watershed for use by public and technical audiences. By 2001, develop and maintain a web-based clearing house of this information specifically for use by educators.
- Beginning with the class of 2005, provide a meaningful Bay or stream outdoor experience for every school student in the watershed before graduation from high school.
- Continue to forge partnerships with the Departments of Education and institutions of higher learning in each jurisdiction to integrate information about the Chesapeake Bay and its watershed into school curricula and university programs.
- Provide students and teachers alike with opportunities to directly participate in local restoration and protection projects, and to support stewardship efforts in schools and on school property.
- By 2002, expand citizen outreach efforts to more specifically include minority populations by, for example, highlighting cultural and historical ties to the Bay, and providing multi-cultural and multi-lingual educational materials on stewardship activities and Bay information.

Community Engagement

- Jurisdictions will work with local governments to identify small watersheds where community-based actions are essential to meeting Bay restoration goals—in particular wetlands, forested buffers, stream corridors and public access and work with local governments and community organizations to bring an appropriate range of Bay program resources to these communities.
- Enhance funding for locally-based programs that pursue restoration and protection projects that will assist in the achievement of the goals of this and past agreements.
- By 2001, develop and maintain a clearing house for information on local watershed restoration efforts, including financial and technical assistance.
- By 2002, each signatory jurisdiction will offer easily-accessible information suitable for analyzing environmental conditions at a small watershed scale.

- Strengthen the Chesapeake Bay Program's ability to incorporate local governments into the policy decision making process. By 2001, complete a reevaluation of the Local Government Participation Action Plan and make necessary changes in Bay program and jurisdictional functions based upon the reevaluation.
- Improve methods of communication with and among local governments on Bay issues and provide adequate opportunities for discussion of key issues.
- By 2001, identify community watershed organizations and partnerships. Assist in establishing new organizations and partnerships where interest exists. These partners will be important to successful watershed management efforts in distributing information to the public, and engaging the public in the Bay restoration and preservation effort.
- By 2005, identify specific actions to address the challenges of communities where historically poor water quality and environmental conditions have contributed to disproportional health, economic or social impacts.

Government by Example

- By 2002, each signatory will put in place processes to:
    1. Ensure that all properties owned, managed or leased by the signatories are developed, redeveloped and used in a manner consistent with all relevant goals, commitments and guidance of this Agreement.
    2. Ensure that the design and construction of signatory-funded development and redevelopment projects are consistent with all relevant goals, commitments and guidance of this Agreement.
- Expand the use of clean vehicle technologies and fuels on the basis of emission reductions, so that a significantly greater percentage of each signatory government's fleet of vehicles use some form of clean technology.
- By 2001, develop an Executive Council Directive to address stormwater management to control nutrient, sediment and chemical contaminant runoff from state, federal and District owned land.

Partnerships

- Strengthen partnerships with Delaware, New York and West Virginia by promoting communication and by seeking agreements on issues of mutual concern.
- Work with non-signatory Bay states to establish links with community-based organizations throughout the Bay watershed.

BY THIS AGREEMENT, we rededicate ourselves to the restoration and protection of the ecological integrity, productivity and beneficial uses of the Chesapeake Bay system. We reaffirm our commitment to previously-adopted Chesapeake Bay Agreements and their supporting policies. We agree to report annually to the citizens on the state of the Bay and consider any additional actions necessary.

<u>June 28, 2000</u>

FOR THE CHESAPEAKE BAY COMMISSION _____ Bill Bolling _____

FOR THE STATE OF MARYLAND _____ Governor Parris N. Glendening _____

FOR THE COMMONWEALTH OF PENNSYLVANIA _____ Governor Thomas J. Ridge _____

FOR THE COMMONWEALTH OF VIRGINIA _____ Governor James S. Gilmore _____

FOR THE DISTRICT OF COLUMBIA _____ Mayor Anthony A. Williams _____

FOR THE UNITED STATES OF AMERICA _____ Administrator, U.S. Environmental Protection Agency, Carol M. Browner _____

APPENDIX C:
CHESAPEAKE BAY TIMELINE

Nature Line	Governance Line
1000 B.C. Chesapeake Bay achieves its approximate modern configuration	
A.D. 1572 Brother Carrera, a Spanish priest, says of the Chesapeake: "It is called the Bay of the Mother God, and in it there are many deep water ports, each better than the next."	
1608 Captain John Smith Describes the bay: "A faire bay compassed but for the mouth with fruitful and delightsome land (where) heaven and earth never agreed better to frame a place for man's habitation."	
	1632 Virginia enacts legislation restricting the planting of tobacco, both to conserve soil resources and to assure an adequate supply of other agricultural products to the settlers of the colony.
1660 European settlers in the bay region reach a population of 60,000.	

Nature Line	Governance Line
	1680 William Penn directs that for every 4 acres of land cleared for farming, 1 acre must be kept in woodland.
1683 William Penn notes: "Of shellfish we have oysters, crabs, cockles, conchs and mussels; some oysters six inches long and one sort of cockles as big as the stewing oyster; they make a rich broth."	
1700 Port Tobacco, in Maryland, becomes so silted that it is closed to ocean-going vessels. Many acres of forests in the watershed are cut for growing tobacco and other farming, resulting in increased sediment loads to the bay.	
	1776 Baltimore enacts an "Act to Remove a Nuisance in Baltimore town" destroying what was described as a large miry marsh giving off noxious vapors and putrid effluvia.
	1785 George Washington intervenes to resolve conflicts in oystering between Virginia and Maryland. This meeting eventually results in the Constitutional Convention in Philadelphia in 1787, giving rise to the U.S. Constitution.

Nature Line		Governance Line	
1850	The ports of Georgetown and Bladensburg are closed due to siltation. By now perhaps as much as 50 percent of the forested land in the watershed has been lost to farming and timbering.		
1876	The shad harvest is at 4 million pounds—gigantic by today's standards but a "worrisome" decline by standards of the time.		
1884	Oyster harvest reaches its historic peak of around 20 million bushels.		
1894	Referring to the Potomac, the U.S. Public Health Service notes that "at certain times of the year the river is so loaded with sediments as to be unfit for bathing as well as for drinking and cooking purposes."		
		1905	Pennsylvania enacts a statute to protect water quality for human consumption.
		1913	The first modern sewage treatment plant in the nation is constructed at Baltimore to protect oyster beds of the upper bay from human waste contamination.

Nature Line	Governance Line
1919 The Commissioners of Fisheries of Virginia note: "One of the greatest questions for the future is that of pollution. The pollution of sewage of our ever increasing population and the waste from our rapidly growing industries is affecting the entire fish and oyster industry in and around Hampton Roads."	
	1927 The Chesapeake Biological Laboratory is founded at Solomons, Maryland, to investigate the conditions of resources in the bay.
1928 Conowingo Dam, most downstream dam on the Susquehanna River, is completed. It totally blocks migratory fish passage to the greatest of the bay's tributaries.	
	1938 A sewage treatment plant is constructed at Blue Plains, in Washington, D.C., at the direction of President Roosevelt, to improve the water quality of the Potomac River.
1940 H. L. Mencken is still moved to note that "Baltimore lay very near the immense protein factory of the Chesapeake Bay, and out of it ate divinely."	

Nature Line	Governance Line
	1948 Congress enacts the first federal Water Pollution Control Act.
	1952 First baywide cruise to conduct scientific investigations of conditions in the bay.
1957 The U.S. Public Health Service declares the Potomac unsafe for swimming.	
1961 The Virginia Fisheries Commission notes that "contamination of our natural waters by pollution of various types is one of the most pressing programs facing our Commonwealth today."	
	1967 Chesapeake Bay Foundation established.
	1968 First Chesapeake Bay water quality conference.
	1970 First Earth Day.
1972 Tropical Storm Agnes inundates the bay with volumes of freshwater not seen in historical times.	1972 Enactment of the modern federal Water Pollution Control Act, designed to achieve fishable and swimable waters and provide substantial federal financial assistance for the construction of sewage treatment plants. EPA bans DDT, resulting in gradual return of the bald eagle and osprey.
	1975 Illegal kepone discharges at Hopewell, Virginia, force closing of the James River to fishing for a decade.

Nature Line		Governance Line	
		1976	The bay's largest oil spill occurs at Smith Point, Virginia.
		1977	Second bay water quality conference held at Patuxent Naval Air Station. Scientists raise concerns, but the overall condition of the bay is held to be fairly good. An upper bay phosphorus strategy is adopted, leading to a commitment to remove phosphorus from major plants in Pennsylvania and Maryland.
		1978	Chesapeake Bay Commission established to bring together state legislators and officials.
		1979	Chesapeake Bay agreement signed between Maryland and Virginia, committing them to work together on Bay issues.
1980	Maryland closes its shad fishery.		
1983	The EPA documents the death of over 90 percent of the bay's underwater grasses.	1983	EPA issues a major study on the bay's condition confirming a widespread and worsening decline. Maryland, Pennsylvania, Virginia, D.C., the federal government, and the Chesapeake Bay Commission sign an agreement making specific commitments to restore the Chesapeake's water quality and natural resources.

Nature Line		Governance Line	
1984	Underwater grasses reach low point of 37,000 acres.	1984	Maryland passes its Critical Area Act restricting zoning in an area 1,000 feet back from the shoreline and extending around the entire bay and tributaries to the head of tide.
1985	Maryland closes its striped bass fishery.	1985	Maryland passes a ban on phosphates in detergents.
		1986	D.C. passes a phosphate ban.
		1987	Virginia passes a phosphate ban. Maryland, Pennsylvania, Virginia, D.C., the federal government, and the Chesapeake Bay Commission sign a new agreement to clean up the bay. The key target is a 40 percent reduction of nutrients by the year 2000.
		1988	Virginia's Chesapeake Bay Preservation Act enacted.
		1989	Nontidal Wetlands Act passed in Maryland.
1990	Striped bass populations and spawning success increase; moratorium lifted.		
		1991	Sewage treatment authorities begin adopting biological nitrogen removal process, first on Patuxent River plants.
		1993	Pennsylvania becomes one of the first states to pass legislation requiring agricultural nutrient management plans (regulations went into effect in 1997).

Nature Line		Governance Line	
1994	Lowest oyster harvest on record.	1994	Virginia enacts nutrient management law for hogs, cattle.
1997	*Pfiesteria*, a dinoflagellate, blooms in Pocomoke and other bay rivers. Fish kills and a newly observed illness in people results. Testing throughout the bay finds the microbe.		
		1998	Maryland enacts a nutrient management law for farms.
		1999	Virginia enacts a nutrient management law for poultry.
		1999	Maryland enacts Smart Growth legislation.
Through the decade	The volume of water without oxygen adequate to support most marine life expands.	2000	Fish passage opens York Haven Dam to shad migration, allowing spawning runs to Binghamton, N.Y.
2000	Pipeline to power plant breaks, spilling 110,000 gallons of oil in sensitive marsh at Chalk Point on Patuxent River.	2000	Partners of the Chesapeake Bay Program sign *Chesapeake 2000,* a new, goal-oriented agreement to remove the bay from the nation's dirty waters list by 2010.
		2000	Nontidal Wetlands Act passed in Virginia. Bi-State Blue Crab Commission creates management plan to restore blue crab numbers.

Nature Line	Governance Line
	2000 Chesapeake Bay Program goal of reducing controllable nitrogen by 40 percent missed.
	2000 Overboard disposal of dredge spoil ended in Maryland.
	2000 Chesapeake Bay Commission estimates cost of implementing *Chesapeake 2000* will be approximately $20 billion.
2002 Acreage of underwater grass (85,000 acres) highest since low point (37,000 acres in 1984). Four-year drought reduced sediment and nitrogen and phosphorus runoff, resulting in water clear enough for grasses to rebound.	
2002 Shad populations growing as result of moratorium, restocking. Most shad in two decades passed over Conowingo Dam.	
2002 Notices to anglers advising them to limit the numbers of fish they consume because of the concentrations of toxic materials in fish flesh increase.	

GLOSSARY

The definitions here are not meant to be exhaustive or to split scientific hairs but to reinforce the meanings of certain words within the context of this book.

acid rain Rain or other precipitation whose pH, a measure of acidity, is substantially more acidic than normal. Acid rain has become a major pollutant of streams and lakes throughout much of the industrialized world in recent decades.

airshed An area within which air pollutants are transported and deposited on land and water surfaces; boundaries may vary with weather conditions, but for the Chesapeake Bay the airshed may include pollution sources as far away as the Ohio River Valley.

algae Generally, any of a large class of plant life in the bay, either floating freely, growing in filamentous form on the bottom, or forming a coating on other plants such as submerged, rooted aquatic vegetation; used here as distinct from the floating plant life of the bay (see *plankton*).

anadromous Migrating upstream from the direction of the sea, usually to reproduce.

anoxic Without oxygen.

aquatic Living in the water.

benthos Bottom-dwelling organisms, such as oysters, clams, and burrowing worms.

best management practices (BMPs) A wide variety of agricultural techniques aimed at increasing soil productivity and reducing pollution; examples include plowing along the land's natural contours, rather than straight up and down slopes, to reduce erosion from rainfall, planting winter grasses to reduce wind erosion, and storing manure under cover to keep rain from washing it into streams.

biotechnology A range of techniques being used to manipulate life in the bay to raise its production of seafood; can range from simple aquaculture, such as growing oysters in rafts to avoid losses to predators, to genetic engineering of organisms to make them grow faster or more uniformly.

buffer strip A strip of varying width left in forest or other permanent vegetation between waterways and land uses such as agriculture or development to intercept and filter out pollution before it runs off into the bay or its tributaries.

catadromous Migrating downstream in the direction of the sea, usually to reproduce.

catch per unit effort (CPUE) The number of fish or other species harvested per a standard measure of fishing effort (such as per crab pot, per mile of net, or per man-hour of fishing time); considered a truer measure of trends in a species' abundance than simply looking at pounds caught.

discharge permit Legal contracts negotiated between federal and state regulators and industries or sewage treatment plants that set limits on many water pollutants or polluting effects from the discharges of their pipes to the public waters.

dissolved oxygen Levels of oxygen in the water; above 5 parts oxygen per million parts of water is considered healthy; below 3 ppm is generally stressful.

ecosystem Interrelated and interdependent parts of a biological system; sometimes popularly expressed as "everything is connected to everything."

estuary A coastal water body where freshwater from rivers mixes with salt water from the ocean.

eutrophic Overenriched or overfertilized.

fishery The commercial or sport catch of a given fish species.

groundwater Subsurface collection of rainwater that percolates through the earth rather than running immediately off into waterways; ranges from water a few inches deep to aquifers far below the surface; a significant source of water to the bay.

homeostasis Literally, keeping the house in order; the mechanism whereby organisms, or even whole ecosystems, maintain stability and orderly functioning (e.g., sweating when hot cools the body back down by evaporation).

hypoxic A deficiency of oxygen; in the bay, usually applied when there is less than 2 parts oxygen per million parts of water.

isohaline The lines of constant salinity running laterally across the bay.

landings Catches (as in "landings of fish are up this year").

larvae An early life stage or stages, often following the egg stage; a period of high vulnerability for most organisms.

metals Materials such as cadmium, lead, arsenic, mercury, and copper that enter the bay from both human and natural sources; in high enough amounts they may be extremely toxic to biological life and may accumulate from low levels in the water to dangerous levels in the flesh of organisms high in the food web.

nitrogen One of two principal nutrients in human sewage and farm fertilizers that are polluting Chesapeake Bay.

nutrient A basic food essential for the growth of plankton in the waters of the bay; in the Chesapeake, usually nitrogen and phosphorus.

Pfiesteria *Pfiesteria piscicida* is a type of alga associated with fish lesions and fish kills, and with the loss of short-term memory in humans. It occurs throughout the Chesapeake and other coastal waters, usually in nontoxic forms. But it can become toxic under certain circumstances that may include elevated levels of nutrients, key pollutants of Chesapeake Bay.

phosphorus One of two principal nutrients in human sewage and farm fertilizers that is polluting Chesapeake Bay.

phytoplankton Floating plant life.

plankton Floating plant and animal life.

pre-treatment The removal of certain wastes from sewage before it is discharged to a sewage treatment plant; usually applied to industrial toxics and heavy metals.

primary production Plant life (in the water, algae and rooted aquatic vegetation); the organisms that first convert sunlight into food and are then consumed by higher organisms; the base of the food web.

priority pollutant Chemicals designated by the U.S. Environmental Protection Agency as high priority for control or removal from waste discharges because of their toxicity or potential to cause cancer or mutations.

progging Exploring. A *progger* is someone who loves to roam the marshes and beaches of the Chesapeake for a variety of reasons that range from trapping muskrats and picking up oysters and soft crabs, to plucking wild asparagus and collecting arrowheads, driftwood, and pottery.

resilience The natural ability of the Chesapeake ecosystem to counter natural and human stresses such as pollution, floods, and drought.

runoff The movement of pollutants from the land via water from rainfall.

salinity The amount of salt, by weight, in the water; a salinity of 10 means there are 10 ounces of salt for every 1,000 ounces of water; freshwater has a salinity of zero; the ocean is about 33 parts salt per thousand parts of water.

scrape A type of dredge, 3 to 4 feet across at its mouth, used by soft-crabbers; dragged through grass beds, it scoops crabs into its mesh bag; instead of teeth, the scrape has a smooth bar so it does not bite deeply into the bottom, which would uproot the grass beds.

sediment The soil from farms, construction sites, and eroding shorelines that runs into the water in rainstorms; a significant pollutant of the bay.

sludge The semisolid residue formed from removing wastes from sewage discharges or industrial discharges.

Smart Growth Smart Growth recognizes that compact patterns of land development in and around existing cities and towns are superior to sprawl—environmentally, socially, and financially. Smart Growth applies to any number of strategies that combine preserving the countryside with encouraging development in areas already built or planned for growth.

spat The microscopic, free-floating larval form of the oyster; it must attach and begin forming its shell soon after hatching, or die.

spawning Reproduction in fish.

stormwater Rainwater that runs off the land, usually paved or compacted surfaces in urban and suburban areas; it can be a significant source of pollution.

stratification In the Chesapeake, stratification occurs when there is little mixing between the lighter freshwater sliding down the bay near its surface and the heavier ocean water moving up the bay near its bottom; this can lead to oxygen declines in the deeper waters of the bay.

submerged aquatic vegetation (SAV) Vegetation rooted in the bottom of the bay's shallows (usually in depths of no more than 10 feet); important both in controlling water quality and as food and habitat for wildlife; more than a dozen varieties are found in the Chesapeake.

watershed Drainage basin; lands that slope toward a particular water body, channeling all the rain that falls on them toward that body of water.

wetlands Vegetation that is periodically flooded or saturated by water; may range from coastal salt marsh, inundated on every high tide, to nontidal wetlands far inland that are dry most of the time; wetlands have high values for wildlife and for water quality.

zoea A larval stage of the blue crab during its early weeks of life; a stage in which the crab is quite vulnerable to environmental stresses.

REFERENCES

GENERAL SOURCES OF INFORMATION

Alliance for the Chesapeake Bay, Towson, Maryland; Harrisburg, Pennsylvania; Richmond, Virginia.

Chesapeake Bay Commission, Annapolis, Maryland; Harrisburg, Pennsylvania; Richmond, Virginia.

Chesapeake Bay Foundation, Annapolis, Maryland; Harrisburg, Pennsylvania; Richmond, Virginia.

EPA Bay Program, U.S. Environmental Protection Agency, Annapolis, Maryland.

PREFACE

Alliance for the Chesapeake Bay. "Amending the Bay Agreement: Two perspectives." *Bay Journal*, September 1992, p. 14.

Alliance for the Chesapeake Bay. "Past political leaders reflect on restoration effort's past, future." *Bay Journal*, May 2001, p. 3.

Chesapeake Bay Commission. *The Cost of Clean Bay: Assessing Fund Raising Needs throughout the Watershed.* Annapolis, Maryland, January 2003.

Fortune. Special Issue: The Environment: A National Issue for the Seventies. New York.

CHAPTER 1: The Bay Connects Us, the Bay Reflects Us

Baltimore Sun. "Victory at Fort Meade." Editorial, August 15, 1991, p. A4.

Blond, Georges. *The Great Migrations of Animals.* New York: Collier Press, 1962.

Boynton, W. R., Kemp, W. M., and Keefe, C. W. *A Comparative Analysis of Nutrients and Other Factors Influencing Estuarine Phytoplankton Production.* New York: Academic Press, 1982.

Cronin, L. Eugene, and Mansueti, Alice J. *The Biology of the Estuary.* Chesapeake Biological Laboratory. Solomons, MD. March 1971.

Gerritsen, J., Ranasinghe, J. A., and Holland, A. F. *Comparison of Three Strategies* to *Improve Water Quality in the Maryland Portion of Chesapeake Bay.* Columbia, Maryland: Versar, Inc., ESM Operations, 1988.

Horton, Tom. *Bay Country.* Baltimore: Johns Hopkins University Press, 1987.

Morton, Rogers C. B. *Statement for the Governor's Conference on the Chesapeake Bay Proceedings.* Volume II, pp. 173–178. Wye, Maryland, September 12–13, 1968.

Nixon, Scott W. "Chesapeake Bay nutrient budgets—A reassessment." *Biogeochemistry* 4 (1987):77–90.

U.S. Environmental Protection Agency. *Chesapeake Bay: Introduction to an Ecosystem.* Washington, D.C.: EPA, 1989.

White, Christopher P. *Chesapeake Bay: A Field Guide.* Centreville, Maryland: Tidewater Publishers, 1989.

Wolfe, Douglas A. *Estuarine Variability.* New York: Academic Press, 1985.

CHAPTER 2: Pollution

Alliance for the Chesapeake Bay. "Bay program falling short of 40 per cent goal to cut nutrients." *Bay Journal,* October 2002.

Alliance for the Chesapeake Bay. "Caps, not upgrades, are plants' greatest concern." *Bay Journal,* July–August 2001.

Alliance for the Chesapeake Bay. "Criteria for a clean Chesapeake." *Bay Journal,* July–August 2001.

Alliance for the Chesapeake Bay. "Nutrient reduction bill wins support from PA senators." *Bay Journal,* September 2001.

Alliance for the Chesapeake Bay. "Nutrients and the Chesapeake Bay." *Bay Journal,* January–February 2001.

Alliance for the Chesapeake Bay. "Sediment happens." *Bay Journal,* July–August 2002.

Alliance for the Chesapeake Bay. "Study finds auto emissions to be leading source of some bay toxics." *Bay Journal,* November 2000.

Blue Ribbon Citizens Pfiesteria Action Commission. *Final Report.* Annapolis, Maryland, November 1997.

Boicourt, W. C. *The Influences of Circulation Progresses on Dissolved Oxygen in Chesapeake Bay.* Cambridge: University of Maryland Systems Center for Environmental and Estuarine Studies, 1990.

Boynton, W. R., Garber, J. H., Summers, R., and Kemp, W. M. "Inputs, transformations, and transport of nitrogen and phosphorus in Chesapeake Bay and selected tributaries." *Estuaries* 18, no. 18 (1995):285–314.

Cameron, Diane. *NRDC's Poison Runoff Index for the Washington Metropolitan Region.* Washington, D.C.: Natural Resources Defense Council, 1989.

Chesapeake Bay Commission. *Seeking Solutions.* Annapolis, Maryland, 2001.

Chesapeake Research Consortium. *The Economics of Stormwater BMPs in the Mid-Atlantic Region.* Edgewater, Maryland, 1997.

Correll, David L. *Contaminant Problems and Management of Living Chesapeake Bay Resources.* Chapter 14: "Nutrients in Chesapeake Bay." Edgewater, Maryland: Smithsonian Environmental Research Center, 1987.

Correll, David L., and Peterjohn, William T. *Nutrient Dynamics in an Agricultural Watershed: Observations on the Role of a Riparian Forest.* Edgewater, Maryland: Smithsonian Environmental Research Center, 1983.

Correll, David L., and Weller, Donald E. *Factors Limiting Processes in Freshwater Wetlands: An Agricultural Primary Stream Riparian Forest.* Edgewater, Maryland: Smithsonian Environmental Research Center, 1990.

DeCicco, John, and Kliesch, James. *ACEEE's Green Book—The Environmental Guide to Cars and Trucks.* Washington, D.C.: American Council for an Energy-Efficient Economy, 2002.

Dewar, Heather. "MDE warns about fish—New advisories on fish consumption." *Baltimore Sun,* December 13, 2001, p. A1.

Dewar, Heather, and Horton, Tom. "Nitrogen's deadly harvest." *Baltimore Sun,* September 24–28, 2000, p. A1.

Dorfman, Mark. *Testing the Waters 2002: A Guide to Water Quality at Vacation Beaches.* New York: Natural Resources Defense Council, July 2002.

Garreis, Mary Jo, and Murphy, Deirdre L. *Survey of Organochlorine Pesticide and Metal Concentrations in Chesapeake Bay Finfish.* Baltimore: Maryland Department of the Environment, Water Management Administration, 1983.

Governor's Oil Spill Prevention Advisory Committee. *Final Report.* Annapolis, Maryland, December 2002.

Klein, Richard. *Preventing Damage to 600 Miles of Maryland Streams, Wetlands, Rivers and Tidal Waters—Why Improvements to Maryland's Stormwater Management Program Are Urgently Needed.* Owings Mills, Maryland: Community and Environmental Defense Services, 2000.

Lanyon, L. E. *Perspectives for Sustainable Agriculture from Nutrient Management Experiences in Pennsylvania.* University Park: Pennsylvania State University, Department of Agronomy, 1990.

Lanyon, L. E., Partenheimer, E. J., and Westphal, P. J. *Plant Nutrient Management Strategy Implications for Optimal Herd Size and Performance of a Simulated Dairy Farm.* University Park, Pennsylvania: Agricultural Systems, 1989.

Lynch, J. A., Bowersox, V. C., and Grimm, J. W. "Acid rain reduced in eastern United States." *Environmental Science and Technology* 34, no. 6 (2000):940–949.

Lynch, J. A., Horner, K. S., and Grimm, J. W. *Atmospheric Deposition: Spatial and*

Temporal Variations in Pennsylvania—2000. University Park: Pennsylvania State University, Environmental Resources Research Institute, 2001.

Malone, Thomas C. *Effects of Water Column Processes on Dissolved Oxygen: Nutrients, Phytoplankton and Zooplankton.* Cambridge, Maryland: Center for Environmental and Estuarine Studies, 1990.

Marshall, Harold G. "Toxin producing phytoplankton in Chesapeake Bay." *Virginia Journal of Science* 47 (1996):29–37.

Marshall, Harold G., Gordon, Andrew S., Seaborn, David W., and Dyer, Brian. "Comparative culture and toxicity studies between the toxic dinoflagellate *Pfiesteria piscicida* and a morphologically similar cryptoperidiniopsoid dinoflagellate." *Journal of Experimental Marine Biology and Ecology* 255 (2000):51–74.

Maryland Department of Natural Resources. *From the Mountains to the Sea: The State of Maryland's Freshwater Streams.* Annapolis, December 1999.

Maryland Department of the Environment. *Facts about TMDLs.* Baltimore, December 1, 1998.

Maryland Department of the Environment. *Task Force on Upgrading Sewerage Systems, Final Report.* Baltimore, December 2001.

McCord, Joel. "Pennsylvania lags in efforts to clean bay." *Baltimore Sun,* September 2, 2001, p. B1.

National Oceanic and Atmospheric Administration (NOAA). *Chesapeake Bay— Status and Trends of Contaminant Levels in Biota and Sediments.* Washington, D.C.: NOAA, 1998.

Pennsylvania Department of Environmental Protection. *305 (b) Report of Water Quality Assessment.* Harrisburg, April 1998.

Prince Georges County Department of Environmental Resources. *Low Impact Development Design Manual.* Bowie, Maryland, 1997.

Schueler, Thomas R., and Holland, Heather K. *The Practice of Watershed Protection—Techniques for Protecting Our Nation's Streams, Lakes, Rivers, and Estuaries.* Ellicott City, Maryland: The Center for Watershed Protection, 2000.

Shelsby, Ted. "Cows dining on grass put the farmer in clover." *Baltimore Sun,* January 29, 2002, C1.

U.S. Environmental Protection Agency. *Airsheds and Watersheds III: A Shared Resources Workshop.* Annapolis, Maryland: EPA, November 2000.

U.S. Environmental Protection Agency. *Chesapeake 2000 and the Bay—Where Are We and Where Are We Going?* Washington, D.C.: EPA, November 2001.

U.S. Environmental Protection Agency. *Remember the Past, Protect the Future.* Washington, D.C.: EPA, 2000.

U.S. Environmental Protection Agency, Chesapeake Bay Program. *Backgrounder:*

Fish Consumption Advisories in the Chesapeake Bay Watershed. Annapolis, Maryland: EPA, 2002.

U.S. Environmental Protection Agency, Chesapeake Bay Program. *Chesapeake 2000.* Annapolis, Maryland: EPA, June 2000.

U.S. Environmental Protection Agency, Chesapeake Bay Program. *Chesapeake Bay Basin Toxics Loading and Release Inventory.* Annapolis, Maryland: EPA, May 1999.

U.S. Environmental Protection Agency, Chesapeake Bay Program. *Managing Stormwater on State, Federal, and District-Owned Lands and Facilities.* Annapolis, Maryland: EPA, December 2001.

U.S. Environmental Protection Agency, Chesapeake Bay Program. *Targeting Toxics—A Characterization Report.* Annapolis, Maryland: EPA, June 1999.

U.S. Environmental Protection Agency, Chesapeake Bay Program. *Toxics 2000 Strategy.* Annapolis, Maryland: EPA, November 2000.

U.S. Environmental Protection Agency, Chesapeake Bay Program. *Toxics 2000 Strategy.* Annapolis, Maryland: EPA, December 2000.

U.S. Fish and Wildlife Service. *Migratory Fish Restoration and Passage on the Susquehanna River.* Harrisburg, Pennsylvania, 2000.

U.S. General Accounting Office. *Pipeline Safety.* Washington, September 2001.

U.S. Geological Survey. *Factors Affecting Nutrient Trends in Major Rivers of the Chesapeake Bay Watershed.* Richmond, Virginia, 2000.

U.S. Geological Survey. *Nitrate and Selected Pesticides in Ground Water of the Mid-Atlantic Region.* Baltimore, 1997.

U.S. Geological Survey. *Pesticides in Surface Water of the Mid-Atlantic Region.* Baltimore, 1997.

Weber, A. J., and Kellogg, R. L. "Assessing loadings of nitrogen and phosphorus from agriculture in the Chesapeake Bay watershed." Presented at *Proceedings of the Integrated Decision Making for Watershed Management Symposium,* January 7–9, 2001. EPA Chesapeake Bay Program Office.

CHAPTER 3: Harvests

Atlantic States Marine Fisheries Commission. *Interstate Fisheries Management Plan for the Striped Bass of the Atlantic Coast from Maine to North Carolina.* Washington: Versar, Inc., 1990.

Brooks, W. K. *The Oyster.* Baltimore: Johns Hopkins University Press, 1996.

Chesapeake Bay Commission. *The Chesapeake Bay Blue Crab—Harvest Trends and Dockside Values,* Report No. 2. Annapolis, Maryland, 2001.

Chesapeake Bay Commission. *Keeping the Agreement.* Annapolis, Maryland, 2000.

Chesapeake Bay Foundation. "Menhaden: Key part of the bay's food web in trouble." Save the Bay (Fall 2001). Annapolis, Maryland: Chesapeake Bay Foundation.

Chesapeake Bay Foundation. *Restoring Chesapeake Gold: The Ecologic and Economic Benefits of Oyster Restoration to the Chesapeake Bay.* Annapolis, Maryland, 2000.

Kennedy, V. S., Oesterling, M., and Van Engel, W. A. *History of Blue Crab Fisheries on the U.S. Atlantic and Gulf Coasts.* Cambridge, Maryland: Center for Environmental and Estuarine Studies. Unpublished draft, 2001.

Norton, Virgil, Smith, Terry, and Strand, Ivar (eds.). *Stripers—The Economic Value of the Atlantic Coast Commercial and Recreational Striped Bass Fisheries.* College Park: Maryland Sea Grant, University of Maryland, 1984.

St. Pierre, Richard. *Historical Review of the American Shad and River Herring Fisheries of the Susquehanna River.* Harrisburg, Pennsylvania: U.S. Fish and Wildlife Service, 1979.

U.S. Environmental Protection Agency. *Strategy for Removing Impediments to Migratory Fishes in the Chesapeake Bay Watershed.* Washington, D.C.: Chesapeake Bay Program, 1988.

U.S. Fish and Wildlife Service. *Restoration of American Shad to the Susquehanna River.* Washington, D.C., 1999.

CHAPTER 4: Resilience

Baltimore Regional Partnership. *Planning for Sprawl: A Look at Projected Residential Growth in the Baltimore Region.* Baltimore, Maryland, 2001.

Chesapeake Bay Commission and the Trust for Public Land. *Keeping Our Commitment: Preserving Land in the Chesapeake Watershed.* Annapolis, Maryland, and Washington, D.C., 2001.

Chesapeake Bay Executive Council. *Habitat Requirements for Chesapeake Bay Living Resources.* Washington, D.C., 1988.

Costanza, Robert, d'Arge, Ralph, de Groot, Rudolf, Farber, Stephen, and Grasso, Monica. "The value of the world's ecosystem services and natural capital." *Nature* 387 (May 1997):253–259.

Environmental Law Institute. *Forests for the Bay.* Washington, D.C., 2000.

Grace, Russell E., Kearney, Michael S., and Stevenson, J. Court. *Marsh Loss in Nanticoke Estuary, Cheapeake Bay.* Washington, D.C.: American Geographical Society of New York, 1988.

Harris, Larry D. *The Fragmented Forest.* Chicago: University of Chicago Press, 1984.

Hershner, Carl, Havens, Kirk, Varnell, Lyle, and Rudnicky, Tamia. *Wetlands in*

Virginia—Special Report No. 00-1. Gloucester: Virginia Institute of Marine Science, 2000.

Hillyer, Saunders C. *The Maryland Critical Area Program: Time to De-mythologize and Move Forward.* Annapolis: Chesapeake Bay Foundation, 1988.

Hylton, Tom. *Save Our Land, Save Our Towns.* Harrisburg, Pennsylvania: R. B. Books, 1995.

Jackson, Jerome A. "Preface." In *The Past, Present, and Future of North American Ecosystems and Their Avifaunas.* Madison: University of Wisconsin Press, 1989.

Kearney, Michael S., and Stevenson, J. Court. *Sea-Level History of the Chesapeake Bay Over the Last Few Centuries.* College Park and Cambridge: University of Maryland Department of Geography and Horn Point Environmental Laboratories, 1989.

Kearney, Michael S., and Stevenson, J. Court. *Sea-Level Rise and Marsh Vertical Accretion Rates in Chesapeake Bay.* College Park and Cambridge: University of Maryland Department of Geography and Horn Point Environmental Laboratories, 1985.

Maryland Department of Natural Resources. *The Maryland Forest Conservation Act: A Five-Year Review.* Annapolis, Maryland, 2000.

Teal, John, and Teal, Mildred. *Life and Death of the Salt Marsh.* New York: Audubon/Ballantine, 1975.

U.S. Department of Agriculture, Forest Service. *Conserving the Forests of the Chesapeake: The Status, Trends, and Importance of Forests for the Bay's Sustainable Future.* Annapolis, Maryland, 1996.

U.S. Department of Agriculture, Forest Service, and Society of American Foresters. *Forest Fragmentation in the Chesapeake Bay Watershed.* Bethesda, Maryland, 1998.

U.S. Environmental Protection Agency, Bay Program. *Chesapeake Bay Wetlands.* Annapolis, Maryland, 1997.

U.S. Environmental Protection Agency, Bay Program. *Perspectives on Chesapeake Bay: Nitrogen Dynamics in Forest Lands of the Chesapeake Basin.* Annapolis, Maryland, 1996.

U. S. Environmental Protection Agency, Bay Program. "Prime farmland lost to development." *Bay Journal,* June 2001, p. 15.

U.S. Environmental Protection Agency, Bay Program. *Riparian Forest Buffers—Linking Land to Water.* Annapolis, Maryland, 1999.

U.S. Environmental Protection Agency, Mid-Atlantic Integrated Assessment. *What Is the State of the Environment in the Mid-Atlantic Region?* Ft. Meade, Maryland, 2001.

U.S. Fish and Wildlife Service. *Status and Trends of Wetlands in the Conterminous United States, 1986–1997.* Washington, D.C., 2000.

CHAPTER 5: The Ultimate Issue: People

Alliance for the Chesapeake Bay. "Bay states at odds over definition of sprawl, how to measure it." *Bay Journal,* July–August 2001, p. 15.

Alliance for the Chesapeake Bay. "Study predicts rapid growth for Maryland unless sprawl is contained." *Bay Journal,* July–August 2001, p. 15.

American Farmland Trust. *Farms for the Future: A Strategic Approach to Saving Maryland's Farmland and Rural Resources.* Northampton, Massachusetts, 1998.

Baltimore Regional Partnership. *Planning for Sprawl: A Look at Projected Residential Growth in the Baltimore Region.* Baltimore, Maryland, 2001.

Beck, Roy. *Re-Charting America's Future.* Petoskey, Michigan: The Social Contract Press, 1994.

Beck, Roy. *The Case Against Immigration.* New York: W. W. Norton, 1996.

Bleken, Marina A. "Global N enrichment by agriculture: A matter of diet?" Volume 1, *Proceedings, Fertilization for Sustainable Plant Production and Soil Fertility,* 11th International World Fertilizer Congress. September 7–13, 1997. Belgium: Gent University.

Brookings Institution Center on Urban and Metropolitan Policy. *A Region Divided—The State of Growth in Greater Washington, D.C.* Washington, 1999.

Brower, Michael, and Leon, Warren. *The Consumers Guide to Effective Environmental Choices.* New York: Three Rivers Press, 1999.

Chesapeake Bay Commission, The Trust for Public Land. *Keeping Our Commitment: Preserving Land in the Chesapeake Watershed.* Annapolis, Maryland, February 2001.

Chesapeake Bay Foundation and 1000 Friends of Maryland. *Making Smart Growth Smarter.* Annapolis and Baltimore, 1999.

Chesapeake Executive Council. *Population Growth and Development in the Chesapeake Bay Watershed to the Year 2020.* Annapolis, Maryland, 1988.

Chesapeake Research Consortium. *The Bi-state Conference on Chesapeake Bay.* Edgewater, Maryland, 1977.

Czech, Brian. "Economic growth as the limiting factor in wildlife conservation." *Wildlife Society Bulletin* 28, no. 1 (2000):4–15.

Daily, Gretchen C. (ed.). *Nature's Services: Societal Dependence on Natural Ecosystems.* Washington, D.C.: Island Press, 1997.

Epstein, Lee R. "Where yards are wide: Have land use planning and law gone astray?" *William & Mary Environmental Law and Policy Review* 21 (1997):345.

Frank, Robert H. *Luxury Fever*. New York: Simon & Schuster, 1999.

Guy, Chris. "Bay Bridge Spans Debate." *Baltimore Sun*, August 4, 2002, p. B1.

Hawken, Paul. *The Ecology of Commerce*. New York: HarperCollins, 1993.

Hillyer, Saunders. *An Evaluation of the Maryland Critical Area Program*. Unpublished draft. Baltimore: Abell Foundation, 2001.

Hirschhorn, Joel S. *Growing Pains: Quality of Life in the New Economy*. Special publication. Washington, D.C.: National Governors' Association, 2000.

Hostetler, John A. "Toward Responsible Growth and Stewardship of Lancaster County's Landscape." *Pennsylvania Mennonite Heritage* 12, no. 3 (1989):12–35.

Hylton, Thomas. *Save Our Land—Save Our Towns*. Harrisburg, Pennsylvania: R. B. Books, 1995.

Jackson, Richard J., and Kochtitzky, Chris. *Creating a Healthy Environment—The Impact of the Built Environment on Public Health*. Sprawl Watch Clearinghouse Monograph Series. Washington, D.C., 2001.

Lieberman, George. "The modernization of zoning: Enabling act revision as a means to reform." *Urban Lawyer:* 23 (1991) 1.

Maryland Department of Planning. *Smart Growth In Maryland*. Baltimore, 2001.

Numbers USA. *Three Possible Causes of Biggest U.S. Population Boom Ever*. Washington, D.C., 2001.

Numbers USA. *Urban Sprawl—Population Growth Is Half the Problem in Sprawl*. Washington, D.C., 2001.

1000 Friends of Maryland. *Smart Growth: How Is Your County Doing?* Baltimore, 2001.

Prince Charitable Trusts, and Chesapeake and Potomac Regional Alliance. *Smart Growth Proposal*. Washington, D.C., 2001.

Redefining Progress. *Indicators for Measuring Progress*. Oakland, California, 2001.

Siegel, Eric. "Immigrants seen as key to city's growth." *Baltimore Sun*, November 10, 2002, p. B1.

Stennett, Edwin. *Our Best Efforts—Sprawl, Smart Growth, and Rapid Population Growth*. Unpublished draft, 2001.

Stennett, Edwin. *In Growth We Trust*. GEM Report No. 1. Gaithersburg, MD: Growth Education Movement, Inc., July, 2002.

U.S. Bureau of the Census. *Total Population Projections 2000–2005: For the U.S. and States*. Washington, D.C., 2001.

Yaro, Robert. *Dealing with Change in the Connecticut River Valley: A Design Manual for Conservation and Development*. Center for Rural Massachusetts, Amherst, MA.

CHAPTER 6: Recommendations

Chesapeake Bay Foundation. *The Chesapeake Crisis: Turning the Tide.* Annapolis, 1990.

Costanza, Robert, and Daly, Herman E. *Toward an Ecological Economics.* Baton Rouge: Coastal Ecology Institute, Center for Wetland Resources, and the Department of Economics, Louisiana State University, 1987.

Hiss, Tony. "Reflections: Encountering the countryside—1." *New Yorker,* August 1989.

Hiss, Tony. "Reflections: Encountering the countryside—2." *New Yorker,* August 1989, pp. 37–62.

Morris, Ian. "The future of the Chesapeake Bay and its resources." Speech. Cambridge, Maryland, 1986.

Westinghouse Ocean Research and Engineering Center. *Proceedings of the Governor's Conference on Chesapeake Bay.* Annapolis, Maryland, 1968.

ACKNOWLEDGMENTS

Writing prescriptions for the health of the environment is as much art as science, as dependent on developing a feel for the mesh of humans and their environment as on the results of water quality tests. No author can do that alone. This book, and its substantial rewrite a decade after initial publication, represents a collaborative effort that involved hundreds of people who willingly gave time and energy to the authors. Below are a few of them.

Will Baker, CBF's President, was full-time editor of the original book, invaluable both for his advice and for his rare ability to know when not to give it. Michael Shultz, CBF's Vice-President for Public Affairs, most ably took over the editing role during this first rewrite of *Turning the Tide*.

The original book benefited immensely from a board of scientific advisors: Bob Biggs, Les Lanyon, Karl Hirschner, Walt Boynton, Bill Richkus, and Bob Huggett. Most of them were still around a decade later to provide guidance in the rewrite. Sorely missed was the late Gene Cronin, CBF trustee and longtime bay scientist, who added invaluable insight to the original book.

The staff at the EPA Chesapeake Bay Program were extremely helpful in the rewriting of *Turning the Tide*, responding to flurries of calls for up-to-date information, despite being under a heavy workload. Kelly Shenk, Maggie Kerchner, Russ Mader, and Jeff Sweeney deserve special mention.

Among the CBF staff, several took considerable time to review and comment on the rewrite of this book: Joe Maroon, Roy Hoagland, Mike Hirshfield, Bill Goldsborough, Michael Heller, Theresa Pierno, Lee Epstein, Matt Ehrhart, Jenn Aiosa, Bill Street, Kim Coble, Joe Lerch, Ann Jennings, Jeff Corbin, and John Page Williams. To update the book's illustrations, we were fortunate to have the services of a talented mother-and-daughter team of graphic artists, Karen Ashley and Tamzin Biles Craig. CBF's Elizabeth Buckman ably managed the logistics of that operation. Joseph Hutchison, now at the *Los Angeles Times,* created the original graphics and kindly granted us the rights to use them as our base for this book.

Finally, thanks to Heather Boyer of Island Press for sticking with the rewrite through numerous stops and starts, and to Sita Culman of the Abell Foundation for her personal interest and thoughtful questions. All of us involved with the project deeply appreciate the Abell Foundation's strong financial support, which has made both the original book and this rewrite possible.

INDEX

Tom Horton was born and raised on the Eastern Shore of Maryland. He grew up hunting, fishing, and consorting with watermen. As a reporter on the Chesapeake Bay for the *Baltimore Sun* (1972–1987), he won numerous local and national awards, including the National Wildlife Federation's Conservation Communicator of the Year, the Scripps-Howard Meeman award for best conservation series (on the Amazon jungle), and the Kenny Rogers World Hunger Media Award (for reporting on the Ethiopian famine). Horton's first book, *Bay Country,* a series of essays on the Chesapeake, won both the John Burroughs Medal for the country's best natural history book of 1988 and a similar award from the Wildlife Society. From 1987 until 1990, Horton and his family lived in the village of Tylerton, on Smith Island, Maryland, where he managed the Chesapeake Bay Foundation's education center, offering three-day field trips to students and summer workshops to teachers. He detailed his experiences there in his book *An Island Out of Time.* Since moving back to the mainland, he has returned to the *Sun,* where his column "On the Bay" appears every Friday.